Dennis Schulting
Kant's Deduction From Apperception

Kantstudien-Ergänzungshefte

Im Auftrag der Kant-Gesellschaft
herausgegeben von
Manfred Baum, Bernd Dörflinger
und Heiner F. Klemme

Band 203

Dennis Schulting
Kant's Deduction From Apperception

An Essay on the Transcendental Deduction of the Categories

Second Revised Edition

DE GRUYTER

First published 2012 as „Kant's Deduction and Apperception. Explaining the Categories"
(Palgrave Macmillan)

ISBN 978-3-11-071026-7
e-ISBN (PDF) 978-3-11-058430-1
e-ISBN (EPUB) 978-3-11-058287-1
ISSN 0340-6059

Library of Congress Control Number: 2018950636

Bibliographic information published by the Deutsche Nationalbibliothek
The Deutsche Nationalbibliothek lists this publication in the Deutsche Nationalbibliografie;
detailed bibliographic data are available on the Internet at http://dnb.dnb.de.

© 2020 Walter de Gruyter GmbH, Berlin/Boston
This volume is text- and page-identical with the hardback published in 2019.
Printing and binding: CPI books GmbH, Leck

www.degruyter.com

FOR CRISTIANA
per sempre

I have to do merely with reason itself and its pure thinking [*ihrem reinen Denken*]; to gain exhaustive acquaintance with them I need not seek far beyond myself, because it is in myself that I encounter them, and common logic already also gives me an example of how the simple acts of reason may be fully and systematically enumerated.
—*Critique of Pure Reason*, Axiv

Metaphysics is not a science, not scholarship, but rather merely understanding acquainted with itself [*bloss der sich selbst kennende Verstand*], [...] it is logical self-cognition [*logische Selbsterkenntnis*].
—R4284, AA 17: 495 (NF: 125)

The mind is [...] itself the archetype [...] of such a *synthesis* through original and not through derivative thinking.
—*Duisburg Nachlass*, R4674, AA 17: 647 (NF: 160)

Contents

Preface to the New Edition —— XIII

Preface to the First Edition —— XXV

Key to Abbreviations of Cited Primary Works —— XXVII

1 **Introduction: The Categories and Apperception** —— 1

2 **The 'Herz' Question** —— 20

3 **The Quid Juris** —— 28
3.1 Introduction —— 28
3.2 Deduction: Justification or Proof? —— 31
3.3 Original Acquisition, Reflective Judgement and the Categories: A Critical Remark on Longuenesse —— 41
3.3.1 Kant on 'Reflective' and 'Determinative' Judgement —— 42
3.3.2 Reflection and the Categories —— 44
3.3.3 A Lockean Deduction? —— 51
 Excursus: The 'Quaestio Facti' and Empirical Deduction —— 54
3.3.4 A Conflation of Levels —— 59

4 **The Master Argument** —— 63
4.1 Introduction —— 63
4.2 The Ostensible Gap —— 64
4.3 The Reciprocity Thesis —— 70
4.4 Is the Deduction a Regressive or Progressive Argument? —— 81
4.5 On Guyer —— 101

5 **The Unity of Thought: On the Guiding Thread** —— 111

6 **Apperception and the Categories of Modality** —— 123
6.1 Introduction —— 123
6.2 The Categories of Modality —— 124
6.3 The 'I think'-Proposition: The Analyticity of Apperception —— 128
6.3.1 The Austere Reading of Apperception —— 136
6.3.2 A Formal Analysis —— 141
6.3.3 Rigorous Coextensivity —— 150

| 6.4 | Deriving the Categories of Modality —— 154 |

7	**Apperception and the Categories of Relation** —— 168
7.1	Introduction —— 168
7.2	'Substance' —— 168
7.2.1	Substance and the 'I Think' in the First Paralogism —— 172
7.2.2	Substance in the Transcendental Deduction —— 178
7.3	'Causality' —— 180
7.3.1	Spontaneity as Action of the Understanding or 'Self-Activity' —— 182
7.4	Combination, Synthetic Unity, and 'Community' —— 186
7.5	Deriving the Categories of Relation: Summary —— 194

8	**Apperception and the Categories of Quality** —— 195
8.1	Introduction —— 195
8.2	Sensation and the Categories of Quality —— 196
8.3	Sensation, Consciousness, and Apperception —— 202
8.3.1	First-Order Consciousness and Apperception —— 210
8.3.2	Consciousness, Unconsciousness, and Obscurity —— 214
8.4	Transcendental (Self-)Consciousness, 'Negation', and 'Limitation' —— 216
8.5	Deriving the Categories of Quality: Summary —— 223

9	**Apperception and the Categories of Quantity** —— 225
9.1	Introduction —— 225
9.2	'All My Representations' and 'Each Representation': About Two Types of 'Accompanying' in § 16 —— 228
9.3	The Analytic Principle of Apperception and Sense Datum Experience —— 235
9.4	Hossenfelder on the 'I Think' and Analytic Unity —— 241
9.5	Numerical Identity: 'Totality is the Unity of Plurality' —— 247
9.6	Deriving the Categories of Quantity: Summary —— 253
9.7	The Conclusion of the D-Argument —— 254

10	**From Apperception to Objectivity** —— 258
10.1	Reciprocity Again: The Argument of § 17 —— 258
10.2	From Objective Unity to Judgement: the Argument of § 19 —— 265
10.3	Kant's 'Master Argument': How the P*- and R-Arguments Interlock —— 280

10.4	The Metaphysically Modest Nature of M: The Analysis of Knowledge —— 283
11	**On the 'Second Step' of the B-Deduction —— 290**
11.1	Introduction —— 290
11.2	Kant's Goals in the Deduction —— 291
11.3	The 'Two-Step' Argument —— 296
11.4	Figurative Synthesis and the A Priori Possibility of Representing a Particular —— 299
11.5	Figurative Synthesis and the Sui Generis Unity of Space —— 305
11.6	The Distinction Between Metaphysical and Geometric Space —— 309
11.7	What Has Kant Actually Proven in the 'Second Step' of the B-Deduction? —— 313
11.8	The Idealism of Nature —— 318

Bibliography of Secondary Literature —— 323

Index of Names —— 332

Index of Subjects —— 335

Preface to the New Edition

What are the desiderata for new systematic-interpretatively guided research on Kant's Transcendental Deduction of the Categories (henceforth Transcendental Deduction or the Deduction for short)? As James Conant, in his excellent programmatic recent essay (Conant 2016), delineates in detail in terms of what he calls 'exegetical puzzles', there is, first, the issue of the relationship between the Transcendental Deduction and the Transcendental Aesthetic, secondly, the relation between the A- and B-Deduction, and thirdly, the relation between the so-called 'first' and 'second steps' of the B-Deduction. Some aspects of these 'puzzles' have recently been debated more intensely than before; for example, a spate of articles on Kant's notion of space in relation to the role of the understanding (Messina 2014, McLear 2015, Onof & Schulting 2015, Williams 2018; see also Vinci 2015) have brought to light the difficulties in assessing the first 'exegetical puzzle'. In addressing this puzzle in the context of interpreting the structure and argumentative thrust of the Deduction, the results of this newer research must be taken into account. Conant fails to do this, however, when he discusses the relevant issues concerning space and intuition.

There is also, I think, a fourth exegetical puzzle—which Conant does not mention—that needs more investigation, namely the relation between the Transcendental Deduction and the so-called 'Metaphysical Deduction'. Kant refers to the sections that precede the actual Transcendental Deduction only once as the Metaphysical Deduction at B159 (at the start of § 26, which concerns the pivotal 'second step' argument), but those sections have in the literature long been referred to as such. There have been three major studies of the Metaphysical Deduction, but the three existing studies (Reich 1986/2001, Brandt 1991, Wolff 1995) have not gone beyond suggestions as to how the Metaphysical Deduction is related to the Transcendental Deduction (Klaus Reich has gone furthest by suggesting that the derivation question is really only solved by looking at the role of the objective unity of apperception, which is summarily dismissed by Brandt—I have tried to build upon Reich's suggestion in the current book; see below).[1]

Perhaps there is even a fifth desideratum, although not directly related to the argumentative structure of the Deduction; there is also the risk, here, of the old patchwork theory, namely the prevalence of historical reconstruction of the text over philosophical interpretation of the arguments. This fifth desideratum concerns the relation between the Transcendental Deduction and the historical de-

---

[1] Also Longuenesse (1998) has used arguments from the Metaphysical Deduction to propound her reading of the centrality of figurative synthesis in the B-Deduction argument.

velopment of its argument over the course of Kant's so-called pre-Critical career, in particular during the so-called 'silent decade'. In the 1980s, especially Wolfgang Carl (1989a, b) and Paul Guyer (1987) have written extensively about the Deduction in the *Duisburg Nachlass*, but on the basis of their analyses of the textual evidence of the *Nachlass*, they came to rather negative conclusions about the philosophical tenability of the arguments in the Deduction. Latterly, Henry Allison has devoted quite some space to the historical development of Kant's arguments in the Deduction, including the *Duisburg Nachlass*, in his new book on the Deduction (Allison 2015).

By characterising four possible interpretative 'choice-points', as he calls them, which decide on the way in which the three relationships or exegetical puzzles that he distinguishes are taken, I believe that Conant (2016) has at any rate provided us with a clear and helpful methodology for interpreting the arguments of the Deduction. Each choice-point reflects the way in which as an interpreter one is committed to a certain view of how the argument of the Deduction proceeds, and thus decides on the specific route that one takes in approaching the Deduction as a whole. This mainly concerns the question of how one reads the relationship between the 'first' and 'second steps' of the B-Deduction, but it goes beyond Henrich's stipulation that the Deduction be read as consisting of two clearly definable argumentative steps. Conant differentiates the following four choice-points:

1) Restrictive vs. nonrestrictive conceptions of subjectivity;
2) Two-stage vs. anti-two-stage readings of the relation between the Aesthetic and the Analytic;
3) Two senses of the term 'intuition';
4) The relation between the subjective and objective unity of consciousness.

One may of course beg to differ about the particular choices Conant himself makes at each of these choice-points, in particular with a view to the ways in which he aims to dismantle what he aptly calls the 'Layer-Cake Conception of Human Mindedness', according to which the conditions of our sentience and sapience are separately intelligible and yield absolutely independent and separable forms of cognition—and I myself critically discuss these choices in Schulting (2017d).

There is however one element that Conant does not regard as a separate exegetical puzzle or choice-point, though he does discuss an aspect of it in the context of his second and fourth choice-points. What I mean is the formal role of *apperception* or the 'I think' in the proof-structure of the argument of especially the B-Deduction (but, *mutatis mutandis*, also in the A-Deduction). This is of course related more to the internal logic of Kant's argument than to the relation between text parts (the issue from which Conant's analysis of exegetical puzzles takes its cue), although one could say, if we look at the B-Deduction, it concerns the relation between § 16, in which Kant argues for the transcendental conditions of self-consciousness, and § 17, where he argues for the transcendental conditions of the cognition of an object, with § 18 as a corollary of those arguments. Structurally, this is an important issue, especially since many interpreters have in the past flagged fundamental problems with Kant's reasoning *from* the conditions for self-consciousness (the principle of apperception) *to* the conditions for consciousness of objects, or indeed the conditions of the knowledge of objects. These problems can generically be termed the problem of 'the Gap' (see Schulting 2017a, e, 2018a). This is a serious problem for Kant if these commentators are right, for it directly undermines the central claim of the Deduction, namely the argument that the subjective conditions of cognition are also the objective conditions of cognition (A89/B122). Apperception is the premise of this argument. Evaluating apperception is therefore of paramount importance for assessing the argument. I argue in this book (and elsewhere)[2] that the criticism against Kant's argument that the subjective conditions are also the objective conditions, namely, the objection that there is a gap in Kant's central argument, is based on a fallacious, metaphysically intemperate reading of the principle of apperception as an analytic principle (B135). *None* of the existing interpretations, including Strawson's, is free from this fallacy. This is one of the most significant failures of research on the Deduction.

In the present book, which is here offered in its revised and expanded edition,[3] I concentrate on this role of apperception for the argument about the transcendental conditions of cognition. My claim is that apperception provides the clue to the structure of the B-Deduction as a two-step reflection-logical procedure, in that the transcendental conditions of cognition, that is, the *categories*, are straightforwardly, *analytically* derivable from apperception—this could, *mutatis mutandis*, be explored in a similar fashion for the A-Deduction, but I focus on the B-Deduction. Hence the title of the book (in its revised edition):

---

[2] See Schulting (2017a, c, e).

[3] Apart from corrections and just a few additional references, the only significant changes in this edition compared to the previous edition (Schulting 2012b), which is now out-of-print and replaced by the current edition, concern the change of title and the integration into the main text of longer passages that appeared in the endnotes in the previous edition, as well as the addition of a chapter on the so-called 'second step' of the B-Deduction (Chapter 11). I have also expanded the discussion of objectivity and judgement in Chapter 10. I have not attempted—in most cases at least—to consider the relevant secondary literature that appeared after the publication of the first edition, which would have required expanding the text significantly or adding *more* cumbersome footnotes, rather than cutting them back.

'Kant's deduction *from* apperception'.⁴ I present a narrowly focused interpretation of the 'first step' of the B-Deduction (running through §§ 15–20), including the introductory sections 13 and 14. I also dedicate a chapter to § 10, i.e. the Third Clue Section, that is, the section in the Metaphysical Deduction where Kant catalogues the categories (A76–83/B102–9), after having furnished the famous guiding thread (*Leitfaden*) to finding the categories. The central hypothesis I advance is—and no Kantian in his or her right (orthodox) mind, bar Klaus Reich (1986/2001) and a few others following in his wake, has dared to make this claim so far—that, to put it very boldly, in the Transcendental Deduction Kant effectively derives the categories 'from scratch'.⁵ This is not entirely accurate, as Kant of course starts with the premise, or undisputed fact,⁶ of the discursivity of the human mind, the very general characteristics of which he first lists in the first two sections of the Metaphysical Deduction (leading up to the table of judgement), which I do not discuss in the book (I believe the arguments in the first two sections of the Metaphysical Deduction are exhaustively and conclusively dealt with by Wolff 1995). So to be more precise, contrary to the standard reading, my claim is that in the Transcendental Deduction Kant derives the categories *from* the discursivity of the human mind, or, *from* the capacity to think, thus confirming the validity of the *Leitfaden* provided in the Metaphysical Deduction, which argues that the table of judgement, or more precisely the table of the discursive functions of thought in judgement, and the table of categories neatly correspond. (Notice that the derivation starting with the factual premise of our discursivity does not make it therefore empirical. The derivation takes place a priori from the laws of our discursive capacity for thinking, *given* that we have such a capacity, and no other.)

The derivation claim that I explore explains why Kant, in § 16 of the B-Deduction, starts with the famous proposition 'The *I think* must *be able* to accom-

---

⁴ The publisher of the first edition rejected the original working title 'Kant's Deduction From Apperception' for fear of it being misunderstood, but in my view it nicely captures the thrust of my main claim, namely, that Kant's Transcendental Deduction is about the deduction or derivation of the categories *from* the unity of apperception.

⁵ More precisely, Reich is concerned with deriving the *functions of judgement* from the objective unity of apperception, for which he looks for textual support outside the *Critique*. By contrast, I claim that the *categories* are derivable from the unity of apperception (the 'I think'), but since the categories *are* the functions of judgement, insofar as they determine intuitions as objects, de facto my claim comes down to the same as Reich's. Unlike Reich, however, I contend—and this was my novel claim—that the evidence for the derivation claim can be gathered from the arguments in the Deduction itself.

⁶ Well, of course Hegel is one who disputes that discursivity is the most basic fact about our thought. See Chapter 1, this volume, and Schulting (2017a), ch. 8.

pany all my representations', which is the principle of discursive thought, or indeed the principle of apperception.[7] The dense, some might say convoluted, argument that ensues in the next paragraphs in §§ 16 and 17 contains, in my view, the argument for the logical derivation of the twelve categories, *from* apperception, which are thus shown to be the necessary and formally sufficient transcendental conditions for the possibility of discursive thought in general and hence also of the more specific thought of an object, that is, of what enables us, as discursive minds, to think or conceive of an object at all. By showing exactly how each and every category is effectively derivable from the 'I think'-proposition or the principle of apperception, and thus constitutes the capacity for discursive thought, Kant, so I argued, can show that these *subjective* conditions of thought have *objective* validity (A89/B122); in other words, the derivation argument shows that the same set of conditions, or functions of thought, governs the possibility of both subjective thought and thought of an object—these functions being the categories, when specifically referring to the *objects* of thought.

The derivation of the categories *from* apperception has not been a popular view among Kantians, and gathering from the criticisms against my take on it, one may safely assume it is not going to be the standard view any time soon. For example, Dyck (2014) has questioned my interpretation of B142 as a basis for the idea that the categories are derived from the unity of apperception or thought in the sense that the categories can be deduced (strictly) logically from the unity of thought as a premise in an argument. He believes that I should have considered alternative readings, readings that take 'derivation' in a looser sense, that is, in a sense different from *logical* deduction, because Kant himself uses the term in different senses at e.g. B238/A193, B140, and B127–8, where it seems clear that 'derivation' cannot be taken to mean (strict) logical derivation from a premise in an argument.[8]

---

[7] On the constitutive features of discursivity, see Chapter 5, this volume, and Schulting (2017a), ch. 3.

[8] The passage at B127–8 seems less clear-cut in my opinion, as Kant here refers to the kind of derivation of the pure concepts of the understanding (or ideas, in their case) that Locke and Hume had in mind, that is, 'an *empirical* derivation' or a derivation from experience, namely in accordance with the psychological laws of association. This would appear to be an inductive derivation from experience as a premise, that is, one that is *mutatis mutandis* comparable to Kant's deductive derivation from thought itself (Kant speaks of Locke's 'physiological derivation' [A86/B119], but also in terms of an 'empirical deduction' [B117/A85]; see further Chapter 3). In both the Lockean and Kantian cases, some sort of logical inference or reasoning is at work, albeit that in the one (Locke's) case the inference is from a psychological principle or empirical fact(s), and in the latter (Kant's) case it is from a general principle (or logical facts) of thought.

First, my thesis that the categories are derivable from apperception does not hinge on the correct interpretation of B142 as such, or the correct interpretation of the term 'derive' or its cognate 'derivation' (Kant's *ableiten* and *Ableitung* respectively). B142 textually supports my reading. Evidently, the term 'derivation' can have variant meanings in different contexts, but mostly Kant just means 'deduction' in the standard sense (see further the discussion in Chapter 3). Secondly, a parallel passage in *Prolegomena* § 39 (*Prol*, AA 4: 322), where Kant expounds on 'the system of categories' and its deduction, pretty clearly leaves no other reasonable option than to read 'derivation' in purely logical terms, especially if we take the context of § 39 into account—basically, this section is the *Prolegomena*'s version of the Metaphysical Deduction. Notice that, a bit later in that section, Kant in fact equates *Ableitung* and *Deduktion* (*Prol*, AA 4: 324.31–2). In the passage in § 39, Kant writes:

> Nothing can be more desirable to a philosopher than to be able to derive, *a priori* from one principle, the multiplicity of concepts or basic principles that previously had exhibited themselves to him piecemeal in the use he had made of them *in concreto*, and in this way to be able to unite them all in one cognition. (*Prol*, AA 4: 322 [TPhb: 114])

Here, Kant contrasts two ways of exhibiting the pure concepts: either by a priori derivation from a principle, or by a posteriori gradual aggregation. The latter is not a viable way to proceed for Kant. Kant further explains, in this section, that the functions of the understanding can be 'fully surveyed', and that the 'pure concepts' 'arise' from them, 'determined *exhaustively* and *with precision*' (*Prol*, AA 4: 323 [TPhb: 115], emphasis added). What Kant means by this is that the 'kind of cognition' that we are after in an analysis of pure concepts is not a loose 'aggregate' of concepts, but a 'division' whose 'necessity' we comprehend, as in a 'system' (*Prol*, AA 4: 322 [TPhb: 114]), 'founded on a universal principle', and which 'forms a closed circle' (*Prol*, AA 4: 325–6 [TPhb: 117]), in which each and every part is reciprocally integrated.[9] In the introduction to the Clue sections in the *Critique*, Kant similarly writes:

> Transcendental philosophy has the advantage but also the obligation to seek its concepts in accordance with a principle, since they spring pure and unmixed from the understanding, as absolute unity, and must therefore be connected among themselves in accordance with a concept or idea. Such a connection, however, provides a rule by means of which the place of *each* pure concept of the understanding and the *completeness* of all of them together can be *determined a priori*, which would otherwise depend upon whim or chance. (A67/B92, emphasis added)

---

[9] Cf. Kant's letter of 7 August 1783 to Garve (*Corr*, AA 10: 340).

This rule for the a priori determination of each of the pure concepts lies in the act of the understanding as a capacity to judge (see *Prol*, AA 4: 323). The derivation consists in a step-by-step demonstration—by virtue of an '*analysis of the faculty of understanding*' (A65/B90)—of the way in which each single pure concept, or category, forms an integral part of the nature of the discursive understanding, and how they all hang together systematically as jointly constituting the capacity to think, which for Kant is a capacity to judge. Each of the twelve categories corresponds to or is identical to each of the twelve functions of the understanding (or judgement), and so each category 'analytically pertains', as I put it in the book, to the unity of thought (cf. A80 – 1/B107).

It is in this way that I claim that the categories can all be derived *from* the 'I think', *from* apperception as being the capacity to think, since together they constitute the unity of thought, which Kant claims is intrinsically *objectively* valid. A different way to describe the close relation between the categories and the unity of thought or the unity of apperception would be to emphasise the 'conformity' between the categories and the subjective conditions of thought, which are their grounds, precisely as Kant asserts this in his later essay *On a Discovery*, where he says that the original acquisition of the categories 'presupposes nothing innate save the subjective conditions of the spontaneity of thought (*conformity with the unity of apperception [Gemäßheit mit der Einheit der Apperzeption]*)' (*Disc*, AA 8: 223 [TPhb: 313, trans. emended and emphasis added]). I take this to confirm my view that the categories are a priori derivable from, or 'analytically pertain to', apperception.

One of the reasons why I remain convinced of, not just the plausibility, but indeed the *unavoidability*, of the claim that the categories derive a priori from the unity of apperception, is that the categories, as logical functions of judgements (B143), are nothing but so many modes of unitary consciousness (cf. *Prol*, AA 4: 305; A401). This becomes clear, among other places, at A109, where Kant reasons that the 'pure concept of this transcendental object', which is constituted by the categories that are the 'fundamental concepts for thinking objects in general for the appearances' (A111), is 'that which in all of our empirical concepts in general can provide relation to an object, i.e., objective reality'. This concept of the transcendental object 'concerns nothing but that unity which must be encountered in a manifold of cognition insofar as it stands in relation to an object', whereby '[t]his relation [...] is nothing other than the necessary unity of consciousness' (A109), that is, the transcendental unity of apperception. Indeed, the very possibility and necessity of the categories rests on the relation between all appearances to the original apperception (A111). In the understanding, which *is* '[t]he unity of apperception in relation to the synthesis of the imagination', are 'pure *a priori* cognitions that contain the necessary unity of the pure synthesis of the imagination in regard to all possible appearances', which 'are the *categories*, i.e., pure concepts of the understanding' (A119). The categories thus *are* the concepts of necessary synthesis (see B151),[10] and hence are a priori, analytically derivable from transcendental or 'pure apperception' as the 'principle of the synthetic unity of the manifold in all possible intuition' (A116–17).

To deny that the categories are analytically derivable from the unity of apperception would rather create a problem as to how to explain the very *possibility* and *necessity* of the categories (A111), when the original apperception is what lends them this necessity and even constitutes their possibility. If the combination of the understanding (*Verstandesverbindung*), which is the intellectual synthesis, is that which is 'thought in the mere category' (B151), how then could the categories *not* be seen as analytically related to the unity of apperception? There is a widespread assumption among commentators that categories are different things or functions than acts of synthesis, but textual evidence and philosophical reasons show that they cannot be. And if they are not, then neither can they be seen as separable from the unity of apperception, since acts of a priori synthesis are nothing but so many modes (twelve, to be precise) of the unity of apperception.

Especially nonconceptualist readings of Kant appear to want to see a priori synthesis and acts of conceptualisation—which involve the categories and/or the understanding and/or judgement (depending on whether one sees acts of the understanding, and the involvement of the categories, as acts of judgement, in which alone categories are instantiated[11])—separated. But such readings are vulnerable to what has aptly been called the 'schmimagination vicious regress problem' (Hanna 2013), the problem namely that if acts of a priori synthesis come separated from acts of the understanding or conceptualisation, or from acts of judgement, it is not clear which *more* original (i.e. more a priori) act of synthesis, or more originary productive imagination, could, *per impossibile*, be considered responsible for *their* synthesis. Separating the various formally distinguishable elements of synthesis as an act of the understanding, both intellectual and fig-

---

10 'This *synthesis* of the manifold of sensible intuition, which is possible and necessary *a priori*, can be called *figurative* (*synthesis speciosa*), as distinct from that which would be thought **in the mere category** in regard to the manifold of an intuition in general, and which is called combination of the understanding [*Verstandesverbindung*] (**synthesis intellectualis**)' (B151, boldface mine).

11 Despite Kant being clear about the fact that the act of the understanding is an act to judge (A69/B94) and that categories are functions of judgement (B143), some commentators, both conceptualist and (quasi-)nonconceptualist (Longuenesse 1998, Grüne 2009, Land 2015), attempt to prise apart the understanding, and the use of concepts, and acts of judgement. See my critique of nonconceptualist readings in Schulting (2015b; 2017a, ch. 5; 2018c).

urative, invites an obvious explanatory regress, where a priori synthesis was supposed to provide the explanation stopper. If a priori synthesis is conceived by Kant as the '*original*-synthetic unity of apperception', in its various guises as productive imagination or mere intellectual synthesis (the understanding), then there cannot be an even more original synthesis that lies at the root of the productive imagination and the understanding, and a priori combines them. The 'schmimagination' problem also holds, *mutatis mutandis*, for the view that not all concept use, or not all acts of understanding, involves judgement (Land 2015). Given the above, there are thus good reasons to believe that the deduction of the categories can best be seen as a logical derivation from the unity of apperception, because the categories are analytically related to it.

My central claim in the book is that the Transcendental Deduction demonstrates by way of the derivation argument—which is an ostensive proof in the sense that Kant indicates at A789/B817—that there is no discrepancy between what enables us to *think* in general and what enables us to think *of an object*. In fact, I believe it is only if we read the Transcendental Deduction in terms of the derivation argument that we can really understand how Kant is able to show that thought itself is intrinsically objectively valid, that subjectivity itself is constitutive of objectivity, and that *therefore* the categories apply to the objects of experience. By showing that Kant's argument for what, following Henry Allison, I call the 'reciprocity thesis', stands up to scrutiny, I go against persistent strands of criticism of the validity of this thesis, which is the central thesis of the 'first step' of the B-Deduction, and I would argue of the Deduction as a whole.[12] The criticism namely is that Kant does not account, among other things, for the difference between a claim that says that self-consciousness, and so the subjective conditions or functions of thought, are necessary for the thought of an object, and the ostensibly different claim that self-consciousness is *sufficient* for such a thought of an object. Hence, as I suggested earlier, it is commonly argued that there is an unbridgeable gap between the two claims that invalidates the main claim of there being an entailment relation between the subjective conditions of thought and the categories as the objective conditions of experience, which Kant proposes in §§ 16 and 17. I explain, in great detail, that this criticism is based on a false, i.e. psychological, reading of transcendental self-consciousness, an inflated interpretation of the scope of the analyticity of apperception,

---

[12] In the 'second step' of the B-Deduction, Kant further argues for the necessary connection between the *thought* of an object and the *perception* of an object; I expound on the central issues relating to the 'second step' in Chapter 11. See also Schulting (2015b, 2017a, ch. 5; forthcoming) and Onof & Schulting (2015).

and a misapprehension of the relation between the analytic unity of consciousness and the original-synthetic unity of apperception.

These are complex issues. But they are clearly important for evaluating the success of the Transcendental Deduction. If Kant's critics are right regarding the reciprocity thesis, the Transcendental Deduction must be considered a failure, given how central this claim is to it. One might perhaps want to argue that in the Transcendental Deduction Kant does not argue for the sufficient conditions of objective thought (and, if we take in the 'second step' as well, the conditions of objective *experience*), but merely for the very general thesis that the categories are only the *necessary* conditions of objective experience, that is, that the categories are necessarily applicable to objective experience.[13] But these commentators—if not the majority of readers of the Deduction—confuse Kant's argument in the Analogies with the one in the Deduction (hence, they often hastily turn to the Analogies for the specifics regarding what constitutes categorially determined experience).[14] Moreover, in the Deduction, Kant must show *how* and not just *that* the categories are necessarily applicable to objects of experience. The 'how' provides insight into the manner in which the subject of thought and the object of thought are necessarily a priori linked, and how each of the twelve categories is an a priori constitutive element in and of this connection. A detailed account of the mutual implicatedness, or what I call the 'rigorous coextensivity', of the synthetic and analytic aspects of transcendental apperception shows this. The exposition of the a priori grounds of experience in the Transcendental Deduction is philosophically more fundamental, and thus more general, than the account of the principles of experience offered in the Analogies. To suggest

---

[13] But even here, there is an ambiguity: does that more modest argument mean that the categories are necessarily applicable to experience of objects only, or also to the objects of experience? For an account of these issues, see further Chapter 4, this volume, and also Schulting (2017a), ch. 4.

[14] That is to say, often one complains that in the Transcendental Deduction Kant is not specific enough about what the categories are—how they are defined—and how they are supposed to be applied to experience, or that the deduction of the categories is not 'complete' until the Analogies, or even until the *Metaphysical Foundations of Nature*. Hence, commentators turn to the Analogies because only there does Kant, so they argue, enter into detail about the particular categories and their application to experience. But this is to confuse the roles of the Analogies and the Transcendental Deduction. I agree with Michael Friedman that the *Critique* and the *Metaphysical Foundations* 'have different yet complementary perspectives on [the] same phenomenal world, about which they establish different yet complementary conclusions' (2015: 563–4). I disagree with Friedman's overall stance though that the scientific laws addressed in the *Metaphysical Foundations* are entailed by the transcendental principles of experience addressed in the *Critique*, such that the superseding of those empirical laws post-Einstein has, as Friedman argues, a direct bearing on the status of the transcendental principles of experience.

that we need the Analogies to understand the Deduction thus rests on a misunderstanding of the order of fundamentality of the different sections in the *Critique*.

In the book, I also assess the question of the sense in which we must read Kant's distinction, in § 13 of the Deduction, between the *quid juris* and a *quid facti*, and what Kant in fact means by a transcendental deduction of the categories. I look at arguments provided in this context by Henrich (1989), Longuenesse (1998), Proops (2003), Seeberg (2006), and most recently Callanan (2011). I particularly criticise Longuenesse and Callanan for blurring the distinction between the transcendental and empirical orders in Kant's reasoning. I also consider the vexed interpretative issue whether the structure of the argument of the B-Deduction is either regressive or progressive. Most commentators hold either of the two possibilities to reflect accurately the structure of Kant's argument in the B-Deduction. I argue that the argument of the Deduction (either in the A- or B-version) is both, and necessarily so[15]; this view ties in seamlessly with my claim concerning the a priori derivation of the categories from the 'I think'.

In the last chapter of this book I address pivotal questions that are related to the 'second step' of the B-Deduction, primarily the way Kant argues that apperception ties in with the *perception* of spatiotemporal objects and that thus the principle of apperception is also the constitutive transcendental condition of our objective *sensible* experience and hence of spatiotemporally determined nature itself, which provides the conclusion to the argument of the B-Deduction, namely a concluding answer to the question how subjective conditions of our thinking are also the objective conditions of our knowledge of objects. Elsewhere (Schulting 2017a, ch. 3; 2017c; forthcoming), I expand on the important issue of how apperception is 'adverbial', so to speak, to any judgement about objects, and thus involves an element of recognitive reflection that has to do with Kant's emphasis on the spontaneous agency of the subject of judgement. This ties in with my claim, in the present book, that the logical functions of judgement, and so the categories, are analytically derivable from apperception. For the principle of original-synthetic apperception *itself*, as the set of the categories as so many functions of necessary synthetic unity among my representations, constitutes the objective validity of a judgement, and so the instantiation of the categories in any judgement. In another paper (Schulting 2017c), I address more precisely the question of the relation, and differences, between transcen-

---

[15] I concentrate on the B-Deduction, but the argument applies, *mutatis mutandis*, to the A-Deduction as well. For my analysis of the A-Deduction account of the threefold synthesis see Schulting (2017a), ch. 6.

dental apperception, *sui generis* self-consciousness and the possibility of self-knowledge, an aspect that is left undiscussed in the current book.

In his very thoughtful critique of the previous edition of this book, Marcel Quarfood expressed the hope that the book would 'stimulate a renewal of the debate' (2014: 88) surrounding the derivation of the table of categories. Thus far, besides his co-critics Corey Dyck and Andrew Stephenson in *Studi kantiani*, the only other commentators who have specifically taken note of my attempt of a derivation are Thomas Land in his sympathetic review for *Kantian Review* (2018), Robert Watt in his excellent discussion of my latest book (Schulting 2017a), and Allison in his earlier mentioned masterful new book on the Transcendental Deduction, although the latter does not discuss it.[16] It seems that, apart from the above-mentioned scholars, the book has so far largely been ignored, both in Germany and in the English-speaking world of Kant scholarship. At any rate, it has not occasioned a major new debate on the role of apperception in the deduction or derivation of the categories from a principle or, at the very least, it has not been the lucky subject of a serious refutation—to be sure, Dyck, Stephenson and Watt offer various arguments contra my thesis, but they rehearse familiar objections; only Quarfood endorses the possibility of a derivation from apperception and addresses potential problems for it in some detail. It is to be hoped that this second edition will provide the opportunity for serious scholars of the Metaphysical as well as Transcendental Deduction to take up the gauntlet.

* * *

Some parts of this preface, Chapter 11 as well as part of a section in Chapter 10, are based on material from my book *Kant's Radical Subjectivism: Perspectives on the Transcendental Deduction* (Schulting 2017), for the reuse of which I acknowledge the permission of Palgrave Macmillan. I thank Christian Onof for his comments on an earlier draft of the preface for this revised edition, on which I worked during the summer of 2017. I thank Walter de Gruyter for publishing the book in its current edition, and Manfred Baum, Bernd Dörflinger and Heiner Klemme for their willingness to include it in the prestigious longstanding book series *Kant-Studien Ergänzungshefte*. I rededicate the book to Cristiana Battistuzzi, who always provides the means *sine qua non*.

Germany, Dennis Schulting

---

16 See Dyck (2014), Stephenson (2014), Allison (2015: 352n.33), Watt (2017), and Land (2018). For my long response to Watt (2017), see Schulting (2017f), which provides additional arguments and textual evidence for endorsing the derivation claim that I make in the present book. For further references to recent literature on the Transcendental Deduction, see Schulting (2018b).

Preface to the First Edition

This book has had an unconscionably long gestation. Many of its ideas have grown out of my doctoral thesis, which concerned a study of transcendental apperception in Kant's theoretical philosophy. After having submitted the thesis to the Department of Philosophy of the University of Warwick, in the autumn of 2003, it dawned upon me that, contrary to received opinion, Kant actually provided, in the Transcendental Deduction of the Pure Concepts of the Understanding in the *Critique of Pure Reason*, an account of the derivation of *each* of the categories from the principle of transcendental apperception. The result of the work that I then began to undertake is what now makes up the greater content of this book. After initial work on it in the spring and summer of 2004, the project had lain dormant for a good five years until after I completed an edited volume on Kant's idealism (*Kant's Idealism. New Interpretations of a Controversial Doctrine*, Springer 2011). The final write-up took me the last months of 2011 and early 2012 and I am glad the book has finally seen the light of day. It contains my attempt at understanding what is arguably the core of Kant's First *Critique* but also one of the most abstruse parts of his philosophy. I am very pleased that the book appears with the same publisher with whom Norman Kemp Smith published, back in 1929, his translation of the *Critique of Pure Reason* and a decade earlier his *Commentary to Kant's Critique of Pure Reason*.

I wish especially to thank Stephen Houlgate for not only his encouragement but also his unflagging criticisms and the vigorous discussions about Kant and Hegel we had while I was at Warwick, which bore fruit in the way that I learned to balance more evenly my criticisms against Hegel and my reverence for Kant. Thanks to Stephen, Hegel has been a major background influence ever since on my thoughts regarding the broader context of the reception of Kant's philosophy. However, while recognising Hegel's own legitimate concerns I staunchly defend Kant against Hegelian critique. Contrary to what Hegel will have us believe, we do not need Hegelian systematicity to understand Kant. The reader can rest assured that this book presents a thoroughly Kantian interpretation of Kant wholly undistorted by Hegelian worries.

I further thank Christian Onof and Jacco Verburgt, both stalwart Kantians, who have read earlier drafts of the manuscript and offered their comments and criticisms, which led me to revise some of the arguments or the way in which they were presented. All remaining obscurities and mistakes are of course mine. I should also like to thank Kees Jan Brons, who at the beginning of my philosophical endeavours taught me to carefully parse philosophical texts without hastily projecting one's own preconceptions and to value both their comparative strengths *and* limits.

I would be remiss if I did not mention the greatest debt that I owe to Cristiana Battistuzzi. The work I have carried out, the definitive result of which can be studied here, would not have been remotely possible if it were not for her unfailing love and support. She also proofread the whole manuscript. Naturally, I dedicate this book to her.

* * *

The following material has appeared earlier in a different form: Parts of my article 'On Strawson on Kantian Apperception', in *South African Journal of Philosophy*, vol. 27(3) (2008), a special issue that contains the proceedings of an international conference on P.F. Strawson held in 2007 in Johannesburg, appear here in altered and hopefully improved form; Chapter 8 contains parts of a paper that is published in the collection *Kant's Philosophy of the Unconscious*, edited by P. Giordanetti et al. (Berlin/New York: de Gruyter, 2012). I kindly acknowledge permission from the editors of the *South African Journal of Philosophy* and from Walter de Gruyter Verlag to reprint copyrighted material here.

(Ealing, London, Dennis Schulting)

Key to Abbreviations of Cited Primary Works

All English language quotations from Kant's works in this book are from *The Cambridge Edition of the Works of Immanuel Kant*, ed. P. Guyer & A. Wood (Cambridge: Cambridge University Press, 1992 ff.), except for the following: The *Prolegomena* is used in the Ellington/Carus edition (see details below), but sometimes I make use of the Cambridge translation (which is indicated by the abbreviation TPhb). For the *Anthropology* I employ the Dowdell translation (see details below), unless otherwise indicated. Occasionally I make use of Kemp Smith's translation of the *Critique of Pure Reason* (Palgrave Macmillan, 2003 [1929]). Where a translation was not available I provided my own.

AA	*Kants Gesammelte Schriften*, ed. Königlich Preußischen, später Deutschen Akademie der Wissenschaften zu Berlin (Berlin: de Gruyter, 1900–)
Anthr	*Anthropology from a Pragmatic Point of View* [AA 7], trans. V. L. Dowdell and ed. H. H. Rudnick (Carbondale and Edwardsville: Southern Illinois University Press, 1978, 1996)
Anthr-C	*Anthropology, History, and Education*, trans. and ed. G. Zöller & R. Louden (Cambridge: Cambridge University Press, 2007)
Anthr-Fried	*Anthropology Friedländer* [AA 25]
AT	*Oeuvres de Descartes*, ed. Charles Adam & Paul Tannery, quartercentenary edition in 11 volumes (Paris: Vrin, 1996)
Beweisgrund	*The only possible argument in support of a demonstration of the existence of God* [AA 2]
CJ	*Critique of the power of Judgement* [AA 5]
Corr	*Correspondence* [AA 10–13], trans. and ed. A. Zweig (Cambridge: Cambridge University Press, 1999, 2007)
CPrR	*Critique of Practical Reason* [AA 5]
Disc	*On a Discovery whereby any new critique of pure reason is to be made superfluous by an older one* [AA 8]
Essay	John Locke, *Essay Concerning Human Understanding*, ed. P. H. Nidditch (Oxford: Oxford University Press, 1975)
FI	First Introduction to the *Critique of the Power of Judgement* [AA 20]
Groundwork	*Groundwork of the Metaphysics of Morals* [AA 4]
GuW	G.W.F. Hegel, *Glauben und Wissen*, in *Gesammelte Werke*, Band 4, ed. H. Buchner & O. Pöggeler (Hamburg: Meiner, 1968)
ID	*On the form and principles of the sensible and intelligible world* [Inaugural Dissertation] [AA 2]
Inquiry	*Inquiry concerning the distinctness of the principles of natural theology and morality* [AA 2]
JL	*Jäsche Logic* [AA 9]
LL	*Lectures on Logic*, trans. and ed. J. M. Young (Cambridge: Cambridge University Press, 1992, 2004)
LM	*Lectures on Metaphysics*, trans. and ed. K. Ameriks & S. Naragon (Cambridge: Cambridge University Press, 1997, 2001)
Logic-Blom	*Blomberg Logic* [AA 24]

Logic-DW	Dohna-Wundlacken Logic [AA 24]
Logic-Hechsel	Hechsel Logic
Logic-Vienna	Vienna Logic [AA 24]
Met-Dohna	Metaphysik Dohna [AA 28]
Met-Herder	Metaphysik Herder [AA 28]
Met-L_1	Metaphysik L_1 [AA 28] = Metaphysik Pölitz I
Met-L_2	Metaphysik L_2 [AA 28] = Metaphysik Pölitz II
Met-Mron	Metaphysik Mrongovius [AA 29]
Met-Schön	Metaphysik von Schön [AA 28]
Met-Vigil	Metaphysik Vigilantius [AA 29]
Met-Volck	Metaphysik Volckmann [AA 28]
MFNS	Metaphysical Foundations of Natural Science [AA 4]
ND	A new elucidation of the first principles of metaphysical cognition [nova dilucidatio] [AA 1]
NF	Notes and Fragments, trans. and ed. P. Guyer et al. (Cambridge: Cambridge University Press, 2005)
OKT	On Kästner's Treatises [AA 20], trans. and ed. C. Onof & D. Schulting, in Kantian Review 19(2) (2014): 305–13.
OP	Opus Postumum [AA 22]
OT	What does it mean to Orient oneself in Thinking? [AA 8]
Prol	Prolegomena to Any Future Metaphysics [AA 4], trans. P. Carus in newly revised version of J. W. Ellington (Indianapolis: Hackett, 1977)
R	Reflexionen [AA 14–19]
Real Progress	What Real Progress has metaphysics made in Germany since the time of Leibniz and Wolff? [AA 20]
Tone	On a recently prominent Tone of superiority in philosophy [AA 8]
TPha	Theoretical Philosophy 1755–1770, trans. and ed. D. Walford (Cambridge: Cambridge University Press, 1992, 2003)
TPhb	Theoretical Philosophy after 1781, trans. and ed. H. Allison, P. Heath et al. (Cambridge: Cambridge University Press, 2002)

1 Introduction: The Categories and Apperception

One of the most important pieces of philosophical argument is undoubtedly Kant's 'Transcendental Deduction of the Pure Concepts of the Understanding' (hereafter the Transcendental Deduction or the Deduction for short) in his *Critique of Pure Reason*. It offers arguably the best solution to a perennial topic in philosophy, namely the secure grounding for knowledge. At the same time, it is considered one of the most obscure texts in the whole of philosophy, condensed as it is into a mere 23 *Akademie* pages (in the B-version). There is no unanimity among scholars as regards the structure, meaning and validity of its argument. In this book, I make a claim about the Transcendental Deduction that, in at least one respect, goes wholly against received opinion. Contrary to existing interpretations of the Transcendental Deduction, I contend that we should take absolutely seriously Kant's assertion—most explicitly articulated at B142 in the B-Deduction—that the categories (or, to be more precise, 'principles of the objective determination' as he calls them there) are deducible or derivable from a principle, namely the principle of apperception, or, the transcendental unity of apperception.[1] As the title of this book indicates, I want to suggest that the deduction indeed proceeds *from* apperception. Until now, the majority of Kant scholars have been in ostensible agreement that such a claim, if indeed it is Kant's claim, is presumptuous and cannot be defended.[2] Paul Guyer (2001:

---

[1] In *Prol* § 39, Kant speaks of the 'multiplicity of the concepts' as capable of being 'derive[d] *a priori* from a principle [*aus einem Princip a priori ableiten*]' (AA 4: 322; cf. 323; trans. emended), and identifies 'derivation' with 'deduction' at AA 4: 324 (cf. B393/A336). Crucially, in § 21 of the B-Deduction Kant observes that the 'unity of apperception' is brought about 'by means of the categories' (*nur vermittelst der Kategorien* [...] *derselben Einheit der Apperception a priori zu Stande zu bringen*) (B145), suggesting the close correspondence between apperception and the categories. Also, in MFNS, AA 4: 474n., the categories are identified as 'determinations of our consciousness'. In a letter to Garve of 7 August 1783, Kant is even bolder when he claims that the *Critique* is the first work to undertake the project of 'deducing [*ableiten*] out of its own nature [of the faculty of '*a priori judging* reason', D.S.] all the objects within its scope, enumerating them, and proving their completeness by means of their coherence in a single, complete cognitive faculty'. Indeed, he claims that '[a]bsolutely no other science attempts this, that is, to develop a priori out of the mere concept of a cognitive faculty (when that concept is precisely defined) all the objects, everything that can be known of them' and that '[l]ogic, which would be the science most similar to this one, is in this regard much inferior' (*Corr*, AA 10: 340). How exactly the derivation from a principle works will be addressed in due course. It is at any rate *not* a derivation from a *self-standing* principle (cf. A67/B92).

[2] See very recently Düsing (2010: 140–1). Wunderlich (2005: 175) denies that the categories are directly related (or 'reducible', as he puts it) to apperception.

70) has claimed even that the deduction of the individual categories ultimately depends on the *natural* conditions of our existence, as much as our empirical experience is dependent on them. The Transcendental Deduction cannot, on that account, be considered an a priori affair in terms of a derivation from a principle. In contrast to Guyer, I firmly believe, first, that Kant does put forward such a derivation claim and, secondly, that given the assumptions of Kant's Critical project it can indeed be upheld. The Transcendental Deduction does not depend on empirical conditions but rather proceeds completely a priori, that is, in abstraction from experience (cf. B89–90/A65).³

In this book, I provide a systematic defence of the derivation claim and explain how, in effect, each of the categories conceptually 'develops out of' the unity of apperception. This can be done by virtue of a '*dissection [Zergliederung] of the faculty of the understanding* itself', thus 'by looking for [concepts a priori] in the understanding alone, as their birthplace' (A65–6/B90, trans. Kemp Smith). I also believe it is only thus that the thrust of Kant's reasoning in the Transcendental Deduction can be fully grasped. A central claim of the book is that one of the thorny issues involved in recent debates concerning the Transcendental Deduction—namely whether Kant is licensed to argue from the unity of apperception to cognition of objects in §§ 16–17 of the B-Deduction and whether this, Kant's 'master argument' is not tantamount to a 'gross *non sequitur*' (this is the so-called reciprocity claim)⁴—can be solved once the derivation question has been answered. Therefore, the question regarding the derivability of the categories bears directly on the question of the meaning of the main argument of the Transcendental Deduction. I contend that the Deduction cannot be really understood absent an account of the derivation of the categories.

One might argue that in the A-preface of the First *Critique* Kant suggests that it is not required to fully get to grips with the subjective deduction—that is, the question 'How is the *faculty of thinking* itself possible?' (Axvii)—in order to understand the chief aim of the Transcendental Deduction, namely showing the objective validity of the pure concepts of the understanding; and that, given this, it would seem superfluous, or at most of merely secondary interest, to attempt a reconstruction of the derivation of the categories from 'the faculty of thinking itself' (by showing how the latter is possible).⁵ However, Kant also says that con-

---

3 Cf. *Prol* § 4, where Kant states that 'making inquiries into pure reason itself and endeavoring in this source to determine the elements as well as the laws of its pure use according to principles' is based 'on no data except reason itself [...] without resting upon any fact' (AA 4: 274).
4 Cf. Pereboom (2010: 161–2).
5 Cf. *Met-Vigil*, AA 29: 984, where Kant is reported to have said that 'it is possible to bring all possible concepts of the understanding into classes, and *derive* [them] *from the faculty of the un-*

sidering the understanding 'in a subjective relation' is 'of great importance in respect of my chief end', but does not 'essentially' belong to it (Axvi–xvii). This is admittedly cryptic, but I believe Kant means this last observation as a gesture of writer's generosity towards the reader who might find herself grappling with the intricacies of such an exposition while not getting to the main point of the Transcendental Deduction—which is to establish *that* the categories are required for the possible experience of objects. But this does not detract from the fact that an account of the subjective aspects of the understanding, of cognition—the question, namely, of *how* the categories are acquired—is an important element in achieving that goal.[6]

Commentators often complain that Kant does not give a specific account of the categories in the Transcendental Deduction, apart from mentioning, in a rather perfunctory manner, some of the categories in the so-called 'second step' of the B-Deduction (see B149, B162–3) or, briefly, the concept of 'cause' at A112.[7] My claim is that Kant does in fact provide—albeit couched in a densely

---

derstanding so that it is thereby exhausted with respect to its extent' (LM: 453–4, emphasis added). Understanding and unity of apperception, which I claim to be the source of the categories, might be taken to be different, but I shall show that they are in fact the same function of unity.

6 In the preface of MFNS, Kant makes a similar observation as in the A-preface of the *Critique* to the effect that proving *that* the categories are necessary conditions of experience is the primary goal of the Transcendental Deduction, and that showing '*how* the categories make such experience possible' is not 'compulsory'. Kant writes: '[I]f we can prove *that* the categories which reason must use in all its cognition can have no other use at all, except solely in relation to objects of possible experience (insofar as they simply make possible the form of thought in such experience), then, although the answer to the question *how* the categories make such experience possible is important enough for *completing* the deduction where possible, with respect to the principle end of the system, namely, the determination of the limits of pure reason, it is in no way *compulsory*, but merely *meritorious*' (MFNS, AA 4: 474n.). But from the subsequent observations in the same note (MFNS, AA 4: 475–6n.36ff.), it is clear that the how-question 'has great importance nonetheless', this being the reason why Kant proposes to deal with the obscurity of the Transcendental Deduction with 'the next opportunity' (i.e. the B-Deduction) by solving the how-question with reference to a clear definition of judgement. Whatever Kant means exactly by his newfound solution, what he says here indicates that the Transcendental Deduction is certainly concerned with the how-question. For a different approach to the A-preface passage (Axvi–xvii), see Bauer (2010: 434–5, 444–5), who associates the issue of the subjective deduction's purported inessentiality with what he calls 'worry passages' (2010: 445ff.) in section III of the A-Deduction.

7 Cf. Allison (2004: 191, 199–201). Allison complicates matters by holding the view that whereas, as on the standard reading, the argument in the first part of the B-Deduction concerns the *general* validity of the categories, in the second part, presumably contrary to the standard read-

argued presentation that has to do, partly at least, with Kant's peculiar method of proof—a very specific account of *all* of the twelve categories in §§ 15–19, on which this book focuses.

In attending to the self-explaining dynamic of the Transcendental Deduction, I am able to explicate how precisely the categories together necessarily apply to objective experience (that is, to the extent that the *thought* of an object in general is concerned) by demonstrating how each of them is conceptually deducible from transcendental apperception, or, the principle of discursive thought. My basic claim is that the story about the categories as the conditions of objective experience or cognition is exactly congruent with a story about the logical constraints of the capacity for discursive thought, namely the unity of apperception. Put simply, it is discursive thought itself, by virtue of the unity of apperception, which operates the categories by virtue of which it is primordially linked to the objective world. This also involves a reappraisal of the so-called 'guiding thread', which Kant specifies at A79/B104–5 in the Metaphysical Deduction. The Archimedean point in the dynamic of this two-tier story is transcendental apperception, as a principle governing not only objective experience (cognition) itself but also the *theory* of objective experience (cognition), or more precisely, the argument that establishes that the categories are the necessary (and formally sufficient) conditions of possible experience (cognition). It is against this backdrop that the thesis of derivability from a principle will become understandable.

In focusing on the systematic deduction of the categories from a principle, I take up anew the controversial project of the eminent German Kant scholar Klaus Reich, whose monograph *The Completeness of Kant's Table of Judgments*[8] made the case that the logical functions of judgement can all be derived from the objective unity of apperception and can be shown to link up with one another systematically (A67/B92),[9] albeit that according to Reich Kant himself did not actually proceed to provide a clear account of such a derivation in the *Critique* itself.[10] More recently, Michael Wolff (1995) has built on Reich's pioneering work and has provided us with a detailed account of the derivation of the functions (or forms)

---

ing, Kant must, but presumably in the end fails to, provide an account of the 'different category types' for each of the 'different experiential functions' they operate (2004: 201).

8 I give references to Reich in the German versions of 2001 and, in square brackets, 1932 (1986), and where a quotation in English is provided, the English translation of 1992 (in this order).

9 Kant himself thinks that there is what he calls a 'closed circle' (*geschlossenen Kreis*) (*Prol*, AA 4: 325) that shows the completeness of the table of the a priori concepts of cognition and enables complete cognition.

10 Prien (2006: 44) proposes to do the same for Kant's theory of concepts.

of judgement that, in my view, decisively settles the question regarding the derivation and the completeness of the table of judgement. However, although Reich's book is considered something of a minor classic in Kant scholarship, Reich has been roundly criticised for his views on the idea of a derivation *from apperception*.[11] Common opinion among Kantians today has it that not only did Kant not mean to derive the functions of judgement, and accordingly the categories, from the principle of apperception, but also that such a derivation would a fortiori be patently speculative and unfounded, stemming from the preoccupations of the post-Kantian idealists[12] rather than something to do with the Critical philosophy itself. I challenge this standard view and aim to resuscitate the main motivation behind Reich's project. I shall argue, in agreement with Reich's main thesis concerning the derivability of the functions of judgement, that Kant indeed does mean to derive, in full a priori fashion, the categories from the principle of apperception.[13] I also believe that, given the general assumptions of the Critical philosophy, Kant's derivation argument is successful.

Yet, unlike Reich, I approach the question from the perspective of the categories rather than the functions of judgement. I seek to give an account of the derivation of the categories—and not, as Reich does, the functions of judgement—from the unity of apperception. I shall also have next to nothing to add to Reich's and Wolff's thoroughgoing analyses of the first two 'Clue' sections.[14] While I look, in Chapter 5, at the Third Section of the Metaphysical Deduction—in particular the passage where Kant effectively provides the so-called 'guiding thread' for finding the categories (A79/B104–5)—I concentrate on Kant's own primary goal of providing a transcendental deduction of the *cat-*

---

11 Cf. Falkenstein (1996: 455). Brandt (1991) is especially responsible for the current consensus among the majority of Kantians about the alleged failure of Reich's project. See also the most recent sharply critical approach by Forster (2008: 70–5, 133–5n.27). The only exceptions in the most important recent literature that I know of are Baum (1986, 2001), Wolff (1995), Longuenesse (1998) and Prien (2006), but neither of them develops Reich's idea of a derivation from apperception in the way I do here. Aportone (2009) points out that Reich's analysis of the Third 'Clue' Section (§ 10 of the Deduction) must be expanded.
12 Cf. Düsing (2010: 140–1).
13 See also Baum (2001: 36ff.) My view, expounded here, concurs with Baum's, though Baum does not develop his views concerning the role of apperception in the way I do here.
14 For a good brief systematic account of the Metaphysical Deduction, which also paints the historical background and its reception, see Longuenesse (2006). See also Allison (2004: 133–56).

egories in the chapter of the *Critique* that bears that name (B116–69 in its B-edition).[15]

I believe, contrary to Reich's suggestion, that Kant *did actually*, in the Deduction itself, provide an account of the specific derivation of all of the categories from one source, albeit by way of a dense, though perhaps poorly presented, argument. Although Kant does not *explicitly*, discursively expound the derivation of each of the categories, I contend that the thrust of the argument in the Deduction is such that it accounts, in the typical mode of a *prima philosophia*, for each of the categories as one of the grounding functions of transcendental apperception as the source of objectively valid thought. I also depart from Reich in that I reconstruct the derivation from the 'I think'-proposition, that is, the *analytic* unity of apperception, not the *objective* unity of apperception, which in my construal is only the conclusion of Kant's deduction. The argument proceeds from the 'I think' *to* objective apperception, of which the definition of judgement is an immediate corollary.

Unlike most commentators[16] I follow Reich, however, in regarding the argument in the Metaphysical Deduction as of a piece with the *transcendental* story from the very start of the chapter 'the Analytic of Concepts' (A65–6/B90–1; in particular, cf. A67/B92). In the introductory section to 'the Analytic of Concepts', Kant writes:

> I understand by an analytic of concepts not their analysis, or the usual procedure of philosophical investigations, that of analyzing the content of concepts that present themselves and bringing them to distinctness, but rather the much less frequently attempted *analysis of the faculty of understanding* itself, *in order to research the possibility of* a priori *concepts by seeking them only in the understanding as their birthplace and analyzing its pure use in general; for this is the proper business of a transcendental philosophy*; the rest is the logical treatment of concepts in philosophy in general. (A65–6/B90–1, emphasis added)

It is clear from the start of the Analytic that the story is transcendental through and through. In the second remark on the table of judgement, Kant is clear that we are discussing '*transcendental* logic' (A71/B97, emphasis added), and the table is a '*transcendental* table of all moments of thinking in judgments' (B98/A73, emphasis added), although in the *Prolegomena* he contrasts the 'logical'

---

15 The logical *functions* of judgement are, to be sure, exactly the categories in their unschematised form, or more precisely, without sensible intuition (see *Prol* § 39, AA 4: 324.20–3). See also R4638, AA 17: 620: 'The *determinate* logical function of a representation in general is the pure concept of the understanding' (NF: 152, emphasis added).
16 There are fortunately exceptions. See e.g. Greenberg (2001: 137–57).

table of judgement with the 'transcendental' table of the categories (*Prol* § 21, AA 4: 302–3).[17]

This is not to say, as has often been the charge, that the argument of the Metaphysical Deduction is constrained by presupposing the argument of the Transcendental Deduction to the effect that the table of judgement is *made* to cohere with the required kinds and right amount of a priori concepts of knowledge, which makes the claims about the correspondence between the tables viciously circular. The background assumption of the claims advanced in this book is that from the very start of the Transcendental Analytic, if not the *Critique of Pure Reason* as such, the story concerns the legitimacy of *objectively valid cognitions*, that is, possible experience as a whole, and so also addresses judgement as *the quintessential form of objectively valid cognition*, that is, as the *essential form* of possible experience. This means that the common denominator of the Metaphysical as well as the Transcendental Deduction is our capacity to cognise objects, to have a capacity for understanding, to judge. One might object to this that holding that the perspective from the very start of the Metaphysical Deduction is *transcendental* does after all imply that the Metaphysical Deduction is geared to the objective of the Transcendental Deduction, viz. an explanation of cognition or experience, and so is made dependent on the latter, which effectively means that the derivation of the table of categories from the table of judgement amounts to a *circulus in probando* (cf. Allison 2004: 152–3). However, this objection assumes a certain conception of the Metaphysical Deduction—that is, of the meaning of the table of judgement and specifically its connection with the table of categories—which is misleading, to say the least, and in fact itself begs the central question.[18]

Notwithstanding my different approach, the overall result of my analysis of the Transcendental Deduction complements Reich's (and Wolff's) conclusions regarding the table of judgement, given the 'parallelism'[19] or coextensivity of the categories and the logical forms of discursive thought. The results of the inquiry into the derivation of the categories will therefore have an effect on how to read the derivation of the functions of judgement (and the way that the table of

---

17 Cf. Wolff (1995: 29, 31). See also the heading of the first of the 'Clue' sections, which is titled 'On the *Transcendental* Clue for the Discovery of all Pure Concepts of the Understanding' (A67/B92, emphasis added).
18 See Wolff (1995) and Greenberg (2001: 137–57) for proper ways of reading the Metaphysical Deduction.
19 Kant's main claim is that the 'pure concepts of the understanding [...] will come out exactly parallel to [that which belongs to judgments in general, and the various moments of the understanding therein]' (*Prol* § 21, AA 4: 302 [TPhb: 96]).

the categories links up with the table of judgement), which I do not address in this book. However, in Chapter 5 I look at the 'guiding thread', which Kant introduces in the run-up to the Transcendental Deduction proper (at A79/B104–5), and explain that thought itself, that is, the understanding as such, and objective experience or objectively valid judgement are based on the same basic functions underlying judgement. The role of the categories is to specify how these functions are applicable to possible *objects* of thought; only to the extent that they have this particular role are they formally distinguishable from the functions of discursive thought as mere logical functions in judgements. I believe that the categories also underwrite the operationality of the logical basic functions of judgement or concept analysis, even when a judgement is considered in abstraction from its objectively valid purport, so from the perspective of what Kant calls general logic (that is, in terms of looking at a judgement as merely a proposition consisting of two or more terms, whose positions are exchangeable, or at a mere relation of concepts in terms of the subordination of one concept under a higher one).[20] However, our investigation concerns these basic logical functions only insofar as they express objectively valid thought,[21] namely as categories.

Nevertheless, the functions of thought and the categories are reducible to the one overarching unitary function, which Kant identifies as the transcendental act of synthesis of the understanding as the capacity for cognition. The account of the Transcendental Deduction is therefore logically, and not just contingently, consistent with an understanding of the necessary logical functions in a judgement. In other words, there is no sense in which the logical functions in judgement and the categories come apart, other than for the purpose of the philosophical explanation of what Kant refers to as possible experience in contrast to mere conceptual analysis. Their distinction is purely formal, and uniquely serves the goal of a *transcendental* story about the constraints of possible experience. Put differently, the distinction between the logical functions of judging and the categories is made solely within the context of the analysis of knowledge with which only transcendental logic is concerned.

Central to my account will thus be the attempt to explicate the way in which the categories and their deduction are coextensive—in a logically rigorous rather than merely loose or analogical sense—with accounting for the unitary logical moments or functions of discursive thought, which Kant at one point says 'are

---

20 See further Schulting (2017b).
21 'Transcendental logic [...] is that general logic applied to objective *a priori* cognition, [and] contains these functions <*functiones*> of thinking or forms of judgment [...]' (*Met-Vigil*, AA 29: 985 [LM: 454]).

so many possible ways of uniting representations in a consciousness' (*Prol* § 22, AA 4: 305 [TPhb: 98]), thereby directly linking the logical moments in a judgement to transcendental apperception. This explication of the parallelism of the categories and the logical moments of discursive thought will be carried out by looking closely at the relation between the analytic and synthetic unities of consciousness.²² An understanding of this logical coextensivity comes down to a proper understanding of Kant's guiding thread. Showing this coextensivity comports with the systematic derivation from the principle of apperception as the principle of discursive thought. It also explains Kant's at first blush cryptic remark in the note appended to B134—that apperception is 'the highest point to which one must affix *all use* of the understanding, even the whole of logic' (emphasis added).²³ For the *systematically coherent use*²⁴ of the functions of discursive thought in judgement and the *systematically coherent use* of the categories of experience reduce to the same original synthetic act of apperception, which is the act of the understanding as a capacity to judge (A69/B94). The logical coextensivity that I claim obtains between the logical functions of judgement and the categories thus concerns their systematically coherent uses of the capacity of understanding, which de facto is a single use, although it is only in transcendental logic that this is made manifest.²⁵

In keeping with the basically Reichian approach outlined above, this book is the first in Kant scholarship to actually expound, with supporting arguments, how *each* of the categories systematically 'develops out of', or originates from, the unity of thought, and hence how all categories hang together in a 'system', precisely as Kant claims (A67/B92), and thus form a 'closed circle' (*Prol* § 39, AA

---

22 Note again that I do not address here the complex questions concerning the logical functions and *their* derivation per se, as to my mind this problem has been successfully solved by Wolff (1995).
23 Cf. *Prol* § 36, AA 4: 318, where Kant says that apperception 'underlies [...] all thinking' (TPhb: 111) as well as the understanding. See further Schulting (2017b).
24 By 'systematically coherent use' I mean 'usage in accordance with the logical connection of each constituent part in a system' (cf. A64–5/B89 and A832/B860).
25 General logic and transcendental logic are only distinguishable from within the transcendental perspective—it is a transcendental distinction. They do not have distinct domains of application in the sphere of experience, or even in the activity of abstract thought; put simply, you could not instantiate a rule of general logic in a judgement or carry out a conceptual analysis without thereby, implicitly, invoking transcendental logic. Neither would there be any point in making a statement of transcendental import, judging that such and such is the case, without thereby framing it in accordance with the forms studied by general logic (forms of judgement, rules of inference). One could of course *abstract* from this transcendental requirement and merely look at the logical relation between concepts (or judgements, or inferences).

4: 325). This origination or 'epigenesis' of pure reason—as he calls it at one point (B167)—by way of a special kind of causality occasioned by, but not logically dependent on and so not caused by experience, a causality that Kant refers to as self-activity, is intimately linked up with the self-explaining dynamic of the Transcendental Deduction. In paying close attention to this methodological aspect, the book goes beyond the standard approach in the literature, which, first, shies away from deriving the categories from a single source and, secondly, is content to give an account of their applicability 'en bloc' to experience.[26] It will be shown that Kant's argument for the applicability of each of the categories to objects of possible experience[27] is integral to a logical, a priori exposition of the constraints of discursive thought as such, of which the principle of apperception is the focal point.[28] This dependence of the argument for the applicability of the categories on the exposition of thinking itself explains the a priori reason for the applicability of each particular category to possible experience. It provides the philosophical *proof* of Kant's general argument that categories must be presupposed for experience to be possible.

In this way, also the complex, dual structure of Kant's derivation argument as a kind of logico-deductive line of reasoning can be clarified. Until now the argument has been construed as either progressive or regressive. I contend that it is both. I explain this by drawing attention to the fact that the dynamic of Kant's reasoning, which underpins the thrust of the Deduction, is such that the argument is not only *about* the conditions of objective experience but also self-explaining. Accordingly, it will be shown that transcendental self-consciousness or apperception, as having to do with a kind of reflective activity, is an indispensable integral part of that explanatory story and is effectively its systematic ground. In short, this book will offer, without unduly relying on interpretative

---

[26] See e.g. Bird (2006: 261). It is almost standard practice among commentators to claim that in the Transcendental Deduction itself Kant does not deal with explaining how each individual category applies to experience; this, it is alleged, is first done in the Analytic of Principles. See Banham (2006: 49), Watkins (2010: 151), and Golob (2016: 29).

[27] That is, at any rate to the thought of an object in general, on which my account focuses. I abstract from the further necessary conditions of *empirical cognition* of objects. This is first discussed in Chapter 11.

[28] Therefore, the direction of dependence is the reverse of what is usually assumed, namely, that the deduction of the logical functions of judgement is made dependent, by Kant, on the scope and objective of the Transcendental Deduction. The proof of the Transcendental Deduction is rather such that the account of the Metaphysical Deduction must *logically precede* the account of the Transcendental Deduction, for it provides the necessary *logical* or *analytical* foundation for the critical, self-reflexive account of the philosophical legitimacy of the categories. Why precisely this is so will become clearer in due course.

aids that are foreign to Kant's manner of thinking, a full-scale and careful analysis of the way in which Kant's reasoning itself, the mode of his theorising in the Deduction, exhibits and supports the derivation of the categories, in accordance with a principle (A67/B92), *from* the mode of discursive thought itself.

The aim of the book is primarily interpretative. It is a contribution to Kant studies. I attempt a precise, systematic,[29] text-based exposition of Kant's arguments. Although no strictly immanent interpretation is possible or even desirable, I shall refrain from weighing up Kant's arguments against standards in current philosophy (the so-called historical fallacy), or reconstructing them in ways that might be more palatable to the analytic mind-set. I think it is better to defer a broader philosophical assessment of Kant's pronouncements to another occasion and, for now, to concentrate on interpretative issues, although I firmly believe that historical and exegetical work is not simply separable from doing philosophy properly.[30]

An additional feature of the book, which is prima facie of more historical interest, is that it presents Kant as to some extent pre-empting the project of a systematic philosophy from a principle as it was ardently pursued by the German Idealists who came immediately after Kant—such as Reinhold,[31] Fichte, and the early Schelling—while steering clear of their egregious mistakes regarding issues of modality. I contend that the systematicity of the procedure in the Transcendental Deduction is congruent with Kant's critical, at base metaphysically modest, approach to the question of the possibility of knowledge and its philosophical explanation. Consequently, I believe that Kant's systematic derivation of the categories does not incur the standard criticisms that, with some justification, have been raised against the speculative pretensions of post-Kantian idealism. If what I shall advance here is true, then much of what the German Idealists

---

29 By 'systematic' I do not allude to the idea of comprehensiveness or system-building (as, in some people's views, was the German Idealists' wont), but what in German would be termed the *Sachstatus* of Kant's claims. In Puntel's (2001) classificatory scheme, my approach would be labelled 'interpretative-systematic', whereby interpretation of Kant's enunciations forms the basis for a systematic understanding of their argumentative thrust.

30 Cf. Ameriks (2001b: 20). Heiner Klemme has put this aptly: 'Systematic philosophy without history of philosophy is deaf, history of philosophy with no systematic ambition is merely learned' (Klemme 2001: 93).

31 Reinhold is not usually counted among the German Idealists strictly speaking. At first, he was a strong defender of more or less orthodox Kantianism (see Schulting 2016a). But given that his prime goal was to provide a systematic philosophy based on a first principle, which is a chief characteristic of German Idealism (excepting Hegel and the later Schelling), he can be considered the inaugurator of German Idealism in at least this essential respect. See Ameriks (2000b, 2006).

claim is wrongheaded in Kant's transcendental philosophy—in particular with respect to his alleged failure to provide a genuine deduction of the categories—rests on interpretative mistakes on the part of these post-Kantian thinkers themselves and issues, not infrequently, from philosophical fallacies underlying their own lines of reasoning. In reality, with the German Idealists it is often difficult to tell apart their interpretative mistakes from their philosophical fallacies. Whatever the case may be regarding the merits of their particular criticisms against Kant, it is almost a foregone conclusion that Hegel will be cited as the most prominent (and undoubtedly most perceptive) among those who charged Kant with not having in effect provided a deduction in the strict sense of a logical derivation and simply relying instead on the de facto givenness of the forms of logic.[32] In this regard, it is instructive to quote a lengthier passage from Stephen Houlgate (2006) on the opening sections of the first part of Hegel's Greater Logic, namely the logic of Being, where Houlgate addresses this issue. Houlgate notes:

> First, Kant—in common with many other philosophers—does not investigate fully *whether* the basic activity of thought is in fact judgment or '*whether* the form of the judgment could be the form of truth' (*EL* 66/94 [§ 28], my emphasis). He simply assumes that it is because it is deemed to be such by traditional formal logic. Second, Kant simply accepts the various kinds of judgment he *finds* in formal logic. That is to say, he takes over the different kinds of judgment (and therewith the categories) '*from formal logic* as given' (*SL* 789/2: 505). In the doctrine of the concept (part 3 of the *Logic*), Hegel claims that formal logicians themselves simply *found* certain kinds of judgment and categories to be fundamental to thought (*SL* 613/2: 289). He thus understands Kant to base his account of the categories on various kinds of judgment that he *finds* in formal logic after they had themselves been *found* by formal logicians in thought. It is this reliance on what he *assumes* thought to be and on what he *finds* in formal logic, not any alleged recourse to empirical, sensuous experience, that makes Kant's procedure in Hegel's eyes 'empirical'.
>
> Kant's 'empirical' approach to thought, judgments, and the categories falls short of what is demanded in a science of logic, Hegel believes, because it does not demonstrate that thought itself requires the categories to be conceived in a particular way. It does not prove that thought *by its very nature* is the activity of judging and that the categories thus have to be taken from the various kinds of judgment, but it simply assumes the primacy of judgment. Furthermore, Kant does not show that the specific kinds of judgment that he takes to underlie the categories inhere in thought necessarily. Kant thus fails to determine the proper way to conceive of the categories because his own account lacks neces-

---

[32] In his review of Kant's *Prolegomena*, Pistorius had already charged Kant with relying on the empirical origin of the forms of logic in the logic books in accounting for the categories' progeny, while it is precisely an a priori proof that is sought. See *Allgemeine Deutsche Bibliothek*, vol. 59 (1784): 322–57, here p. 335.

sity. Indeed, it simply follows in the footsteps of ordinary, everyday consciousness by *taking for granted* what it is to think and how to understand the categories.

If we are to determine how the categories have to be conceived, our conception of them must be based not just on what thought is found or assumed to be but on what thought *proves itself* or *determines itself* to be. In other words, our conception of the categories has to be derived or deduced from—and so necessitated by—thought's own self-determination. According to Hegel, such a deduction would involve demonstrating that certain categories understood in a certain way arise directly from the very nature of thought as such; that is to say, it would entail 'the exposition of the *transition* of that simple unity of self-consciousness *into* these its determinations and distinctions' (*SL* 789/2: 505, my emphasis). But, Hegel laments, 'Kant spared himself the trouble of demonstrating this genuinely synthetic progress' by simply taking the basic character of thought (and therefore of its categories) for granted. (2006: 15–16)

Houlgate's account of Hegel's criticisms against Kant in the particular respect of deducing the categories from thought itself is exactly to the point. It shows very well how the now standard reading of the Deduction, also among Kantians, is rooted implicitly or explicitly in Hegel's verdict on Kant, although Hegel goes further than any Kantian would go in criticising Kant, as Houlgate points out, for insisting on the basic judgemental nature of our thinking activity. The central objection against the Deduction that Houlgate cites concerns Kant's alleged failure to legitimate the assumption of the given-once-and-for-all status of the forms of thought in traditional logic,[33] that is, Kant's ostensible 'empirical procedure'.

This is a common objection that can also be found in the standard Kant literature on the Metaphysical Deduction. In a classic article, Lorenz Krüger (1968) bases his interpretation of Kant's claim about the completeness of the table of judgement on the same assumption underlying this objection—namely that Kant's purported systematising of the functions of the understanding is but an empirical cumulation of existing forms of logic—while claiming with reference to B145–6 that a fortiori Kant did not *intend* to derive the functions of judgement (and thus the categories) from an original source but rested content with their de facto occurrence in logic. For Krüger, the objection can be countered by undermining the force of the claim to which Kant would be committed on a Hegelian reading. That is to say, if it can be shown that Kant is not committed to claiming to derive the functions of judgement from a single source, then the objection no

---

[33] The basis for this criticism lies in Kant's observation in the *Prolegomena* (§ 39, AA 4: 323–4) that '[h]ere, then, the labors of the logicians were ready at hand, though not yet quite free from defects; and with this help I was enabled to exhibit a complete table of the pure functions of the understanding, which were however undetermined in regard to any object.' See further Wolff (1995: 130 ff.) on how this passage should be read.

longer holds sway. However, this reading has several problems of its own. First, although this strategy may, in one reading, be able to explain the passage at B145–6,[34] it contradicts Kant's own remarks about such a derivation and the claim for an a priori account of the pure concepts of the understanding earlier at B142 (AA 3: 114.15–19) and A67/B92 (AA 4: 57.30–58.4/AA 3: 84.30–85.4), and, secondly, it assumes that the de facto status of the forms of logic, that is, the fact that Kant simply takes them over from the tradition, stands in opposition to systematically deriving or 'generating' these forms, or more precisely the *functions* of thought, from a single source, 'from a common principle' (A80/B106), that is, from the understanding as the capacity to think. And this last assumption rests on an erroneous notion of a derivation from a principle. It is not a matter of course that the de facto or 'empirical' status of the logical forms of thought, as they can be found in the handbooks of traditional logic, conflicts with a logical derivation from a principle, given these forms.[35] Although they are situated at either extreme of evaluating Kant's derivation claim, both Krüger (and the majority of Kantians) and Hegel are equally mistaken about the relation between the empirical status of the forms of logic that Kant adopts and the claim regarding their possible a priori derivability.[36]

Thirdly, if Krüger is right about Kant, then although Hegel would be wrong about Kant's intentions I believe he would appear to be right about the lack of probative force of a deduction that is not an a priori derivation from a single source in thought, since, as Houlgate notes quite rightly, it would simply 'lack necessity'. Kant's Deduction would have to be considered a failure, or else not

---

34 But cf. Wolff (1995: 180–1). Against Krüger, Wolff asserts that 'Kant an keiner der zitierten Stellen behauptet, eine Begründung der Annahmen über Arten und Anzahl der Verstandesfunktionen sei unmöglich, sondern im Gegenteil an allen drei Stellen [the one at B145–6, the 'Herz' letter of 1789 and *Prol* § 36, D.S.] sagt, eine "fernere" oder "weitere" Begründung sei unmöglich'. Cf. *Prol* § 39, AA 4: 324. See also Baum (1986: 24–5).

35 Cf. Wolff (1995: 180–1) and Baum (1986: 25). Aportone (2009) appears to believe that the way the logical functions can be classified as they are 'found' excludes the possibility of deriving or producing them: 'Die verschiedenen möglichen Urteilsarten (bzw. Grundtypen von Verstandeshandlungen) sind somit gegeben, und also entdeckt, nicht abgeleitet oder hervorgebracht' (2009: 169–71).

36 It would be odd for Kant to insist, so often, on the deduction being carried out systematically, and not 'rhapsodically', and still to believe that the deduction is *merely* an empirical 'assembl[y]' (*Prol* § 39, AA 4: 322 [TPhb: 114]) of basic concepts or principles. Kant does not consider it inconsistent to take the 'work of the logicians', 'already finished though not yet wholly free of defects', and on this basis to present a 'system of categories, by which it is distinguished from that ancient rhapsody (which proceeded without any principle)' by means of which 'the true signification of the pure concepts of the understanding and the condition of their use could be exactly determined' (*Prol* § 39, AA 4: 323–4 [TPhb: 115–16]).

really a deduction in the strict philosophical sense, as Dieter Henrich (1989) and, following him, Seeberg (2006) have indeed argued (see on this Chapter 3, this volume). Of course, in defence of Krüger's reading of Kant one could then raise doubts about Hegel's high hopes with regard to the necessity of a logical derivation of the functions of thought. However, I firmly believe one would do better to take those claims seriously and to investigate whether Hegel's criticisms against Kant hold up without resorting to deflationary readings of the Deduction such as Krüger's.

The best way to proceed, then, is not by playing down the significance of Hegel's charge but by proving him wrong in his reading of Kant by showing that what Hegel believes is lacking in Kant is already provided, in some sense and to a certain extent, by Kant himself. As Houlgate rightly asserts, our conception of the categories must be based not on what we *commonly take* the forms of thought to be, but on a *demonstration* of how these forms themselves *prove* to be the ground for the categories, 'on what thought *proves itself* or *determines itself* to be', hence how the categories 'arise directly from the very nature of thought as such'. In other words, a deduction of the categories must be grounded in a self-explaining story that explicates the necessary linkage between thinking itself and category-governed possible experience, notwithstanding the fact that the forms of thought have their status firmly entrenched in traditional logic. Evidently, in his defence of Hegel, and for reasons that have to do with Hegel's own project in the *Science of Logic*, Houlgate believes Hegel is quite right to say that Kant did not tell this self-explaining story. More in particular, Kant supposedly did not expound the transition from self-consciousness (i.e. the unity of apperception) to the set of categories. Furthermore, Houlgate (2006: 22–3) notes that Hegel criticises Kant's presumed view that the categories are *distinct* from, and thus have no *intrinsically* deducible relation to, each other.[37]

The present study wants to correct precisely this picture of Kant's procedure in the Deduction. I do not claim that what Kant does is exactly the same as what Hegel later undertakes in his project of a presuppositionless derivation of concepts; nor do I claim that Kant's Deduction makes Hegel's project redundant (or even Fichte's or Schelling's). However, in my view, Kant *does* show, first, how the categories issue from thought itself and are derivable from it, by in effect 'demonstrating this genuinely synthetic progress' from the unity of thought, that

---

[37] This is an interesting claim and I believe that Hegel might be taken to have a point here against Kant. Although the three *moments* of each title of category are necessarily connected, as I shall show, it is prima facie more difficult to see how each of the titles *necessarily* entails the others. Hegel's analysis in the *Science of Logic* is, of course, more overtly a logic of the intrinsic entailments between each separate category.

is, from the unity of apperception, *to* the synthetic a priori, which consists of the set of categories and underlies the objective unity of apperception that defines a judgement. This is the story of the derivation of the categories from apperception. Secondly, the categories are not singly 'applicable' to objectively valid thought, and hence to the experience of objects, but are so applicable in virtue of the *systematicity* of discursive thought itself, that is, in their systematic connection (cf. A64–5/B89). No category comes apart from the other categories,[38] although in any one actual empirical judgement, the surface form of judgement of course always takes a particular judgemental *logical form* (either hypothetical, disjunctive, or merely categorical as to its relation; either affirmative, negative or limitative as to its quality, and so on)—and thus one category (e.g. substance in a categorical judgement) *appears* more clearly involved than others. In the whole of possible experience, however, *all* categories are necessarily instantiated for experience, any instance of experience, indeed to *be possible*. And given that any *particular* empirical judgement is grounded in possible experience (and thus always involves, in the background as it were, a whole of hypothetical judgements, categorical judgements, and so on), it is implicitly governed by the entire set of categories. Kant's argument for the legitimate necessary application of the categories concerns possible experience, not any arbitrary occurrence of empirical experience or judgement, which is in itself a contingent event that of course can only take place *within* the realm of possible experience (cf. B142).

I should like to point out that though the present book is not intended as a commentary on the Transcendental Deduction (in either version), it can be used as such for the first part of the B-Deduction in particular. I do not address the historical background of Kant's account of the categories in the School metaphysics and earlier, or the developmental story behind both the A- and B-Deductions.[39] I also disregard various not unimportant aspects of the Transcendental Deduction that are not central to the theme of my book, the addressing of which would result in a cumbersome work (e.g. the precise relation between

---

38 Cf. R5932, AA 18: 391.18–22.
39 For an account of the historical background, see Heimsoeth (1956: 19–92; 1963), and specifically with respect to the categories of quality, see also Maier (1930). For a commentary on the A-Deduction, see Carl (1992). Carl (1989a, b) offers crucial accounts that enable an understanding of the preparatory work for the deduction of the categories that Kant undertook in his so-called silent decade, especially regarding the *Duisburg Nachlass*. Also Guyer (1987) and Kitcher (2011) provide important insights into Kant's argument in this period. I shall refer to some of Kant's *Reflexionen* from this period that bear on the role of apperception, particularly in regard to the categories of relation (Chapter 7). Since the first edition of this book, Henry Allison has published a major volume dedicated to the Transcendental Deduction, including an expansive account of its historical development and context (see Allison 2015).

transcendental and empirical apperception, self-knowledge and the issue of self-affection).

In Chapter 2, the origin of the project of a deduction of the categories is explored in the famous letter of 1772 to Marcus Herz, in which Kant reported on his efforts to address the problem of intellectual knowledge, after he had presented in his *Inaugural Dissertation* a theory of intelligible knowledge and his already fully-fledged theory of time and space as the necessary conditions of sensible knowledge. The 'Herz' letter contains important initial clues to Kant's discovery of the need for a deduction of the categories and the chief principle of such a deduction.

In Chapter 3, I consider two interpretative issues concerning the well-known juridical metaphor that Kant invokes in an introductory section (§ 13) which addresses the 'principles of a transcendental deduction in general' and, more in particular, introduces the Transcendental Deduction as an argument that proves the *legitimacy* of the categories as necessary conditions of objective experience. The Transcendental Deduction is presented as having a validatory purpose, but also as providing an 'explanation of the way in which concepts can relate to objects *a priori*' (B117/A85), thus giving it an explanatory role. The first issue I consider is whether the type of argument in the Transcendental Deduction is a justification or a proof. I discuss Dieter Henrich's well-known view that the Transcendental Deduction is a philosophical analogue of a legal deduction. The second issue concerns the correct interpretation of Kant's notion of 'original acquisition', which is closely linked to the topic of § 13. I scrutinise Béatrice Longuenesse's thesis that reflective judgement plays a grounding role in the 'acquisition' of the categories, which seems to weaken the transcendental status of the categories.

In Chapter 4, I present a case for Kant's principal claim, his 'master argument' (Pereboom 2001), namely that transcendental self-consciousness or transcendental apperception establishes objective experience, or more precisely, in the first instance the thought of an object in general, and even what it is for objects to *be* objects for us. This claim is argued by Kant in §§ 16 and 17 of the B-Deduction. I defend this claim, the reciprocity claim, against persistent strands of criticism. I particularly look at Guyer's reading of apperception and the reciprocity claim. I also address the literature regarding whether Kant's argument must be construed as progressively or as regressively structured. This is relevant for an assessment of the reciprocity claim, as the premises are different for the progressive and regressive arguments.

Chapter 5 explores the groundwork of the argument of the Transcendental Deduction in the Metaphysical Deduction, where Kant expounds the main characteristics of discursive thought or judgement, which he lists in a table of elementary functions of judgement from which he then, controversially, derives the table of the categories. I am here not specifically concerned with the thorny technical questions regarding both tables, but focus on the *Leitfaden* issue in the Third Section of the Metaphysical Deduction (A76ff./B102ff.). The chapter emphasises Kant's major claim that the coextensivity of judgement and the intuition of an object, which together constitute the possibility of having an objective cognition or experience, rests on a single function of thought, namely an operation of a function of unity among one's various representations. It is the singular importance of this single function that must guide an inquiry into the rationale behind the metaphysical derivation of the categories from the table of judgement, and subsequently the transcendental derivation of the categories from the principle of the unity of apperception, which is the subject of this book. Most importantly, I maintain that this function is equivalent to the original–synthetic unity of self-consciousness or transcendental apperception, which is the Archimedean point of Kant's reasoning.

In Chapters 6 to 9, I undertake detailed analyses of the deduction of each of the twelve categories. This is the meat of the book. It is also its most contentious and enigmatic part.

In Chapter 10, I address the ramifications of the derivation of the categories for the reciprocity claim (having first been discussed in Chapter 4), by looking closely at Kant's argument for it in § 17 and the definition of judgement as its corollary, argued by Kant in § 19. I also put into clearer perspective the way in which the progressive argument coheres with its apparent opposite, the regressive argument, having now demonstrated how the deduction of the categories works. Contrary to construals that read Kant's Transcendental Deduction as either progressive or regressive, I contend that the Transcendental Deduction must be approached simultaneously on two different levels: the progressive argument is based on a logical derivation of the categories from the principle of apperception and concerns the explanatory purport of the Deduction, while the regressive level exhibits the validatory nature of the Deduction, taking objective experience or knowledge as its premise.

Though I believe that it is not strictly speaking part of the deduction *of the categories*, in Chapter 11 I address the 'second step' of the B-Deduction, in which Kant provides an analysis of *perceptual* knowledge that accords with the constraints of our forms of sensibility—effectively an analysis of the connection between transcendental apperception and perception. Although the specific problem which Kant addresses there is relevant to the discussion of the proof-structure of the argument as a whole, I believe that the 'second step' contains no *new* arguments that would add to an understanding of the basic thrust of Kant's reasoning in the '*first step*', that is, make clear what was not already made clear earlier in §§ 15–19. The *argument* of the 'first step', namely the actual deduction of the twelve categories from the unity of apperception, is thus complete by the end of the first half,⁴⁰ even though the Transcendental Deduction continues with a separate, (relatively) independent explanation of the connection between apperception and perception of sensible objects (and the experience of nature in general), which concerns the explanation of the possibility of *experience* rather than merely the possibility of the thought of an object in general.

My reading of the 'first step' of the B-Deduction has of course a bearing on how to read the 'second step'. In the 'second step', Kant undertakes to show how the determinacy of the categories ties in with the synthesis that locates and 'individuates' an object spatiotemporally, within the realm of empirical experience or nature of which all objects, and the particular space they occupy, are parts. Kant thus shows how the modality of space/time, and thus the possible relation to the external world, is coextensive with the modality of thought itself. However, consequent on my interpretation of the 'first step', I would take issue with the received reading of the structural role of the 'second step'. Rather than arguing that Kant's claims in the 'second step' commit him to the metaphysically intemperate view that all perceptions that are had by a perceiver are necessarily subject to the categories (even if not de facto categorially determined), my claim is that Kant is basically committed to the rather more modest view to the effect that necessarily, perceptions are subject to the categories *if and only if* they are to contribute to knowledge. This view of Kant's argument in the 'second step' is in conformity with the hypothetical reasoning underlying the globally regressive argument of the 'first step', which I explain in the course of this book.

---

40 At B159 Kant refers back to §§ 20–1 as summarising the concluding results of the *transcendental deduction*. Cf. Baum (1986: 12–13), who rightly speaks of the first part of the Transcendental Deduction as a proof of the 'ontologische Bedeutung der Kategorien'.

2 The 'Herz' Question

On 1 May 1781, shortly before its publication, Kant wrote in a letter to Marcus Herz (*Corr*, AA 10: 266) that the *Critique of Pure Reason* would finally appear, almost ten years after he first indicated to Herz that he was working on a book under the title 'The Bounds of Sensibility and of Reason' (*Corr*, AA 10: 123), and more than nine years after he had announced he was 'in a position to bring out a critique of pure reason [...] [and] to publish it within three months' (*Corr*, AA 10: 132). The writing took evidently much longer than Kant had anticipated.[1] The only recorded evidence of Kant's thoughts concerning his project in the so-called silent decade between 1770 and 1781, in which he published next to nothing of significance, are his *Reflexionen*, in particular the so-called *Duisburg Nachlass* from around 1774–75, and a series of letters to Herz.[2]

The letter dated 21 February 1772 (hereafter the 'Herz' letter) is an important source for early clues about Kant's main plan for the *Critique*. In it, Kant observed that a central element, in fact 'the key to the whole secret of metaphysics' (*Corr*, AA 10: 130), was missing in his previous endeavours, in particular referring to *On the Form and Principles of the Sensible and the Intelligible World*, his *Inaugural Dissertation*, published two years earlier, which had argued that the forms of sensible cognition, space and time, and the forms of intellectual knowledge were irreducibly distinct. The element missing was an account of how, through the understanding, we come to know the object that we are affected by in sensibility and what 'the *source of the intellectual* elements in our cognition' (*Corr*, AA 10: 278) is.

That the 'Herz' letter looks forward to the *Critique* is disputed by L.W. Beck, who believes that the problem in the letter does not concern the problem of 'how a priori concepts must be applicable to sensible objects', but rather 'the problem of how there can be a priori knowledge of *intelligibilia* without intellectual intuition' (1989: 22–3). Beck believes that Kant is still thinking about how our intellectual representations could represent noumena, not how they can represent conceptually the objects that we intuit sensibly, the problem of the *Critique*. The Copernican turn regarding concepts, which must be seen as applicable only to objects of experience rather than to noumena, first comes *after* the 'Herz' letter, Beck contends. However, a sentence from the letter may provide a solution. Kant says:

---

1 See further Kuehn (2001: 232) on details regarding the publication of the *Critique*.
2 See Carl (1989a, b), Guyer (1987) and Allison (2015) for in-depth accounts of the *Duisburg Nachlass*. I address some aspects of the *Duisburg Nachlass* in Chapter 7.

> I had said [in the *Inaugural Dissertation*]: The sensuous representations present things as they appear, the intellectual representations present them as they are. But by what means are these things given to us, if not by the way in which they affect us [*Wodurch aber werden uns denn diese Dinge gegeben, wenn sie es nicht durch die Art werden, womit sie uns afficiren*]? (*Corr*, AA 10: 131)

That Kant still thinks, as Beck claims, that the intellectual representations represent things as they are in themselves is confirmed by a passage a few lines down (131.22). But it also seems clear, from the last sentence in the above quotation, that the objects of intellectual representations, 'given to us' in a non-affective manner, are the *same* objects that affect us sensibly, namely the things themselves. A further confirmation of this is given by Kant, when in the same paragraph he speaks of the question of the conformity of the understanding to the things themselves as the question

> as to how my understanding may, completely a priori, form for itself concepts of things with which concepts the facts should necessarily agree, and as to how my understanding may formulate real principles concerning the possibility of such concepts, *with which principles experience must be in exact agreement and which nevertheless are independent of experience*. (*Corr*, AA 10: 131, emphasis added)

Now Beck may be right that this is not the theory of the *Critique* regarding the conformity of the understanding to appearances, but rather 'an essentially Leibnizian view of the relation of ontology to phenomenology, of reality to appearance', 'an intrinsic part of the ontology if not the epistemology of the Dissertation of 1770' (1989: 25). However, I think that the essence of Kant's attempt to bridge the gap between the intellectual realm and the phenomenal world is carried forward to the *Critique*, and in that sense the 'Herz' letter provides, *mutatis mutandis*, the first clue to the central problem of the Transcendental Deduction.

In the 'Herz' letter, Kant formulated this problem as the now familiar question:

> What is the ground of the relation of that in us which we call 'representation' to the object? (*Corr*, AA 10: 130)[3]

Only by answering this question, reasons Kant, are we able to determine the agreement between the intellect, which is independent of sensibility, and the object, and so to determine the objective validity of our intellectual representation of the object. Sensible knowledge of the object, the necessary conditions for

---

[3] See also the contemporary *Reflexion* R4473, AA 17: 564–5, which contains very similar material that Kant might have used for formulating the 'Herz' letter.

which Kant already had argued in the *Inaugural Dissertation*, is unproblematic, since

> [i]f a representation comprises only the manner in which the subject is affected by the object, then it is easy to see how it is in conformity with this object, namely, as an effect accords with its cause, and it is easy to see how this modification of our mind can *represent* something, that is, have an object. (*Corr*, AA 10: 130)

The relation between our sensible representations and the object is thus fully 'understandable'. The same would be the case for an intellect that were related to its object in a manner in which it *produced* the object, 'if the object itself were created by the representation' (*Corr*, AA 10: 130). Kant refers to the contrast between *intellectus archetypus* and *intellectus ectypus*,[4] where the latter is 'an intellect which would derive the data for its logical procedure from the sensuous intuition of things' (*Corr*, AA 10: 130). The ectypal hypothesis, adopted by broadly realist positions, is reflected in the view of, as Ameriks (2003b: 100) puts it, 'dogmatic realists [who] say that objects directly produce our representations'. But, as Ameriks further notes, '[o]ne difficulty with the ectypal hypothesis [...] is that by itself it is insufficient to explain the peculiarity of *epistemic* representation as such'. Ameriks continues:

> To say that a particular representation somehow comes into being as the result of the world's impact or 'affection' is not yet to say how that representation comes to have the complexity requisite for being considered a human cognitive state, i.e., a state that does not simply 'match' the world in some sense—as a mirror image might match something—but is such that it can be true or false, justified or unjustified. (2003b: 100)

Importantly, as Ameriks points out, 'any such causal account would appear at best to be able to explain only *contingent* effects'. Hence, Kant rules out the ectypal hypothesis for an explanation of the 'ground of the relation' of the intellect to its object, as the ectypal hypothesis is insufficient for explaining the fact that intellectual representations involve aprioricity and thus, in his view at least, necessity.[5] But the archetypal hypothesis, which argues that our representations are

---

4 Cf. *Tone*, AA 8: 391 (TPhb: 432), where Kant links the archetypal–ectypal distinction to Plato's recollection theory. He also makes reference to Plato further on in the 'Herz' letter (*Corr*, AA 10: 130). In R3825, AA 17: 304, Kant associates *cognitio prototypa* with the cause of things (*causa rerum*) and *cognitio ectypa* with what is caused (*causatum*).

5 I believe that Ameriks (2003: 101) is furthermore right to point out, with reference to *Prol* § 9, that for Kant it is not only a priori knowledge that is seen to be impossible on a causal account of experience, but even in '*non*-apriori cases' it remains 'mysterious' how 'accidents of objects' might be thought of as 'migrat[ing] into finite intuiting subjects'. In other words, Kant has 'a gen-

the causes of the object, is equally problematic, as save for the moral will the intellect does not 'bring the object itself into being' (*Corr*, AA 10: 130).⁶ As Kant observes in his *Lectures on Metaphysics:*

> We have no archetypal intellect <*intellectum archetypum*> which would be the productive cause of things so that the object arises concurrently with the representation. (*Met-Mron*, AA 29: 797–8 [LM: 151])

But if, as Kant says, intellectual representations or indeed 'the pure concepts of the understanding' are neither caused by, nor 'abstracted from' (*Corr*, AA 10: 130) sense perception, nor themselves causing the object qua existing thing, then how are pure concepts of the understanding, representations that refer to an object, possible 'without being in any way affected by it' (*Corr*, AA 10: 131)? 'And if such intellectual representations depend on our inner activity, whence comes the agreement that they are supposed to have with objects [...]?' What is at issue here is the 'determination of the origin and validity of our cognitions', the fundamental question namely

> as to how my understanding may formulate real principles concerning the possibility of such concepts, with which principles experience must be in exact agreement and which nevertheless are independent of experience. (*Corr*, AA 10: 131)

In one of a series of *Reflexionen* that are more or less contemporaneous with the 'Herz' letter, Kant formulates the operative question that will be central to the project of the *Critique* thus:

> How can cognitions be generated in us the objects of which have not yet been exhibited to us[?] Where the objects must not be guided by our cognitions, but the latter by the objects, it seems that they must, at least as far as their fundamental elements are concerned, be given to us before they can be thought. It is therefore *the possibility of a priori cognition which is constant for itself without having been created by the objects themselves that constitutes our first and foremost important question.* (R4633, AA 17: 615–16 [NF: 149], emphasis added)

---

eral objection to empiricism', although the problem could lie in 'ectypalism of any sort', namely any type of theory asserting that 'a representation com[es] to "copy" some object outside it because of the causal "impression" of that object', which could equally be empirical and non-empirical.

6 In the *Critique of the Power of Judgement*, in the well-known § 77, Kant identifies our discursive understanding as an *intellectus ectypus*, which contrasts with an *intellectus archetypus* (AA 5: 408). See Quarfood (2011) for an account of Kant's distinction between discursive understanding and intellectual intuition, with special attention to §§ 76–7.

Kant is clear about the fact that 'this question, of how the faculty of the understanding achieves this conformity with the things themselves[,] is still left in a state of obscurity' (*Corr*, AA 10: 131). He is also clear about the uselessness of all of the various rationalist attempts—he specifically mentions, along with Plato, the theories of hyperphysical influx and pre-established harmony and hits out at Crusius's preformation theory in particular[7]—at explaining the gap between the intellect and the things themselves and to provide 'insight into the [...] ground' of '*a priori* cognitions', since they in fact already presuppose what they are supposed to explain, and are thus viciously circular.[8] Such attempts 'run all philosophy into the ground'. Instead, Kant suggests that the solution to the question of '[h]ow a relation and connection are possible, where only one of the *relatis* is given, must be sought in the nature of cognition in general' (R4473, AA 17: 564 [NF: 139]). '[T]he primary source of the pure concepts of the understanding and of first principles' must not be sought in something exogenous (such as the aforementioned explanatory theories suppose), but endogenously, in the very systematic arrangement of the pure concepts of the understanding itself, so that in this way it could be determined 'how my understanding may, completely a priori, form for itself concepts of things' with which those things 'should necessarily agree' (*Corr*, AA 10: 131).

The answer to the question regarding the a priori agreement between representation and object to which Kant resorts eventually in the *Critique* is a modification of the archetypal hypothesis, which could be labelled the 'representation-making-object-possible' model (cf. A92/B125–6) with the important proviso that our representation of the object 'does not produce its object as far as its *existence* is concerned' (A92/B125), but only provides the *necessary* ground for the possibility of objects or experience *in general*.[9] This ground is

---

[7] See Hogan (2010: 31–2).

[8] Kant reiterates this argument against rationalist hypotheses regarding the '*necessary* agreement of experience with the concepts of its objects' at the end of the B-Deduction (B166–7).

[9] Longuenesse (1998: 20 ff.) has argued that Kant in fact breaks with the idea, still present in the 'Herz' letter, that there is a *causal* relation between the object and the intellect by instead talking, in § 14 of the Deduction, about the relation between object and representation that is of the 'make possible' type (cf. Carl 1989a: 27). Longuenesse argues that an important reason for this change is 'a more fundamental shift' in the way that the object has now been 'internalized' in representation, where the relation between object and representation cannot be one of causation, for 'the problem of the "relation of a synthetic representation to its objects" as stated in the Transcendental Analytic no longer involves any direct relation to an object *outside representation*' (1998: 22), involving Kant's idealism about objects of experience. I concur with her view that the relation between object and representation in the *Critique* is not one of a straightforward cause–effect relationship, since we no longer have to do with the putative cognition of the 'caus-

the set of categories as 'concepts of an object in general' (B128), whose validity therefore 'rests on the fact that through them alone is experience possible (as far as the form of thinking is concerned)' (A93/B126). This model he associates with 'a system of the *epigenesis* of pure reason' (B167). According to this system, the a priori agreement, or original relation, between intellectual representation and object thus consists in the fact that by means of a priori concepts intellectual representation first establishes the objectivity of objects. That there might seem to be an ambiguity about Kant's use of the terms 'object' and 'experience' in his argument for the necessary conditions of experience is, on closer analysis, not the case. It is not prima facie evident that conditions for experience are also conditions for the objects of experience. But that the necessary conditions for the object in general are the same as the conditions of possible experience is because possible experience is that 'in which all objects of cognition are found' (A94/B127), all possible objects being instantiations of an object in general. For Kant, objects are by definition objects *of experience*. '[T]hings that cannot be given to us through any experience are nothing for us' (R4634, AA 17: 618 [NF: 150]).[10] At the end of the B-Deduction, after having expounded how the categories should be seen as establishing the concept of an object in general, Kant draws the conclusion from the arguments he put forward regarding the legitimacy of the application of the categories to experience, that indeed they agree necessarily with experience. He writes:

---

al relation between things existing "in themselves" and (mental) representations, but a relation between appearances as ("internalized") objects of empirical intuition and representations formed by [...] discursive reflection on what is given in sensibility' (1998: 23). However, apart from the fact that I think that Longuenesse's 'internalization' reading of the relation between representation and object, though informative in some sense, runs the risk of a short argument to idealism (but see my own account in Schulting 2017a, ch. 1), I do not believe that one must inevitably see a disjunction between the causal language that Kant uses in the 'Herz' letter and the 'making possible' language in § 14 of the Deduction. In the first set of drafts for a deduction, collated as *Reflexionen* 4629–34, which Kant wrote in the first half of the 1770s, Kant already speaks in terms of the categories as *conditions of the possibility* of experience (see esp. R4631, AA 17: 615.18–23 and R4633, AA 17: 615–16). On the other hand, there is, in the Critical context, also still a sense in which the thing in itself affects our senses, which Longuenesse seems to acknowledge (1998: 22), and also a sense in which, in my view, Kant adopts a qualified archetypal reading of how the role of the understanding consists in being the origin or ground of the form of an object in general, where the category of cause, in its purest form, plays a fundamental role. The notion of cause as such a ground will be discussed in Chapter 7.

10 This is an important early *Reflexion*, from around the period of the 'Herz' letter, which contains an early version of Kant's argument in § 14 of the Deduction. For discussion, see Carl (1989b: 6–11).

> Now there are only two ways in which a *necessary* agreement of experience with the concepts of its objects can be thought: either the experience makes these concepts possible or these concepts make the experience possible. The first is not the case with the categories (nor with pure sensible intuition); for they are *a priori* concepts, hence independent of experience (the assertion of an empirical origin would be a sort of *generatio aequivoca*). Consequently only the second way remains (as it were a system of the *epigenesis* of pure reason): namely that the categories contain the grounds of the possibility of all experience in general from the side of the understanding. (B166–7)

It is also significant that already in the 'Herz' letter Kant explicitly indicates that the way to go about his quest 'for the sources of intellectual knowledge' is to 'reduce transcendental philosophy (that is to say, all the concepts belonging to completely pure reason) to *a certain number of categories*', which are arranged 'according to the way *they classify themselves* by their own nature, following a few fundamental laws of the understanding' (*Corr*, AA 10: 132, emphasis added).[11] Kant is rather confident when he writes to Herz:

> Without going into details here about the whole series of investigations [...] I can say that, so far as my essential purpose is concerned, I have succeeded and that now I am in a position to bring out a critique of pure reason [...]. (*Corr*, AA 10: 132)

This optimistic tone might suggest that he already had a clear vision of the entire project by the time he wrote to Herz, but the fact that it took him another nine years until publication clearly shows that he had not. Nevertheless, the idea of some sort of deduction of the categories as the source of the relation between the intellect and its object of knowledge was born. Notice furthermore the wording of the proposed proof procedure: 'according to the way *they classify themselves* by their own nature, following a few fundamental laws of the understanding [*so wie sie sich selbst durch einige wenige Grundgesetze des Verstandes von selbst in classen eintheilen*]'. This gives the impression that Kant also already had an idea of how to go about proving the a priori origin of the categories from how the understanding itself works.

However, that it took him so long to finish up the work he thought he could quickly complete comes as no surprise, since Kant himself acknowledged, in the Preface to the A-edition of the *Critique*, that the Deduction constituted the investigation 'that [had] cost [him] the most [...] effort' (Axvi). From the evidence of the *Duisburg Nachlass* and the various other *Reflexionen* from this period, it can be seen that Kant struggled for the best part of the 1770s—and indeed even after the first publication of the *Critique*—to find the right formulations for the central idea

---

11 Cf. Wolff (1995: 193).

of the Deduction of the Categories, namely the idea that the origin of the relation between our representations and objects must be sought within the understanding itself.

3 The Quid Juris

3.1 Introduction

In this chapter, I consider two interpretative issues concerning the well-known juridical metaphor that Kant invokes in a section of the Deduction (§ 13) which addresses the 'principles of a transcendental deduction in general' and, more specifically, introduces the Transcendental Deduction as an argument that proves the *legitimacy* of the categories as necessary *a priori* conditions of objective experience. The Transcendental Deduction is presented as having a validatory purpose, but also as providing an 'explanation of the way in which concepts can relate to objects *a priori*' (B117/A85), thus giving it an explanatory role.[1] The first issue is about whether the type of argument in the Transcendental Deduction is either a justification or a proof. This is relevant for my central claim concerning the derivability of the categories. The second is about how to interpret Kant's notion of 'original acquisition' (*Disc*, AA 8: 122–3), which is not mentioned in § 13 but is germane to its subject matter. It concerns the *a priori* and *transcendental* status of the categories. This point is relevant for my second central claim, namely the rigorous coextensivity of the synthetic and analytic unities of consciousness, which I shall argue (in Chapters 5 and 6.3.3) underlies Kant's so-called reciprocity thesis concerning the a priori relation between thought and object, which I first address in Chapter 4.

In § 13, Kant speaks about the Transcendental Deduction as concerning a *quaestio juris* or *quid juris*, rather than a *quaestio facti* or *quid facti* (B116/A84).[2] What he means by this is that the Transcendental Deduction is not a mere 'explanation of the *possession* of a pure cognition' (B119/A87), of a priori

---

1 Cassam (2007: 67 ff.) identifies three roles for the Transcendental Deduction: 'revelatory', 'validatory', and 'explanatory'. Cassam (2007: 70) is right that 'revelatory' accounts of the Transcendental Deduction miss the central point of the Deduction as, not 'showing that we do use categorial concepts in our thinking', but as 'showing that we are entitled to use them', which indicates the 'validatory' motivation of the Transcendental Deduction. 'Kant wouldn't be trying to show that we are entitled to use the categories unless he thought that we do actually use them, but it is a presupposition of his argument that we actually use categorial concepts in our objective thinking; *that* this is what we do is not what he is trying to prove' (2007: 70). Cassam does not think that there is much to a supposed 'explanatory role' for the Transcendental Deduction (2007: 80–4). However, I think there is an explanatory role for the Deduction, in the way that it explains, by means of ostensive proof, which functions of thought (or categories) are required for the possibility of objectively valid knowledge.
2 Cf. *Met-Mron*, AA 29: 764.

https://doi.org/10.1515/9783110584301-006

concepts, which is not in dispute,³ but a justification of these concepts as necessarily and a priori relating to objects and the external world, something that is specifically called for in the case of a priori concepts, which cannot be proven on the basis of mere experience (B117/A85).⁴ It concerns the question regarding

---

3 However, what role the *quaestio facti* plays is perhaps not so clear. Proops (2003: 210) believes that 'Kant fails to make clear whether he introduces this notion simply as a neutral foil to the entitlement-establishing "question of right" (*quid juris*), or whether he conceives of it, more interestingly, as corresponding to an initial stage in the argument of the Deduction', thus providing a justificatory role for the *quid facti*. See further below Section 3.2. I believe that Kant indeed means the notion 'as a neutral foil' and accords it no individual role within the proof of the legitimacy of the categories. Cf. *Real Progress*, AA 20: 275, where Kant says that '[t]he principle, that all knowledge begins solely from experience, concerns a *quaestio facti*, and is thus not at issue here, since the fact is unreservedly granted [*die Thatsache wird ohne Bedenken zugestanden*]' (TPhb: 366, trans. emended).—Regarding the *possession* of knowledge and the role of the Transcendental Deduction, Callanan (2011: 14 ff.) seems to me to mistakenly conflate the fact of our possessing knowledge, as an underlying, unproblematic assumption of the Transcendental Deduction, and the specific task of the Transcendental Deduction, which contrary to the standard reading Callanan claims 'does proceed by reflection upon the conditions *under which the Categories are possessed*, that is, on categorical concepts' acquisition procedure', albeit that such a procedure does not 'involve "facts" in the sense of requiring reference to the given perceptual matter of sensory particulars' (emphasis added). I concur with Callanan's view that in the Transcendental Deduction a reflection on a particular kind of acquisition of the categories (i.e. *original* acquisition; see below Section 3.2.3) is concerned, but to frame this in terms of the provision of 'the *possession*–conditions for the Categories' (2011: 1) strikes me as unwarranted by Kant's text in § 13. Callanan says that 'it is the *lack* of doubt regarding our rightful possession of knowledge that is the appropriate starting point for the inquiry of the Deduction' (2011: 15, emphasis added), but clearly the *rightful* possession of a priori knowledge is precisely what first needs to be established beyond any doubt. Indeed, the de facto possession of the categories is not in doubt (they have been the stock in trade of metaphysics since Aristotle) and does not require any explanation (cf. per contra Callanan 2011: 16), but the *right* to our using them is and so requires a deduction. However, more charitably, Callanan might be taken to argue that the reflection upon the original acquisition of the categories has an explanatory function as well, not just a validatory. That is, the Transcendental Deduction must *explain how* the use of the categories that we possess '*purports to represent* how things must be in accordance with necessary laws' (Callanan 2011: 16).

4 Often it is assumed that in the Transcendental Deduction Kant wants to justify *the use* of the categories, but it seems from the concluding remark of the B-Deduction (B169) that this task is reserved for the second book of the Analytic of Principles. However, at B117/A85 Kant does also seem to suggest that a 'transcendental deduction' does concern 'their right to be so employed' [*Befugnis ihres Gebrauchs*; note that Kant speaks of entitlement to 'pure *a priori* employment' of concepts]; the 'pure *a priori* employment' would be the 'manner in which concepts can thus relate *a priori* to objects' (trans. Kemp Smith). The use here is not in any way concerned with an effective employment, but rather with how categories can be seen as instantiated in *pos-*

the 'birth certificate' (A86/B119) of the pure concepts of the understanding. In *Metaphysik Volckmann*, from the period 1784–85, this is described as follows:

> We call the explanation of the possibility of such cognitions [*Erkenntnisse*] deduction and this retains here the same meaning which it has in Law [*beym Jus*], namely I ask: *quid juris?* or, with what right can you assert that these concepts can be used a priori, and with respect to objects of experience, for otherwise I can dispute [*streitig machen*] that this cognition is *a priori*, and that experience stands under these concepts. A deduction of the concepts of understanding is therefore a proof [*Beweis*] of the validity of cognition; whether it is pure *a priori* without experience. (AA 28: 399, trans. mine)

The precise meaning of this claim, of *how* Kant establishes our entitlement to the use of the categories and their objective validity and how this ties in with the structure of the argument of the Transcendental Deduction, will be discussed in Chapter 4 and following. Here, I am interested in two recent interpretations of the Transcendental Deduction that are different from my reading specifically in regard to evaluating the *quid juris* question. The first interpretation (Section 3.2) is the one advanced by Dieter Henrich (1989) and later expanded on by one of his students, Ulrich Seeberg (2006), which claims that the Transcendental Deduction is not a standard philosophical deduction but a philosophical analogue of contemporary legal arguments. This conflicts with my reading of the Transcendental Deduction as a philosophical deduction in a more or less logically standard sense, namely deduction as in 'derivation from a principle' (albeit a non-axiomatic one).[5] The second interpretation with which my reading conflicts is the one offered by Béatrice Longuenesse (Section 3.3), whose interpretation differs from mine in the way that I believe her ingenious reading of the 'original acquisition' of the categories as grounded in an act of reflective judgement threatens their status as *a priori*, unabstracted concepts and, in addition, makes it difficult to understand how the categories apply to experience. As her reading is an influential but problematic one, my account of Longuenesse will be somewhat longer. My difference with Henrich and Seeberg does not so much concern the fact that Kant's proof is a philosophical analogue of legal de-

---

sible experience. This is indicated by the heading of § 26 ('Transcendental deduction of the universally possible use of the pure concepts of the understanding in experience').

[5] In the *Prolegomena* (§ 39, AA 4: 324.31–2), Kant clearly associates 'deduction' with 'derivation' (see also *Met-Schön*, AA 28: 474 [1785–90]) and earlier he also speaks of 'deriv[ing] *a priori* from one principle [*aus einem Princip a priori ableiten*]' of all the concepts of the understanding (*Prol*, AA 4: 322 [TPhb: 114]). This is connected with the idea of a 'system' of categories, which shows up 'the necessity of [its] division', and is 'a comprehending' rather than the mere comparison associated with an 'aggregate' of cognitions.

ductions, which I do not dispute, as their sharp contradistinction between a proof modelled after such legal deductions and an (implicitly) strong deductive way of reasoning.

3.2 Deduction: Justification or Proof?

In the wake of an influential article by Henrich (1989), it seems that there is a consensus among interpreters about the idea that Kant's Deduction is not in fact a deduction in the philosophical sense of the word, that is, a premise–conclusion style argument.[6] At first sight, Kant does indeed not seem to argue in such a way, although of course it is not the case that no such arguments at all can be found in the Transcendental Deduction. The attention is focused foremost on § 13, in the run-up to the Transcendental Deduction, where Kant discusses the *quid juris/quid facti* distinction. I want to address the issues brought up by Henrich and then more in depth by Seeberg, concerning the question whether the Transcendental Deduction is a philosophical proof *sensu stricto* or rather a justification in the style of contemporary legal procedures. I do not dispute Henrich's and Seeberg's findings that Kant's Transcendental Deduction can fittingly be seen as an analogue of contemporary juridical procedures. I also concur with Henrich's account of the idea of 'reflection' as integral to Kant's mode of reasoning in the Deduction. However, I disagree that it is thereby excluded that the Deduction is a logical proof in some sense. One good illustration of why a legal deduction is not incompatible with a clear syllogistic schema, for example, is provided by Kant himself in his *On the wrongfulness of unauthorised publication of books* (1785). Here, Kant presents a legal argument 'contained in a syllogism that establishes the *right*', in this case, '*of a publisher*' (AA 8: 79). Nor do I believe that Kant does not want to provide an *apodictic* philosophical corroboration of the claims he makes by means of an ostensive proof.[7] I think that Seeberg distinguishes too sharply between, on the one hand, mathematical proof as deduction or demonstration and, on the other, philosophical justification, whereby the latter, in his view, cannot be a proof. Contrary to what Seeberg suggests, Kant does allow philosophical apodictic proof that is not a mathematical demonstration.

Henrich (1989: 31) argues that deduction as a 'logical procedure' is not 'the only, and not the most common, usage [of the term] in eighteenth-century aca-

---

6 But see already Heidegger (1995: 306 ff.).
7 Cf. Baum (1986: 10): '[F]ür Kant [stehen] die juristische Argumentationsweise der Deduktion und die syllogistische Form eines Beweises in keinerlei Konflikt miteinander [...].'

demic language'. He argues plausibly that, since Kant was perfectly capable of organising his thoughts in syllogistic form, in the *Critique* and elsewhere, and since (apparently) he did not fashion his arguments in the Transcendental Deduction in this way, we have 'good reason to look for a reading of the term "deduction" in Kant's sense, one that does not make the meaning of his very program entirely dependent upon the design of a chain of syllogisms'. Such a reading is provided by considering the juridical background of the use of the term 'deduction', which Kant himself in fact alludes to when he refers to 'jurists' demanding 'proofs' of the lawfulness of entitlements (B116/A84). Looking at this background is appropriate—all the more so since Kant frequently invokes legal metaphors to characterise the role of a critique of pure reason. Strikingly, at A751/B779, he labels the 'critique of pure reason' itself 'the true tribunal for all disputes of pure reason [...] [which] is directed to the determining and estimating of the rights of reason in general [...]' (trans. Kemp Smith). At Axi–xii, Kant likens the 'critique of pure reason' to 'a court of justice, by which reason may secure its rightful claims while dismissing all its groundless pretensions, and this not by mere decrees but according to its own eternal and unchangeable laws', which, significantly, he links to reason's 'self-knowledge'.[8] Henrich (1989: 32) refers to the contemporaneous practice of *Deduktionsschriften* in natural law, which were aimed at justifying 'controversial legal claims between the numerous rulers of the independent territories, city republics, and other constituents of the Holy Roman Empire'. In these *Deduktionsschriften*, 'extensive arguments about the way in which a claim had originated and had been maintained over generations had to be given'. He writes further:

> In order to decide whether an acquired right is real or only presumption, one must legally trace the possession somebody claims back to its origin. The process through which a possession or a usage is accounted for by explaining its origin, such that the rightfulness of the possession or the usage becomes apparent, defines the deduction. (1989: 35)

Henrich (1989: 33) claims that Kant would have assumed that 'his audience would understand him when he transferred the term "deduction" from its juridical usage to a new, philosophical one'. He states that although the deduction is a proof, and that its results are brought together, in the conclusions, through syl-

---

[8] See further Schulting (2009a). As Seeberg (2006: 169) notes, the juridical term *deductio* means to summon a witness to appear in court, or in general to bring a case to court, or to take 'legal action', which as Kant writes at A751/B779 is precisely the way in which the *Critique* 'secures to us the peace of a legal order, in which our disputes have to be conducted solely by the recognised methods of *legal action*' (trans. Kemp Smith). Cf. A787/B815.

3.2 Deduction: Justification or Proof?

logistic reasoning (cf. § 20 [B143] and § 26 [B161] in the B-Deduction), 'its being a "deduction" is not defined in terms of a chain of syllogisms' (1989: 39).[9]

Henrich asserts that Kant is not so much interested in fashioning his arguments in strict syllogisms as in the manner of how the investigation is supported by reflection. It is more important 'to ascertain the reliability of premises (of *Beweisgründe*, that is, of the notions and reasons that proofs can rely upon)' (1989: 41), rather than the inferences based on them. Henrich observes:

> The very notion of a deduction is compatible with any kind of argumentation suitable for reaching the goal—namely, the justification of our claims to *a priori* knowledge. As a matter of fact, several types of argument operate within the text of the deduction before it begins to establish its results by means of a syllogistic proof. (1989: 39–40)

This suggests that Kant's line of reasoning is not a single, linear one, but a 'weaving together of considerations' (Kitcher 2011: 87). This, however, appears to conflict with Kant's assertion in a section of the chapter 'The discipline of pure reason in regard to its proofs' (A787–9/B815–17) that a dogmatic, transcendental proof, can only be a single one and that the 'ground of proof can therefore only be unique [*ein einziger*]'. There is thus reason to suspect that in respect of its most crucial aspect, the analogy between Kant's Transcendental Deduction and the practice of *Deduktionsschriften*, where it is customary to proffer different forms of proof—'lawyers throw the kitchen sink at a case', as Patricia Kitcher (2011: 89) aptly says—breaks down. Kant's observation is revealing (note the reference to 'parliamentary advocate'):

> Where reason would conduct its business through mere concepts, only a single proof is possible if any proof is possible at all. Thus if one sees the dogmatist step forth with ten proofs, one can be sure that he has none at all. For if he had one that proved apodictically (as must be the case in matters of pure reason), for what would he need the rest? His intention is only that of every parliamentary advocate: one argument for this one, another one for that, in order to take advantage of the weakness of his judges who, without getting into the business deeply and in order to get rid of it quickly, just grasp at the first argument that occurs to them and decide accordingly. (A789/B817)

Nevertheless, it could be said in defence of Henrich that *within* the single proof a manifold of argumentative approaches is adopted by Kant. As said, Henrich points out that at any rate reflection is a fundamental 'pre-condition of rationality' (1989: 42) and should be seen as intimately connected with the procedure of a deduction. Indeed, as Henrich (1989: 43) further observes, 'no deduction can

---

[9] See also Henrich (1988: 42).

get under way unless it relies primarily on arguments that refer directly to what is revealed by reflection', and that 'constitute the core of every transcendental reflection'. This is why he, rightly, believes that the 'key notion of the deduction in the First *Critique* is, without doubt, the unity of apperception', and that the 'I think' as the mode of reflection is 'the origin of the system of the categories and the point of departure for the deduction of the legitimacy of their usage' (1989: 44–6). This will also be the approach taken in this book, although I am less sure about Henrich's (1989: 37) notion of apperception being the philosophical analogue of the legal *factum* to which the claim to be justified is to be traced back and from which it originates.[10]

Following Henrich, Seeberg (2006: 12) also believes that the method of the Transcendental Deduction is not modelled after a deductive derivation of conclusions from premises and that the transcendental nature of the Deduction is not intelligible if it is explained simply in terms of syllogistic deduction (2006: 179). He associates such a model of deduction with a mathematical deductive grounding of propositions from axioms, which he contrasts with the Deduction's 'synthetic–explicative' method.[11] He also suggests a connection between the typical brevity and 'avoidance of subtlety' of *Deduktionsschriften* as well as their linguistic style and the notorious compactness of Kant's Transcendental Deduction (2006: 175–6). Seeberg's (2006: 64, 68–9, 72, 81) central point about the self-reflexive character of Kant's procedure in the Transcendental Deduction, and for the project of the *Critique* as a whole as a 'self-understanding' of reason that sets itself limits, is well-taken.[12] Also his view that, as a whole, the *Critique* is concerned with showing the rules that govern knowledge of reality as an accountable, self-conscious human activity (2006: 115, 124) is one I concur with. I take issue, however, with his sharp contrast between a mathematical proof and a philosophical model of demonstration in regard to the Transcendental Deduction. Seeberg appears to present an exclusionary choice between *either* strictly mathematical deductive proof *or* philosophical *non*-deductive types of reason-

---

10 Proops (2003: 211, 215–16) also disputes this. However, he considers the factum to be the Metaphysical Deduction, where not the validity (legal) question is asked but where the deduction should be understood in its broad sense of being a derivation. This ties in with Proops's view that the *quid facti* is the first stage in Kant's deductive argument. I doubt though that the Metaphysical Deduction can be seen in terms of the *quaestio facti* that Kant means in § 13.
11 In Seeberg's view, the Transcendental Deduction does not present an 'analytisches Urteil [...], dessen Prämissen hypothetisch angenommen oder axiomatisch gesetzt werden könnten', but requires 'stattdessen eine selbstbezügliche Vergegenwärtigung spontaner, synthetischer Urteilsakte' (2006: 58).
12 See Schulting (2009a). Cf. Seeberg (2006: 78). See further in particular Seeberg (2006), ch. 3.

3.2 Deduction: Justification or Proof? — 35

ing. I propose that although Kant's reasoning is not *explicitly* modelled after a strict axiomatical deduction, and is thus not a direct proof from concepts *sans phrase*, it is still a deductive proof from concepts, but one that is so implicitly or mediately, namely by having recourse to possible experience.

It is clear that Kant thinks that transcendental philosophy also proceeds by way of strict proofs, albeit that these are necessarily different from mathematical demonstrations (*Logic-Vienna*, AA 24: 894), and that a deduction, in terms of the answer to the *quid juris*, is *as such* a proof nonetheless (*Met-Volck*, AA 28: 399) and even one that carries apodictic certainty, as Kant insists in the preface to MFNS (AA 4: 474n.).[13] In a note towards the end of the B-preface of the *Critique* Kant makes it clear that the hypothetical nature of his argument in the preface must make way for an apodictic proof of the truth of the Copernican hypothesis in the body of the book itself. What there had been proposed 'as a hypothesis' must

> in the treatise itself [...] be proved not hypothetically but rather *apodictically from the constitution of our representations of space and time and from the elementary concepts of the understanding*. (Bxxiin., emphasis added)

In § 20 of the B-Deduction, Kant clearly refers to the first part of the Transcendental Deduction as a 'proof' (B145). Also, philosophical proofs must be apodictic (Axv), whose certainty is not less than mathematical certainty, only different in kind, namely discursive or dogmatic rather than intuitive (*Logic-DW*, AA 24: 734 ff.).[14] In the introductory section of the 'System of the Principles of the Understanding' at A161–2/B201, Kant makes a distinction between the 'intuitive certainty', 'as regards their evidential force [*Evidenz*]', of the mathematical principles (not: principles of mathematics) as opposed to the 'merely discursive certainty' of the dynamical principles, 'even while we recognise that the certainty is in both cases complete [*obzwar beiderseits einer völligen Gewißheit fähig sind*]' (trans. Kemp Smith). Towards the end of the B-preface, Kant is adamant

---

[13] At A233/B286, Kant appears to see deduction and proof as disjunctives: 'When, therefore, a determination is added *a priori* to the concept of a thing, then for such a proposition if not a proof then at least a deduction of the legitimacy of its assertion must unfailingly be supplied.' However, a few lines above this passage it is mathematically immediate certainty that is contrasted with 'justification or proof' or a 'deduction' (A233/B286).

[14] Cf. *Logic-Vienna*, AA 24: 830–1, 892; R2454, AA 16: 376; R5645, AA 18: 291, 293; R2714, AA 16: 480; MFNS, AA 4: 474n. Nevertheless, in the *Jäsche Logic* it is stated that since philosophical proof is *probatio*, and not *demonstratio*, it cannot provide apodictic certainty (AA 9: 241); also that direct proofs, which Kant says are what transcendental proofs must be (see below), are not apodictically certain (AA 9: 233–4).

that '[c]riticism is not opposed to the *dogmatic procedure* of reason in its pure cognition as science'. For Kant, 'science must always be dogmatic, i.e., it must prove its conclusions strictly *a priori* from secure principles'.[15] He points out that the *Critical* philosophy rather 'is opposed *only to dogmatism*' (emphasis added), which is 'the presumption of getting on solely with pure cognition from (philosophical) concepts according to principles, which reason has been using for a long time without first inquiring in what way and by what right it has obtained them'. Kant is not opposed to the dogmatic *method* to the extent that it means to proceed a priori and in accordance with the strict rules of logic (further on in the passage he refers to the 'strict method of the famous Wolff, the greatest among all dogmatic philosophers'). But he opposes dogmatism insofar as its 'procedure of pure reason' does '*without an antecedent critique of its own capacity*'. Kant makes it quite clear, however, that the method of transcendental philosophy has nothing in common with popular philosophy ('loquacious shallowness under the presumed name of popularity'), but should instead prepare the way for metaphysics as 'a well-grounded science, which must necessarily be dogmatic, carried out systematically in accordance with the strictest requirement, hence according to scholastic rigor' (all quotations from Bxxxv–xxxvi).[16] In The Architectonic of Reason, Kant similarly points out that '[w]hat we call science [...] arises architectonically, for the sake of its affinity and its derivation from a single supreme and inner end, which first makes possible the whole', and that 'such a science *must be distinguished from all others with certainty and in accordance with principles*' (A833–4/B861–2, emphasis added).

For Kant, furthermore, transcendental proofs must be 'ostensive', or 'direct', meaning that a transcendental proof is a proof that 'is combined with the conviction of truth and simultaneously with insight into its sources', as contrasted with 'the apagogic proof', which 'can produce certainty, to be sure, but never comprehensibility of the truth in regard to its connection with the grounds of its possibility'. Whereas apagogic proofs are closer than ostensive proofs to 'the intuitiveness of a demonstration' in mathematics (A789–90/B817–18), direct (ostensive) proofs, which prove the truth of a cognition by relating it to its grounds, appear only to give 'comparative certainty' (*Logic-Blom* § 196, AA 24: 233–4), which would seem to contradict Kant's emphasis, as pointed out

---

[15] Cf. letter to Herz of January 1779, *Corr*, AA 10: 247.
[16] See also the remarkable *Reflexion* R5031 from the late 1770s: 'I have chosen the scholastic method and preferred it to the free [...] motion of the spirit and wit, although, since I want every reflective mind to take part in this inquiry, I found that the dryness of this method would scare away precisely readers of this sort who seek the connection with the practical' (AA 18: 67 [NF: 206]).

above, on the need for apodicticity, also in transcendental philosophy. (The 'comparative certainty' is akin to the earlier mentioned 'discursive certainty' of the dynamical principles, in contrast to the 'intuitive certainty' of the mathematical principles.)[17] Ostensive proofs, which Kant also calls 'genetic proofs', reveal 'not only truth but also at the same time its *genesis*, its generative source' (*Logic-Blom* § 196, AA 24: 233 [LL: 186]).[18] This connects ostensive proof with the idea of a transcendental deduction as the answer to the *quid juris*, the question regarding the source of one's entitlement to the use of the categories. And indeed, in the section 'The discipline of pure reason in regard to its proofs', at A794/B822, Kant explicitly associates a 'transcendental deduction of its ground of proof', that is, 'discovering a title for [one's] assertions', with direct (ostensive) proof.[19]

Of course, that transcendental proofs are direct proofs does not imply that they rest on mere conceptual analysis, or that they are not really distinguishable from just any inferential link among the set of premises. The proof of a synthetic *a priori* proposition

> does not show [...] that the given concept (e.g. of that which happens), *leads directly* to another concept (that of a cause), for such a transition would be a leap for which nothing could be held responsible; rather it shows that experience itself, hence the object of experience, would be impossible without such a connection. (A783/B811, emphasis added)

In transcendental proofs, the possibility of the *a priori synthetic* connection between concepts and their application to the object or objective event must be established and cannot just be analytically inferred from given concepts. It belongs to the essence of transcendental proofs that the objective validity of a priori concepts and the way that they are synthetically connected must be *justified*, for which 'possible experience' serves as the 'special clue', the 'guideline'

---

17 See also B761–2/A733–4, where Kant distinguishes 'discursive principles' from 'intuitive ones, i.e. axioms', the former of which 'always require a deduction'. Discursive principles can never lay claim to the self-evidence of axiomatic certainty. 'Philosophy [...] must content itself with justifying [its *a priori* principles'] authority through a thorough deduction.' Cf. B199–200/A160–1.

18 This additional feature of ostensive proofs marks out transcendental proof as different from just any logical proof (cf. Gram 1984: 140–1; Gram is highly critical of Kant's account of the four rules of transcendental proof, but that is because he fails to understand the singular status of transcendental proofs, as not singling out a particular type of argument among other arguments as Gram consistently believes, but as characterising, at least in Kant's eyes, the *unique* mode of philosophical proof).

19 In *Real Progress*, Kant however appears to dissociate direct proof from a 'deduction of the legitimate claim of reason to a priori determinations' of the domain of metaphysics (AA 20: 320).

(A782–3/B810–11). Kant alludes to 'possible experience', more specifically 'the unity of apperception', as that in which lies 'the possibility of synthetic judgments' and which is the necessary 'third thing [...] in which alone the synthesis of two concepts can originate' by means of which one 'must go beyond a given concept in order to compare it synthetically with another' (B194/A155; cf. R5643, AA 18: 284 [*Loses Blatt* C3]). But this justification, guided by possible experience, occurs fully *a priori*. Kant explains that

> although we can never pass *immediately* beyond the content of the concept which is given us, we are nevertheless able, in relation to a third thing, namely, *possible* experience, to know the law of its connection with other things, *and to do so in an a priori manner.* (A766/B794, trans. Kemp Smith and emphasis added)

Also, the fact that a transcendental proof does not prove the truth of a synthetic judgement 'directly from concepts, but rather always only indirectly through the relation of these concepts to something entirely contingent, namely *possible experience*', does not make the proof itself any less 'apodictically certain' (A736–7/B764–5).[20] The sense in which a transcendental proof is a direct proof is thus not because it proves 'directly from concepts' as if it concerned mere conceptual analysis, but because unlike apagogic proofs it 'is combined with the conviction of truth and simultaneously with insight into its sources' (A789/B817).

To hark back to Henrich's emphasis on the role of reflection, I believe that in the Transcendental Deduction, and in the *Critique* as a whole, a transcendental reflection (cf. A263/B319) takes place, as a reflection on the relation of thinking to the world, which eo ipso involves a sense of self-reflexivity. It concerns thinking *about* how *thinking* hooks up to the world. This reflection, which takes place in the Transcendental Deduction and is an *a priori* reflection on the 'third thing', is not predetermined by the rules of logic, or the rules of inference, since here it is that the logical functions—insofar as they are objectively valid, hence as categories—must first be derived from scratch, as it were, without presupposing putatively pre-given definitions or principles by means, or on the basis, of which chains of syllogisms can be generated and conceptual analyses can be carried

---

[20] See further Stapleford (2008: 40–57). Stapleford rightly observes: '[T]ranscendental proofs seek to uncover the conditions of instantiating certain concepts. As Kant puts it: "In the case of the transcendental propositions [...] we start always from *one* concept only, and assert the synthetic condition of the possibility of the object in accordance with this concept" (A787/B815). The proof specifies what it would be like for an object to fall under the given concept: "[I]t can contain nothing more than the determination of an object in general in accordance with this one single concept" (A788/B816). So transcendental proofs do not investigate simply the meanings of terms but the conditions of their application' (2008: 45).

out. This does not mean that the logic of Kant's reasoning is free from the rules of logic, although a certain freedom or spontaneity is involved, which is reflected in the way that Kant refers to 'self-activity' (B130) in § 15 and the 'spontaneity' of the 'I think' in § 16 as conditions of objective cognition.[21] This is not just the self-activity or spontaneity of a judging self that makes a judgement *about* some *x*, but also of the transcendental self that reenacts, as it were, the performance of such a judging self—much like Descartes' meditator who reflects, from the subjective standpoint of a thinker, on what any thinker must be able to reflect for herself.

What is at issue here is the methodology of 'first philosophy' concerning metaphysical questions that are not reducible to questions of logic (precisely the mistake Leibniz made, according to Kant, in constructing his 'intellectual system of the world' [A270/B326]), and so in fact precedes logical conditions and rules and indeed *grounds* logic itself, as Kant claims (B134n.).[22] The methodical mode of transcendental reflection is to argue by way of the 'original-synthetic unity of apperception', which rests upon an act of the self-active rational agent contemplating the necessary constraints of objective experience, her *own* experience. This links up with the self-explanatory dynamic of reason shown in the way that Kant argues for the necessary applicability of the categories to objective experience. The explanatory theory that Kant presents in the Transcendental Deduction must itself provide its own method for thinking about its subject matter—indeed, it is the transcendental method, 'the altered method of our way of thinking' (Bxviii), that is applied while carrying out the reflection.[23] It cannot proceed just by virtue of the 'dogmatic procedure of reason', by reasoning from definitions, and simply adopting the rules of inference, let alone construct a system *more geometrico*, as Spinoza attempted. The Transcendental Deduction forms part, the pivotal part, of the actual carrying out of the project of a 'self-knowledge' of reason (Axi).[24]

This is, of course, not to say that Kant's method of transcendental reflection in the Transcendental Deduction conflicts with the rules of logic. Also in transcendental proofs, 'audacious leaps' (Bxxxvi) in the argumentation must be prevented. It means that the exposition of the elements of cognition and experience should 'move', to put it in Hegelian language, in a careful, analytic, step-by-step procedure that expounds the elements of 'analysis' that could not be shown by simply adhering to rules for logical or conceptual analysis and presenting argu-

---

[21] See further Chapter 7, this volume, and Schulting (2017a), ch. 3.
[22] For an account, see Schulting (2017b).
[23] See further Schulting (2009a).
[24] See further on transcendental reflection, Chapter 10, this volume.

ments in clear premise–conclusion style. The transcendental character itself of a priori cognition, and hence the transcendental relation of the categories to experience, can only come to the fore in an idiosyncratic exposition that is itself transcendental in nature. Logical rules, which are in fact grounded in transcendental logic, cannot be the *ground* of the exposition of the transcendental, pure concepts of the understanding (if they were, then there would be no need for transcendental logic in the first place). That Kant's analysis in the Transcendental Deduction does not manifestly *show* the rigorous mode of syllogistic reasoning is due to the transcendental nature of inquiry. However, this transcendental procedure does not detract from the rigorous nature of a derivation from a principle —a deduction in the standard philosophical sense—in the same way that the intentionally reflexive style of Descartes' *Meditations* does not conflict with the strict deductive rules for logical inference that Descartes stipulated for philosophy in the *Regulae* (AT X: 365, 368, 369–70, 379–80).

What the transcendental reflection in the Transcendental Deduction accomplishes is precisely what a transcendental proof as an ostensive proof sets out to establish: providing insight into the systematic coherence of all of the constitutive elements of synthetic a priori cognition. These constitutive elements are, insofar as the conceptual aspect of the analysis of a priori cognition is concerned, the pure concepts of the understanding which 'spring pure and unmixed from the understanding, as absolute unity, and must therefore be connected among themselves in accordance with a concept or idea' (A67/B92).[25] What Kant proposes to do in the Transcendental Deduction is to determine, by means of an 'analysis of the faculty of understanding' (A65/B90), the systematic interconnection between all of the categories. The transcendental reflection that is carried out in the Transcendental Deduction is in fact the mode of explanation of this systematic coherence. Such an explanatory role for the Transcendental Deduction, as one of its roles, hangs together with what is commonly referred to as the regressive argument, which regresses from given knowledge to its necessary grounds, while the precise step-by-step ostensive proof, which is a deduction in the philosophical sense of the word, as a derivation from a principle or premise, is provided by means of the progressive argument (see Chapter 4). At the same time, this explanatory role for the Transcendental Deduction reinforces

---

[25] In the 1772 'Herz' letter, discussed in Chapter 2, Kant speaks of the arrangement of the categories 'according to the way *they classify themselves by their own nature*, following a few fundamental laws of the understanding [*so wie sie sich selbst durch einige wenige Grundgesetze des Verstandes von selbst in classen eintheilen*]' (*Corr*, AA 10: 132, emphasis added), suggesting a self-explicatory structure of the interconnectedness of the categories by which Kant's transcendental proof is informed.

its general validatory function in terms of a legitimisation as a philosophical analogue of a legal *Deduktionsschrift*, as Henrich and Seeberg have emphasised.

3.3 Original Acquisition, Reflective Judgement and the Categories: A Critical Remark on Longuenesse

In the Introduction to the *Critique of the Power of Judgement*, in both the unpublished first (FI) and second versions, Kant makes a distinction that holds Béatrice Longuenesse's special attention in her justly acclaimed book *Kant and the Capacity to Judge* (1998), one of few modern day classics of Kant scholarship. She thinks that it must be linked to an explanation of the possibility of judgement in general, and hence to the transcendental account regarding the possibility of knowledge in the First *Critique*. It concerns the distinction between a 'merely reflecting' or 'reflective' judgement and a 'determining' or 'determinative' judgement. This distinction prompts Longuenesse to argue that reflection has a constitutive role to play for determinative judgement, a type of judgement that she directly associates with the general notion of 'judgement', which Kant argues in the Transcendental Deduction corresponds with the determination by the understanding of an object, or indeed with the objective unity of apperception (TD §§ 17, 19; cf. R5933, AA 18: 392–3, *Prol* § 19, AA 4: 298–9) (see further Chapter 10). In her account of judgement and the transcendental conditions governing judgement, Longuenesse insists on the grounding role of reflection for the possibility of judgement in general, and so on the necessary role of reflection for knowledge, that is, for the understanding.

My observations here concern a critique of Longuenesse's apparent attempt to argue for the *transcendental* role of logical reflection for the possibility of judgement, or, the understanding. I think that the view that reflection has such a role is mistaken and threatens the transcendental nature of Kant's argument in the Transcendental Deduction. I shall point out why I think this, although I shall not be able to offer here anything in the form of a sufficiently argued critique of Longuenesse's richly documented take on judgement in her book. The main criticism concerns what I take to be Longuenesse's confusion of the logical and the transcendental conditions of judgement, which forms the backdrop for my account of the original acquisition of categories and is linked to my discussion, in this chapter, of the *quid juris*. On Longuenesse's view, it seems that the categories lose their privileged status as exclusive transcendental conditions of knowledge, something for which she has also been criticised by Allison (2000). Moreover, her view threatens to undermine Kant's definition of judgement as an *objective* unity of apperception.

3.3.1 Kant on 'Reflective' and 'Determinative' Judgement

In FI, Kant states that

> [t]he power of judgment can be regarded either as a mere faculty for *reflecting* on a given representation, in accordance with a certain principle, for the sake of a concept that is thereby made possible, or as a faculty for *determining* an underlying concept through a given *empirical* representation. In the first case it is the *reflecting* [*reflectirende*], in the second case the *determining* [*bestimmende*] power of judgment.

He goes on to write:

> *To reflect* (to consider), however, is to compare and to hold together given representations either with others or with one's faculty of cognition, in relation to a concept thereby made possible. The reflecting power of judgment is that which is also called the faculty of judging (*facultas diiudicandi*). (FI, AA 20: 211; see also CJ, AA 5: 179)

For Kant, the distinction between the reflecting and determining power of judgement is important for arguing for the possibility of finding among the multiplicity of the empirical objects of nature a common ground for their unity and arriving at empirical concepts and their thorough interconnection into empirical laws. In Kant's account of the general form of the objects of nature, or nature as such (*natura formaliter spectata* [B165]; cf. A114, A125), in the First *Critique*, it was clear that the reflective power of judgement had 'its directions in the concept of a nature in general' (FI, AA 20: 212), and hence in the a priori concepts of the understanding that provide the rules for schematising these and apply the schemata to the empirical synthesis of intuitions. In that case, the reflective power of judgement is not just reflective but also determining, Kant points out, in that 'its transcendental schematism serves it at the same time as a rule under which given empirical intuitions are subsumed' (FI, AA 20: 212). In short, here the universal is given, under which the power of judgement subsumes the particular (CJ, AA 5: 179).

But in the case of particular experiences or intuitions, for which no empirical concept is yet given, the reflecting power of judgement

> proceeds with given appearances, in order to bring them under empirical concepts of determinate natural things [...] in accordance with the general but at the same time indeterminate principle of a purposive arrangement of nature in a system. (FI, AA 20: 213–14)

The power of judgement in its 'merely reflective' mode ascends from the particular to the universal, which comes down to a classification of the manifold,

3.3 Original Acquisition, Reflective Judgement and the Categories — 43

> i.e., a comparison with each other of several classes, each of which stands under a determinate concept, and, if they are complete with regard to the common characteristic, their subsumption under higher classes (genera), until one reaches the concept that contains the principle of the entire classification (and which constitutes the highest genus). (FI, AA 20: 214)

The principle that is central to Kant's argument in the *Critique of the Power of Judgement* is

> the suitability for the capacity of the power of judgment itself for finding in the immeasurable multiplicity of things in accordance with possible empirical laws sufficient kinship among them to enable them to be brought under empirical concepts (classes) and these in turn under more general laws (higher genera) and thus for an empirical system of nature to be reached. (FI, AA 20: 215)

This is what he calls the 'principle of the *technique* of nature' or 'the *purposiveness* of nature' (FI, AA 20: 216)—i.e., 'the concept of an objectively contingent but subjectively [...] necessary lawfulness' (FI, AA 20: 243)—for our power of judgement, which is a transcendental principle that stipulates that nature in the specification of the transcendental laws of understanding, 'i.e., in the manifold of its empirical laws, proceeds in accordance with the idea of a system of their division for the sake of the possibility of experience as an empirical system' (FI, AA 20: 243). This stands in contrast to the '*nomothetic* of nature' (FI, AA 20: 215), which conversely is the principle of the set of transcendental laws that govern nature only formally and determine what it is to have a general concept of nature (*natura formaliter spectata* [B165]) (see further Chapter 11).

Kant then further argues that in 'the mere reflection understanding and imagination mutually agree for the advancement of their business, and the object will be perceived as purposive merely for the power of judgment', which is merely subjective, and 'for which [...] no determinate concept of the object at all is required nor is one thereby generated, and the judgment itself is not a cognitive judgment' (FI, AA 20: 221). This is what Kant terms an aesthetic judgement of reflection, a judgement that is not logical, not cognitive, merely subjective, and does not lead to a determinate concept of an object, but still has universality encoded in it, in that it makes a claim to universal validity or a certain necessity (FI, AA 20: 239). It is this type of judgement, whose ground is entirely subjective but *a priori*, 'even though it can never provide a determinate concept of the object' (FI, AA 20: 239), that is Kant's major concern in the first part of the Third *Critique*.

3.3.2 Reflection and the Categories

In her account of Kant's notion of the 'capacity to judge' in the context of the First *Critique*, Longuenesse is particularly interested in the way that Kant appears to suggest that whereas the power of judgement is clearly reflective in the context of aesthetic judgement that does not lead to a determinate concept of an object, and it is determinative in the case of a cognitive judgement that does determine an object for a concept, a determinative judgement is not thereby not reflective. Longuenesse thinks that Kant's designation 'merely' in 'a merely reflecting judgment' (FI, AA 20: 220) (and he also speaks of an aesthetic judgement that is 'not determining at all, but only reflecting' [FI, AA 20: 247]) indicates this. Although reflection in an aesthetic judgement is not logical, logical reflection, more in particular, the combined logical act of comparison/reflection/abstraction (CRA for short),[26] plays a necessary role in the constitution of an empirical *determinative* judgement,[27] where a determinative judgement is a true or false statement about an actually existing object or objective state of affairs—more specifically an assertion where a particular is subordinated under a universal in accordance with the transcendental laws that govern such subordination. One could say that CRA is, apart from the categories, an additional enabling condition for the possibility of an empirical determinative judgement, while it is uniquely constitutive of an aesthetic judgement of reflection.

Longuenesse thus argues that in fact the categories are themselves products of reflective activity, operating, to put it in Allison's (2001: 16) terms, 'pre-reflectively', the level at which as logical functions of judgement they 'guide' sensible syntheses of imagination, as well as 'post-reflectively as concepts under which

---

26 See JL § 6, AA 9: 94–5. Cf. A260/B316.

27 This is suggested by Kant, among other places, in e.g. *Prol* § 21a: 'The judgment of experience must therefore add to the sensuous intuition and its logical connection in a judgment (*after it has been rendered universal by comparison*) something that determines the synthetic judgment as necessary and therefore as universally valid' (AA 4: 304, emphasis added). Kant does not, however, hint here at a *transcendental* role for 'comparison' for the determination of a judgement as objectively valid, which is what Longuenesse needs. Indeed, such mere logical connection by means of CRA does not at all 'generate' what is necessary for objectively valid judgement, namely categories: 'Hence it is not, as is commonly imagined, enough for experience to compare perceptions and connect them in a consciousness through judgment; from that *there arises no universal validity and necessity* of judgment, by virtue of which alone consciousness can become objectively valid and be called experience' (*Prol* § 20, AA 4: 300, trans. emended and emphasis added).

objects are subsumed in objectively valid judgments of experience'.[28] This suggests that reflective judgements involve the categories as much as determinative judgements do, albeit in different ways.[29] It is not clear how, nor certain whether, Kant would allow this, or whether it might not conflict with Kant's transcendental theory of objective experience. Allison, who follows Longuenesse's account,[30] states that

> reflection and determination are best seen as complementary poles of a unified activity of judgment [...] rather than as two only tangentially related activities pertaining to two distinct faculties.

He continues:

> Accordingly, every ordinary empirical judgment involves moments of both reflection and determination. [...] [E]very determinative judgment involves reflection (as a condition of the very concepts under which particulars are subsumed) [...]. (2001: 44)

Longuenesse strongly believes that Kant's account of reflective judgement in the Third *Critique* is connected, in a more than superficial manner, to the account of judgement in the *Critique of Pure Reason*, more specifically to the exposition on pre-discursive synthesis, or the threefold synthesis (synthesis of apprehension, reproduction and recognition) in the A-Deduction (cf. Longuenesse 1998: 116n.29). This has to do, as Longuenesse (1998: 196) believes, with the fact that perceptions or representations are intrinsically (she talks about a 'conatus' that is as it were encoded in them) amenable to being subsumed under concepts, or being conceptualised. The capacity that makes this possible is the capacity to judge, more specifically here the capacity to reflectively subsume particular empirical representations under a concept. Longuenesse writes:

> [A]cts of discursive thinking sift the sensible given with an eye to generating, inseparably, concepts to be bound in judgments and thus representation of objects [...] to be reflected under those concepts. (1998: 111)

---

28 According to Longuenesse, the categories have an 'evolving' status and are applied in two stages (1998: 243–4): they 'have a role to play as it were at each end of the activity of judging' (1998: 196); see further below.
29 Similarly, since Longuenesse associates this analysis with Kant's distinction between judgements of perception and judgements of experience (see below), judgements of perception seem to already involve, in some way, the categories (cf. Schultz's criticism in Sassen [2000: 213–14]), thus contradicting Kant's statement in the *Prolegomena* that judgements of perception do not require the categories (*Prol*, AA 4: 298).
30 But see his criticism of Longuenesse on the role of the categories in Allison (2000).

According to Longuenesse, in opposition to what she labels the common reading, namely the 'reading of Kant that deliberately privileges the *determination* of the empirical by the *a priori* (i.e. by the categories and by mathematical concepts) to the detriment of the *reflective* relation between the intellectual forms and the sensible' (1998: 112), we can find at the heart of the First *Critique* 'a conception of judgment in which *reflection* plays an essential role, contrary to the common view that *reflection* is a theme exclusive to the third *Critique*' (1998: 163). The First *Critique*'s concern is commonly considered to be with the legitimate use of the categories that relates only 'to the *application* of universal concepts, and so to determinative judgments, the function of which is "to find the particular for the universal"' (1998: 163), and not with the reflective power of judgement. But Longuenesse thinks that opposing the two *Critiques* in this way is misguided, for the reason already indicated that notwithstanding the fact that aesthetic judgement and teleological judgements are indeed 'merely reflective' since they fail to form concepts, cognitive, or 'logical', judgements are *also* determinative, that is, both reflective and determinative. Again, Longuenesse argues that the peculiar feature of aesthetic and teleological judgements is not that they are reflective judgements, for in her view Kant thinks that *every* judgement about empirical objects as such is reflective, but it is rather that they are *merely* reflective judgements, judgements in which reflection can never arrive at conceptual determination. More specifically, Longuenesse claims that if we 'suppose that the first *Critique* is concerned only with *determinative* and not with *reflective* judgment' we 'miss the fact that even in the first *Critique* the *application* of the categories is inseparable from a thought process that has a *reflective* aspect' (1998: 164). That is to say, the application of the categories, according to Longuenesse, *presupposes* what she calls a 'progress from sensible representations to discursive thought' (1998: 164), and this is precisely what we found in the account of reflective judgement the power of judgement does in its reflective mode, finding a universal for a given particular. In other words, Longuenesse says, the '"application" [of the categories, mathematical and empirical concepts] is itself indissociable from a reflective use of the power of judgment, that is, an activity of comparison/reflection/abstraction' (1998: 112n.17). 'It is only by paying sufficient attention to the acts of comparison in judgment', Longuenesse reasons, 'that one can hope to understand how judgments formed by comparison of representations may eventually lead to the subsumption of appearances under categories, and so to what Kant calls "judgments of experience"' (1998: 123).

She then argues that when Kant, in § 19 of the B-Deduction, describes judgement as 'the way to bring given cognitions to the *objective* unity of apperception'

(B141), which is one of his various definitions of judgement,[31] this reflective procedure of finding a universal for a given particular is what should first come to mind. Naturally, Longuenesse does not want to claim that this procedure is merely reflective in the way that an aesthetic judgement is, as it is a reflective procedure that is at the same time determinative, for it leads to the determination of the concept of an object. She argues that 'both directions of judgment, *reflective* as well as *determinative*, collaborate in relating concepts to objects and allowing concepts to "become clear", reflected explicitly as concepts' (1998: 117). At any rate, to be able to apply the categories as 'universal representations of synthesis' (1998: 196) to empirical objects one must first have reflected these objects under concepts in empirical judgements—or put differently, one must have progressed through the process of CRA from the manifold of representations to a universal representation that is the common representation under which the manifold is subsumed. What is not clear is how according to Longuenesse (1998: 118) the 'determination of the concept will *result* from the act of comparison', while at the same time 'the concept must already be present in an "undetermined" state, that is, in an intuitive state, or more precisely, as a still unreflected, "obscure" rule for the synthesis of intuition'.

It appears that Longuenesse steers the analysis of judgement towards a genetic account of how judgement is formed from the bottom up, as it were, whereas the received reading has it that Kant's account in the Transcendental Deduction concerns a regressive analysis of the transcendental possibility of synthetic a priori cognition, which constitutes what a judgement is, *given* a particular judgement.[32] The account does not appear to concern, as Longuenesse thinks it does, an analysis of the possibility of perceptions being such that they *lead to*, by virtue of whatever inner dispositional power or force, forming concepts or being subsumed under predicates in a judgement. The language of Longue-

---

31 See further Schulting (2017a), ch. 3.
32 Kant's account of objective experience is globally regressive. This is often repeated by Kant, most explicitly in § 21a of the *Prolegomena*: '[I]t is first of all necessary to remind the reader that the discussion here is not about the genesis of experience [*dem Entstehen der Erfahrung*], but about that which lies in experience [*von dem, was in ihr liegt*]' (AA 4: 304 [TPhb: 97]). Accounts of the 'genesis of experience' 'belong to empirical psychology', as Kant says (cf. B152). Although the argument for the possibility of the thought of an object in general, in the 'first step' of the Transcendental Deduction, is progressive—namely from self-consciousness as its origin to the objective unity of apperception that is constitutive of the thought of an object in general—and thus in some sense genetic, it is a completely *a priori* argument from the formal 'I think', not from mere (empirical) representations that are reflected upon, compared and abstracted from so as to form universal concepts. On the regressive as well as progressive nature of Kant's main argument, see further Chapters 4 and 10.

nesse's description of the possibility of judgement is indicative of a certain strategy, motivated by a particular interpretation of especially the A-Deduction, to read the account regarding a priori synthesis in terms of a bottom-up procedure, guided by the combined act of CRA, that ultimately leads to what she terms 'universally reflected concepts', i.e. the categories. For example, Longuenesse claims that '[b]y means of the logical forms of our judgment we *strive* to bring about the "objective unity of given representations"' (1998: 83, emphasis added).[33] She also says that every judgement 'aims at objectivity' or at 'conformity to the object' (1998: 83), even though the particular judgement may remain 'subjective' to a greater or lesser degree.[34] This is a reference to Longuenesse's controversial defence of judgements of perception, which are not objective, but may or may not lead to judgements of experience, which are objective by definition. Longuenesse links judgements of perception to associative combination, i.e. a reproductive imagination, which has only subjective validity and is in fact *contrasted*, by Kant, with judgement (B141). Longuenesse believes that also a judgement of perception, and so, by implication, an act of reproductive imagination, requires unity of apperception.[35] So even here, in Longuenesse's view, the subjectively valid combination of representations is due to the objective unity of appercep-

---

[33] The language of 'striving' occurs frequently in Longuenesse's arguments, for example in respect of how sensible intuitions are worked up to form judgements, by means of an '*effort toward judgment* affecting inner sense' (1998: 243). See also Longuenesse (1998: 253).

[34] Note that in the *Jäsche Logic* (§ 5), it is quite clearly stated that logic considers concepts only 'in respect of [their] form, i.e., only *subjectively*; not how it determines an object through a mark' (AA 9: 94 [LL: 591], my underlining). Reflection only concerns the '*logical* origin of concepts—the origin as to their mere form' (AA 9: 94 [LL: 592]). On this account, reflection does then not seem to be concerned with the objective validity of concepts. Cf. A260/B316, A262–3/B318–19, A269/B325.

[35] To be fair to Longuenesse, this is also suggested by Kant himself in the *Prolegomena* (see § 20, AA 4: 300 and § 22, AA 4: 304). My account in the following chapters of the intimate relation between the 'I think' and the categories might be seen as in conflict with the one that Kant gives here in the *Prolegomena*, where he suggests that the unity of representation that is 'relative to the subject and is contingent and subjective' is a judgement that is 'merely subjective', since 'representations are referred to a consciousness in one subject only and are united in it', in contrast to objective judgements, whose representations 'are united in a consciousness in general, that is, necessarily'. This approach is evidently linked to Kant's distinction between judgements of perception and judgements of experience, which Longuenesse takes seriously and has given a very intricate account of that certainly merits further investigation. However, I take Kant to have given up this distinction in the B-Deduction (see footnote below), implying that the 'I think', which is pure and not empirical apperception (cf. B132), can ipso facto no longer be identified with a 'merely subjectively valid' unity of consciousness, given that Kant argues in § 18 that the transcendental unity of apperception is an objective unity of consciousness *in contrast to* a subjective one.

tion, and so given the definition of judgement, in some way geared to becoming predicates in a judgement. I believe this is hugely problematic, since in §18 of the B-Deduction (B139–40) Kant contradistinguishes clearly the objective and subjective unities of consciousness, where only the *objective* unity of consciousness is considered objectively valid and thus, given the definition of judgement that Kant provides subsequently at B141, coextensive with judgement. A subjective unity of consciousness, which is merely subjectively valid, does not constitute a combination of representations that pertains to a judgement, nor does it constitute a unity of representations that show a necessary *combinability* by the original, objective unity of apperception so as to constitute the combination definitional of a judgement of experience (see further Chapter 10).[36]

Longuenesse further makes a couple of prima facie puzzling observations about the relation between the objective unity of apperception, original–synthetic unity of apperception, analytic unity of consciousness, the subjective unity of consciousness and judgement. For example, 'judgment [is] the mediating element between, on the one hand, the *original synthetic* unity of apperception' 'as producing the synthesis of the manifold of sensible intuitions', and, on the other, 'the *objective* unity of apperception' 'as relating the synthesis to objects'; or, judgement is 'the form of conceptual universality, or the "analytic unity of consciousness", [which] is the means by which (synthetic) objective unity of consciousness is realized in judgment' (1998: 105–6), suggesting that judgement is merely the analytic relation between the predicates and not also the transcendental content which is the result of the very synthetic act of judging (in conformity with the *Leitfaden* passage at A79, Longuenesse's account of which is otherwise illuminating and one I am in broad agreement with). These views reveal what I believe are mistaken readings of the interconnection between the var-

---

[36] I agree with Pollok's (2008: 324, 326) account of Kant's very probable change of mind regarding judgements of perception between 1783, the year of the publication of the *Prolegomena*, where the distinction is made, and 1786, when he published the *Metaphysical Foundations of Natural Science* (MFNS), whose preface contains the famous note on a proposal for a deduction from a definition of judgement, which would appear to exclude the possibility of merely subjectively valid judgements of perception. In the MFNS footnote (AA 4: 475–6n.), Kant responds to Schultz's review of Ulrich's *Institutiones logicae* from 1785, in which Schultz criticised Kant's distinction between judgements of perception and judgements of experience (see Sassen 2000: 213–14). In reaction to this, in the B-Deduction ('the next opportunity') Kant then undertakes to rework the solution to the question how experience is 'possible by means of the categories' by seeing it as evolving out of the 'precisely determined *definition of a judgment in general*' (AA 4: 475n., emphasis added), suggesting that anything that is not an objectively valid experience of objects cannot be seen as corresponding to a judgement of whatever type. The distinction between judgement of perception and judgement of experience thus falls away.

ious *formally* distinguishable unities that are involved in Kant's argument for what constitutes objectively valid thought and hence judgement, but also of Kant's careful reasoning as regards the specific goal of the Transcendental Deduction as well as its proof structure. From Chapter 6 onwards, I shall present my own view of how these unities of consciousness do connect up.

True, Longuenesse sees associations or reproduced representations as issuing in judgement only 'if they have themselves been *predetermined* by the activity of judging, which relates all cognition to the objective unity of apperception' (1998: 83, emphasis added). Or, indeed, syntheses of imagination 'will ultimately lead to the representations of *determined* objects (*phenomena*) only if they are "brought under" the unity of apperception', i.e. 'by *transcendental* imagination' (1998: 109). But, in Longuenesse's view, even empirical associations 'are acts of relating representations to objects, and this is why they eventually lead to genuine "judgments of experience", with a claim to hold "for everybody, always"' (1998: 84). Again the language is striking here, as if some conative striving were involved in the reproductively associated representations themselves, which links them intrinsically to judgement. I believe that this view would not be endorsed by Kant; nor is there any reasoning in the text of the Transcendental Deduction that supported a reading that argues that representations themselves necessarily entail their being connected, through a certain a priori rule-governing, such that they form, potentially, objective, determinative judgements; or indeed, that there would be 'subjective predispositions [*eingepflanzte Anlagen*] for thinking, implanted in us along with our existence [...]' (B167). Nothing in Kant's reasoning points to a putative dispositional force or capacity that makes our representations or appearances *combinable* for judgement, and hence subject to categorial determination.[37] Kant cannot argue that, for if categories were indeed preformed or 'implanted predispositions for judgments', it would mean that there is a 'postulated harmony of categories and experience'. This would leave the necessary status of the categories in doubt, since any one category could in that case be a mere concept as 'divine predisposition' (Quarfood 2004: 100) and so not a '*self-thought a priori* first principle' (B167), and consequently 'the relation between a predisposition to think in a certain way and what actually

---

[37] The language in some passages in the A-Deduction, such as at A112–13 and A124, does seem to suggest a conative aspect in the appearances themselves, which makes them disposed to being united in the objective unity of apperception. But compare A112, where Kant emphasises, with regard to the concept of cause, that 'experience teaches us that one appearance customarily follows another, *but not that it must necessarily follow that*' (emphasis added), which implies that nothing in the appearances themselves suggests ipso facto necessary connection or an objective ground for association. Cf. A121–2.

3.3 Original Acquisition, Reflective Judgement and the Categories — 51

is the case would be entirely contingent' (Quarfood 2004: 100). The latter problem arises in particular for Longuenesse, as it seems that she is not able to explain in which cases categories and representations or perceptions are in complete agreement and in which cases they are not.

3.3.3 A Lockean Deduction?

It appears that on Longuenesse's reading, as she herself notes (1998: 116), schemata are acquired *before* the concepts of which they are the schemata. This strikes one as paradoxical, to say the least.[38] She argues that the Transcendental Deduction inquires

> into the formation or acquisition both of 'rules for the determination of our intuition' and of concepts [...] [while] it seems clear that the 'rules for the synthesis of intuition' must first have been *acquired* at the outcome of the operations described in the A-Deduction (apprehension, reproduction, and recognition) in order to be *reflected* as discursive concepts, 'universal or reflected representations'. We are here concerned with this empirical acquisition of 'rules for the synthesis of intuition'. (Longuenesse 1998: 116n.29)

This, I believe, shows a mix-up on Longuenesse's part of the empirical and transcendental explanations of how concepts are generated. The process of CRA applies to empirical concept formation, as Kant points out in the *Critique of the Power of Judgement*, especially in the Introductions, but not to how the categories are 'originally' acquired (which Kant describes as 'a system of epigenesis' at B167; see on this below).[39] Longuenesse thus appears to interpret the threefold synthesis in the A-Deduction in terms of an empirical, generative process of concept formation from the particular to the universal; by contrast the synthesis or syntheses Kant talks about are clearly pure, a priori and transcendental, not empirical (A99 [AA 4: 77.24–30]; A115) and are 'inseparably combined' with one another (A102), and so amount to a transcendental combined act of syntheses that provide universal rules for the determination of the concept of an object in general, under which one's empirical intuitions must be subsumed.[40] The rule-governed operation of synthesis is not just a logical process, which supposedly establishes objectively determinate knowledge, but it is the *transcendental* ground of such logical processes (either in conjunction with the perception of objects, as

---

38 See also the critique formulated by Sedgwick (2000: 86).
39 Cf. Prien (2006: 73–5).
40 For a detailed account of the threefold synthesis, see Schulting (2017a), ch. 6.

in actual judgements of experience, or in abstraction from it, when we only consider the relation among conceptual representations or predicates, or in judgements of perception for that matter). One cannot then argue—as Longuenesse appears to do by regarding reflection as co-constitutive of the acquisition of discursive concepts or categories—for the *logical* ground (which would be empirical) of such a transcendental ground or the categories without hugely begging Kant's question.

There are a few general problems that I would like to stress here: (1) an act of comparison is a logical act of *analysis* (even if one supposedly 'under *sensible* conditions' [Longuenesse 1998: 127]), not a specifically transcendental act of *synthesis*, which is in fact presupposed by the logical act. It seems as if Longuenesse wants to say here that the determination of the concept is grounded upon comparison that leads to the concept, out of which the determination 'results' (1998: 118). It is not clear what she means by 'result', and how it comes about.[41] It seems to me that she confuses the levels of explanation, what is supposed to explain what, that is, what is the *explanans*, and what the *explanandum*. The transcendental act of synthesis is the ground of any logical analysis (cf. B134n.), so how can transcendental synthesis—or, the set of categories or universal and reflected representations, as Longuenesse frequently puts it—*result from* what it in fact *grounds*?

This is related to her view of the two-stage application of the categories. She argues for an 'initial "application"' (1998: 244), which is carried out by the *synthesis speciosa*, but in which the categories 'are not reflected as concepts', hence leaving the synthesis undetermined. At this stage, there is only 'blind' synthesis of imagination. Categories as concepts ('clear concepts', 'universal representations'), on the other hand, come about through the formation of empirical judgements on the basis of an analysis of the *synthesis speciosa*, at which point the categories get applied 'in a second sense'—namely in the sense that a claim to objective validity for the combined representations is made. Only at this point is the object of representation really subsumed 'under a concept of pure understanding' (1998: 244). Longuenesse also frequently speaks of the categories 'guiding' the syntheses in intuition, which is supposed to reflect the two-stage process of the generation of the categories—namely first 'as *schemata* [...] as rules of sensible synthesis generated with a view to forming judgments' and then, in the second instance, 'as "clear concepts" [...] as "universal representations" of pure synthesis according to rules [...]' (1998: 253). It is hard to see

---

[41] In a commentary on Longuenesse's book, Sedgwick (2000: 84) expresses a similar puzzlement.

how this two-stage process corresponds with Kant's view of the instantiation of the categories without landing us in an infinite regress, which Kantian a priori synthesis is in fact supposed to block (cf. Longuenesse 2008: 515). If categories first 'guide' the sensible synthesis with a view to forming judgements and only subsequently get applied in that the thus synthesised representations are subsumed under pure concepts of the understanding in an objectively valid judgement, then the question arises as to which function or functions regulate(s) the categories' actual instantiation (their 'second application') in contrast to their mere 'guiding' function (their ostensible 'first application'). The infinite regress that threatens concerns the question of which even more original act would lie at the basis of this difference between 'mere' guiding and effective instantiation, and would be the ground of possibility of getting us from the former to the latter.

(2) Furthermore, Longuenesse's view of the acquisition of the universally reflected concepts, the categories, not just empirical concepts, as resulting from CRA, strikes me as suggestive of an *empirical* deduction of the categories, something Kant deemed impossible. As Longuenesse herself percipiently notes (1998: 125), such a view of the acquisition of the categories looks very much like a Lockean sensitivisation of the concepts of the understanding as if they were empirical, abstracted concepts of reflection (A271). Longuenesse poses the operative question herself:

> Should we consider that this dependence of concepts on their 'application in comparison' holds not only for empirical concepts, but also for a priori concepts—categories and mathematical concepts? Should one say also of the latter that they are generated through 'comparison, reflection and abstraction' from given representations, and that they have no universality other than that generated by these acts? (1998: 120)

She asks rhetorically:

> Could one not reproach me with having attributed to Kant precisely the 'sensualization of the concepts of the understanding' he criticized in Locke? (1998: 125)[42]

Indeed, Kant explicitly states that attempting to search 'in experience' for 'the occasional causes [*Gelegenheitsursachen*] of their generation [i.e. of the catego-

---

[42] In the section On the Amphiboly of Concepts of Reflection, in which he takes Leibniz to task in particular for regarding rational reflection as providing the basis for 'a supposed system of intellectual cognition' (B336/A280), Kant criticises Locke for '*sensitiviz*[ing] the concepts of understanding in accordance with his system of *noogony* [...], i.e., interpret[ing] them as nothing but empirical or abstracted [*abgesonderte*] concepts of reflection' (A271/B327).

ries], where the impressions of the senses provide the first occasion for opening the entire power of cognition to them and for bringing about experience', that is, a 'tracing of the first endeavors of our power of cognition to ascend from individual perceptions to general concepts' is something Locke carried out,[43] but is altogether different from a *transcendental deduction* of pure concepts, which 'does not lie down this path at all', namely the path of a 'physiological derivation, which cannot properly be called a deduction at all because it concerns a *quaestio facti*, the explanation of the *possession* of a pure cognition' (A86–7/B118–19). In Kant's view, Locke 'committed the error of taking the occasion for acquiring these concepts, namely experience, as their source' (R4866, AA 18: 14 [NF: 197]). Any effort to read the *origin* of the pure concepts in such an empirical way is an 'entirely futile work' (A85/B118), since any empirical deduction of the *subjective* origin of these concepts would not eo ipso amount to a proof of the *objective* validity of these concepts.[44]

Excursus: The 'Quaestio Facti' and Empirical Deduction

Ian Proops (2003) has argued regarding § 13, where Kant makes the *quid juris/ quid facti* distinction, that one must actually distinguish between an empirical deduction, which Kant says is 'useless' (B119/A87, trans. Kemp Smith) for the explanation of the employment of the categories, and a Lockean 'physiological derivation', which can have its usefulness (B118–19/A86–7), and which concerns a *quaestio facti*. Proops appears to uncouple empirical deduction and the *quaestio facti*, which most commentators assume to be intimately related (cf. Carl 1992: 127n.25); on the standard reading, the answer to the *quid facti* would seem to be an empirical deduction (cf. Carl 1992: 113n.4). It is not prima facie clear, in § 13, whether the distinction to which Proops calls attention is in fact heeded by Kant, since he says similar things both with regard to the procedure of an empirical deduction ('which shows the manner in which a concept is acquired through experience and through reflection upon experience', precisely what Longuenesse has in mind; note that the quotation proceeds, 'and which therefore concerns, not its legitimacy [*Rechtmäßigkeit*], but only the fact [*Factum*] from which the possession has arisen' [B117/A85, trans. emended]) and with regard to Locke's endeavours ('Such an investigation of the first strivings of our faculty of knowledge, whereby it advances from particular perceptions to universal con-

---

[43] Cf. R3930, AA 18: 352.
[44] It is all the more striking that Hegel precisely objected to Kant's formalist approach to the intellect as nothing more than 'extended Lockeanism' (GuW: 326, 333).

cepts [...]' [B118–19/A86], again what Longuenesse appears to have in mind). By dissociating the two, Proops understandably wants to provide an explanation for Kant's otherwise puzzling observations that 'to seek an empirical deduction [of *a priori* concepts] would be labour entirely lost' (A85/B118) and is 'an utterly useless enterprise' (B119/A87), whereas to carry out a Lockean investigation of 'seek[ing] to discover in experience [...] the occasioning causes of their production' 'is undoubtedly of great service', as an 'explanation of the *possession* of pure knowledge' (B118/A86, trans. Kemp Smith[45]). This seems confirmed by a statement from *Real Progress*, where Kant asserts, while differentiating it from a *quaestio facti*, that the affirmative answer to the *quaestio juris* whether 'all knowledge' must 'also [...] be derived solely from experience, as the supreme ground of knowledge [...] would inaugurate the empiricism of transcendental philosophy', suggesting an empirical deduction of the origin of knowledge, which would amount to 'self-contradiction',

> for if all knowledge is of empirical origin, then regardless of what may be grounded *a priori* in the understanding, and can ever be admitted, by the law of contradiction, to reflection and its logical principle, the synthetic in knowledge, which constitutes the essence of experience, is still purely empirical, and possible only as knowledge *a posteriori*; and transcendental philosophy is itself an absurdity. (AA 20: 275 [TPhb: 366])

This is in line with Kant's statement in § 13 in the *Critique* that an 'attempted physiological derivation [...] cannot properly be called a deduction at all because it concerns a *quaestio facti*, the explanation of the *possession* of a pure cognition' (A86–7/B119), of which only a transcendental deduction and not an empirical one would be meaningful as an answer to the *quaestio juris*. This, then, suggests, as Proops (2003: 219) points out, that an empirical deduction is not the answer to a *quid facti*, but the wrong answer to the *quid juris*.

However, Proops also wants to reserve an independent role for the *quaestio facti* as 'a necessary first step in the proof of the *quid juris*' in Kant's argument (2003: 219), and locates this first step in the Metaphysical Deduction (2003: 223), the *quid juris* being the proof of the legitimacy of the categories, in the Transcendental Deduction, *on the basis* of the answer to the *quaestio facti*, which would concern the derivation of the categories from the functions of judgement.[46] Notice that Allison (2001: 67) makes a similar *quid facti/quid juris* distinction in regard to the argument of the *Critique of the Power of Judgement*.[47] How-

---

45 In this excursus, all foregoing quotations from Kant's text in § 13 are from Kemp Smith.
46 Aportone (2009: 180–1) also appears to see the Metaphysical Deduction as concerning a *quid facti*.
47 Allison (2004: 475n.47) accepts Proops's proposal.

ever, although in the Metaphysical Deduction pure concepts are expounded that we already possess (cf. A85/B118), I believe the argument of the Metaphysical Deduction is not an 'explanation of the *possession* of a pure cognition' (B119/A87), as Proops argues, but rather a first premise in the overall argument of the Deduction, which concerns an identification or inventory of the pure concepts, and is thus indeed a first stage in Kant's overall justificatory argument, but not a *quid facti* issue. I do not see evidence in Kant's text for Proops's interpretative move that sees a resemblance between a Lockean physiological derivation and a Kantian derivation (deduction in the broader non-legal sense). Moreover, it would be odd for Kant to compare his own endeavour, in the Metaphysical Deduction, to establish the origin of the categories in the functions of judgement (B159) to a Lockean-type *quaestio facti* regarding the *occasioning* cause of the categories in *experience*, whose comparability he would also surely have emphasised more if their procedures in this regard had indeed been comparable. It seems to me that, for Kant, a *quaestio facti* has no transcendental-philosophical relevance, as the above-quoted passage from the *Real Progress* indeed suggests.

* * *

Longuenesse acknowledges that a Lockean procedure of tracing the occasioning causes of experience would be more appropriate for empirical concepts, but does not think a similar procedure for a priori concepts is automatically disqualified:

> Since the example Kant gives to illustrate these operations clearly has to do with empirical concepts ('I see a spruce, a willow, and a linden...'), one may doubt the three operations mentioned[48] are capable of clarifying the 'made' character of a priori concepts. Yet, we *should not exclude this possibility too quickly.* (1998: 120–1, emphasis added)

However, I find Longuenesse's subsequent attempt to explain that her reading is not in fact vulnerable to the objection of it amounting to a Lockean derivation unconvincing. I think it is evident that her view that 'the operation of comparison/reflection/abstraction is indeed the discursive act par excellence, through which the very form of conceptual universality is produced, *whichever kind of concept we consider*' (1998: 121, emphasis added), cannot serve as support for an account of the originality of categories, which are not just *any* concepts, or 'forms of conceptual universality', but *a priori* concepts of the understanding, concepts that have a unique status that is absolutely distinct even from the most abstract empirical concepts. They are neither empirically derived, 'empirical products' (B124/A92) nor innate; rather they are 'original concepts' that 'must

---

[48] Longuenesse (1998: 120) refers to JL § 6.

3.3 Original Acquisition, Reflective Judgement and the Categories — 57

have arisen entirely *a priori*, independently of experience', 'mixed in' in our sensible experiences (A2).[49] Kant distinguishes between a *generatio aequivoca*, which points to an empirical origin for the pure concepts, 'encountered [...] in experience', as Locke did (B127), and an epigenetic system, which means that 'the categories contain the grounds of the possibility of all experience in general from the side of the understanding' and are objectively necessary '*self-thought* [*selbstgedachte*] *a priori* first principles of our cognition' (B167); here, '*the understanding itself*, by means of these concepts, [is] the originator of the experience in which its objects are encountered' (B127, emphasis added).

In *Disc* (AA 8: 221–3), Kant writes about the way categories are acquired in terms of an original acquisition in contrast to *acquisitio derivativa*, meaning that our cognitive faculty 'brings them about, *a priori*, out of itself', thus originally (which might be called their only innate aspect).[50] They are nonetheless *acquired* in the sense that they are applied, or instantiated, only in the context of de facto sensible experience, in response to sensory stimuli (and have no objective sense beyond experience). Kant appears to adopt a qualified dispositional model of the understanding, in which nothing is innate except the formal ground of the categories, which are first uncovered on the occasion of the encounter with objects in experience.[51] *Acquisitio derivativa*, on the other hand, concerns 'determinate *concepts* of things that are in accordance with this form [i.e. space] [...] [and] *already* presupposes universal *transcendental* concepts of the understanding' (emphasis added). Longuenesse's view that categories, like empirical concepts, which are however acquired 'derivatively', are arrived at through the logical

---

[49] Also, if, as Longuenesse claims, the operations of CRA ground the categories, and given that they are also involved in the formation of empirical concepts, what would the categories 'add' to them, that is, what role would be left for the categories? I thank Christian Onof for raising this point.

[50] See also R4851, AA 18: 10. See Quarfood (2004: 77–117) for an account of Kant on *acquisitio orginaria* and innatism and the relation to epigenesis and the latter term's biological origin. Quarfood (2004: 85–6) explains that the use of the legal term *acquisitio originaria*, meaning the acquisition of something 'which before the acquisition did not belong to anyone', is precisely reflected in Kant's notion of 'our cognitive faculty' bringing these pure concepts about 'out of itself' and a priori. In *Met-L$_2$* Kant is reported as having said: 'We have no innate concepts (<*notiones connatae*; G: *angebornen Begriffe*>) at all, but rather we attain them all, or we receive acquired concepts <*notiones acquisitae*>. The understanding acquires concepts by its paying attention to its own use' (AA 28: 542 [LM: 309]).

[51] Cf. A66/B91: 'We will therefore pursue the pure concepts into their *first seeds and predispositions* in the human understanding, where they lie ready, until with the opportunity of experience they are finally developed and exhibited in their clarity by the very same understanding, *liberated from the empirical conditions attaching to them*' (emphasis added). Cf. Callanan (2011: 23n.28).

process of CRA would appear to conflict with the idea of *acquisitio originaria*.[52] Longuenesse reads the acquisition of categories in such a way that they must be seen as

> *acquired* not only because they would not be reflected as concepts unless impressions had struck our senses and given rise to acts of sensible synthesis, *but also because they presuppose the empirical concepts under which appearances are thought, as well as the combination of these concepts in empirical judgments.* (1998: 253, emphasis added)

The statement in this last italicised passage is at variance with Kant's statement in the above quotation from *Disc* that it is in fact 'determinate *concepts* of things' that *presuppose* the categories. Also, in the *Prolegomena* Kant is quite clear that the categories 'which make the judgment of experience objectively valid' are 'special *concepts originally generated in the understanding* [im Verstande ursprünglich erzeugte Begriffe]' (*Prol* § 18, AA 4: 298).[53] To put it in the words of the student report in *Met-L₂*: 'The understanding acquires concepts *by its paying attention to its own use*' (AA 28: 542 [LM: 309], emphasis added). The categories are thus acquired by the understanding independently of, and logically prior to, the processes by means of which the acquisition of empirical concepts takes place, even if the latter are of course required for an actual act of the understanding to yield an objectively valid cognition. The transcendental and empirical levels regarding the original acquisition of the categories and the derivative acquisition of empirical concepts respectively should not be conflated.

It seems to me that Longuenesse is not able to allay the worry that her account of the generation, or indeed emergence, of the categories as what she calls 'clear concepts' through the act of CRA—and which she appears to base entirely on Kant's *Reflexionen* on logic and in particular the problematic handbook on logic, compiled by Jäsche—comes close to a Lockean type deduction of a priori concepts, if not an *acquisitio derivativa*. In the *Jäsche Logic* (§ 5), it says that 'this *logical* origin of concepts—their origin as to their mere form—consists in reflection, whereby a representation common to several objects (*conceptus communis*) arises as that form which is required for the power of judgement' (JL, AA 9:

---

[52] For Longuenesse's understanding of original acquisition, see Longuenesse (1998: 221n.17, 222, 252–3).

[53] See also ID, § 8, where Kant writes that intellectual concepts, the predecessors of the categories, are not '*innate* concepts' but concepts 'abstracted from the *laws inherent in the mind* (*by attending to its actions* on the occasion of an experience)' (AA 2: 395 [TPha: 387–8], emphasis added). It is in this sense that these concepts are '*acquired* concepts'. Kant further states in the same section: 'Such concepts never enter into any sensory representations as parts, and thus they could not be abstracted from such a representation in any way at all.'

94 [LL: 592]), which in my mind does not include the categories as transcendental concepts unless *transcendental* reflection were at issue here. In my opinion, Longuenesse does not seem to fully heed the transcendental nature of the argument regarding the categories as the original concepts, derived from the unity of apperception, which is the highest point to which even logic must be affixed (B134n.). The synthetic unity in which different representations are held together, in virtue of the set of categories, is a prerequisite for these different representations having an analytic unity of consciousness in common that makes the latter into a *conceptus communis*. However, this synthetic unity is brought about by an act of apperception, which, it is true, implies an act of simultaneously apprehending, reproducing and recognising, which is synthetic, but not a reflective act (CRA) that supposedly *precedes*, or *leads to*, the analytic unity that is a 'universally reflected concept' in terms of a category, let alone one whereby the universal concept is *empirically* acquired; the synthetic and analytic unities are contemporaneous in that the principle of apperception is the *transcendental condition* of any empirical logical act of CRA. The act of reflection at issue, if synthesis is one, would be a *transcendental* reflection of reason that is entirely a priori and basic, underived from some given particular representations or judgements. CRA is therefore not an *a priori* synthetic act; it is rather the case that CRA presupposes it for its own possibility.[54]

3.3.4 A Conflation of Levels

I am not claiming of course that reflection, or more precisely the combined act of CRA, does not play any role in what in the *Critique of the Power of Judgement* Kant calls determinative judgement, i.e. an actual judgement that subsumes a particular under a given universal in accordance with a priori rules and thus determines an object of knowledge. Reflection in fact plays an indispensable role in judgement; one should even say it is a *necessary* logical condition of any empirical judgement, since any given empirical judgement presupposes the capacity for concept formation (and, of course, it is also a transcendental condition for the possibility of 'merely reflective' judgements such as aesthetic judgements). But—and here I disagree with Longuenesse—logical reflection is not a transcendental condition, viz. a *constitutive* condition, for the inherently objective purport

---

[54] The Transcendental Deduction is a piece of transcendental reflection on the possibility of judgement or experience. But there is nothing transcendental about judgement or experience per se. Cf. B80–1.

of a judgement, and thus is not a transcendental ground of the original acquisition of the categories. Longuenesse conflates the transcendental and logical conditions of an empirical judgement, and at the same time, she appears to simply confuse 'determinative judgement' with the determinative *act of the understanding*, namely the objective unity of apperception, which constitutes the a priori determination of an object that of course always only occurs in an empirical judgement. What makes a judgement 'determinative' is the determining or determinative act of the understanding in general, what in the Second Introduction Kant terms the 'legislative' function of the understanding that a priori provides the transcendental laws in accordance with which the power of judgement subsumes under general rules (universals) (CJ, AA 5: 174, 177, 179). However, any determinative judgement or the determining power of judgement in general is not the same as the determinative *act of the understanding* in general consisting of the set of transcendental laws that 'sketch out [...] *a priori*' (CJ, AA 5: 179) the laws governing the determining power of judgement. We have to be careful here about the order and levels of arguing. Any empirical determinative judgement requires the capacity of the understanding, namely the capacity to categorially determine an object. But that does not imply conversely that the capacity of the understanding, or categorial determination, *is* itself a determinative judgement. Categorial determination, and so the determinative act of the understanding, is a transcendental operation whereas a determinative judgement is, as such, an empirical event.

John Callanan (2006) has given an account of the justification of the categories that likewise appears to invert the transcendental and empirical orders of Kant's reasoning. However, in his case it is not reflection that is presumed to have a grounding role, as Longuenesse believes, but the '*activity* of judgment' (2006: 377). There are a few problems with Callanan's approach. I do not think it is true to say that Kant's transcendental strategy for proving the legitimacy of the employment of the categories *cannot*, as Callanan maintains, 'rely upon rational grounds as their source of justification' (2006: 376). Callanan reasons, as part of an otherwise illuminating, novel account of Kant's answer to Hume, that 'Kant's account cannot rely solely on the identification of those concepts as part of our cognitive capacities as a reason for their validity'. He continues:

> Although for Kant the Categories are necessary for judgement about the world, he does not suggest that it is these rational concepts that act as the *ground* of our judgements about the world—it is not the fact that we are so constituted to make judgements in accordance with certain *a priori* concepts that *entitles* us to assume that our judgements reveal the true character of nature. (Callanan 2006: 376)

3.3 Original Acquisition, Reflective Judgement and the Categories — 61

This would, according to Callanan, be something like a preformation system, which Kant rejects (B167–8).[55] Instead, looking to the introduction to the Analytic of Principles (A132–3/B171–2) for support, Callanan argues that while Kant 'takes Hume's arguments as conclusive against any attempt to ground rationally the relation between a representation and its object in judgement', Kant's view is not that the ground of judgement lies in the rules of the understanding but that 'the role of the understanding can only be understood in relation to the practice or *activity* of judgement' (2006: 377). However, Callanan is wrong to infer, on the basis of A133, from the fact that Kant asserts that judgement cannot be learnt but only practised, that 'the rules of the understanding [...] cannot serve as the ground of judgment' (2006: 377)—by which I assume Callanan means the a priori concepts or transcendental rules of the understanding. In this passage, Kant speaks only of the power of judgement and rules in general (from the perspective of general logic), not transcendental rules, which Kant argues later on in the section are the 'determinate rules' through which '*transcendental* logic' 'correct[s] and secure[s] the power of judgment in the use of the pure understanding' (B174/A135). Callanan subsequently argues that, in line with Hume's 'resolution of the sceptical *impasse*', Kant 'accepts that it must be a *non-rational* faculty of thought that serves as the ground of our activity of judgement', that is, '[i]t is the *imagination* that serves as the ground of the relation between a representation and its object' (2006: 378), so that 'the *a priori* concepts of the understanding could be justified by reference to the activity of judgement itself' (2006: 379).

I think Callanan inverts the transcendental and empirical orders here. It is not the activity of judgement, by virtue of a non-rational factor—presumably

---

[55] Although Kant indeed rejects a 'preformation-system' (B167), Callanan (2006: 376) is wrong to conclude from this that—presumably in reaction to Hume's critique of rationalist accounts of the employment of rational concepts (such as cause)—by implication Kant would reject an account that seeks to demonstrate the 'rational grounds as their source of justification' for the employment of the a priori concepts. For Kant associates a preformation system with a view—he refers to Crusius's model of a priori knowledge (cf. *Prol* § 36n., AA 4: 319)—of the categories as '*subjective* predispositions for thinking', which would only yield '*subjective* necessity' (B167–8, emphasis added), whereas his own preferred rational system ('epigenesis') aims at validating the categories as *objectively* necessary (see further Hogan 2010: 30–2 and Quarfood 2004: 91ff.). The fact that Kant rejects accounts based on our (merely) subjective constitution does not imply that he rejects 'any such explanatory theory which purports to offer human beings' rational constitution as adequate justification for rational judgement' (Callanan 2006: 376). In fact, he offers one in the Transcendental Deduction: '(as it were a system of the epigenesis of pure reason): namely that the categories contain the grounds of the possibility of all experience in general *from the side of the understanding*' (B167, emphasis added). See further Motta (2007: 101–5) on Kant and Crusius.

transcendental imagination—that provides a justification of the categories, but a *rational*, a priori, independent and systematic deduction from the understanding (the unity of apperception) which shows that the activity of judgement, and so experience, is only possible on condition of the licit application of the *a priori* concepts or rules of the understanding. It is not the empirical activity of judgement that legitimates the employment of the categories, but it is rather that the pure categories, as necessarily applicable in judgement, enable the activity of judgement. It is true to say that the categories can only be licitly used in the activity of judgement—or put differently, that their legitimacy is shown by showing their necessary employment in judgement—but that does not make the latter the original, supposedly non-rational, ground *of the concepts of the understanding*. That would be tantamount to claiming that an empirical, essentially contingent event grounds transcendental functions, that is, that *necessary a priori* concepts or rules would be *rationally* dependent on something *non-rational*, which clearly cannot be what Kant has in mind. Moreover, Kant makes it clear (B151–2) that it is the *rational* understanding *by means of* the imagination,[56] and not simply the imagination, which is responsible for the 'application' of the categories.

To conclude, my main worry with Longuenesse's argument is that it seems on her view that the independent status of the a priori concepts—the categories as underived, unabstracted concepts—is at risk. And although she is perfectly aware of this worry, as I have indicated, I find her attempt—also in response to the critiques by Sedgwick (2000) and Allison (2000)—to allay it to be unsatisfactory. Also, as said, her claim that reflective judgement is co-constitutive of objectivity, in that it somehow grounds the acquisition of the categories as 'universally reflected concepts', is problematic. In my view, in Kant's transcendental view objectivity, and hence judgement, is established by the categories and the categories alone, as I shall show in the following chapters. And although I agree that reflection forms an ineliminable part of an *actual given* determinative judgement, and is not just an aspect of aesthetic judgements, I do not think it is true to say that logical reflection has any a priori constitutive, that is, *transcendental* role to play regarding the a priori concepts that govern the possibility of an object or nature in general. Hence, I believe that logical reflection is not somehow the ground for the acquisition, original or otherwise, of the categories.

---

56 More precisely, the transcendental synthesis of imagination, or productive imagination, is the 'effect' of the understanding itself as operative in sensibility, and nothing numerically separate from it. See further Chapter 11. See also Schulting (2017a), chs 5 and 6.

4 The Master Argument

4.1 Introduction

In the Transcendental Deduction Kant makes the striking claim, his 'master argument' in fact, that transcendental apperception not only establishes the possibility of the *experience* of objects but also constitutes what it is for objects to *be* objects. In view of what Kant asserts explicitly at B197/A158 (and earlier at A111), transcendental apperception appears to be both the necessary condition of the experience of objects and the condition sufficient for the existence of the objects that are being experienced (at least insofar as an *object in general* is concerned). In this chapter, I seek to defend this twofold claim against various strands of criticism, in particular against the standard reading of the principle of transcendental apperception and its allegedly problematic relation to objectivity and objective experience, which it is supposed to ground. The main criticism is that there is a gap in Kant's argument from self-consciousness to objective experience. Such a defence warrants a wholesale reassessment of the principle of apperception and a reconsideration of its operative role in the argument of especially the B-Deduction. This involves revisiting the contentious issue of the derivation of the categories from apperception, which I undertake in detail in the chapters that follow. Prior to that, various problems germane to such an investigation must be canvassed, not least the above-mentioned issue of an ostensible conflation of two apparently distinct sets of conditions, one set constraining the unity of consciousness or self-consciousness and one set governing the consciousness or experience of *objects*. That is what I shall do in this chapter against the backdrop of a survey of the secondary literature. In Section 4.2, I introduce the main problem of Kant's 'master argument'. In Section 4.3, I expand on the so-called 'reciprocity thesis' concerning the relation between self-consciousness and objective experience, more particularly between self-consciousness and the concept of an object in general. In Section 4.4, I reflect on the relevant question of whether the argument in the Transcendental Deduction is regressive or progressive, and in Section 4.5 I elaborate on Guyer's critical interpretation, which in my opinion is one of the most incisive and important critiques of Kant's theory of apperception.

4.2 The Ostensible Gap

In the B-edition of the Transcendental Deduction Kant argues that

> the unity of consciousness is that which alone constitutes the relation of representations to an object, thus their objective validity, and consequently is that which makes them into cognitions and on which even the possibility of the understanding rests. (B137)

In a subsequent passage, Kant continues:

> The synthetic unity of consciousness is therefore an objective condition of all cognition, not merely something I myself need in order to cognize an object but rather something under which every intuition must stand *in order to become an object for me*. (B138)

In the A-Deduction, Kant writes similarly:

> It is clear [...] that since we have to do only with the manifold of our representations, and that *X* which corresponds to them (the object), because it should be something distinct from all of our representations, is nothing for us, the unity that the object makes necessary can be nothing other than the formal unity of the consciousness in the synthesis of the manifold of the representations. Hence we say that we cognize the object if we have effected synthetic unity in the manifold of intuition. (A105)

Questions have been raised by many a commentator as to the soundness of Kant's apparent inference from the synthetic unity of consciousness to the possibility of the experience or cognition of objects. That is to say, how can it be possible that the mere unity of one's consciousness, if we understand it as having to do with *self*-consciousness as is clear from a section prior to the one quoted above (B131–2), establishes the cognition or experience[1] of objects? Does Kant

---

1 Technically speaking, Kant does not yet speak here, in the 'first step' of the B-Deduction, of 'experience' (in the 'thick' Kantian sense). It is only in the first real new proposition in the 'second step'—in § 22, where he identifies 'experience' with 'empirical cognition', and then more in detail in the conclusion of the Deduction in § 26—that the application or use of the pure concepts *in experience* is addressed. Kant defines experience as 'an empirical cognition, i.e., a cognition that determines an object through perceptions' (B218). We are here solely concerned with the *cognition*, or even more precisely the *thought*, of an object *in general*. But I shall continue speaking of 'experience' *sensu latiori*, since it appears to be customary among some commentators, and because I believe it is warranted by the thrust of Kant's global argument about possible experience as consisting of two integral constituent elements, concepts and intuition; the argument with which I am concerned here, namely the argument regarding the constraints of the *concept* of an object, is part and parcel of that global argument. I also want to avoid using the term 'representation', as some others do (see below), as it suggests a short argument to connot thus run together the *necessary* requirements for the possible experience of objects and the *sufficient* conditions of objective experience?[2] There is an additional ambiguity here, for Kant's assertion in the quoted passage at B138 suggests that the synthetic unity of consciousness is indeed the condition under which alone an object can *be* an object for a cognising subject, not just the condition under which a self-conscious subject can have *experience* of an object (cf. again A111 and B197/A158). As has often been the sticking point for interpreters, Kant thus seems to be making two unargued-for claims that moreover are confused into one:

> 1) that the ostensibly subjective unity of self-consciousness is also an *objective* unity of consciousness (a claim that is prima facie at odds with the distinctions stipulated by Kant in the following § 18 of the B-Deduction)

and

> 2) that objective unity of consciousness *constitutes* (in the constituting sense) the object as distinguishable from one's consciousness of it.

Furthermore, on what grounds can Kant link the categories (and hence judgement), these being the so-called rules or conditions for the cognitive representation of objects (B128), to the putative conditions of the unity of consciousness, of self-consciousness? Are they the same conditions, or if not, what is the ground of their relation?

In this context, I should note that Carl (1989a, b) has advanced the compelling, but I believe ultimately mistaken, view that Kant himself vacillated between opting to construct the Transcendental Deduction as based on the premise of the *Faktum* of objective experience *or* as based on the premise of merely subjective experience, as a result of which we are faced with various attempts to present a deduction of the concepts either with recourse to transcendental apperception (predominantly in the B-edition of the *Critique*) or without it (mainly in A, the *Prolegomena* and an oft-referenced footnote in MFNS). Carl interprets this appa-

---

ceptual idealism (see Ameriks 2000b). For an account of the 'second step' of the B-Deduction, see Chapter 11 and also Schulting (2017a), ch. 5.

2 See Guyer (1992: 138, 144 ff., 151) and Guyer (1987: 117 ff.); cf. Carl (1989b: 15 ff., 1989a: 96, 99), and Cassam (2007: 60); see also Carl (1998: 197 ff.) for a succinct and clear presentation of the problem. Both Carl and Guyer give prima facie valid philosophical grounds for their respective adverse criticisms of Kant regarding an alleged modal fallacy underlying the claims concerning the unity of consciousness and objective experience, but I believe that their criticisms are not germane to Kant's real argument. For Guyer see further Section 4.5 below.

rent equivocating strategy on Kant's part in terms of the difference between, on the one hand, an *epistemologically*, essentially regressively, structured argument about the conditions of objective experience and, on the other hand, an *ontological* claim about the unity of consciousness (see Carl 1989a: 89–93, Carl 1989b: 11–16; cf. Guyer 1992: 125 ff.). He also claims that there are 'deficiencies in his notion of apperception in 1775' (1989b: 5). The problem regarding Kant's ostensible equivocation would seem to amount to the problem noted here regarding the relation between the conditions for subjective experience and those for the experience of objects. According to Carl, it is clear that Kant wants to combine the two noted strategies, but it is also clear, Carl contends, that he fails to provide the required link between the two. In order for the conditions of the mind, governed by transcendental apperception, to become conditions of any objective unity of experience, the subjective functions would have to be 'changed into objective ones', as Carl points out (see Kant's own remarks on this head in R4674 and R4675 in AA 17: 647–8 and R5927 in AA 18: 388), and only then could the functions of apperception be considered concepts of the understanding that together constitute what it is to represent objects. Carl writes:

> Kant effects this change by moving from a necessary condition to a necessary and sufficient condition. He first claims that all appearances, being objects of perceptions, presuppose a unity of the mind—a unity that, according to his notion of apperception, is a necessary condition of perceptions as conscious representations. He then concludes that this is sufficient for a unity of these representations themselves. (1989b: 15)

In Carl's view, Kant fails to establish, in the *Duisburg Nachlass* and subsequently in the *Critique*, the link between subjective and objective conditions of experience, but unjustifiably identifies the categories with the subjective functions of apperception *tout court* and 'simply drops the change' (Carl 1989a: 96). Carl supports his reading of apperception in the *Duisburg Nachlass* (dating from 1774–75) with the fact that Kant would not as yet have discovered the paralogisms of pure reason, which according to Carl thus explains his attempt to identify the categories directly with the functions of apperception (Carl 1989b: 19; cf. Klemme 1996: 126 ff., esp. 127n.173). This might or might not be the case (also depending on how the arguments for a rationalist psychology itself and Kant's developing relation to the latter are interpreted), but the thesis has I believe no immediate consequences for Kant's theory of apperception in the B-Deduction, where any putative rationalist remainders in regard to the self would appear to have been eliminated.³ I am also not so sure about Carl's claim about the ontological assumptions underlying Kant's apperception theory in the *Nachlass*; I suspect that Carl imposes his own reading of the unity of consciousness on Kant, in the same way that readers of the A- and B-Deductions impose an 'ontological' reading of sorts on the unity of apperception, the reading that I aim to undermine. But to confirm this suspicion, more evidence would have to be found in the *Nachlass* itself, which I must leave for another occasion. At any rate, I firmly believe that on an attentive reading of the B-Deduction there is no reason to suspect that Kant espouses a rationalist, i.e. dogmatic, view of self-consciousness there (see further Chapter 7).

Guyer (1992: 144 ff.), among others,⁴ passes adverse criticisms on Kant's claim that unity of self-consciousness constitutes the objects of our representation, for 'it ignores the idea that there is an essential difference between the self and its representations on the one hand and the objects they may represent on the other'. Guyer further argues:

> [E]ven if the conditions for the possibility of apperception are also necessary conditions for the representations of objects, there must be some additional condition necessary to represent objects that is not a condition for self-consciousness as such. Yet if we were to ignore this requirement and grant Kant's present claim that the conditions for the unity of apperception are sufficient for the representation of objects, then it would become obscure how we can ever represent mere conditions of the *self* without also representing an object.

Apparently, such a claim would effectively result in, as Guyer says, 'equating transcendental apperception with an experience consisting *exclusively* of knowledge of objects' (1992: 138).⁵ Therefore, Guyer considers the thesis that transcendental apperception is not only a necessary condition for the representation of

---

3 See further Klemme's critical comments on Carl's reading of the *Duisburg Nachlass* in Klemme (1996: 128 ff., esp. 130, 135)
4 For further criticisms of Kant in respect of the issues at hand here, see Thöle (1991: 87, 229–35, 260–1), Carl (1989b: 14–15) and Hanna (2011). Cf. *per contra* Allison (1983: 146), Baum (1986: 68 ff., 105 ff.) and, more recently, Greenberg (2001: 190–1) and Banham (2006: 72–3). See also Hoppe (1983: 126, 210 ff.). Henrich (1988: 48–9) focuses on Kant's failure to distinguish between three different notions of 'objective'. According to Henrich, construing the Transcendental Deduction as taking its point of departure in the putative correspondence between the unity of self-consciousness and objective unity is in itself insufficient. Henrich's well-known claim is that we must see the argument as starting with a priori knowledge of the self's identity.
5 Cf. Guyer: '[Kant] just equates the transcendental unity of apperception with knowledge of objects by fiat, instead of demonstrating a synthetic connection between them (in either direction). That is, Kant does not develop an argument that self-consciousness as such has special *a priori* conditions which also apply to objects, whatever the source of the latter' (1987: 118).

objects but also sufficient for it an 'excessive assumption' (1992: 151) on Kant's part. Clearly, Guyer finds fault with Kant's most fundamental claim, expressed in the above-quoted passages in the B-Deduction, that the conditions for the transcendental unity of apperception and the conditions for the knowledge of objects intersect or are indeed the same.[6]

Pereboom (2001: 95–9), for one, denies that the argument from §§ 17–20, where Kant presents his 'master argument', is premised on the necessary unity of apperception argued for in § 16. According to Pereboom,

> the transcendental unity, and more precisely, the synthesis that explains our consciousness of the identity of the subject, is *merely a necessary* condition for the representation of objects [...]. (2001: 95, emphasis added)[7]

Pereboom dismisses the tenability of the claim that the unity of apperception would be sufficient for the representation of objects, because such an argument 'would have Kant demonstrating the existence of objects (in some sense) on the grounds of certain premises about self-consciousness' (2001: 95). These 'certain premises about self-consciousness' concern Kant's alleged claim that the synthetic unity of my self-consciousness implies the existential unity of representations that I have (or possibly have had or will have) that are subsequently correspondent with an objectively valid unity of representations. Pereboom develops a different strategy for reading the argumentative structure of the first half of the Transcendental Deduction, in order to save Kant from the sufficiency claim attributed to him by other commentators. He argues that in § 17 Kant proposes 'merely a necessary condition for the representation of objects' (Pereboom 2001: 95), which he then first demonstrates in § 18; this claim is, according to Pereboom, not based on the argument presented in §§ 15–16. The distinction between these two arguments is, he believes, reflected by the distinction between an argument from above (§§ 15–16) and one from below (§§ 17–20). I think this

---

[6] Cf. Hossenfelder (1978: 128 ff.). Recently, Prien (2006) has strategically advanced the idea of two distinct kinds of synthetic unity, a 'weaker' and a 'stronger' reading, only the latter of which grounds objective validity (and not just subjective validity for which the weaker sense of synthesis suffices). Apart from the fact that Kant's text nowhere warrants outright any such distinction, despite Prien's attempts to read certain passages in this way (he is well aware of the lack of strong textual evidence for such a distinction), this strategy does not work for it invites a regress problem regarding how the unity of self-consciousness and objective unity *do* connect up. A strategic interpretative distinction between two synthetic unities is thus only a cosmetic cover-up of the embarrassment arising from Kant's controversial claim here, the reciprocity claim that is under scrutiny. See further on Prien, Chapter 5, this volume.

[7] See also earlier Pereboom (1995: 20).

4.2 The Ostensible Gap — 69

view, presumably modelled on the structure of the A-Deduction, is hugely implausible, both textually and interpretatively, as is Pereboom's claim, consistent with his denial of the sufficiency claim, that synthesis, which is necessary for the unity of consciousness, can take place 'without being the source of a relation of representations to objects' (2001: 97). I do not think that in any arbitrary actual judgement a priori synthesis fails to be 'the source of a relation of representations to objects', although a synthetic relation can of course be considered formally in abstraction from that relation.[8]

Similarly, in an earlier article (Pereboom 1995: 22), Pereboom contends that the claim that 'unification under a concept *of an object* is both a necessary and sufficient condition of the representation of an object' is not shown, in § 17, from principles established in § 16. Pereboom argues that (Kant's) claim that 'the unity of consciousness is that which alone constitutes the relation of representations to an object' 'does not entail that the synthesis that explains knowledge of the unity of consciousness cannot take place without producing a relation of representations to objects' (1995: 23). It may very well be, as Kant appears to claim, that the relation to an object is 'produced by the same process of unification, synthesis, that explains knowledge of the unity of consciousness' (1995: 23). But, according to Pereboom, unity of consciousness is not exhausted by the synthesis that constitutes the relation to an object, which thus leaves a 'gap' in Kant's argument for the derivation of object knowledge from self-consciousness. However, against Pereboom it can be objected that this suggests that the 'process of unification' guaranteeing both the relation to an object and the synthetic unity of self-consciousness is in some sense distinct from the unities it produces, either the synthesis that constitutes the relation to an object or the synthesis that explains unity of consciousness. In Chapter 7, I argue that given the a priori nature of the unity at issue there is no discrepancy between the process, or more precisely, the function of synthetic unification and its 'products', implying that relation to an object and synthetic unity of consciousness are reciprocally dependent and that thus the transcendental unity of self-consciousness is exhausted by the relation to an object.

It is further alleged by Kant's interpreters that there is a certain 'looseness of [...] connection', to put it as Guyer (1979: 159) describes it,[9] between transcendental apperception and the theory of judgement, which is linked up with Kant's strategy for determining the conditions of object cognition, namely the categories. Again, the reasoning is that the fact that a judging of an objective state

---

8 See also Pereboom (2010: 155–65).
9 Cf. Henrich (1988: 48).

of affairs requires unity of consciousness does not imply that, inversely, the unity of consciousness constitutes or establishes the objectivity that is coterminous with objectively valid judgement. Accordingly, it is argued that the categories are not directly related to, let alone derivable from, transcendental apperception. Presumably, then, there is no 'direct transition from the unity of apperception to the objective form of judgment' (Guyer 1979: 160).[10]

In what follows, I shall provide preliminary reasons, reasons that can be made out from closely observing the line of argumentation in the first half of the Transcendental Deduction in its B-version, for upholding Kant's claim that there is an a priori and necessary connection between synthetic unity of consciousness, or the transcendental unity of self-consciousness (B132), and objectivity and the consequent claim that synthetic unity of consciousness is sufficient for objectivity. (Note that, for now, I simply take objectivity and objective unity as equivalent; evidently, this assumption needs explanation.) The operative question is: is Kant able to show that the transcendental unity of apperception is indeed an objective unity as opposed to merely a subjective unity of consciousness, as he maintains in § 18 of the B-Deduction seemingly without having offered anything in the form of supporting arguments in the foregoing sections? I shall argue that he is and that the arguments for it are provided in the preceding §§ 16 and 17 of the B-Deduction.

4.3 The Reciprocity Thesis

Following Henry Allison (1983: 144 ff.; 1996: 49, 51, 58; 2004: 173–5), I call the claim, made by Kant in the above-quoted passage at B138, that synthetic unity of consciousness is necessary and sufficient for objectivity 'the reciprocity claim' (henceforth Reciprocity for short).[11] By Reciprocity I mean the conceptual circumstance that, in an a priori way, synthetic unity of consciousness establishes objective unity, and hence objectivity, while objective unity constitutes what it means to have a synthetic unity of consciousness. In short, the objective and synthetic unities coincide. This fundamental feature of Kant's reasoning in the Transcendental Deduction calls for an inquiry into the precise characteristics and ramifications of transcendental apperception, expressed by the 'I think'-

---

[10] Carl puts it bluntly: 'The claim that the "titles of self-perception" are identical with the categories is not convincing at all. [...] Because the functions of apperception are relations between the self as a mental substance and its perceptions, this identification with the categories is more a fancy than a well-founded suggestion' (1989b: 16–17).
[11] Cf. de Vleeschauwer (1937: 108).

proposition, which is introduced at the outset of § 16 of the B-Deduction as the premise of its argument proper. More precisely, we must examine: (a) in what consists the relation of this 'I think' to the unity consisting of *object-relating* representations, that is, the unity of representations that in some way have objective validity and is thus an objective unity; (b) whether the unity of self-consciousness can be equated with this objective unity, thereby shoring up the reciprocity claim; and (c) in which sense object-relating representations, hence unitary representations, are indeed constitutive of *objects themselves*. In this context, it must also be considered in which sense the categories, being the concepts of what constitutes an object in general (B128), are related to the 'I think'. It will emerge on analysis that the conditions for formal identity expressed by the 'I think'-proposition, which I shall argue constitute the unity of discursive thought, are the *same* conditions that establish the identity, at least in a formal sense, of the *objects* of unitary experience, as indeed Kant suggests at, among other places, A111. This will clarify at least one strand of the sufficiency claim, namely that the *objective unity* of representations is coextensive with *objectivity* formally construed, for what is at issue here are merely the set of *conditions* to which experience *and* objects must be subject for there to *be* both experience and objects of experience. In other words, there is a set of necessary conditions which constrains the experience of objects *and* the objects of a subject's experience, both being elements of *possible* experience. The standard reading of Kant's transcendental story is that the categories are the necessary conditions of experience, but this is only one part of that story regarding *possible* experience, which includes the objects that are being experienced.[12] I contend that these formal conditions of identity, which apply to both subject of experience and object of experience, *are* the categories (at any rate in their pure unschematised form insofar as merely the formal cognition of an object in general is concerned). Contrary to Guyer and the majority of interpreters, I argue accordingly that the categories are a fortiori derivable from the unity of apperception, as Kant himself claims at B142 (Chapters 6–9).

Let me briefly elaborate on Kant's at first blush careless equation of objective unity of consciousness with objectivity *tout court*, that is, with objects or the set of objects or states of objects of which one has or can have experience. Understandably, one may want to make a point of asking what we should take the notion of object as Kant puts it to use in the Transcendental Deduction to mean, since Kant's talk about 'the relation of representations to an object' in the

---

[12] Evidently, the full story about possible experience requires the 'second step' of the Transcendental Deduction and subsequently the Analytic of Principles.

above-quoted passage at B137 (Section 4.1) suggests a deflationary notion of object or objectivity.[13] That is to say, is objective representation, a compound of representations that have objective reference, not clearly different from the object as such that one represents, the object being the referent of one's representations, the represent*ed*? Should we then not first define the notion of 'object'—and thus objectivity as a concept—that is at issue here, or at least disambiguate Kant's use of the notion? This might seem reasonable. However, I think it is hermeneutically unavailing to defer to the urge to answer these questions prematurely and to provide beforehand a definition of what is meant by the term 'object' and based on such a definition to demarcate the difference between an object and its representation. First, doing so would appear to beg the question against Kant's reciprocity claim and would thus not help us understand it. Secondly, the idiosyncrasy of the transcendental reflection that is pursued by Kant in view of grounding the philosophical legitimacy of the categories, of which objectivity is the principal offshoot concept, is precisely such that one cannot simply proceed in the traditional manner of starting out by providing conceptual definitions, as was practice in the School metaphysics, and go about making one's claims based on these definitions. It is conspicuous that the point at which Kant provides an initial definition of 'object' is midway in the analysis. For example, at A104 Kant announces that '*here then* it is necessary to make understood what is meant by the expression "an object of representations"' (emphasis added; cf. A107 ff.). Also in the B-edition, the definition of 'object' is only first provided at B137, in fact practically towards the end of the argument of the actual deduction. At the same time, an interpretative reconstruction of this transcendental reflection would not be served well by defining the terms employed by Kant ahead of construing the exposition of their operational function in the argument of the Transcendental Deduction.

Heeding an Aristotelian differentiated notion of 'definition',[14] what we should take Kant to mean by object and objectivity will only have been fully clarified, or made explicit, and thus clearly (although perhaps not completely)

---

[13] Cf. Guyer (1992: 151). However, Guyer points out that a deflationary conception of an object, that is, 'defining an object as constituted by any conceptual connection of the manifold of intuition whatever', could not explain Kant's claim that the conditions for unity of apperception are not only the necessary conditions for knowledge of objects but also (formally) sufficient for it (that is, sufficient for the cognition of *an object in general*; space and time are, of course, the necessary added conditions to enable the empirical cognition of a spatiotemporal object, which is argued in the 'second step' of the B-Deduction; see for this, Chapter 11 and also Schulting 2017a, ch. 5).
[14] Aristotle, *An. Post.* II.10.93^{b}38–94^{a}3. See also B759n. See further Aportone (2009: 289 ff.).

defined and demarcated, upon his having demonstrated that the categories, which are at first only nominally defined as the 'concepts of an object in general' (B128), are justifiably applied to objective *experience*, that is, after the *de jure* question with regard to our de facto beliefs concerning objective experience or knowledge has been answered, that is, at the end of the Deduction (§§ 26–7).¹⁵ This means that implicitly, that is, pre-theoretically, I may have an idea of what objectivity is,¹⁶ and thus deploy the nominal definition of 'object' whenever I entertain beliefs about it in connection with my experience of an object, but I am as yet not justified in attaching any *philosophically* conclusive definitional value to that idea prior to a philosophical explication that makes the conditions of objectivity and hence my experience of an object explicit. To put it simply, objectivity and its conceptual grasp is precisely what needs explaining. And surely, to provide a definition of object or objectivity before embarking upon the explanation that is called for would be a prime case of begging the question. As Kant says, 'in philosophy, the definition, as distinctness made precise, must conclude rather than begin the work' (A730–1/B758–9).¹⁷

Having said that, to forestall certain persistent interpretative strategies I note that what is at issue is not so much the object qua its existence,¹⁸ but qua its very objectivity, qua that which *makes* it an object (cf. B125 ff.). Objectivity in *this* sense (as *Gegenständlichkeit*) is obviously not the same as objectivity understood

---

15 See further on Kant's account of definitions A727 ff./B755 ff., especially A730 ff./B758 ff. and Kant's note to A731/B759. Cf. Baum (1986: 76). See also A241–2 and A245, where Kant asserts that the categories cannot be defined at all (at least as regards their *real* definition; see Kant's note, which was dropped in the B-edition), for any definition would already presuppose them. At A82–3/B108–9, Kant suggests that definitions of the categories can be given in a 'complete system of transcendental philosophy'.
16 Cf. Ameriks (2003b: 10).
17 At A730/B758, Kant states that 'we must somewhat weaken the stringency of the requirement by which we denied philosophical explanations the honorary title of "definition", and limit this entire remark to this, that philosophical definitions come about only as expositions of given concepts, [...] thus [...] only analytically through analysis (the completeness of which is never apodictically certain)'. In a philosophical definition, concepts are, unlike in the mathematical construction of concepts, only 'explained'. See also L. W. Beck (1984).
18 *That* the object exists (de facto) is already assumed as given for the transcendental analysis of cognition or experience; to the extent that existence *as category* is in need of explanation (*de jure*) it is accounted for in the way the modality of a judgement stipulates that the thing judged about is (absolutely) posited as actually existing, even before an objective determination of it (by means of the categories of quality) is accounted for. But this is not to say that an argument for the sufficiency claim about the representation of objects, based on the unity of self-consciousness, is to prove the existence of objects, as Pereboom (2001: 95) believes it would. Rather, it means to explain what it means when we claim that an object or objects exist(s) (cf. B72).

in any naturalistic sense, as brute factualness, say (whatever that means). Without in the least forswearing empirical realism, as an epistemologist Kant is not interested in mere factuality or even primarily in the empirical significance of our conceptual activity (a worry that much occupies 'analytic' Kantians such as Strawson and McDowell).[19] Harking back to a scholastic conception of object, Kant's central question concerns the intentionality towards an object, to a 'something in general=X' (A104) that corresponds isomorphically to our veridical representation of an object, rather than the subsisting thing itself (the x of judgement), *of which* one has determinate experience (cf. A250).[20] In a way, Kant is interested in establishing the general a priori criterion or criteria by which the knowledge or conception of an object is made possible. Or even more to the point, he is interested in the manner in which we grasp the identity conditions under which there can be knowledge of an object strictly speaking, namely of an object *as* something that is numerically identical and hence as corresponding to the identity of the act of our thinking it. In a certain sense, as is clear from Kant's definition of object in § 17, which I shall argue is the implied logical consequence of Kant's argument for a priori synthesis, the object is that of the posited thing to which the a priori form of our cognition is isomorphically related in order for the thing to *be* an object of our cognition *überhaupt* (cf. A92/B125), that is, in order for it to be called 'object' at all.[21]

As will become clearer in due course, this way of seeing *objectivity* as entirely dependent on our representation will partly explain Kant's at first blush extraordinary claim that the synthetic unity of consciousness is sufficient for the *objects* of experience as well as the *experience* of objects. The sufficiency claim does not mean to establish the existence of objects *simpliciter* (as things that really exist); their existence, which at any rate cannot be cognised a priori, is taken for granted.[22] The sufficiency claim rather specifies what is essential for an object to be represented or experienced *as such*, that is, *as* an object that is before thought, before the identical subject that represents it, in contrast to aggregates of merely

---

19 On McDowell, see Schulting (2017a), ch. 5. On Strawson, see Schulting (forthcoming).
20 For more detailed discussion, see Chapter 10, and also Schulting (2017a), chs 1 and 4.
21 See also the important letter to Herz of 26 May 1789, where Kant writes: '[T]he form in which [objects] are given depends on us,—on the one hand, in its subjective aspect, [objects are] dependent on the specific character of our kind of intuition; on the other hand, they are dependent on the uniting of the manifold in a consciousness, that is, on what is required for the thinking and cognizing of objects by our understanding. Only under these conditions, therefore, can we have experiences of those objects; and consequently, if intuitions (of objects of appearance) did not agree with these conditions, those objects would be nothing for us, that is, not objects of *cognition* at all, neither cognition of ourselves nor of other things' (*Corr*, AA 11: 51).
22 Cf. Erdmann (1878: 45–7).

subjective representations (which, significantly, for Kant do not amount to experience [*Erfahrung*]). Synthetic unity of consciousness will be explained as that which, by dint of its expressing the *objective unity* intrinsic to discursive thought in general, enables this contrast and, at the same time, establishes the *constitution* of an object (*stricto sensu*[23]) itself as the correlate of such an objective unity.

My goal is to defend Kant's reciprocity claim against the persistent criticisms that are raised against it. I contend that Kant's arguments for it are sound, given the assumptions of his conception of logic (some of which I shall discuss in Chapter 5 below) and given the qualifications that I have indicated regarding what we should take objectivity to stand for in the Kantian theory of knowledge (viz. as rule-governed unity among one's representations and not as brute factualness). The burden of the argument, however, will be to show that Kant is licensed to argue that the transcendental unity of apperception *is* an objective unity (TD § 18), for, as I shall show, the conditions for the unity of experience of objects are the *very same* conditions that make possible the unity of discursive thought as such, to which the unity of apperception exactly corresponds, and which are also satisfied if and only if the conditions for the unity of experience of objects are satisfied, namely in judgement.

My auxiliary thesis, to be argued in Chapters 5 and 6, is that the clue to Kant's reciprocity claim lies in the strict coextensivity of the analytic and synthetic unities of self-consciousness, which Kant only formally distinguishes for the purpose of expounding his argument. Both unities are *aspects* of the same function of transcendental apperception, and are reducible to that function.

By the analytic unity of apperception or the analytic unity of consciousness[24] one should understand the unity of all those (conscious) representations that one has which share the same feature of self-consciousness (viz. the representation 'I think' as their common mark)—but *excluding* those that do not share it (viz. representations that may be represented in me, but of which I am not self-consciously aware of being so represented, Leibnizian *petites perceptions*, say).

---

23 By 'object' I (and I claim also Kant) mean the object of thought and cognition, not a putative 'thing in itself' outside the scope of thought or cognition. Again, what is at issue is the possibility for a thing to be an object (and that eo ipso implies: to be an object *of thought*, for what else can talk of an object amount to if it does not concern an, at least potential, object for thought?), not its possibility of *existing* as a thing. The thing in itself is by definition not a thing *for* thought, and so an object of thought. See Schulting (2017a), chs 1 and 4.

24 It appears that Kant uses the expressions analytic unity of *apperception* and analytic unity of *consciousness* and likewise synthetic unity of *consciousness* and synthetic unity of *apperception* interchangeably (see e.g. B133 and B133n.; B138).

Synthetic unity of consciousness is to be understood as the unity of one's occurrent representations that together belong, in a thoroughgoing way as Kant puts it (B133), to the same self-consciousness whose unity they constitute, as heterogeneous parts in a synthetic whole.

The analytic feature of the function of apperception stresses the *sameness* or homogeneity of representations with regard to one's common consciousness (this consciousness being a higher-order representation that is a shared mark or partial representation [*Teilvorstellung*] of all one's representations that are regarded by one as one's own),[25] while the synthetic feature stresses the *combinatory* nature of the unity of consciousness that comprises the various, heterogeneous representations under a common one.

Now, by the coextensivity of the analytic and synthetic unities of apperception or consciousness I mean that there could be no de facto synthetic unity of consciousness or apperception without analytic unity of self-consciousness while there is no analytic unity of consciousness that is not testament to an underlying primordial synthetic unity of representations (cf. B133 and B133 ff. note; see also B134 ff.; I return to these important passages, which are often misinterpreted, in due course).

I thus contend that synthetic apperception and analytic unity of consciousness are equiprimordial. They are not simply analogical, rather they are isomorphically correspondent elements of, and reducible to, one single function. The one does not come without the other. Consequently, I argue that the coextensivity of the analytic and synthetic unities of apperception establishes the formal identity of self-consciousness, which is a *transcendental* unity of self-consciousness (B132 [AA 3: 109.1–2]), as a necessary and sufficient function of thought in general, from which the conditions of objectivity—taken in the aforesaid sense that will need a good deal of further explication—can subsequently be analytically inferred. This coextensivity points to the non-trivial circularity of Kant's global argument, and hence indicates its fundamentally regressive nature (see below Section 4.3 and Chapter 10). It serves to explain Kant's claim that the principle of apperception is analytic. It also explains why the synthesis or the synthetic unity in question must be a priori.

The structural feature of the coextensivity of the unities of apperception will hereafter be more precisely referred to as 'rigorous coextensivity'. By the rigorous coextensivity of the unities of apperception (henceforth Rigorous Coextensivity for short) I mean the strict coextensiveness of the analytic unity of consciousness and the synthetic unity of apperception. The coextensiveness is rigorous, for no 'I

---

25 See Prien (2006: 58–67).

think' applies to a manifold of representations that is not synthetically united by means of an act of synthesis, while no *synthetically* united manifold exists (in the strict sense of 'synthetic unity' that Kant accords it) that is not actually accompanied by an 'I think'.[26]

This view goes against the standard view of transcendental apperception, for which the synthetic function of apperception and analytic unity of consciousness (or 'I think'-accompaniment), although necessarily related as in an entailment relation, come apart or are considered at least not *necessarily* coextensive. I shall argue that the standard view is misguided, textually unsupported and in fact logically unwarranted. For Rigorous Coextensivity textual support can be found at, among other passages, A108, where Kant writes that

> the original and necessary consciousness of the identity of oneself is at the same time [*zugleich*] a consciousness of an equally necessary unity of synthesis of all appearances in accordance with concepts [...]. (AA 4: 82.13–16)

See also B130, where Kant argues that 'this action [i.e. 'action of the understanding' or 'synthesis', D.S.] must originally be unitary and equally valid for all combination, and that the dissolution (*analysis*) that seems to be its opposite, in fact *always* [*jederzeit*] presupposes it' (emphasis added). Another important passage is at B134, which I gloss in Chapter 6.

My central claim is that Rigorous Coextensivity shores up Reciprocity. In Kant's terms, this means that the transcendental unity of self-consciousness, or the original consciousness of self-identity, constitutes an objective unity of apperception. Given that what is to be understood by an object, qua its form, is effectively the determinate unity of a manifold of representations (cf. B137), and keeping in mind my earlier caveats, it also means that the transcendental

---

26 Rigorous Coextensivity does not imply that there could not exist manifolds of representations that show *some* relation of connectedness between them other than synthesis. (Kant means by synthesis mostly *necessary* synthesis, which must be seen as analogous to Hume's 'necessary connexion'—the apodictic, metaphysical knowledge of which is denied by Hume—in contrast to an associative conjunction of impressions that are merely drawn forth by the mind.) It will be argued in Chapter 6 that a distinction should be observed between what Kant terms synthetic unity of apperception, which is consistent or coextensive with analytic unity of consciousness, and any unspecified type of unity of consciousness (i.e. any arbitrary aggregate of mental states). Kant calls this latter a *subjective* unity of consciousness (TD § 18, B139–40), which contrasts with *objective* unity of consciousness and hence, on the reading that I present here, is not consistent or coextensive with an analytic unity of consciousness strictly speaking.

unity of self-consciousness constitutes objectivity *tout court*—compare A108 again, where the passage quoted earlier proceeds as

> [...] i.e., in accordance with rules that not only make them necessarily reproducible, but also thereby [*dadurch*] determine an object for their intuition, i.e., the concept of something in which they are necessarily connected. (AA 4: 82.16–19)

As I shall show, all of this gainsays the view propounded by Guyer and others that Kant does not provide an argument for claiming that the transcendental unity of self-consciousness satisfies the conditions for the constitution of both objective unity of consciousness and objectivity and that there is reciprocity between the two unities.

However, it has been pointed out, by Georg Mohr (1991: 133 ff.) among others,[27] that on a reading of the unity of self-consciousness that puts it on a par with an objective unity of representations, consciousness seems to be possible only if it is consciousness of something *objective*. This would appear to mean that all consciousness is subject to the determinacy of a rule-governed experience of veridical objects and that no room is left for non-veridical awareness of either oneself or objects.[28] Mohr believes, rightly, that such a view would be unintelligible and philosophically indefensible. However, some prominent commentators of Kant appear rather to endorse, and allege that Kant held, the view that indeed there could not be consciousness of oneself, let alone of outer things, that does not entail or directly involve transcendental apperception.[29] I do not think Kant holds this philosophically problematic view. Although I do not specifically address Kant's beliefs regarding subjective (sub-cognitive) consciousness, I shall point out that the possibility of sub-cognitive consciousness

---

27 See also again Guyer (1992: 126 ff., 138, 146), Hoppe (1983: 125, 130–3), Carl (1989a: 95 ff., 100) and Klemme (1996: 182 ff.).
28 Hoppe (1983: 46–7n.) argues for the possibility of 'categorially subjective perception' or consciousness, which is not governed by pure apperception or transcendental self-consciousness, and notes that hints of this more primitive kind of consciousness can be traced in Kant. Notice that Hoppe makes a helpful distinction between 'categorially subjective perception' and 'factically subjective perception', with the latter being a subspecies of 'categorially objective experience'.
29 See e.g. Allison (1983: 153 ff.), where Allison states that categories are required even for consciousness of our mental states. See also Collins (1999: 146 ff). Remarkably, Collins asserts that '[i]f we did not experience enduring, causally connected objects immediately, we would not have experience at all *and could not even be conscious*' (1999: 57, emphasis added) or '[s]ince the route through outer enduring objects is a necessary condition for self-representation, a conscious subject [...] is necessarily a subject conscious of enduring outer objects' (1999: 138).

that does not entail transcendental apperception is in fact *logically* inferable from the 'I think'-proposition itself (see Chapter 8).

I contend that the worry expressed by Mohr and others is based on an inflationary reading of the scope or domain of transcendental apperception (this concerns the modality of the 'I think') as well as on an equivocation over the notion of unity as mere co-presence of mental states and unity as a veridical unity of representations that is objectively valid, only the latter of which, on account of Reciprocity, is coextensive with Kant's transcendental (synthetic) unity of consciousness. Once it is clear that transcendental apperception is *not* a condition of (psychological) consciousness *tout court* and its putative psycho-physiological combinative structure and even of some primitive form of *self*-awareness, Kant's assertion to the effect that transcendental apperception is necessary and sufficient for objectivity and objective unity will turn out to be much less speculative and problematic a claim than appears at first sight. Showing that in a special sense transcendental apperception has a restricted scope as to the extent to which representations are *necessarily* accompanied by it, and so explaining what Kant labels the *analyticity* of the principle of apperception, will prove to be my key strategy in undercutting the criticism against Reciprocity.

Inevitably, in setting out my views, here in this chapter, I can only hint at some of the preliminaries of a much larger complex of arguments, which are in need of further extensive analysis and exegetical back-up. These will be provided in Chapters 6–9, which concern the deduction of the categories proper.

I note that for the purposes of the argument here I employ variously the terms 'cognition' and its cognates as well as 'thought' of an object, when I actually mean the latter, not the *knowledge* thereof strictly speaking (what Kant labels *empirische Erkenntnis*; cf. B165 ff., B288), although occasionally I also employ the term 'knowledge' in a looser sense. Notice that Kant himself too uses the terms 'thinking' and 'cognizing' interchangeably (B137) and speaks of 'cognitions' already in § 17 (B138) and § 19 (B141 ff.), while it is clear that there only the objective validity of *any* discursive kind of cognition is at issue (cognition in the broader sense), not yet the validity of cognition which is bound by the constraints of human sensibility and yields objectively real knowledge. But even here, one should not confuse Kant's notion of sensibly constrained cognition with knowledge strictly speaking, as Kant talks about *possible* knowledge, or possible experience, not knowledge facts or factual knowledge or true knowledge.[30] Discursive

---

[30] Notice that knowledge for Kant can be 'false', although of course for Kant too one has no knowledge of falsehoods strictly speaking (knowledge has a transcendental component in the sense that it precedes falsehoods and true facts; knowledge is always propositional in that

cognition in general is therefore the same as discursive thinking and hence bound by the same conceptual characteristics of thought in general. Henceforth, when speaking of 'thought' I thus mean discursive thought.

There is debate as to whether Kant's *Erkenntnis* should be translated as 'cognition' (as do Guyer/Wood) rather than as 'knowledge' (as does Kemp Smith). The fact that Kant allows false *Erkenntnis* (A58/B83) would seem to indicate that it cannot be translated as 'knowledge' (in our post-Gettier contemporary sense). Moreover, Kant himself appears to identify *Erkenntnis* with the Latin *cognitio* in the *Stufenleiter* (A320/ B376–7). However, we should be careful not to gloss Kant's term *Erkenntnis* as if it signified merely being about the subjective conditions of cognition or a mental act or an epistemic attitude, and not also about the *objective* conditions under we can in fact *know things* or *facts* (in the contemporary sense). While strictly speaking knowledge (*Erkenntnis*) in Kant's sense is, taken as such, not the same as knowledge in our contemporary sense, neither is it *just* cognition as a mere subjective *capacity for* knowing, which would rather be 'to think of an object' on Kant's account, in contrast to knowing one (B146).[31] I employ the terms 'cognition' and 'knowledge' as reflecting Kant's distinction between 'thinking an object' and 'knowing an object' respectively (B146; B165). Notice that Kant's *Erkenntnis* must be divided into its transcendental and empirical meanings, where the empirical meaning of *Erkenntnis* (i.e. *empirische Erkenntnis*) could be identified as knowledge in our contemporary sense (cf. B165–6). The transcendental meaning of *Erkenntnis*, as it is discussed in the Deduction, concerns the transcendental or a priori conditions of such knowledge, but this should not be conflated with the psychological condition or capacity for knowing, nor with the *merely* conceptual capacity or the capacity to think or judge. The transcendental or a priori conditions of empirical

---

one *knows that* some proposition *p* is either false or true). Knowledge, in the Kantian sense, is always falsifiable, indicating that it cannot concern knowledge facts as such.

31 Some point to Kant's term *Wissen* (B850 ff.) as the ostensible Kantian equivalent of 'knowledge', as distinguished from *Erkenntnis* as the ostensible Kantian equivalent of 'cognition'. However, Kant's account of *Wissen* at A822/B850 cannot be read in such a way that the transcendental conditions for *Erkenntnis* are not sufficient for *Wissen*, which Kant defines as a 'taking something to be true' that is 'both subjectively and objectively sufficient'. Transcendental apperception as the transcendental ground of *Erkenntnis* and of truth, as argued in the Deduction, is precisely concerned with a 'taking something to be true' that is 'both subjectively and objectively sufficient' (cf. A125–7). There is nothing beyond what is known in terms of *Erkenntnis*, that would first be satisfied by *Wissen*. It is simply an anachronism to map a contemporary distinction, which is moreover informed by an Anglophone analytic tradition that does not appreciate the Kantian distinction between the transcendental and the empirical, onto an ostensible distinction between Kant's *Erkenntnis* and *Wissen*.

knowledge, which includes pure intuition, is what *makes* empirical knowledge knowledge. It is these knowledge-making conditions that are at issue in the Deduction. There is nothing beyond the knowledge-making conditions that would constitute knowledge, *in addition to* those conditions and given sensible input (empirical intuitions).

Although it is of course important to consider what in the literature has been called the 'second step' of the Transcendental Deduction for a full understanding of the proof-structure of the Deduction, in particular regarding the question how the concept of an object in general links up with the spatiotemporal perception of objects in human intuition, I shall not discuss it until Chapter 11. I believe that discussing in detail the 'second step' is not necessary for an initial assessment of the structure and purport of the argument that is under consideration here, and which I think will amply clarify Reciprocity, which is delineated in its core sense in §§ 16–17. Arguably, the transcendental deduction of the categories is already complete by the end of the 'first step' (cf. B159 [AA 3: 124.16–18]). What is important is first to address the question what it is for an object as such to be *thought* at all by looking at the intentionality, or objective validity, of discursive thought itself. This question lies at the heart of the Transcendental Deduction.

In the following section, I reflect on the interpretative controversy regarding whether the Transcendental Deduction is a regressive or progressive argument. This discussion bears on the proper evaluation of Reciprocity. Controversially, I argue that Kant's argument is *both* progressive and regressive. In doing so, I raise some issues with regard to various interpretations, in particular those of P.F. Strawson, Karl Ameriks and Paul Guyer as examples of the more forceful construals of apperception and the Transcendental Deduction in the Anglophone Kant literature.

4.4 Is the Deduction a Regressive or Progressive Argument?

The prevailing view in the literature, particularly in the 'analytic' school of Kant interpretation, is that in the Transcendental Deduction Kant mounts a progressively structured argument that starts out from the analytic principle of apperception (the 'I think'-proposition) as its premise, disclosing a conceptual truth about *subjective* experience, and concludes that there necessarily is experience of the *objective* as an enabling condition of subjective experience. However, such an argument starting from a basic notion of experience or representation is often presented as proceeding by analysis, rather than by virtue of synthesis as one would normally expect from a progressively structured argument and as indeed Kant himself asserts in a footnote in the *Prolegomena* (AA 4: 276n.; cf. AA

4: 274, 279). Strawson (1968: 87, 108) believes that Kant's key argument starts off from a 'weak' premise concerning a conceptual truth about the possibility of experience or representation, which then proceeds by way of inference to the 'strong' conclusion that objective connectedness is the necessary constraint of experience itself (notice Strawson's variant sense of experience, which does not have the connotation of Kant's *Erfahrung*). The inference from such a 'weak' premise clearly constitutes a progressively structured argument that ascends from a presumed tautology regarding mere experience, experience in a 'thin' sense to use an Ameriksian label, to a 'thick' concept of the objective (see below on Ameriks). However, Strawson (1968: 94–7) famously rejects Kant's underlying synthesis argument and accordingly the connection of the apperception argument with the categories. On his view, the progressive argument has nothing to do with synthetic construction. The central argument is supposedly based on a thoroughly analytic principle, from which the necessity of the concept of the objective can equally analytically be inferred.[32] I should note that various proponents of the progressive reading differ on specific details, and that some admit the synthesis argument but dismiss the cogency of the argument altogether. Guyer, for one, takes one of Kant's strategies to amount to a progressive argument premised on transcendental apperception, which however *includes* a claim to a priori synthesis, but he regards Kant's supporting arguments as thoroughly defective.[33]

Others, however—most prominently Ameriks (1978, 2003a)[34]—have maintained that Kant's argument in the Transcendental Deduction is not progressive

---

[32] In the Strawsonian view, the premise of the argument is the analytic principle of apperception as an unconditioned criterion of the empirical possibility of self-ascription of representations which shores up a so-called transcendental argument concerning the conceptualisability of experience in a broad sense (including any one of one's mere subjectively valid representative states). Such conceptualisability requires a conception of objectivity which first enables a differentiating of one's subjective experiences from the awareness of outer objects. Hence, objectivity, and thus an objective world, is necessary for even the possibility of the self-ascription of one's own experiences. In this way, however, Strawson is unable to see, or in fact dismisses out of hand, the intrinsic conceptual relation between the analytic character of transcendental self-consciousness and a priori synthesis, which first establishes what it is to conceive of objectivity and provides the evidentiary basis for the claims of the Transcendental Deduction. See further Schulting (forthcoming).

[33] Although she appears to privilege the regressive reading, Kitcher (2011: 85ff.) considers whether the Transcendental Deduction can be construed progressively, starting from the 'I think'.

[34] See also Allison (1996: 31) and Collins (1999: 91–3); cf. Cassam (2007: 57ff.). An approach in the early English-language Kant literature that is in many ways similar to Ameriks's regressive interpretation can be found in Watson (1880). Strikingly, Watson's account is a proto-Ameriksian

at all. That is, it is not progressive in the distinctively Strawsonian sense of an argument that proceeds from a 'weak' premise concerning mere representation to a 'strong' conclusion to the effect that a proof of the necessity of objective experience is furnished, which shows objectivity to be the enabling condition of such representation. What Kant does aim at, Ameriks suggests, is just to explain through analysis what it is that makes objective experience the valid kind of experience we normally claim it is. The experience that is meant here is to be interpreted in the 'thick' sense (Ameriks 2003a: 197), namely as 'common experience',[35] although not exclusively in the strong sense of scientific (Newtonian) experience (Ameriks 2003b: 87).

On Ameriks's construal of the structure of the argument Kant should not be taken to argue progressively from some (putatively) uncontroversial definition concerning the mere self-ascribability of one's basic mental states, or experiences in the 'thin' or 'weak' Strawsonian sense, *towards* the objectivity of experience (in the 'thick' sense). Rather, he should be seen as arguing on the basis of the givenness of such a rich concept of experience and subsequently analysing and thus making explicit its implicit a priori marks, that is, regressing to a priori concepts (see again AA 4: 276n.).[36] This Kant does by showing that certain a priori concepts necessarily apply to the objects of such experience.

The crucial difference between the regressive and the progressive readings, then, is that on the regressive reading Kant's premise is not simply a supposedly analytic truth about representation *tout court* (or experience in the 'thin' Strawsonian sense) but must instead be taken to be the *actuality* of full-blown objective experience. On the regressive reading, the premise is therefore obviously synthetic, not merely analytic as with Strawson. What the Transcendental Deduction is supposed to achieve, on Ameriks's reading, is to account for the legitimacy of our synthetic claims to knowledge or experience of objects by showing the necessary applicability of the categories to such knowledge or experience. The regressive nature of a transcendental proof of a synthetic a priori proposition such as 'Everything that happens has its cause' concerns the fact that it is a prin-

---

retort against Arthur James Balfour's proto-Strawsonian reconstruction of Kant's argument as an anti-sceptical transcendental argument of sorts, which spawned an entire debate in subsequent issues of the journal *Mind*. See e.g. Watson (1880: 547) and Balfour (1878: 482ff.). See further Gram (1984: 146n.18).

35 See Ameriks (2005). It concerns our ordinary beliefs about objects of experience. Cf. Kant on 'common knowledge' in morality in *Groundwork*, AA 4: 392. In the *Logic-Hechsel* (LL: 419), the connection is made between ordinary beliefs and the 'analytic method'.

36 See also the references in Ameriks (2003b: 87n.120). Cf. *Inquiry*, AA 2: 276, 278, 281ff., 286, 289.

ciple which 'first makes possible its ground of proof [*Beweisgrund*], namely experience, and must always be presupposed in this' (A737/B765).

Although some have riposted that such a construal of the argument would make Kant's main claim trivially tautological if not viciously circular,[37] and a fortiori open to a sceptic's attack, it seems that, at first glance, Ameriks has provided a plausible reading of Kant's argument in the Transcendental Deduction as on the whole being fundamentally regressive, for the Deduction is basically meant to be an *explication* of possible experience (cf. B117/A85).[38] A regressive argument need not be trivial, for it may yield knowledge that was not previously explicitly known (see e.g. *Prol* § 4, AA 4: 274.37–275.5).[39] Nor is a regressive argument simply begging the question (in that it offers an argument the conclusion of which appears among its premises), since what is presupposed is not the *philosophical* legitimacy or necessary truth of synthetic a priori knowledge or experience as such (which is in need of establishing) but just its *actuality*—notice also that the argument is not concerned with explaining experience *quoad materiale* or how experience emerges.[40]

In the literature there appears to be some ambiguity about what precisely Kant regards as the premise of the regressive argument.[41] In the distant past, the great Kant commentator Hans Vaihinger (1881: 388 ff., 412 ff.) provided an elaborate account of the difficulties involved in determining the precise nature of the premise of Kant's argument in both the *Critique* and the *Prolegomena*. If we disregard the controversy—topical among the neo-Kantians of the Marburg School—regarding the question whether the *nervus probandi* of Kant's argument is the legitimacy of Newtonian science rather than our ordinary beliefs about objects, there are two main possibilities to construe the regressive argument: (1) assume the actuality of objective knowledge and prove its legitimacy, or (2) assume the legitimacy, and hence also the actuality, of objective knowledge and show its conditions of possibility. Vaihinger shows that Kant's reasoning is not so clear as to allow a complete disambiguation of his various lines of argumentation; Kant does not clearly distinguish between the two indicated strategic starting-points of his proof. His foremost concern, in the *Critique* as well as the *Prolegomena*, is to explain the possibility of object cognition (construal 2), which he does by showing that certain concepts are implicit in such cognition. But it is also true that, to defeat dogmatism in metaphysics, Kant is concerned to prove that the

---

[37] See also Strawson (1968: 73 ff., 85, 92) on trivial readings of the Transcendental Deduction.
[38] Cf. Ameriks (1978: 281 ff.) See further Ameriks (2001a: 42 ff., 46). Cf. also *Inquiry*, AA 2: 289.
[39] Cf. *Inquiry*, AA 2: 286 and *Logic-Blom*, AA 24: 131.
[40] Cf. *Prol* § 4, AA 4: 274 ff., 276, 279, and § 21a, AA 4: 304.
[41] For this, see Thöle (1991: 22 ff. n.20). See also in this regard the views of Prauss (1971: 62 ff.).

pure concepts of the understanding have legitimate application to our experience of objects (construal 1), in other words, to first prove their restricted legitimacy within the realm of possible experience.[42] As Vaihinger suggests, these two aims are interconnected.[43]

At any rate, the conclusion of the proof is, on Ameriks's regressive reading, not already assumed to be true, for the goal of the argument is explicitly philosophical. That is to say, the argument aims at justification by way of a transcendental explanation of what is assumed in the premise in terms of the existence, and commonly accepted authority, of ordinary beliefs about objects (entertained by science as well as in common experience). What is presupposed in experience, more particularly in judgements, in terms of necessary a priori concepts (the categories) must be legitimated *philosophically* to fully warrant ordinary beliefs about objects. This is the Transcendental Deduction as the answer to the *quaestio juris* (see again Chapter 3). Consequently, Ameriks and the 'progressivists' could agree on the fact that the specific (philosophical) explanation of synthetic knowledge cannot be at any rate the *principium cognoscendi* of Kant's argument on pain of begging the central question.

However, I propose yet another approach. To an important extent, my interpretation agrees with Strawson's belief that there is an 'analytical connexion' (1968: 96) between the premise and the conclusion of the argument. Nevertheless, I also concur with Ameriks, against Strawson, over the fact that the premise of the argument does not concern a merely conceptual truth about representation *simpliciter*. On a certain level, it is true to say, as does Ameriks, that the premise of the Transcendental Deduction reveals a de facto commitment to objective experience, the actuality of which is thus not subjected to doubt and as a consequence first in need of being shown to obtain in order to refute epistemic scepticism, as Strawson argues. To explain this apparent contradiction in my interpretation, I contend that Kant's argument must, in some sense, be seen as both progressive and regressive, while avoiding the shortcomings of both Strawson's and Ameriks's construals and also meeting the criticisms raised by Guyer and others in regard to Reciprocity.

Before filling out some of Guyer's misgivings about Kant's claims (see Section 4.5 below) I should like first to stake out my own position on the structure of Kant's argument in the Transcendental Deduction. I maintain, first, regarding the progressive argument, that its premise consists in the strict logical or formal

---

[42] In Cassam's (2007) terms, the first strategy would be validatory, whereas the latter would be revelatory.
[43] Cf. Kemp Smith (1999: 44 ff.).

identity of self-consciousness, which is born of the formal analytic unity of consciousness,[44] in a way that does not conflict with the de facto commitment to objective experience. Secondly, I maintain that, given Rigorous Coextensivity, this premise provides an a priori certain foundation for the transcendental exposition of the synthetic grounding structure for the cognition of objects, namely the exposition of the *origin* and objective *validity* of such knowledge.[45] That exposition proceeds synthetically in the actual argument of the 'first step' of the B-Deduction (more precisely §§ 16–17). The certainty that I am here talking about is of course not mathematical certainty, but still, to put it in Kant's terms, a certainty 'to the degree of conviction', a certainty 'in virtue of rational principles' (*Inquiry*, AA 2: 292).[46] The foundation that is at issue is that which should provide the formal ground, not simply for the representation of objects but for their very constitution as bona fide *objects* of cognition, as indeed Kant appears to claim in the passage at B138, quoted at the outset of this chapter. Transcendental philosophy has the peculiar trait that it is able to specify in an a priori way both the rules for objective experience and the case to which these rules must be applied, that is, to that of which the experience is (cf. B174 ff./A135 ff.). It is this fundamental point around which Reciprocity centres. As noted earlier, it is not the object per se 'as far as its existence is concerned' (A92/B125; cf. B72) that is the concern of Kant's reasoning, but the a priori possibility of an object *as object*, qua its objectivity, as well as the a priori conditions of objective knowledge or experience.[47] It is only for these a priori conditions of knowledge and the a priori possibility of *objects* of knowledge that a certain foundation can be established, which Kant argues lies in the unity of apperception. This is the chief reason

---

44 This is of course in need of further clarification. What, among other things, is the relation between the identity of self and the analytic unity of consciousness? Is identity the same as analytic unity? I explain this in due course.
45 I broadly agree with Allison on this score; see esp. Allison (1996: 32, 49) and also (2004: 173 ff.).
46 See again Chapter 3, Section 1.
47 Cf. A720/B748: 'The matter of appearances, however, through which *things* in space and time are given to us, can be represented only in perception, thus *a posteriori*. The only concept that represents this empirical content of appearances *a priori* is the concept of the *thing* in general, and the synthetic *a priori* cognition of this can never yield *a priori* more than the mere rule of the synthesis of that which perception may give *a posteriori*, but never the intuition of the real object, since this must necessarily be empirical.' See also R5643 (1780–88): 'I cannot cognize *a posteriori* that something is objectively determined, without determining it objectively in accordance with an *a priori* rule; for everything that is objectively determined must be able to be determined *a priori* from the concept of the object, *to be sure not as far as its matter is concerned but still as far as the form of connection is*' (AA 18: 284 [NF: 269], emphasis added).

why Kant can make the prima facie surprising, if not shocking, claim at A129, in the conclusion to the A-Deduction, that the objects of which we have cognition 'are one and all in me, that is, are determinations of my identical self', which is 'only another way of saying that there must be a complete unity of them in one and the same apperception' (trans. Kemp Smith).

The type of knowledge that is the object of Kant's investigation concerns only that element of objects of which, in virtue of reason's own capacity, we may demonstrably have formal a priori knowledge.[48] In general, by invoking the explanatory model that he does Kant aims to explicate, *mutatis mutandis*, the assumed traditional correspondence-theoretical notion of truth, namely the putative *adaequatio* between the concept of a thing and the thing itself to which such a concept must be applied (cf. B82ff./A58ff.).[49] The central question concerns the epistemological issue in what manner the terms of this correspondence are a priori related, and so exhibit a sense of sameness or identity, while amounting to objectively real knowledge of that which is *different* from the thinking mind itself, whereby it should be noted that the straightforwardly ontological reading of *adaequatio* is of course rejected by Kant. More precisely, it concerns the possible determination of a 'general and certain criterion of truth' that does not abstract from the content of cognition but is genuinely 'alike' to it, thus a 'sufficient and yet at the same time general sign of truth' (B82–3/A58–9). The fundamental problem at issue here is how something external to thought must simultaneously necessarily be *different from* and *identical to* thought so as first to be capable of being thought as *that which is over against* (cf. A104), and thus an *object for*, thinking; the meaning of 'correspondence', or *adaequatio*, acquires another sense in Kant's theory of truth, for it can no longer be assumed as a matter of course that the correspondence relation between the constituents of knowledge is one of identity in terms of sameness or equality *tout court*—what Frege termed *Gleichheit*.

If, then, Kant is indeed out to explicate truth as sufficient ground of the cognition of objects, given that explicating such truth should nonetheless yield a general criterion of knowledge, then he will only be able to establish the *formal* characteristics of truly cognised objects, namely only insofar as one's perceptions are determined such that they constitute an objectively real order to which things or events in the world must be a priori taken to belong, to be 'alike' (cf. B82ff./A58ff.). These formal characteristics are the categories, which

---

48 Cf. R5936, AA 18: 394. See also A129–30 and Bxviii, where Kant writes the familiar dictum that 'we can cognize of things *a priori* only what we ourselves have put into them'.
49 See Schulting (2009a: 60ff.).

in the truly Aristotelian sense are the ultimate and most general ontological predicates that must be attributed to things as objects of propositional knowledge (expressed in judgements).

It is the *regressive* explication of these conditions, through a *progressive* exposition from a principle, which is the central concern of the Transcendental Deduction. Kant calls the 'fact that these concepts [i.e. the categories, D.S.] express *a priori* the relations of the perceptions in every experience' (B269/A221), and hence provide the 'sufficient and yet at the same time general sign of truth' (B83/A59), their 'transcendental truth' (B269/A221–2), their *veritas transcendentalis*, which is tantamount to the objective reality of a priori concepts and is to be shown in a deduction.[50] Establishing objective reality is thus in line with ascertaining, wholly independently of experience, the transcendental truth of the categories, to which the objective order of the perceptions of which experience is constituted must isomorphically conform in order to yield objectively valid knowledge. Consequently, the type of necessity that the truth of our cognition amounts to is a conditional necessity, which points to an essentially regressive type of reasoning. Notice that the conditional necessity concerns the truth of our cognition, not the truth of the philosophical proof that establishes this necessity,[51] which must be apodictically certain (in the non-mathematical sense), that is, the proof must yield 'apodictic (philosophical) certainty' (Axv).[52] The knowledge thus arrived at is conditional in the sense that objects as appearances are known in terms of their causal relations in an *empirically* real world, for which possible experience is the mediating factor, not in terms of their putative substantial properties in the metaphysical sense.[53]

I shall argue that the formal identity of self-consciousness, from which the progressive argument proceeds, must not be taken to issue in a trivial tautology regarding the possibility of self-consciousness that has no corollary for the theo-

---

[50] With regard to the formal nature of material or objective truth, to which Kant appeals, see also B236/A191. Cf. *Met-Volck*, AA 28: 415: 'Wahrheit ist eigentlich Uebereinstimmung mit dem Object, das principium der Wahrheit im logischen Verstande besteht darin, daß das Mannigfaltige des Objects in den Erkentnißen unter einander zusammenstimme. Betrachte ich ein Object überhaupt so ist es Einheit, die Einheit der mannigfaltigen Bestimmung ist transcendentale Wahrheit.'

[51] Cf. *Met-L₂*, AA 28: 557–8: 'The cognition of necessity is therefore a hypothetical cognition. All things have derived necessity <*necessitatem derivativum*>; I can cognize them *a priori* in some respect <*secundum quid*> from grounds of experience. [...] Real possibility is the agreement with the conditions of a possible experience. The connection of a thing with experience is actuality. This connection, insofar as it can be cognized *a priori*, is necessity' (LM: 322–3).

[52] Cf. *Logic-Vienna*, AA 24: 830ff. Cf. R5645, AA 18: 291.

[53] Cf. A227/B279–80 and also A225/B272.

ry of knowledge. The clue to the progressive argument is, I believe, precisely the notion of transcendental apperception as a general and a priori certain criterion, indeed an analytic principle, of objective or *material* truth (cf. A60/B85) as different from merely logical validity.[54] Transcendental apperception is the principle of the 'logic of truth' (A62/B87), whereby truth is to be understood not merely as formal validity of the logical relation between the terms of a proposition but as rule-governed correspondence between intellect and extra-intellectual thing, subject and object. Crucially, the principle of apperception, which underlies and so grounds the correspondence, does not stipulate a definitional or conceptual truth about mere experience or consciousness, from which, in the fashion of a Strawsonian analytical argument, consequences could be teased out as to the necessity of the employment of concepts of the objective for even being able to have purely subjective experiences (in Strawson's sense). The progressive argument rather bears out that the principle of apperception is the *original* ground (*principium*) on which objectivity is grounded (*principiatum*),[55] and which thus first enables both the experience and constitution of objectivity and hence the constitution of objects in general. Objectivity is the *explanandum*, not the *explanans* as it is in Strawson's reconstruction. Neutralising the persistent assumption in the literature that the principle of apperception concerns mere experience (in Strawson's sense) or self-awareness as such in terms of the possibility of self-ascription goes a long way towards resolving the problem that solicited the criticisms levelled against Reciprocity.

The progressive argument (P), which roughly runs from B131 (§ 16) to B138–9 (§ 17) with §§ 18–20 giving the implications of the preceding sections (for present purposes a discussion of these sections can be left out, as I want to concentrate on Reciprocity, which we are addressing here), may to a first approximation be schematised as follows:

P1. 'The: *I think* must *be able* to accompany all my representations' (B131), which is tantamount to the identity between the I that thinks *its* representations and all representations that have in common the indexical 'I', viz. all *my* representations. (*operative premise*)

---

[54] Notice though that apperception is also 'the highest point to which one must affix [...] even the whole of logic', as Kant states at one point (B134n.). See Schulting (2017b).
[55] What is meant is the argument from *principium ad principiata*, that is, from ground to grounded, which amounts to a qualitative synthesis (see ID, AA 2: 388n.). This is the argument from the 'highest principle' to synthetic a priori cognition. Cf. *Logic-Hechsel*, LL: 418–19; and JL § 117, AA 9: 149.

P2. Given the formal nature of the 'I think',[56] the identity of 'all my representations' is equal to the analytic *unity* of 'all my representations', or, the 'I think' is the analytic *unity* of apperception (AUA) (B132).

P3. AUA is rigorously coextensive with the original *synthetic* unity of apperception (SUA); Rigorous Coextensivity constitutes the analytic *principle* of apperception (B133–5). (*central argument of § 16*)

P4. The coextensivity of AUA and SUA or Rigorous Coextensivity is an a priori fact of discursive thought (B135).

P5. SUA coincides with an objective unity (B136–7). (*main thesis of § 17*)

P6. Therefore, AUA corresponds in an a priori way with an objective unity (B137; B138–9). (*upshot of §§ 16–17*)

P7. Therefore, the opening statement of the argument (the 'I think'-proposition) is the premise of the objectivity argument and as such is the necessary and sufficient ground of objectivity. (*Reciprocity*)

This is not an adequate exposition of Kant's reasoning by a long chalk. It is a rough outline of the P-argument as I construe it, which will be fleshed out in the chapters to come. It does not explain the terms 'analytic unity' and 'identity', and 'synthetic unity' and 'objective unity' as regards their interrelatedness, such that the inference of the P-argument would be plain for all to see. Furthermore, it assumes rather than explains Kant's definition of an object, which thus leaves Reciprocity still unaccounted for. It leaves out an explication of the role of judgement and does not address the conclusion of the argument (§ 20). Lastly, but not unimportantly, it also does not give an explication of why the start of the P-argument is prefaced by a section (§ 15). In Chapters 6 and following, I shall expound the rational proof that I take Kant to have produced and which I believe is sound, given the basic premises of his view of discursive thought (to be discussed in Chapter 5).

---

[56] That the 'I think' should be taken in a merely formal sense is argued in detail by Kant in the Paralogisms chapter of the *Critique* (see e.g. A354 and B404 ff.). However, the 'I think's formality follows from the nature of discursive thought, as Kant explains this in the Metaphysical Deduction, and so is not something that is only first established in the Paralogisms. It already essentially informs the argument in the Transcendental Deduction, based on Kant's definition of thought as a function of unity (A69/B93). Evidently, Kant must start out from the presuppositionless position of a merely logical and non-substantial thinking 'I', the necessary agent of discursive thought, whose content or substantial identity cannot already be taken for granted. That the 'I' of the premise of the Transcendental Deduction is indeed merely formal will become clearer in the course of a more detailed exposition of the P-argument in the Chapters 6 and following.

4.4 Is the Deduction a Regressive or Progressive Argument?

Whatever the case may be in detail, having just sketched the main thrust of the P-argument, I also contend—and this constitutes the other component of my dual interpretation—that the P-argument licenses, on a different level of reasoning, a *regressive* argument that concerns the entitlement to the employment of the pure concepts that are implicit in the objective experience already assumed as actual in the premise of the regressive argument.[57] This is the argument as Ameriks construes it. I believe that the global argument Kant presents constitutes the general argument about the justification of the application of necessary a priori concepts to objects of experience, which Kant explains in A92–4 (TD § 14). It is these a priori concepts that Kant, in general fashion, seeks to uncover as implicitly presupposed in what we take ordinarily to be objective empirical knowledge (notice again that Kant identifies objective experience [*Erfahrung*] with empirical knowledge [B147; B165–6]). This argument is the transcendental deduction of the categories in terms of the legitimation of their use, broadly taken. The regressive argument (R) may be roughly schematised as containing the following steps (for the present moment ignoring all attendant premises):

R1. There is knowledge of objects or a standard claim to the possession of such knowledge which shows a commonly shared experience (the *fact* of experience).

R2. Knowledge or experience of objects presupposes the implicit use of primitive concepts which ground it.

R3. These primitive concepts are the categories, which can be defined as the necessary concepts that first establish what it is to experience or know objects.

R4. The categories cannot simply be abstracted from the objects experienced or known.

R5. Hence, categories must be a priori.

R6. Therefore, the a priori application of categories to experience or knowledge of objects is legitimate, for they are the necessary grounds of objective experience or knowledge.

R7. Therefore, the claim to the possession of objective knowledge or to knowledge of objects is (philosophically) justified.

However, it is the P-argument which settles the principal assertion of the Transcendental Deduction that not only do certain pure concepts, the categories, govern the experience of objects by being presupposed as its necessary conditions, but also that these concepts genuinely refer to the objects and indeed first constitute them *as* objects. The R-argument does not tell us *how* the a priori concepts

---

[57] Regressive is the argument *a principiatis ad principia*, that is, from grounded to ground (amounting to a qualitative *analysis*). This is the argument from 'what is sought, as if it were given', viz. synthetic knowledge, ascending to 'the only condition under which it is possible' (*Prol* § 5, AA 4: 276n.; cf. B364/A308). See also Thöle (1991: 36–8).

are inferentially derivable from a premise so as to yield a philosophically apodictic proof.[58] It does not tell us the manner in which the necessary form of an object is constituted, and how the categories yield the sufficient condition for objectivity. That is, the analytic method of a regressive argument does not provide us with the rational knowledge regarding which *specific* conditions are necessary and sufficient for the cognition of objects and, even more crucially, *in what way* they are to be seen as necessarily applicable to such cognition.[59] Put differently, the R-argument only tells us *that* the a priori concepts are legitimately applied as the necessary conditions of possible experience. But the rational ground for the claim of legitimacy is missing. A purely regressive construal of the Transcendental Deduction is not capable of demonstrating that the categories are the necessary and sufficient conditions, not only of the cognitive representation of objects, but also of their very constitution as objects of possible experience.[60]

In other words, one fails to address the reciprocity claim that is central to Kant's reasoning in the Transcendental Deduction if one merely attends to the regressive nature of the Deduction's legitimating task. Through deductively demonstrating that the categories are a priori derivable from a premise one makes it clear that one does not betray an evasion of the fulfilment of the burden of proof (namely by basing the proof on the objective experience of which the categories must first be *shown* to be the necessary conditions). Although, as I said earlier, a regressive argument need not at all be trivial, or indeed viciously circular, a regressive argument does not constitute a proof strictly speaking, that is, it does not amount to a philosophical demonstration in terms of a rational explanation from a principle. A regressive argument in itself is not sufficient to provide a genuine legitimation, a deduction, of the categories. I explain at the end of the book (in Chapter 10) how the P-argument is to clinch Reciprocity and in what sense that argument interlocks with the R-argument, after having shown (in Chapters 6–9) how the derivation of the categories makes up the P-argument.

Importantly, as I said earlier, Kant does not intend in any sense, at least not in the Transcendental Deduction, to demonstrate the *actuality* of objective expe-

---

[58] Cf. Henrich (1976: 93). Henrich here points out the requirements for a *Begründung* of the Deduction, the criterion of which he famously links with a priori *knowledge* of the self's identity.
[59] Only the P-argument as a proof of the validity of the argument regarding the necessary (and sufficient) conditions of objective experience is a *deduction* properly speaking (see Chapter 3). Concurring with Baum in this respect, I believe that an interpretation that merely considers the regressive argument does not even address the Transcendental Deduction strictly speaking, that is, the subjective deduction from § 15 onward, but restricts itself to the transitional §§ 13 and 14, or even merely A92–3 (see Baum 1986: 64 ff., 71 ff.; cf. Axvii).
[60] Cf. Baum (1986: 202).

rience or knowledge—Kant grants *that* there is objective experience or knowledge[61]—let alone its metaphysical necessity,[62] or indeed the *existence* of objects.[63] As already noted, for Kant it is not the existence of objects (objects 'in the weighty sense', as Strawson [1968: 73] puts it) nor the conception of objective connectivity as the presumed necessary (material) condition of subjective experience that is the *terminus ad quem* of the Transcendental Deduction. Kant's goal is rather, first, to demonstrate the necessary and sufficient conditions under which the *concept* of an object, its capability of being thought and hence an object's very essence (its objectivity, *Gegenständlichkeit*), is first made possible and subsequently to demonstrate, through showing the a priori relatedness between the thought of an object and the a priori form of the intuition of an object, its capability of being known. The existence of things, their materiality and the percepts thereof are assumed as given and unproblematic.[64]

Rather than arguing, as Strawson does, that conceptualisability of experience and hence objective connectivity is that which first enables the self-ascription of one's experiences, the capacity of which is expressed by 'transcendental self-consciousness',[65] I contend, in conformity with Reciprocity, that conversely

---

61 See e.g. *Real Progress*, AA 20: 275. Carl (1989b: 10 ff.), however, disputes the reading of the Transcendental Deduction as based on a 'Faktum der Erfahrung'—note that Hermann Cohen, whom Carl refers to here, is often seen as the source of this dictum, but he in fact believed that 'die transscendentale Deduktion klar und bündig auf das "Faktum" *der Wissenschaft* gegründet und orientiert [ist]' (Cohen 1907: 53, emphasis added). Indeed, Carl argues, '[i]t is experience itself [...] that has to be proved. To prove the validity of the categories for all appearances is to show that experience as a certain form of organizing our sensory data is the only form in which we can *have* such data' (1989b: 11, emphasis added; cf. Guyer 2006: 83). Carl further asserts that 'the *necessity* of experience must be proved [which] is the aim of a subjective deduction, and because of this aim the notion of apperception is introduced within the framework of a deduction of the categories' (1989b: 11, emphasis added). Carl, therefore, thinks that the subjective deduction is more important than the objective deduction (1989b: 18–19).
62 Cf. Guyer (1987: 123 ff.).
63 Cf. Erdmann (1878: 45–7).
64 Cf. Kant's letter to J.S. Beck of 4 December 1792 (*Corr*, AA 11: 395), where Kant stresses that the idealism of objects, which centrally informs his theory of knowledge (in contrast to empirical-idealist constructs such as Berkeley's), only concerns the necessary (and sufficient) *form* of their representation, not their matter nor their existence (cf. B236/A191: 'only the formal conditions of empirical truth can be inquired after here'). See further Schulting (2017a), chs 1 and 4. See also Chapter 11, this volume.
65 Strawson (1968: 94, 108) speaks of 'transcendental self-consciousness'. However, Kant himself does not usually call it thus, but rather 'transcendental unity of self-consciousness', or indeed 'transcendental consciousness' (A117n.), which *is* self-consciousness strictly speaking. I shall be using 'transcendental consciousness' and 'transcendental self-consciousness' interchangeably.

it is the transcendental unity of self-consciousness—and hence *a priori synthesis* —itself that first enables the conceptualisability and thus the objective connectivity of experience (cf. A121ff.). Obviously, this does not mean that transcendental consciousness literally *produces* objects 'in the weighty sense', namely as existentially instantiated occupants of empirical space (cf. again A92/B125 and B139)—which is of course not to say that the objects *determined* by transcendental consciousness do not exist in the strict sense, as 'weighty' objects. But this only goes to show that the P-argument comports with the overall regressive nature of Kant's epistemological argument, which presupposes the de facto existence of objects as determinable occupants of a spatiotemporal continuum.

That which first constitutes the possibility of connectedness and hence the possibility of an identical sameness, implied as a background condition in the recognition of objects and objective events (even mental states), is not, as Strawson (1968: 117) would have it, a 'course of experience of an objective world, conceived of as determining the course of that experience itself', but rather an unrestricted *principle* of objectively valid identity, indeed the principle of apperception, which is an *a priori* ground of any instantiation of kinds of identical sameness and hence of the determinate course of one's experience. The 'connective point [*Beziehungspunkt*][,] [a] something [...] that is parallel to my "I" [*meinem Ich*]', of which Kant speaks in the *Duisburg Nachlass* in R4675,[66] is not the really existing thing external to my mind, but what in the A-edition of the *Critique* is called the transcendental object—or, in the language of B141, the objective unity of apperception—which is 'parallel' or corresponding to the transcendental *subject* of apperception; this 'object' makes the unity of cognition necessary and, most importantly, is 'nothing other than the formal unity of consciousness' (A105; cf. A114; see also A250). Strawson's empiricist conception of the objective connectivity that putatively enables self-ascription is exactly the reverse of Kant's *a priori* conception of the possibility of objective connectivity.

It is therefore important to bear in mind, following Ameriks, that Kant does not attempt a demonstration of the conceptualisability of empirical experience in any merely 'weak' (Strawsonian) sense nor to show a perception's necessary susceptibility of being categorially determined.[67] Neither does Kant want to es-

---

[66] AA 17: 648.7 and 648.20 respectively (NF: 161, trans. emended); cf. R4676, AA 17: 656.
[67] For example, at A180/B222, in the introductory section to the Analogies, Kant explicitly indicates that '[a]n analogy of experience will [...] be only a rule in accordance with which unity of experience *(not how perception itself, as empirical intuition as such)* is to arise from perceptions [...]' (emphasis added and trans. emended; Kemp Smith has: 'An analogy of experience is [...] only a rule according to which a unity of experience may arise from perception. It does not tell us how mere perception or empirical intuition in general itself comes about.').

tablish *from* the supposedly necessary unifiability of experiences in the 'thin' sense that there must be knowledge of objects as its condition, as Strawson (1968: 88) has it.⁶⁸ With this in mind, one should be mindful of the metaphysical modesty underlying the P-argument. In other words, the P-argument must be construed in keeping with the restrictive argumentative scope of the R-argument as Ameriks has interpreted it.

Now it might appear counterintuitive to maintain, as I do, that the argument is regressive as well as progressive, given the conventional view that the two interpretative strategies are diametrically opposed.⁶⁹ However, I contend that only such a twofold reading enables an appreciation of the intricacies of Reciprocity (and hence of its ramifications for the Transcendental Deduction as a whole), lest one choose simply to reject it. Although, on the whole, I agree with the thrust of Ameriks's regressive reading, my reading differs from his in that I emphasise that Kant's *strategy* or *method* for the Transcendental Deduction as a philosophical proof is, to a certain extent, Cartesian, and thus necessarily progressively structured in a way that Ameriks does not, or at least not explicitly, endorse.⁷⁰ This does not contradict Kant's de facto commitment to a common sense notion of objective experience, which Ameriks is keen to emphasise. But as Guyer (2003: 93) rightly points out in a review of Ameriks (2000b), 'in Kant's view even the reliable claims of common sense must ultimately be validated by their philosophical deduction from a priori sources in the mind'.⁷¹

---

68 For my view on Strawson's reading of Kant, see further Schulting (forthcoming).
69 My dual-level reading is closest to Vaihinger's. He points out with regard to Kant's various lines of argumentation, which he associates with explanation and proof, that 'eben darum schieben sich diese beiden Argumentationszielpunkte [*scilicet* "explanatio" and "probatio"; cf. Vaihinger 1881: 397] abwechselnd vor und lösen sich gleichsam ab; es sind zwei zusammengehörige Brennpunkte einer Ellipse' (Vaihinger 1881: 398).
70 Cf. Ameriks (2003b: 14). Ameriks believes Kant's mode of reasoning is typified by a 'distinctive *non*-Cartesian strategy'. I should note, however, that my view of 'progressive' does not correspond to the usual strong conception of 'progressive', the view that Ameriks is right to repudiate (see Ameriks 1978: 281 ff.). It is in this regard that my view and Ameriks's view of the sense in which the argument may still be said to be progressive in some importantly other sense than the standard progressive reading allows could be aligned.
71 See also Thöle's critique of Ameriks in Thöle (2001). In a *Reflexion* from 1780–83 (R5637), Kant is not so positive about a common sense account of knowledge, among other accounts, that 'supposes that our experience and also our *a priori* cognition pertain immediately to objects and not first to the subjective conditions of sensibility and apperception'. In contrast to other accounts such as empiricism, intellectual intuitionism and innatism, common sense, which he refers to pejoratively as the '*qualitas occulta* of the healthy understanding' or of 'common reason', in fact 'gives no account' (AA 18: 272–3 [NF: 262]).

In my view, the Transcendental Deduction is progressively structured, for a philosophical proof does not allow circularity of reasoning, even if non-trivially, as a satisfactory way of demonstrating the transcendental truth of claims about objects. More importantly, it must be progressive in that, operatively, the proof-structure of the argument, being an *a priori* account of the subjective conditions that govern but also ground objective knowledge, does ex hypothesi not allow an external assumption as its premise. The logical premise of the philosophical argument must at any rate be internal to reason.[72] As Kant puts it, our basic cognitions 'must wholly be derived *in abstracto* from concepts' (*Prol*, AA 4: 279, trans. emended). Kant observes that unlike in the *Prolegomena* he proceeded synthetically in the *Critique*, for the 'system [is] based on no data except reason itself, and [...] therefore seeks, *without resting upon any fact [Factum], to unfold knowledge from its original germs*' (*Prol*, AA 4: 274, emphasis added; cf. B81/A57). This is because, in Kant's view, 'reason has insight only into what it itself produces according to its own design' (Bxiii). The proof in the *Critique* is Cartesian-like because the argument of the Transcendental Deduction itself starts out from the self-confirmatory principle of the identical *cogito*, which bestows logical certainty on the ensuing argument, rather than from the matter of fact of either mere experience or objective experience—there is no properly basic fact or belief from which a philosophical demonstration gets started other than the merest basic *logical* truth of discursive thought itself.

Evidently, this does not mean, for Kant, that the truth of the premise is anything more than formal. Hence, the premise signals nothing but the sheer possibility of discursive thought as the minimal presupposition of any bona fide philosophical investigation into the possibility of cognition. The truth of the premise is corroborated by the inferences that are drawn from it in that the inferred synthetic truths make up, formally, the intension of the 'I think'. This bears out the 'analytical connexion', to use Strawson's words, that is shown by the P-argument, for the conclusion of the argument contains nothing that is not already, implicitly, contained intensionally in the premise, from which it can thus be derived as a necessary consequence. But, contrary to Strawson, I argue that a priori synthesis is part and parcel of the analytical unpacking here. That this is what Kant envisions is I believe signalled in the oft-quoted passage at B135:

---

[72] In this regard, I consider Kant's method in respect of his epistemological intentions to be largely rooted in a Cartesian conception of 'internal' justification, albeit that I am inclined to argue that Kant is committed to weak internalism because for Kant any justification of knowledge must finally be based on possible experience and cannot rest on immediate rational evidence.

> Now this principle of the necessary unity of apperception is, to be sure, itself identical, thus an analytical proposition, yet it explains [*erklärt*] as necessary a synthesis of the manifold given in an intuition, without which that thoroughgoing identity of self-consciousness could not be thought. (trans. emended)

In the A-Deduction, at A117–18, Kant speaks, tellingly, of the '*transcendental principle of the* [synthetic] *unity*' as *including* a synthesis, indicating an intensional-logical moment in the logic of derivation of the categories.

Alluding to Kant's Cartesian-like strategy helps to explain why both Kant's and Descartes' appeals to self-consciousness in the context of epistemology are so strikingly similar, a fact that one assumes is linked up with their rationalist interests. The main differences between Kant's and Descartes' views about the self lie in the extent to which the limits of possible knowledge of the self's *metaphysical* nature, and hence the *metaphysical* implications of a priori grounded knowledge, are accounted for. I contend that there is not so much difference in their approach to the self's *epistemic* function, that is, with regard to the role that the self must play in a philosophically justificatory project. Clearly, for Kant the identity of the 'I think' does not refer to anything like a Cartesian *res cogitans*, which a fortiori has a continuing (diachronic) existence and whose mental states are immediately accessible to it (A349–50),[73] nor even to a self in terms of a basic 'self-familiarity' that precedes actual acts of reflection, of which Henrich (1967)[74] has spoken in this context (by way of contrasting Fichte's allegedly superior insights into self-consciousness with Kant's allegedly reductive conception of the self).[75] This means that no *metaphysical* claims are made with the premise.[76]

With respect to the premise supposedly being tantamount to a primitive psychological notion, as Descartes appears to believe, we should concur with Ameriks, against a broadly Strawsonian construal, on not taking the Transcendental Deduction as departing from the concept of a simple representation or subjective

---

[73] The certainty of the *cogito*, or the validity of the proposition '*The soul is substance*' (A350), does not transfer to the continued existence of the self, and hence cannot be tantamount to a priori knowledge of all one's possible mental states, a view that Guyer imputes to Kant (see below Section 4.5). It is disputable whether such a view can be imputed to Descartes himself.
[74] See also Henrich (1976: 61).
[75] See Schulting (2017c) for a reply to typically Fichtean criticisms of Kant's theory of self-consciousness.
[76] The 'I think' is merely an empty analytical representation that *as such* has no intension apart from its purely *logical* attributes, its 'transcendental predicates' (A343/B401) (substance, simplicity and so on), and not a representation of a collective whole, a putative identical thoroughgoing self that is wholly self-contained (cf. B404/A345–6). Cf. Erdmann (1878: 53–4).

experience (or, mere awareness of oneself). As Ameriks has often pointed out, the 'I' of the Kantian *cogito* is not just an agent of representation but is already a self involved in judgemental acts regarding objects, as the corollary of the P-argument in § 19 indeed confirms (as I argue in Chapter 10). Moreover, Kant already explicitly refers to the possibility of representation of something 'as combined in the object' at B130 (AA 3: 107.20 – 2) in § 15, suggesting a complex kind of representation. Kant thus does not talk about representation *simpliciter*. That the premise already indicates thought's fundamental objective intentionality is not an unwarranted assumption for which no argument is offered, but will be shown to follow from the mere capacity to *think* in the strict sense—that is, from the capacity to judge, and not from the mere capacity to represent or to be aware, as Strawson and others have it.

If, then, we take Kant's P-argument along the lines I suggest, namely in conformity with the R-argument construed along broadly Ameriksian lines, the proof will not cajole a sceptic into admission of its conclusion, for the proof assumes as a fact our ordinary beliefs regarding objectivity, the warrant of which a sceptic blankly rejects. However, to the extent that for the purpose of a philosophical explanation of the possibility of objective experience Kant has proved the objectivity thesis on the basis of the sheer possibility of (discursive) thought, from which Reciprocity issues, it would appear difficult for a sceptic to reject the force of the proof, given that a sceptic too is in the business of formulating judgements, that is, having thoughts that at least have a truth value, which on Kant's account are dependent on the same function as the forming of objective unities of representations. A radical sceptic could of course reject even having such discursive thoughts (e.g. he could reject anything that goes beyond unconnected impressions that are more or less vivid), but it is not clear what the philosophical merit of such a position would be. How could the sceptic formulate this, his own position other than by forming at least logically *valid* claims to that effect? In Kant's view, at any rate, judgement itself is objectively valid and eo ipso commits any judger about objects (whether empirically real or not) to asserting the objective unity of her representations and hence, given the ramifications of Reciprocity, the objectivity of mind-external things, if they exist. This epistemic situation would appear to equally hold for the sceptic. However, whatever the case may be, I believe that, also given his general outlook on the possibility of rational proofs and the hypothetico-deductive method of reasoning he adopted from natural science, Kant's main aim is not to deliver a knockdown disproof of epistemological scepticism along the lines of a so-called 'transcendental argument'—

something that one might argue he attempts to do in the Refutation of Idealism[77] – but to show that a sufficiently intelligible proof can be provided that will validate philosophically our knowledge claims and so to legitimise the application of the categories.

Looking at the Transcendental Deduction in general, Ameriks's regressive reading and my dual construal of Kant's argument are in agreement. At any rate, I concur with Ameriks, contrary to the mainstream progressive construal of the Transcendental Deduction, that Kant does not make the bold claim that genuine empirical knowledge would 'really flow' from *mere* conceptual principles or from the sheer 'fact of consciousness' (1978: 274–5, 283–4). Nothing however precludes Kant's operative argument from being Cartesian in its archetypal methodological sense, namely to the extent that it aims at securing a certain foundation from which possible objective cognition can be deduced a priori, that is, *even* when the argument is rightly taken to show a commitment to a commonly accepted notion of objective experience (which, *mutatis mutandis*, also holds for Descartes himself, for that matter).[78] Therefore, I dispute Ameriks's claim that Kant's mode of reasoning is 'distinctly *non*-Cartesian' (2003b: 14).

Indirect support for my dual-level reading of the argumentative structure of the Transcendental Deduction might be drawn from a section (§ 3) in Kant's account of the a priori forms of sensibility in the Transcendental Aesthetic. In that account, at B40, Kant elucidates what he means by a 'transcendental exposition', clearly the kind of procedure that is similar to that of the Transcendental Deduction. By a transcendental exposition Kant understands 'the explanation of a concept as a principle from which insight into the possibility of other synthetic a priori cognitions can be gained'. He further writes:

> For this aim it is required 1) that such cognitions *actually flow* from the given concept, and 2) that these cognitions are only possible under the presupposition of a given way of explaining this concept. (B40, emphasis added)

I believe that the first requirement points to a progressive argument and, as is evident, the second to a regressive one. The synthetic a priori cognitions of

---

[77] See Stapleford (2008) for a fine account.
[78] Compare Descartes, AT VI: 18 ff. with for example JL, AA 9: 51. See also Kant's approving remarks about Descartes in regard to the principle of '*clarity and evidence of cognition*' as 'criterion of truth' in JL, AA 9: 32 (LL: 543). Nevertheless, to the extent that Descartes must indeed be seen to be the classic foundationalist in the sense that one's epistemic beliefs are grounded in primitive mental states that have privileged status, Kant's epistemological internalism evidently differs from Descartes'.

which Kant speaks in this particular section are the propositions of geometry; these propositions which amount to synthetic a priori cognitions *flow* from the concept as such of, in this case, space as an a priori form of intuition. In the Transcendental Deduction this concept, from which empirical knowledge or cognition is made possible, would be the concept as such of an object in general. Both requirements are in fact two aspects of the same general argument: experience or cognition of an object is, considered in the a priori way, really only possible under the presupposition of a general concept of an object in general, which implies that such experience or cognition really flows from this latter general concept as the principle of the entire, transcendental, argument or exposition.

Having said all this, my reading fits in with almost all of what Ameriks's modest *regressive* interpretation reveals on the general level, that is, the broadly defined goal of the Transcendental Deduction. The central question for Kant is and remains, in general and at each stage of the Transcendental Deduction, 'what is the *condition of possibility* of *x*', whereby *x* must be understood to be the object of experience as well as objective cognition or experience itself (A111).[79] The most important difference with Ameriks's reading, then, boils down to the fact that I would want to insist on Kant's predilection for a typically modern Cartesian-style justification of his arguments. This is borne out, I believe, by what I take to be the progressively structured *method* Kant adopts in the Transcendental Deduction, but even more crucially, by a certain reflective mode that appears to 'accompany' Kant's very reasoning (see further Chapter 10, Section 4). This is not at all to reject the fact that, as Ameriks rightly points out, underlying Kant's reasoning in the Transcendental Deduction is a common sense notion of objective experience, which is deemed unproblematic and intersubjectively accepted. The very construction of the rational argument of the Transcendental Deduction itself shows that Kant's fundamental *parti pris* is towards empirical experience, which he sees as an incontrovertible aspect of human thought. In this regard, Kant may be considered a positivist of sorts, for he accepts empirical experience (taken empirically) as a brute, metaphysically contingent, fact (cf. A737/B765). In fact, I maintain that only a *regressive* view of experience is strictly coherent with the quasi-circular nature of his methodological or *Copernican* solution for providing apodictic or a priori certain knowledge of the external world (notice the implicitly conditional structure of the claim 'we can

---

[79] In *Prol* § 21a Kant 'remind[s] the reader that we are discussing, not the origin of experience, *but what lies in experience*' (AA 4: 304, emphasis added). This clearly indicates the regressive nature of Kant's argument.

cognize of things *a priori* only what we ourselves have put into them' [Bxviii]),⁸⁰ even though it does not provide us the absolute truth about the world as it is *in itself*.

4.5 On Guyer

At this point, it is worth expatiating on the ostensibly orthodox Cartesian reading of the premise of the Transcendental Deduction, propounded by among others Paul Guyer who, although critical of it, advocates a version of the 'strong'⁸¹ progressive construal of Kant's argument. According to this reading, Kant's assertion that the synthetic unity of self-consciousness is constitutive of object cognition (Reciprocity) rests on a gross *non sequitur*. I have already briefly spoken of Guyer's views at the outset of my disquisition in this chapter. Although many Kantian commentators have taken issue with Guyer's interpretation, few have realised how serious the consequences of his incisive philosophical criticisms of Kant's synthesis argument are for the sustainability of Reciprocity. Few have therefore thought it necessary to offer countervailing evidence for the opposing position, which takes Reciprocity for granted. None have discerned that the basic fault underlying Guyer's interpretation is a general mistake regarding the meaning and purport of the analytic principle of apperception (which Guyer at least seems to be aware of by insisting, with reference to the A-Deduction, that the principle is synthetic),⁸² a mistake, I contend, by which all existing interpretations of the Transcendental Deduction have been dogged and consequently one which prohibits a bona fide understanding of Reciprocity. The difference between Guyer and others who defend Kant's synthesis claim is that, given the standard reading of the analyticity of the principle of apperception, Guyer is aware of the potentially philosophically serious problems involved with a priori synthesis whereas Kant's defenders blithely accept a priori synthesis without seeing the ostensible inconsistencies with the analyticity of the principle of apperception. At least, Guyer is *philosophically* consistent in his critique of Kant.

Guyer appears to agree with at least one aspect of Strawson's interpretation by pointing out that, if interpreted austerely, the premise of the argument would

---

80 On Kant's Copernicanism, see Schulting (2009a).
81 I note again that the strong progressive reading is, in general, the construal of the argument as starting from a 'weak' premise concerning the conceptual constraints of (mere) subjective representation leading to a 'strong' conclusion regarding the necessary knowledge or even the necessary existence of an objective world as a precondition for subjective representation.
82 Also Henrich (1976: 59) says the principle is synthetic.

indeed constitute merely a self-explanatory principle concerning the self-ascription of representations. Grounds for such an interpretation are provided by passages such as at B138 (AA 3: 112.13–19). However, acutely aware of the emphasis Kant puts on the a priori synthesis thesis Guyer believes that Kant's actual premise is not just such a (putatively) trivial principle.[83] Consequently, Strawson's 'strong' conclusion regarding (the necessity of) objectivity cannot really be grounded on a 'weak' premise. It is therefore not surprising, and quite consistent for that matter, that Strawson himself dispenses with *a priori* synthesis, for the only synthesis that would seem to follow from the analytic principle of self-ascription of representations, as Strawson understands it, is an *a posteriori* synthetic unity of representations that *actually* have been self-ascribed.[84] In Strawson's view, then, the synthesis can only be the *result* of self-ascription, not its a priori ground.

While apparently agreeing with the thrust and philosophical soundness of an analytical reconstruction of Kant's argument, such as Strawson's, Guyer adheres to the belief, as regards matters of interpretation, that the fundamental premise of Kant's (progressive) argument is such that

> all representations, regardless of what particular empirical significance they may subsequently be discovered to have, are necessarily recognised to belong to oneself: I thus have *a priori* knowledge that all of my representations, whatever they may represent, belong to my single, numerically identical self. (1992: 141)[85]

(It is this latter part of Guyer's assertion concerning the a priori knowledge of an identical self that sets his interpretation apart from readings of the broadly

---

[83] Cf. Guyer (1980: 208). According to Guyer, the notion of apperception, as a consciousness of one's self-consciousness, can only be retained once freed of the 'encumbrance of *a priori* synthesis' (1980: 212).

[84] Cf. Guyer (1980: 205). See also Guyer (1987: 142). Cf. Hossenfelder (1978: 100–2).

[85] Guyer further states that 'Kant reiterates this premise numerous times'. He cites A107, A113, and A116 as ostensible textual evidence. See also Guyer (1987: 137–8). Guyer's reading of Kant's premise in terms of the idea of so-called a priori *knowledge* of the self appears to be indebted to Henrich's (1976: 59, 86–7, *et passim*) appeal to Cartesian certainty, of which later Henrich has said, not that it concerns a priori *knowledge*, but a priori 'ascertainment' (he uses the phrase *apriori zu vergewissern*) of the necessary implications of the consciousness of the identity of self with regard to all her thoughts. See Henrich (1988: 43ff., 59, 62, 70). Nevertheless, Henrich would appear to claim that the a priori certainty regards all possible thoughts as 'belonging to' the subject in a synthetic connection (1976: 58–9) and that the subject has certain a priori knowledge of her numerical identity, so that she 'aller Erfahrung voraus, eine Kenntnis davon haben muß, was es für es heißt, von Vorstellungszustand zu Vorstellungszustand überzugehen' (1976: 86). Henrich's textual evidence is A108.

Strawsonian kind.) Given such an understanding of the premise, it is quite consistent for Guyer subsequently to observe that Kant's putative claim to the effect that a priori knowledge of the synthetic unity of all of one's possible representations constitutes the possibility of a priori knowledge of objects—Reciprocity—cannot in the end be sustained, for it would mean the intemperate claim that all possible (subjective) representations are eo ipso representations of outer objects, and veridical ones at that. Consonant with this criticism, Guyer reasons that if we were to grant Kant's claim

> that the conditions for the unity of apperception are sufficient for the representation of objects, then it would become obscure how we can ever represent mere conditions of the *self* without also representing an object. (1992: 146)

Thus, Guyer has found fault with Kant's reasoning concerning self-consciousness and its foundational role in the Transcendental Deduction on the grounds that (1) Kant unlawfully presupposes, as regards the premise of the constitution argument, the possibility of synthetic a priori knowledge of the identity of a (substantial, Cartesian) self and (2) he lays a fortiori claim, in respect of the conclusion of that argument, to an entailment relation between such synthetic a priori knowledge and the knowledge of mind-external empirical objects.[86] The reasoning behind Kant's claims would furthermore appear to imply that (3) the thinking self as the premise of the constitution argument—which is tantamount to Reciprocity—would presumably be a priori aware of the synthetic unity of all her representations (past, present and future) *prior to* actually reflectively grasping her representations as her own (that is, *self*-ascribing them). Although this would seem to indicate a confusion on Kant's part with respect to kinds of modality (that is, a confusion of de dicto and de re claims regarding the necessary unity of representations), the claim behind (3) does seem important for Kant, for how can one know that indeed *all* of one's representations are united in the transcendental way unless there is such an 'advance guarantee' (Guyer 1980: 208) that they do all come together in ways that agree with a necessary unity? This kind of knowledge surely could not be derived analytically from a 'weak' premise.[87] Kant's alleged reasoning is further such that, by implication of (2), it would mean that (4) a priori knowledge of all one's representations, constituting one's identity as a self, corresponds not just with the knowledge, but also with the *numerical identity*, of the objects of which one claims to have knowl-

---

[86] Cf. Guyer (1992: 141–5). Guyer's most sustained criticism of Kant's apperception argument can be found in Guyer (1987: 133–49).
[87] Cf. Guyer (1980: 205, 208) and Guyer (1987: 140). See also Hossenfelder (1978: 102).

edge, just by assuming an a priori ontological connection between the identity of the thinking self and the identity of the object thought; but, as already noted, also that (5) from an epistemic point of view, *all* of a subject's representations are objectively valid, that is, have objective reference.

Taken at face value, none of these implications (3–5) are philosophically defensible though. First, it would not seem to make sense to posit that I have prior knowledge of my identity as a self even before I (can) actually reflect on my mental states and self-ascribe them to myself. For how do I know that *when*, supposedly, I am primordially acquainted with my identical self *that* it *is*, de re, my identical self that I *believe*, de dicto, I am acquainted with, without operating a basic function, by means of reflection, that provides the rule for determining what it is to be so self-acquainted? In other words, what *determines* self-identity, that is to say, what determines the identity between the de dicto belief about my numerical identity and my de re numerical identity? Postulating an a priori knowable identical self to which all my self-ascribed representations must correspond invites an infinite regress if no such basic function or rule for determining can be shown to apply.[88] I am not self-acquainted with myself as a numerically identical person as a matter of course—such a self-acquaintance would conflict with Kant's criticism of paralogistic reasoning regarding personal identity. When Kant says that 'identity must necessarily *enter into* [hinein kommen] the synthesis of all the manifold of appearances insofar as they are to become empirical cognition' (A113, emphasis added), it seems prima facie clear that for Kant too the identity of self-consciousness cannot be prior (nor temporally posterior I should note) to the act of synthesis, which provides the rule for determining what it means to be self-acquainted. To this extent, Guyer's attribution to Kant of an intemperate claim concerning the putative a priori knowledge of the self's identity would appear to be misguided.

It will be shown in Chapters 6–9 that indeed, for Kant, identity of self-consciousness and a synthetic act of apperception as an act of taking together one's representations and thus ascribing them to one's identical self are equiprimordial, which demonstrates that Kant merely makes a claim to the conditional necessity underlying the relation between my representations and the identity of self, that is, the claim:

---

[88] It is ironic that Henrich (1967) has argued—and has criticised Kant for not appreciating—precisely the opposite, namely, that it does not make sense to posit that I am able (empirically) to self-ascribe my representations to myself, if I were not *a priori* acquainted with my identity, on the basis of which a reflective ascription of a particular representation I have, and which is therefore one that belongs to my self-identity, can first occur. See Schulting (2017c).

> Representations relate, and so belong, to my identical self *if and only if* representations that I have show up synthetic unity, and representations show up synthetic unity *if and only if* they have been apperceived or synthesised, *by me*, so as to belong to my identical self.

If, namely, Kant were to make a claim to the absolute necessity regarding the synthetic unity of one's representations and the identity of one's self, as Guyer believes Kant does, then it is no longer clear why an *act* of synthesis would be necessary for such a unity to obtain, for an a priori synthetic identity that is also a priori knowable would imply, as a matter of course, a sameness (*Gleichheit*) as a basic ground which is in no need of further unification. Kant could simply have dogmatically assumed the synthetic (a priori) unity as a premise. (This might be a reason why Guyer gives priority to the A-Deduction version of the argument, where Kant would seem to assert that the principle of apperception is indeed synthetic, rather than analytic as he states in the B-edition.) However, given the discursive limitations of our mode of thought, Kant could not, and I believe does not, assume a synthetically universal as a premise, but merely an analytically universal (cf. CJ, AA 5: 407 ff.), namely, the merely formal, empty representation 'I think', which is in need of a manifold that it must run through and subsequently take together for it to have a content and hence first to show up a synthetic unity.

Ignoring for now my caveats about Guyer's reading, Guyer is at any rate right to query the intelligibility of a priori synthesis if this is taken to mean a priori knowledge of one's self-identity pure and simple. Nor is it a fortiori philosophically sound, if we pursue the earlier mentioned points 4 and 5 further, to just assume an a priori knowable connection between the numerical identities of self and object. Such a view, if it were Kant's view, has the hallmark of Leibniz's doctrine of pre-established harmony, which, or any version thereof, clearly he repudiated.[89] Even if it were true that I have a priori knowledge of myself, no legitimate basis would thus be provided for postulating, as Kant would seem to do on account of Reciprocity, an isomorphic metaphysical connection between the self's identity and the identity of external objects, such that any occurrence of self-awareness would map onto an occurrence of a mind-external object. Such an inference would be a manifest *non sequitur*. Lastly, it does not seem intelligible, as Guyer is right to point out, to hold that all of the representations that one has eo ipso have objective reference; for at least some of one's representations are *mere* representations or just fancies of the mind and hence lack any, even only potential, objective validity. If Guyer is right, then Kant's arguments seem hopelessly flawed. But is Guyer's interpretation germane to Kant? Is Kant's P-ar-

---

[89] See e.g. *Real Progress*, AA 20: 283 ff.; cf. B166–8.

gument, by means of which he intends to establish the reciprocity between unity of consciousness and objectivity, indeed tantamount to what Guyer has argued is fallacious reasoning?

Having already signalled some possible criticisms of the interpretative avenue that Guyer pursues, I believe there are good systematic as well as exegetical reasons not to accede to Guyer's findings, so that on a more charitable reading of the ostensible textual evidence one need not take the view that Kant is culpable of the grave philosophical mistakes with which Guyer charges him. For one thing, as noted, Guyer (1979: 162ff.) is wrong to suggest that Kant's argument for identity is to be construed along the lines of the claim, conformably with Descartes' *cogito* argument or a version thereof, that *all* of the representations had (de re) are united *existentially* in *my* numerically identical self (for any one instantiation of the *cogito*), which requires an a priori synthetic existential unity, and that a fortiori I have certain a priori knowledge of this. Nor even does it merely concern the ostensible analytic principle of apperception 'that all *my* representations in a given intuition must be subject to that condition under which alone I can ascribe them to the identical self as my representation' (Guyer himself quotes B138), if this is to mean that *any* representation that I *have*, at any one moment, must be connectable to my continuing identity, in fact, that 'I cannot actually have any representation without being capable of connecting it to my continuing identity' (Guyer 1979: 163).[90] Guyer contrasts this rather intemperate principle with the hypothetical principle that

> whenever I am conscious of my continuing identity with respect to a manifold of representations, I must be conscious of their subjection to the condition of my consciousness of identity, namely, their synthesis into a rule-governed complex. (1979: 163)

Only such a kind of argumentation is capable of being apodictically proven, but then *no a priori synthesis*, Guyer argues, would be implied.[91] As a corollary, Guyer (1979: 164) argues consistently that, given the equivocation over the difference between these principles, the 'a priori validity of the categories cannot be derived *directly* from the a priori certainty of numerical identity' for the reason given under point (5) above. Excising, as Guyer suggests, a priori synthesis from apper-

---

[90] See also Guyer (1992: 144, 2006: 86).
[91] See Guyer (1987: 142). Why would an a priori synthesis not be possible on a reading of apperception in terms of a merely conditional principle? I believe it would not be possible only if the unity of consciousness is interpreted possessively or psychologically, which Guyer indeed appears to do. But see Guyer's 'option c' (Guyer 1987: 144ff., esp. 146). This option is eventually equally dismissed by Guyer.

ception effectively undercuts the force of Reciprocity and so undermines the cogency of the P-argument.

However, contrary to Guyer, I contend that no lack of fit exists between Kant's argument for numerical self-identity and the argument concerning the applicability of the categories, for I believe Kant is not ignorant of the difference between an argument for absolute necessity and an argument for hypothetical or conditional necessity with respect to the unity or unifiability of one's own representations.[92] Therefore, I contend that there is no prima facie problem with deriving the categories *directly* from the identity of the subject. All of this hinges, of course, on the interpretation of the passage Guyer cites (B138 [AA 3: 112.13–19]). That is, the operative question is the interpretation of the *analytic* principle of apperception, of what it is that constitutes the principle's analyticity. I believe that the principle of apperception is congruent, as I proceed to show in Chapter 6, with the conditional or hypothetical principle that Guyer sees as shoring up the only defensible argument for a connection between apperception and the categories as the rules for *empirical* synthesis, and is not at all tantamount to the intemperate claim that Guyer attributes to Kant. Guyer separates the viable analytic claim from Kant's so-called 'constitution-theoretic talk' (1979: 166).[93]

I argue conversely that the conditional nature of the principle of apperception, its veritable analyticity, is in fact *solely* comprehensible against the backdrop of an explication of what *a priori* synthesis, indeed synthetic 'constitution', amounts to. This interpretative approach partly ties in with Guyer's justifiably drawing attention to Kant's methodological internalism, which has much in common with Descartes' epistemic foundationalist internalism. Crucially, however, it avoids extrapolating to the Kantian context the dogmatic claim to absolute necessity with regard to the metaphysical identity of the self that (presumably) underlies Descartes' egology, which Guyer wrongly attributes to Kant. The interpretative path that I shall take is in some ways similar to Henrich's more forceful line of argumentation that the Transcendental Deduction must be construed such that it is seen to be grounded upon a system or 'fabric' (*Gefüge*, as he puts it [1988: 68]) of implications, that is, a system of the 'I think' being implied in all possible tokenings of the 'I think', which I take it Henrich means to be *not* mere representations.[94] This implicative system of thought, which involves a sys-

---

92 Cf. *Met-L₂*, AA 28: 556 ff.
93 Guyer quotes Henrich (1976: 105).
94 Cf. Henrich (1998: 39); see also Henrich (1976: 93).

tem of categories, has important repercussions for the possibility of knowledge of objects.[95]

On my reading, Kant's P-argument starting from the identity of the *cogito*, if interpreted in accordance with the thrust of the R-argument, is cogent and analytically coherent. This belief is based upon a formal analysis of the modality of the 'I think'-proposition, the ramifications of which are such that the standard reading of the proposition must be considered mistaken. From my account of the derivation of the categories (Chapters 6–9), it will become clear that Guyer's dismissal of the cogency of Kant's constitution argument (Reciprocity) is rooted in a misunderstanding, on Guyer's part, in respect of the limited scope of the 'I think'-proposition in relation to manifolds of representation. That is, it rests on a misreading of the *analyticity* of the principle of apperception, which results in a misconception of the identity of the thinking self. This misunderstanding has to do mainly with a confusion between the epistemic and possessive senses of the unity of one's consciousness, which results in unjustly charging Kant with confusing a claim to conditional necessity regarding the unity of one's mind with a metaphysical claim to absolute necessity with respect to unitary consciousness.[96]

Although it appears that Guyer (1987: 147 ff.) is aware of the distinction between *recognising* 'some relation among my representations' and the mere existence of a relation 'of possession by my continuing self', it should be noted that, for one thing, the distinction between recognising and possessing is not bijective, as Guyer would seem to suggest it is the case for Kant, so that for each relation of possession there necessarily is an (at least possible) instance of recognition of this relation. In Kant's view too—cf. B133, which is quoted by Guyer, and is discussed in detail in Chapter 9—I could possess an aggregate of representations, of which I also may be *severally* conscious in an immediate sense (and so I may in some sense attend to my mental states by ascribing them *empirically*), *without*, even potentially, grasping these representations as *together*, as a manifold, belonging to my (formally) identical self the consciousness of which would provide one with an objective, conceptual criterion for their recognition (cf. A122, which I believe Guyer interprets wrongly).

The confusion between the epistemic and possessive senses of the unity of one's consciousness is a problem that also besets Strawson's (1968: 98) reading

---

[95] Cf. Henrich's notion of 'das Wissen von den konstanten Bedingungen des Übergangs [of the states of the identical subject, D.S.] als ein Wissen von *Regeln*' (1976: 89).

[96] This is basically also Ameriks's criticism against Guyer (see Ameriks 1983: 183 ff.). Ameriks's critique is directed at Guyer (1980), which contains essentially the same arguments as the later account in Guyer (1987). For use of the term 'possessive' I am indebted to Ameriks (2000b: 281); cf. Hoppe (1983: 113, 117 ff.).

of transcendental apperception as the necessary condition of the belonging together of all of one's variant mental states to a single consciousness, an assumption which unsurprisingly has led some (e.g. Hurley 1994: 141ff.) to expostulate that surely a contingent 'co-consciousness' must be possible that does *not* presuppose self-consciousness and so does not belong, in the strong sense, to the identical self—this suggests the possibility of a co-occurrence of mental states that do not relate to each other in terms of a relation of sameness.[97] Admittedly, Kant's use of words like 'belonging to' (*gehören*) in the context of his argument for the necessary conditions of unity (see for example at B134) might appear to warrant the possessive interpretation of apperception, that is, the interpretation that any representation whatsoever that I *have* belongs eo ipso to my identical self.[98]

Strawson's reconstruction of Kant's argument to the effect that it should be seen to exhibit an 'analytical connexion' between mere experience and objectivity, logically inferable from the presumed tautological truth of the fundamental premise of unitary consciousness, founders, for the inference is effectively based upon such a fallacious possessive reading of unitary consciousness (thereby conflating de dicto and de re modality). That is to say, according to Strawson (1968: 98, 100 ff., 114, 117) the premise of the so-called analytical argument concerns the *necessary* unifiability of *all* of one's experiences in terms of one's subjective mental states, implying that the *existence*, and thus having, of a subjective mental state is such that it conceptually entails the potentiality of self-ascription, which in turn requires another, objective, connectedness.[99] Presumably, no mental state could be considered a mental state that a subject has or is in if it did not entail this potentiality. (This involves Strawson's repudiation of the intelligibility of a sense datum experience, which has no means of differentiating itself from that of which it is an experience and therefore, Strawson argues, is ipso facto logically contradictory to the extent even of merely having such an experience.)[100] This means that the mind as such, qua mental states, is governed by the possibility of self-ascription, of which 'transcendental self-consciousness' is said to be

---

[97] Cf. Kant at B140: '[T]he unity of consciousness in that which is empirical is not, with regard to that which is given, necessarily and universally valid.'
[98] Cf. e.g. Hoppe (1983: 122–5, 210). See also Schulting (2017a: 185n.15).
[99] I note again that Strawson denies Kant's basic claim that the condition of connectivity is satisfied by the activity of transcendental apperception (cf. B134 ff.); rather, according to Strawson it is a 'course of experience of an objective world, conceived of as determining the course of that experience itself' (1968: 117) that is the persistent point of reference which provides the required element of connectivity underlying the identity of experience.
[100] See further on Strawson's critique of sense datum experience, Chapter 9, this volume.

an a priori condition, which in turn invokes the basic condition of objectivity. But it is evident from a study of the modality of apperception (see Chapter 6), that no such necessary potentiality is implied by the 'I think'-proposition for all of the representations or mental states had (by any arbitrary agent of representation).

In essence similar to Guyer's construal, although dispensing with the a priori synthesis thesis, Strawson's reading of the premise of the so-called transcendental argument has Kant committed to far more than he actually argues for. Effectively, Strawson commits a modal fallacy in the way he stipulates how the unity of consciousness should be interpreted, a fallacy of which, ironically, Kant is routinely accused. As already noted, the fallacy of equivocation lies in Strawson's first premise (cf. Strawson 1968: 92ff.). That is to say, Strawson equivocates over taking the premise, on the one hand, as the starting-point of a de dicto claim with regard to the requirements for objective reference of our representations (cf. e.g. 1968: 26ff., 89) and, on the other, as initiating what amounts to a de re claim to the effect that representations, 'even [...] the most fleeting and purely subjective of impressions' (1968: 100), are necessarily unifiable (cf. e.g. 1968: 24). This fallacy is the main—but not the only—reason why I believe Strawson's reconstruction of an ostensibly transcendental core argument in Kant's theory of experience collapses.[101]

My claims are still in need of argumentative support. My own view of the P-argument will be set forth by means of a reconstruction of the rational proof that Kant provides for Reciprocity by closely looking at the derivation of each of the twelve categories from apperception. This will be done in Chapters 6–9. My interpretation of the P-argument is such that it can be aligned with the way in which Ameriks has insisted upon reading the Transcendental Deduction as fundamentally exhibiting a regressive argumentation structure. The main objections that Ameriks has raised against the progressive reading of the Transcendental Deduction can thus be defused. To make this clear, I address the interconnectedness between the P- and R-arguments in Chapter 10.

---

[101] See Schulting (forthcoming).

5 The Unity of Thought: On the Guiding Thread

In this chapter, I consider a central argument of the Metaphysical Deduction in the Third Section of the 'Clue' (A76ff./B102ff.), which will provide me with the auxiliary means to address the derivation of the categories from the unity of apperception in Chapters 6–9. I shall here not be concerned with the thorny questions regarding the derivation of the functions of judgement and the table of judgement per se. I take these arguments for granted, which is not to say that they do not merit closer inspection. However, as I said in Chapter 1, I do think that Wolff (1995), in addition to Reich's book, has amply demonstrated by means of careful exegesis of the First and Second 'Clue' Sections how a systematic reading of the section leading up to the classification of the functions of judgement in § 9 shows that Kant's claims regarding the completeness and derivation question concerning the table of judgement stand up to scrutiny. Therefore, I am not going to rehearse Wolff's meticulous arguments in support of the claims concerning the table of judgement here.

In this chapter, I am mainly interested in Kant's claim that a strong correspondence exists between the functions of discursive judgement and the *categories* (*Prol* § 21, AA 4: 303), so much so that one must regard the categories *to be* those functions of judgement insofar as they determine the intuition of an object (B143, B131; *Prol* § 39, AA 4: 324; *Real Progress*, AA 20: 271). The categories constitute the intrinsic objective validity of judgements. Kant's aim is to show that the functions of the understanding, the elementary logical moments of unity in a judgement, 'what belongs to judging in general [*zum Urtheilen überhaupt*]',[1] correspond strongly to the concepts of the intuition of objects, 'so far as these are determined by one or other of these moments of judging' (*Prol* § 21, AA 4: 302, trans. emended), that is, the categories (cf. B128). Given the logical moments of judgement, or, the functions of judgement, and given the notion that the understanding or the faculty of thought is 'a *faculty for judging*' (A69/B94), Kant presents a table of the categories which corresponds exactly to the table of the elementary functions of judgement. Kant reasons that if

> the logical moments of all judgments [as] so many possible ways of uniting representations in one consciousness [*in einem Bewußtsein*] [...] serve as concepts, they are concepts of the *necessary* unification of representations in one consciousness [*in einem Bewußtsein*] and so are principles of objectively valid judgments. (*Prol* § 22, AA 4: 305, trans. emended)

---

[1] Cf. A68/B93: 'All judgments are [...] functions of unity among our representations.' The unity that is uniquely expressed by discursive judgement is what Michael Wolff aptly calls a 'numerical unity of cognition' or 'epistemic unity' (1995: 84; see also 1995: 113).

These concepts of necessary unification of representations, the categories, map exactly onto 'the logical functions of all possible judgments in the previous table' (A79/B105; Kant refers to the table of the logical functions at A70/B95, usually referred to as the table of judgement). The underlying claim is that the understanding is not just the capacity for thinking, as 'cognition through concepts' (A69/B94), and thus for judging, but also the capacity to unite manifolds of representations in intuitions, as the way in which we relate immediately to an object of experience (A19/B33). What Kant attempts to achieve in the Transcendental Deduction—and to which the *Leitfaden* section is the prelude—is to show the way in which concept and intuition, as the capacity for thinking concepts and 'bringing forth representations itself', 'the *spontaneity* of cognition', and the '*receptivity* of our mind to receive representations' (B75/A51) respectively, are united such that cognition arises. In the Transcendental Deduction, he aims to redeem the promissory note of the introduction to the Transcendental Logic that it is 'just as necessary to make the mind's concepts sensible (i.e., to add an object to them in intuition) as it is to make its intuitions understandable (i.e., to bring them under concepts)' (B75/A51), a task which the Transcendental Logic is specifically put in charge of.

What Kant must show is that there is a single element that is shared by both the capacity for thinking concepts, i.e. for representing by means of analytic unities and unite these in propositions,[2] and the way in which our mind receives representations through the forms of intuition and determines them accordingly. The difficult task that Kant is facing is to try and unite two absolutely separate and irreducible sources of knowledge, while respecting the fact that the faculties of receptivity and spontaneity 'cannot exchange their functions' (B75/A51). This means that two different ways of uniting representations, by means of intuition as an immediate representation of objects and through concepts as a mediate way of representing objects respectively, must be able to be united on a different, higher level, while retaining their irreducible difference.[3] Kant speaks of two types of 'uniting in one consciousness', namely 'either analytic by identity, or synthetic by the combination and addition of various representations one to an-

---

[2] Kant believes that 'the understanding can make no other use of these concepts than that of judging by means of them' (A68/B93). That means that for Kant there is no singular thought (*simplex apprehensio*) of an object by means of a mere concept (see Wolff 1995: 74–5). Since concepts can be used in judgement only, any *mere* consideration of concepts in their relation of subordination is therefore an abstraction of their actual employment in cognition, i.e. in a judgement.
[3] Aportone (2009) speaks of the 'Identitätsthese' concerning the identity of '*zwei* Funktionen der Verstandeshandlung *überhaupt* als Synthesis der Vorstellungen zur Einheit des Bewußtseins: Urteilen *und* Anschauen' (2009: 142–3).

other' (*Prol* § 22, AA 4: 305, trans. emended). These two types of 'uniting in one consciousness' correspond to the unitary functions of thought (or judging in general) and the forms of sensibility as conditions of receiving representations in space and time, and hence of representing spatiotemporal *objects*, respectively, just as Kant had argued in the *Inaugural Dissertation*. As Kant explains in the First 'Clue' Section (starting at B92/A67), the human understanding is a discursive understanding, which means as much as to say that it must think through concepts, which rest 'on functions', in contrast to intuitions which 'rest on affections', although it needs the latter to have material content, that is, designate a real object. Concepts are mere forms of representing that have other representations as their objects, whose content partially corresponds to the content of the concept to which they are subordinated. However, a concept can never have a real object as its content (cf. B234–5/A189–90) and is 'never immediately related to an object, but is always related to some other representation of it (whether that be an intuition or itself already a concept)' (A68/B93). Kant defines function as 'the unity of the action of ordering different representations under a common one' (A68/B93), that is, unification by means of subordinating various representations under a higher representation, which is the partial representation that is analytic to the subordinated representations (the one concept holds of many other representations).[4] This is why this type of unification is 'analytic by identity' (*Prol* § 22, AA 4: 305), or comes about 'by means of the analytic unity' (A79/B105). Crucially, a relation of concepts based on analytic unification, which is always merely 'a representation of a representation' (A68/B93), that is, a representation of partial representations,[5] will never reach the object of intuition, the really perceived object. Only intuition is capable of immediately representing an object (A68/B93). Concepts are merely ways of unifying various other concepts, and as such they are 'predicates of possible judgments' (A69/B94). Hence, the different ways or forms in which the understanding, as the capacity to think concepts, can unite concepts, by means of the analytical unity between various (conceptual) representations, correspond to the 'functions of unity in judgments'. It is in this fairly straightforward way that Kant is able to draw up

---

4 Wolff (1995: 72–3n.68) considers whether 'function' defines the activity of the understanding only, since at A51/B75 Kant seems to associate the term 'function' with both sensibility and understanding. But, as Wolff points out, although sensibility may be ascribed some ordering activity sensations are not representations 'subordinated' in the technical sense that Kant means when he defines 'function' as the activity of the understanding at A68/B93.

5 Kant says that '[j]udgment' itself is 'the mediate cognition of an object, hence the representation of a representation of it'. Wolff (1995: 76) explains how not only concepts but also judgements are 'Vorstellungen zweiter Stufe'.

the table of the functions of unity in judgements in the Second Section of the *Leitfaden*.[6]

How does this relate to the 'uniting in one consciousness' that is 'synthetic by the combination and addition of various representations one to another', which is the way that objective cognition (and hence experience) comes about, namely as 'the synthetic connection of appearances (perceptions) in consciousness, so far as this connection is necessary' (*Prol* § 22, AA 4: 305)? In the Third 'Clue' Section, Kant reflects on the possibility of finding the linking element between unification by means of analytic identity, that is, subordination of representations under a higher one, and unification by means of combination or addition of representations 'one to another'. This is the prerogative of a *transcendental* logic, which

> has a manifold of sensibility that lies before it *a priori*, which the transcendental aesthetic has offered to it, in order to provide the pure concepts of the understanding with a matter, without which they would be without any content, thus completely empty. (A76–7/B102)

Two aspects are conspicuous: (1) transcendental logic is concerned with content, not just with form, and (2) the content is somehow a priori. This last aspect concerns the fact that the manifolds of representations that are received by our sensible faculty of representation are contained in a priori intuitions, space and time, which *as such* are provided to the discursive understanding and are determined accordingly (this requires figurative synthesis, which like intellectual synthesis is a transcendental act of the understanding [B151–2]; see Chapter 11). In the Transcendental Aesthetic, space and time were argued to be the forms by means of which objects can first be represented and were also argued to be wholes that do not contain parts *under* them, analytically like concepts, but *in* them, that is, synthetically as consisting of homogeneous parts. Now the manner in which the unification in one consciousness by way of 'combination or addition of various representations one to another' occurs is by way of the understanding itself, *as faculty of spontaneity*, going through the manifold contained in an intuition—any sensible intuition, but specifically a spatiotemporal one—and taking it together in a concept. Thus, the understanding itself 'combine[s] [the manifold] in a certain way in order for a cognition to be made out of it'

---

[6] This is a very basic cursory exposition of Kant's rationale behind the table of judgement. For a detailed exegesis of the First and Second 'Clue' Sections of the Metaphysical Deduction, see Wolff (1995), chs 1 and 2. See also Greenberg (2001), ch. 9. Prien (2006) presents an illuminating account of Kant's theory of concepts. On Kant's theory of marks and concepts, see also Stuhlmann-Laeisz (1976), ch. 5.

(B102/A77). The action of the understanding that is responsible for this combination is what Kant labels 'synthesis'.

This is as striking a claim as it is straightforward. The very same understanding that was earlier indicated to be responsible for the merely analytical procedure of subordinating concepts as predicates of possible judgements is here presented as the *bridge between* its own analytic procedure and the way that a synthetic connection among representations in the manifold of an intuition is established. Kant defines synthesis as 'the action of putting different representations together with each other and comprehending their manifoldness in one cognition' (B103) and contrasts pure with empirical synthesis to stress the fact that here, in view of the task of the Transcendental Logic as the '*analysis of the faculty of the understanding*' in search of a priori concepts (A65–6/B90), we are concerned only with the possibility of *a priori* synthesis. Synthesis is thus a fundamental characteristic of the understanding (cf. B130), as much as the purely analytic act of ordering different representations *under* a common one is central to the activity of the understanding. Both kinds of unifying actions are reducible to one faculty, namely the understanding as a faculty for judging. It is important to already notice the fact that synthesis is something that the understanding does, and given that the understanding as 'the faculty of thought' (A69/B94) is a faculty for judging, that is, a capacity to judge ('[t]hinking is [...] the same as judging'; *Prol* § 22, AA 4: 304),[7] by implication synthesis happens in judgement.

The above notwithstanding, Kant seems to suggest that synthesis is something that happens *prior to* judgement, when he writes, at B103/A78, that 'synthesis in general is [...] the mere effect of the imagination, of a blind though indispensable function of the soul'; and that only 'to bring this synthesis *to concepts* is a function that pertains to the understanding'. This difference between synthesis as an act of the understanding itself and synthesis as an 'effect of the imagination' is reflected by Kant's arguments for various kinds of synthesis that are involved in the constitution of knowledge in the A-Deduction, where the bringing of synthesis to concepts is presented as synthesis of recognition in the concept (A103ff.) as different from, and additional to, the synthesis of reproduction in the imagination (A100–2), where each of the syntheses (including the synthesis of apprehension) ostensibly reflect different stages in the cognitive process that leads to conceptual knowledge.[8] Similarly, here in § 10, Kant

---

[7] See also A69/B94: '[T]he *understanding* in general can be represented as a faculty for judging'; cf. B106/A80–1: 'the faculty for judging (which is the same as the faculty for thinking)'.
[8] For a more detailed account, see Schulting (2017a), ch. 6.

makes it appear as if there were a staged process from the mere manifold of pure intuition, through synthesis by means of the imagination ('as the second thing' which 'still does not yield cognition') and then towards 'concepts that give this pure synthesis *unity*, and that consist solely in the representation of this necessary synthetic unity', and are 'the third thing necessary for cognition [...] and [...] depend on the understanding' (A78–9/B104). This differentiation between kinds of synthesis is often employed as evidence for the view that not every synthesis is a synthesis performed by the understanding or involving the categories (and hence judgement).

For example, Lucy Allais (2009) argues that synthesising is not yet or not the same as conceptualising and that '[a]lthough concepts always involve synthesis, it does not follow that synthesis always involves concepts' (2009: 396n.35). According to Allais, who defends Kant as a nonconceptualist,[9] intuition requires synthesis, but synthesis itself is not already conceptual. This might be taken to reflect Kant's distinction between synthesis of reproduction in the imagination (or figurative synthesis in the B-Deduction; B151–2) and synthesis of recognition in a concept (the intellectual synthesis). That according to Allais synthesis supposedly is not already conceptual would appear to conflict with Kant's assertion in a note (*Loses Blatt* B12) from the 1780s, where transcendental synthesis of the imagination is said at least to involve 'a concept of the object in general' and by implication the categories:

> The transcendental synthesis of the imagination pertains solely to the unity of apperception in the synthesis of the manifold in general through the imagination. *Through that a concept of the object in general is conceived in accordance with the different kinds of transcendental synthesis.* (AA 23: 18 [NF: 258], emphasis added; cf. A119)

Allais however denies the necessary connection between synthesis and the categories when she writes:

> To say that *we* perform syntheses that *are* governed by the categories (and other concepts), and indeed that we must do this if we are to be able to apply the categories (and other concepts), is not to say that synthesis *per se* is governed by the concepts [...]. (2009: 396)

Her view is mistaken. Although I take it that Allais means the categories by the last mention of 'concepts' in the quotation, not just empirical concepts, she does appear to be intentionally ambiguous about the use of the term 'concept'. If she means 'empirical concept' or just generally 'analytic unity of marks', then of

---

9 On Allais's nonconceptualist reading, see Schulting (2017a), ch. 5.

5 The Unity of Thought: On the Guiding Thread — 117

course synthesis is not conceptual. However, in the context of the Transcendental Deduction Kant means 'concept' generally as 'pure concept' or indeed as 'consciousness of [the] unity of synthesis' (A103). That Allais does believe that synthesis and categories can come separate shows her misunderstanding about the intimate relation between synthesis and the categories, as if synthesis and categorial determination rested on two wholly separable functions, which would go against the very spirit of the *Leitfaden*. For it is unclear how such a reading of the relation between synthesis and the understanding comports with the very notion of the understanding itself being the *same* faculty that brings different representations '*under* one concept analytically' *and* 'bring[s] under concepts [i.e. the categories] not the representations but the *pure synthesis* of representations' (A78/B104). It is at any rate evident that there must be an intimate relation between pure synthesis, which is 'a *synthesis in accordance with concepts [Synthesis nach Begriffen]*' and the categories themselves, as Kant states that '*pure synthesis, generally represented*, yields the pure concept of the understanding' (A78/B104). Indeed this is precisely what the actual formulation of the *Leitfaden* suggests:

> The same function that gives unity to the different representations *in a judgment* also gives unity to the mere synthesis of different representations *in an intuition*, which, expressed generally, is called the pure concept of understanding. The same understanding, therefore, and indeed by means of the very same actions through which it brings the logical form of judgment into concepts by means of the analytical unity, also brings a transcendental content into its representations by means of the synthetic unity of the manifold in intuition in general, on account of which they are called pure concepts of the understanding that pertain to objects *a priori* [...]. (B104–5/A79)

The categories are the logical functions of the understanding insofar as the manifold of representations in the intuitions thought under the subject predicate of a judgement is determined. Each of the twelve categories accounts for one particular manner in which the manifold is *synthetically* united in the intuition and brought to the concept, 'conceptualised'. The 'application' of the categories is an action of the understanding that is contemporaneous with 'bring[ing] the logical form of judgment into concepts by means of the analytical unity', that is, by syntactically uniting predicates as the terms in a proposition.

I claim that it is not only the case that (1) the 'application' of the categories is coextensive with 'synthesising' the manifold in intuition, for the different categories *are* the different ways of synthetically unifying the manifold of representations in an intuition (by definition, categories and synthesis cannot come apart), and they 'express the necessary unity of apperception under which all appearances belong insofar as they belong to one cognition *a priori* and necessarily' (AA

23: 19 [NF: 259]); but also that (2) the synthesis of the manifold of representations in an intuition, which 'brings a transcendental content into' the representations of the judgement that are analytically subordinated by the very 'same understanding', is rigorously coextensive with the analytic unity of representations, or predicates, that pertains to the logical form of any judgement. This comports with Kant's statement at B143, in the conclusion to the 'first step', that the categories *are* nothing but the logical functions or moments of thought in judgements (that is, 'insofar as the manifold of a given intuition is determined with regard to them', namely the intuition underlying the subject predicate of judgement). Categories and logical functions in a judgement do not come apart. Likewise, the synthetic unity by means of which the understanding's functionality, as a capacity for categorial determination of the manifold in intuition, brings transcendental *content* into its representations requires the logical functions in a judgement to bring logical *form* into its representations ('transform them into concepts analytically' [A76/B102]) and must therefore be considered coextensive with the analytic unity of conceptual relations. Content does not come without form. Reciprocally, and more controversially, analytic unity by means of which the understanding establishes the form of the relation among representations, their conceptual relation, likewise requires a priori synthesis, as Kant claims in a note in the Transcendental Deduction (B133–4n.). However, this is a point of transcendental logic and is abstracted from in the perspective of general logic.

It is often claimed that 'synthesis' is 'governed by' the categories (cf. Longuenesse 1998, *passim*). Although Kant often uses (and I have used) the term 'application' when speaking of the relation between the manifold of representations and the categories (see e.g. B149), which can be misleading, to talk about categories 'governing' the synthesis suggests that categories and synthesis are separable, which they are not. Kant makes it clear that

> the categories are nothing other than the representations of something (appearance) in general so far as it is represented through transcendental synthesis of imagination [...].

He further states:

> The manifold, however, cannot thoroughly belong to one apperception except by means of a thoroughgoing synthesis of imagination and its functions in one consciousness. This transcendental unity in the synthesis of imagination is thus an *a priori* unity under which all appearances must stand. *Those* [functions, D.S.] however are the categories, thus the categories express the necessary unity of apperception under which all appearances belong insofar as they belong to one cognition *a priori* and necessarily. (AA 23: 19 [NF: 259], emphasis added; cf. *Prol*, AA 4:305)

The standard reading that synthesis is an activity that is separate or separable from the set of categories itself makes it unintelligible how supposedly by virtue of synthesis the categories get 'applied'. Which function other than synthesis (and we are talking *a priori* synthesis here, naturally) would perform the unification of the synthesis and the categories, if indeed they were to come separately? This leads inevitably to an infinite regress, the threat of which Kant's notion of a priori synthesis is supposed to thwart in the first place. The categories being so many modes of synthesising pre-given manifolds in intuition and the act of synthesis being the combined set of these modes of synthesising, by implication synthesis cannot be separate from the categories. Any other connection that intuitions might have independently of the understanding is not synthesis in Kant's sense (i.e. a priori necessary connection) (see further Chapter 7).

For the purposes of establishing the possibility of knowledge arising from the a priori relation between concept and intuition it is necessary to regard the means by which *concepts* are related to each other analytically as *necessarily and originally connected* with the means by which manifolds of representation in *intuition* are combined synthetically. In other words, the analytic unity that attaches to the logical form of concepts (which are always used in a judgement [A68/B93])[10] and the synthetic unity by means of which intuitions are united (as the objective content of a judgement) are *rigorously coextensive*. The claim of 'rigorous coextensivity' between the analytical unity of apperception and the synthetic unity of apperception (Rigorous Coextensivity for short) is the auxiliary thesis that will prove relevant for a defence of Reciprocity (discussed in Chapter 4), in Chapter 10. I shall provide further arguments for the truth of Rigorous Coextensivity in Chapter 6. Rigorous Coextensivity reflects what Kant calls the 'original-synthetic unity of apperception' (B131; heading), which underwrites the possibility 'for me to represent the *identity of the consciousness*' in the representations of a given manifold (B133), and constitutes the principle that 'the

---

10 Prien (2006) disagrees and claims that '[d]ie Funktion unterzuordnen muss demnach schon *vor* und *unabhängig* vom Gebrauch von Begriffen in Urteilen ausgeführt werden' (2006: 31, emphasis added). Prien (2006: 32–3) disputes Longuenesse's (1998) reading that in judgement a 'Doppelrolle' is fulfilled: on the one hand a predicate is asserted of the subject-concept, on the other hand concepts are connected with objects. Prien: 'Die Handlungen, aufgrund derer Begriffe sich auf Gegenstände beziehen, sind in der Handlung des Urteilens dagegen nicht enthalten'. Prien distinguishes between judgement as the objective relation of 'cognitions' and these cognitions themselves that are independently established, but I think he inflates Kant's view of concepts as in and of themselves, as mere concepts, already having objects *stricto sensu* (at most, they have logical content for an object). The function of objective validity is a function of judgement, so for concepts as cognitions to acquire objective validity they must be predicates in a judgement.

analytical unity of apperception is only possible under the presupposition of some *synthetic* one' (B133). My claim is that the understanding is this principle of 'original-synthetic unity of apperception', and that the categories that 'have their seat in the understanding' (A81/B107, trans. Kemp Smith) are therefore derivable from the principle of apperception.

Bernd Prien (2006: 138) disputes the coextensivity that I claim exists between the analytic and synthetic unities of apperception, and that therefore the analytic unity of apperception accords with the categories. He claims that

> [f]ür das Bewusstsein der eigenen numerischen Identität, also die analytische Einheit der Apperzeption, ist jedenfalls keine *objektive* Einheit der Apperzeption, gemäß den Kategorien, erfordert, **sondern nur irgendeine**. (boldface mine)

Prien (2006: 142–3) refers with *irgendeine* to B133 ('*analytical* unity is only possible under the condition of **some** *synthetic* one'), suggesting that a 'weaker' and a 'stronger' version of synthesis must be distinguished, but he overdetermines the sense of *irgend einer*. The two senses of synthesis that Prien (2006: 103) differentiates are (I'm paraphrasing):

> 1) The synthesis of representations which are accompanied with consciousness and which enables the consciousness of the numerical identity of one's self-consciousness; this synthesis concerns the possibility of uniting representations *nach irgendeiner Regel*, which governs the transition from one state to another (cf. Henrich 1976). Both subjectively and objectively valid representations are united in self-consciousness. It depends on the rule of synthesis whether the unity of representation is objective or merely subjective.

> 2) A synthesis leads to an objective unity, when the rule of synthesis is necessary, which it is when it accords with the categories. Prien says that this concerns a synthesis which is necessary, suggesting that the mere synthesis of representations in self-consciousness is not necessary, but merely contingent (a Humean bundle of representations?), but this contradicts clearly Kant's arguments in § 16.

Prien's view is problematic for several reasons, most crucially: (i) Kant does not make such a distinction between two kinds of synthesis, as Prien acknowledges (2006: 143); (ii) it undermines Reciprocity; and (iii) it leads to a vicious regress: that is to say, which synthesis sees to it that the non-necessary synthesis of representations that make up the unity of consciousness is subjected to a rule such that the synthesis is not just 'subjectively valid' but rather necessary and 'objectively valid'? If the synthesis of representations in the unity of consciousness is already original, as Kant claims, there could not be an even more original representation or function of synthesis that synthesises the unity of consciousness such that it becomes an *objectively* valid, necessary synthesis. Prien claims further that 'die synthetische Einheit der Apperzeption im schwachen Sinne die Bezeichnung transzendental nicht [verdient]' (2006: 147), but this just undermines the force of his claim that two senses of synthesis must be differentiated.

Here, in the Third Section of the *Leitfaden* Kant only provides the clue to finding the categories on the basis of the idea that the understanding as a faculty for judging performs two tasks (two 'actions') simultaneously, as it were, by means of which the subjective conditions of thought, that is, the logical functions of unity in a judgement, are to be considered to be also the objective conditions that constrain possible knowledge of *objects* about which we make judgements. The understanding not only provides the rules for forming judgements, but at the same time, and importantly by means of *'the same function'* and 'the very same actions' (B104–5/A79, emphasis added), also provides the rules by means of which we can determine *a priori* the intuitions that immediately relate to the objects that we perceive in space and time. These rules are of course the categories.

What Kant does not do (nor intends to) in this section of the Metaphysical Deduction is to *prove* that the categories are indeed the ways in which manifolds of representations in intuitions are determined in order to conceive of these representations as representations of *real* objects (rather than as mere objects of concepts). Neither does he prove here (nor does he intend to) *how* the categories must be seen to effectively unite the manifold in an intuition. These two remaining tasks for Kant's project of a deduction of the categories are reserved for the Transcendental Deduction,[11] where the proof *that* the categories are the ways of determining intuition (in fact, the legitimation question or *quaestio juris*) and the question *how* this takes place (the ostensible question 'How is the *faculty of thinking* itself possible?' [Axvii], whose consideration Kant prima facie appears to regard as merely meritorious) are rolled into one proof. If this proof is successful, Kant's clue that the same function of the understanding performs a twofold task that establishes the possibility of cognition as a synthetic a priori relation of concepts and intuitions is fully warranted. The justifiability of Kant's clue (*Leitfaden*) thus depends on the success of the Transcendental Deduction.[12] The method of proof is such that in the Transcendental Deduction itself Kant will start out, not from a definition of the understanding as a capacity for judging, nor from a definition of judgement, but from a more minimal premise, namely the *fact* of discursive thought as cognition through concepts, which is expressed in the principle of apperception.[13] Indeed, by starting the argument from the 'I

---

[11] Cf. Aportone (2009: 179–80).
[12] Cf. Reich (2001: 30 [25–6]).
[13] Cf. Wolff (1995: 181). Wolff rightly points out that the discursivity thesis, which the Metaphysical Deduction 'dogmatically' assumes, is only first shored up in the Transcendental Deduction.

think'—the sheer thought of a subject thinking her thoughts—as its minimal premise, Kant demonstrates, by systematically deducing the twelve categories, what it means to have a discursive mind having objectively valid thoughts. The assumption that the understanding is indeed a capacity for judging will be proven to be justified once Kant has demonstrated that the definition of judgement as a complex relation of *both* the conceptual relations among representations by means of analytic unity *and* a combination of intuitions by means of synthetic unity is the immediate corollary of the argument for the derivation of the categories from the unity of apperception, on which rests the possibility of having a determinate concept of an object. This proof is the subject content of the following chapters.[14]

---

14 For more on the *Leitfaden* passage at A79, see Schulting (2017a, ch. 5; 2017d, f).

6 Apperception and the Categories of Modality

6.1 Introduction

In this chapter and the following ones I expound my own reading of the P-argument. The sense in which the R-argument is thereby necessarily implied will be detailed in Chapter 10, which addresses the interrelatedness of the P- and R-arguments. The argument of Chapters 6–9 involves an elaboration of Kant's controversial claim that the categories must be capable of being derived from the unity of apperception (cf. B142, B144; see also *Prol* § 39, AA 4: 322ff.), the claim that I seek to defend. In Chapter 4, I contended that the P-argument starts from the self-evident principle of the formal-logical identity expressed in the 'I think'-proposition (in § 16 of the B-Deduction) and concludes with the synthetic a priori conception of what constitutes an object in general (in § 17) with §§ 18 and 19 being the corollaries of the argument of the preceding sections. The P-argument should be taken to establish the reciprocal relation between synthetic unity of consciousness and objectivity, Kant's 'master argument'. This concerns the disputed reciprocity claim or Reciprocity for short. I also claimed that what I called the rigorous coextensivity that obtains between the analytic and synthetic unities of apperception, introduced in Chapter 4, explains Reciprocity. Now do these claims carry any weight?

In the previous chapters, I have raised objections against Guyer's take on the P-argument. In Chapter 4, I criticised Guyer for an apparent confusion about the kind of unitary consciousness that is at issue, which results in imputing to Kant a modal fallacy I believe he does not commit. Strawson's argument, also relying on a progressive reading of the Transcendental Deduction, is likewise based on an erroneous interpretation of the premise of Kant's argument, which however brings him to reconstruct the argument in such a way that it shows up merely an 'analytical connexion' between subjective experience in a weak sense and objectivity while dispensing with the need for a priori synthesis altogether. In short, Guyer claims that we cannot have the P-argument without the a priori synthesis, but since a priori synthesis is allegedly based on a modal fallacy, the argument breaks down. According to Guyer Kant's argument in the Transcendental Deduction is a failure. Strawson claims that we can have the P-argument from the unity of consciousness to objectivity, but only without the a priori synthesis. I claim that we can (and must) have both, without the modal fallacy. In setting forth my own view grounds will be provided for my criticisms of Guyer and, by implication, Strawson.[1] This involves an alternative reading of the premise of Kant's P-argument, namely pure or original apperception.

In Sections 6.2–6.3, I provide some preliminary grounds for such an alternative reading with respect to the modality involved in pure apperception. In Section 6.4, I go on to derive systematically the categories of modality from apperception. In the following Chapters 7 to 9, the other categories (of relation, quality and quantity) will be derived from the principle of apperception. This will be done by looking in detail at Kant's reasoning in §§ 16–17. The derivation of all categories will show that, contrary to what Guyer and others believe, Reciprocity can be upheld and that the reasoning behind it is cogent.

But let us first examine the categories of modality, in line with Kant's analytic procedure in the Paralogisms (B418).[2] I believe it is appropriate to begin with the modal categories, as they indicate the minimal conditions of discursive thought, and hence of the thought of an object in general.[3] Kant also starts the P-argument with the 'I think', which in fact expresses the *actuality* of thought (cf. B157), the *fact* of the understanding as the capacity for thought (A69/B94), or also the 'spontaneity of thought' (A68/B93), that was assumed as given in the Metaphysical Deduction. The actuality of thought is then also the *real* premise, from which the P-argument proceeds.

The reading of the modality of the 'I think'-proposition that I advance (1) facilitates an entirely different understanding of the analyticity of apperception; (2) helps one begin to understand the cogency of Reciprocity; and (3) rescues Kant from the charge of making unlawful modal (metaphysical) claims about the *unity* of the thinking self.

6.2 The Categories of Modality

As with the modal logical functions of the understanding in judgement (problematic, assertoric, apodictic), which 'contribute nothing to the content of the judgment' (B100), by which Kant means the propositional content of a judgement, the modal categories—which are 'possibility/impossibility', 'existence/

---

[1] For a more detailed critique of Strawson, see Schulting (2008). See also Chapter 9, this volume, and Schulting (forthcoming).
[2] Cf. Reich (2001: 65–8 [55–7]). Reich writes that 'die die Forderung der Ableitung immanent befriedigende systematische Vorstellung der Denkfunktionen in der allgemeinen reinen Logik in dieser Weise von der Modalität zur Quantität vor sich zu gehen hat' (2001: 69 [58]).
[3] Cf. Natorp (2000: 18).

non-existence', also called 'actuality',[4] and 'necessity/contingency' (A80/B106)—do not add to the content of the thought of an object in general. The transcendental *content* of the thought of an object in general is constituted by the categories of quantity, quality and relation. While the categories of modality 'do not augment the concept to which they are ascribed in the least', they 'express only the relation to the faculty of cognition' (B266/A219). The categories of modality only concern the question 'how is the object itself (together with all its determinations) related to the understanding [...]?' (B266/A219). The possible ways in which the object, which is thoroughly determined, is so related, or posited as Kant calls it (see further below Section 6.4), are 'either as *problematic* or *possible*; *assertoric* or *actual*; and as *apodictic* or *necessary*' (*Met-L₂*, AA 28: 547 [LM: 314]).

As holds for all the categories in their unschematised form, the categories of modality 'have a merely logical significance and analytically express the form of *thinking*' (A219/B267),[5] when they are considered in abstraction from the way that they are used in the principles of modality, namely the postulates of empirical thought. It is true that, as Kant says, if the categories 'are to concern *things* and their possibility, actuality, and necessity, then they must pertain to possible experience and its synthetic unity, in which alone objects of cognition are given' (A219/B267). Categories do not provide representations, but only the way that *given* representations are related to an object, so if they are to yield *knowledge* then an intuition must be added (*Met-Schön*, AA 28: 472). However, the categories

---

4 *Met-Volck*, AA 28: 396; A219/B267; A233/B286.
5 Cf. Kant's letter to J. H. Tieftrunk of 13 October 1797, in which he makes it clear that what J. S. Beck wants to do with his so-called 'Standpoint', namely starting out the Transcendental Deduction from the categories, is rather useless, as one is then 'busying [one]self with the mere form of thinking, that is, concepts without object, concepts that as yet are without any meaning' (*Corr*, AA 12: 463). Although this is in some sense of course true, it seems rather unfair of Kant to say this, as the proof that the categories are applicable to objects must somehow be able to be explained in detail, step-by-step, and thus starting with the categories, as Beck and also Tieftrunk tried (see his letter to Kant of 5 November 1797 [*Corr*, AA 12: 212ff.]), is fully in line with starting out with self-consciousness, as Kant does in the Transcendental Deduction; Kant reflects on the possibility of starting with the categories and seems more positive about Beck's proposal in a contemporaneous *Reflexion* (R6358, AA 18: 683–4; cf. R6353, AA 18: 679). Nevertheless, Kant would be right of course to insist that this procedure cannot consist in *merely* providing definitions of the categories without arguing for them, as Beck might be taken to have done in his *Einzig-möglicher Standpunct aus welchem die Critische Philosophie beurtheilt werden muß* (Riga, 1796), the third volume of his *Erläuternder Auszug aus den critischen Schriften des Herrn Prof. Kant auf Anrathen desselben* (see di Giovanni and Harris 2001: 204–49). Cf. also Kant's more positive view of Beck's 'Standpoint' in the letter to Tieftrunk of 11 December 1797 (*Corr*, AA 12: 223).

as such are the necessary and sufficient conditions for *the form* of any object. Kant writes:

> The pure concepts of the understanding are related through the mere understanding to objects of intuition in general, [...] they are [...] mere *forms of thought*, through which no determinate object is yet cognized. The synthesis or combination of the manifold in them was related merely to the unity of apperception, and was thereby the ground of the possibility of cognition *a priori* insofar as it rests on the understanding, and was therefore not only transcendental but also merely purely intellectual. (B150)

It is in view of this necessary form of any object that we must be able to consider '[t]hinking, taken in itself' (B428) and to look at the categories from a 'purely intellectual' perspective, independently of the way in which the object is given through an empirical intuition[6] (although not independently of the fact that in some sense *a* manifold of representations must be given for thought), just as Kant does by separating the so-called 'two steps' of the B-Deduction.[7] (He writes in the transitional section between the 'two steps', at B144, that in the argument of the 'first step', 'since the categories arise *independently from sensibility* merely in the understanding, I must abstract from the way in which the manifold for an empirical intuition is given, in order to attend only to the unity that is added to the intuition through the understanding by means of the category'.)

Given that Kant argues for the strict parallelism between the functions of the understanding and the categories as the forms under which objects can be thought (A80/B106), it is appropriate to locate the origin, or 'birthplace' (B90/A66) of the categories and to systematically determine their connectedness in the understanding itself (cf. A67/B92) independently of how these categories are instantiated in the principles of modality, viz. the postulates of empirical thinking in general, which define 'the concepts of possibility, actuality, and necessity in their empirical use' (B266/A219). We are here thus concerned with the categories in their mere *logical* meaning, as the *analytic* characteristics, or indeed 'moments',[8] of the understanding of objects in general (cf. again B150).

It is perfectly valid to look for the categories in the pure, simple representation 'I' in abstraction from an empirical manifold which alone would give them objective significance.[9] For example, at A356, in the A-Paralogisms, Kant allows me to say of the 'I' of apperception that 'I am substance', which 'signifies nothing

---

6 Cf. Reich (2001: 34 [29]).
7 Cf. letter from J. H. Tieftrunk of 5 November 1797 (*Corr*, AA 12: 212ff.) and Kant's response in the letter dated 11 December 1797. See also Chapter 8, this volume.
8 Cf. Reich (2001: 36 [31]).
9 Cf. Erdmann (1878: 53ff.).

but the pure category, of which I can make no (empirical) use *in concreto*'. Notwithstanding the fact that I am not licensed to make an empirical use of the concept, I am permitted to say 'I am a simple substance'. In this case,

> the concept of substance is used only as a function of synthesis, without an intuition being subsumed under it, hence without an object; and it is valid only of the condition of our cognition, but not of any particular object that is to be specified. (A356, emphasis added)

Given further that the understanding is *thought* itself (A69/B94) (see Chapter 5), it is appropriate to look for the origin of the categories in thought and thus in self-consciousness, even though Kant says that the '*modi* of self-consciousness in thinking are [...] not yet themselves concepts of the understanding of objects (categories), but mere functions, which provide thought with no object at all' (B406–7). This last statement must be read in the context of the Paralogisms; Kant says this to avoid any paralogistic inferences to real knowledge of the self from sheer categories (cf. A401–2).

The appropriateness of linking the categories to thought or self-consciousness is confirmed by other passages in the Paralogisms. For example, whereas the 'I think' itself is not a category, the 'I think' is

> the vehicle of all concepts whatever, and hence also of transcendental concepts, and is thus always comprehended among them, and hence is likewise transcendental. (A341/B399; cf. A345–6/B404)[10]

And at A401, Kant writes:

> Apperception is itself the ground of the possibility of the categories, which for their part represent nothing other than the synthesis of the manifold of intuition, insofar as that manifold has unity in apperception.[11]

But before I come back to the categories and how they must be seen as 'contain[ed] *a priori*' in the understanding (A80/B106), and hence are derivable from the principle of apperception, let us take a first look at some of Kant's arguments in § 16 of the B-Deduction, and how these arguments have been interpreted in the literature.

---

10 Cf. B401/A343: 'For this inner perception is nothing beyond the mere apperception *I think*, which even makes all transcendental concepts possible, which say "I think substance, cause, etc.".'
11 See further Reich (2001: 31–5 [27–30]).

6.3 The 'I think'-Proposition: The Analyticity of Apperception

At § 16, Kant writes that 'the *I think* must *be able* to accompany all my representations'. Kant calls it a 'principle' (*Grundsatz*) at B135. From the passage that follows it seems that Kant thinks of this 'I think', or the *cogito*, as a kind of representation. It is further identified by Kant as pure apperception or original apperception (B132). Importantly, at A354 Kant identifies the 'I think' as 'the formal proposition of apperception', and at A400 he identifies the 'I' with 'mere apperception' (*bloße Apperception*). As it appears, the 'I think' is also closely linked up with, if not identical to, what is called transcendental self-consciousness or the unity thereof (B132 [AA 3: 109.3 – 4]). In fact, in the Transcendental Aesthetic, at B68, Kant already identified the 'simple [*einfache*] representation of the "I"' as 'consciousness of self' (*Bewußtsein seiner Selbst*) (trans. Kemp Smith). The 'I think', transcendental apperception and self-consciousness are, for Kant, thus equivalent (regarding the topic of consciousness, see Chapter 8).

One of the central issues concerning the role of transcendental apperception in the Transcendental Deduction concerns the question regarding what Kant calls the 'thoroughgoing identity' of 'apperception' (B133) or 'thoroughgoing identity of self-consciousness' (B135). This involves several aspects, not least the *numerical* identity of the thinking self, which will be discussed in more detail in Chapter 9. First note, however, that it concerns an identity or sameness of the subject with respect to a manifold of representations in, as he describes it, 'a certain intuition' (*in einer gewissen Anschauung*) (B132 [AA 3: 109.5 – 6]). At B138 (AA 3: 112.15 – 16), Kant speaks of '*my* representations in any given [*irgend einer gegebenen*] intuition'. Kant means here that the intuition at issue is not already specified as such, but that at any rate *a* manifold in intuition must be *given* for a consciousness of the identical self to be able to relate to her own representations.[12] But the way he puts it in the cited passage at B132 also clearly shows that the intuition with respect to which a thoroughgoing identity of the apperceiving subject exists is not just *any* manifold of representations. The context clearly indi-

---

[12] Earlier, at B135, Kant makes it clear that our form of thought is discursive and thus must be *given* a manifold of representation in a 'distinct' intuition, and that only in this manner is self-identity possible, namely as a form of consciousness of the unity of the representations in that given manifold. The form of discursive thought, the 'simple representation' 'I', does not contain itself a content, a manifold. Our mode of thought is not like an intellectual intuition, which would be an 'understanding, in which through self-consciousness all of the manifold would at the same time be given, would *intuit*'. '[O]urs can only *think* and must seek the intuition in the senses.' On the difference between discursive understanding and intellectual intuition, see further Quarfood (2011).

cates that the manifold must be a synthesised one for the analytic principle of apperception to apply to it. In other words, the identity or sameness of the subject with respect to the intuition must, in some way, be seen as reciprocal with the synthetic unity of that intuition.

Furthermore, from the thrust of § 15 it is already clear that the synthetic unity of apperception that is brought into this 'certain intuition' has to do with a referring relation to an object, of which it is already assumed one has an empirical intuition (regardless of whether this is a spatiotemporal intuition or not). The fundamental 'intentionality' of transcendental apperception, its intrinsic objective value, is suggested here, which is also indicated by Kant's observation regarding the '*transcendental* unity of self-consciousness', which he calls thus 'in order to designate the possibility of *a priori* cognition from it' (B132). Kant advances the notion of synthesis, which establishes synthetic unity in the manifold, specifically 'in order at the same time to draw attention to the fact that we can represent nothing as combined in the object without having previously combined it ourselves' (B130). This passage in § 15 demands further clarification but it is suggested in this and a very similar passage at B134 (AA 3: 110.11–18), and quite clearly at B140 (§ 18), that Kant believes that the identity of apperception which is a '*transcendental* unity of self-consciousness' is by the same token an objective unity of consciousness and hence formally *constitutive of* an object (in general). This belief is tantamount to the constitution claim (Reciprocity) that solicited the criticism levelled at Kant's argumentation by Guyer and others (see again Chapter 4). The criticism is based on a standard understanding of the sense of 'object', as well as a specific notion of the unity of self-consciousness. To be able to dispel the criticism we must explain Kant's sense of 'object', and how it must be seen as *originating* in self-consciousness.

The 'thoroughgoing identity of self-consciousness' (B135), which is the same as the 'thoroughgoing identity of the apperception of a manifold given in intuition' mentioned at B133, and which is articulated in the 'I think'-proposition that functions as the operative premise of the constitution argument (the P-argument), is that which rationally underwrites the synthetic, and hence objective, *unity* of representations as universally warranted. Reciprocally, no a priori identity of self obtains, however, other than that which serves to warrant the objective validity of the synthetic unity of one's representations in this 'certain intuition' which is *actually* accompanied by the thinking 'I' (a manifold of representations that are thus '*my* representations' strictly speaking [B132]). Identity and synthetic unity of self-consciousness are co-constitutive or reciprocal, which underpins the constitution claim (i.e. Reciprocity). Therefore, as will become clearer in the course of my account of the derivation of the categories, the identity of self is merely the 'identity of the function' (A108) of synthesis among one's *epistemically* relevant unitary representations, namely among those that, from what § 15 tells us, were already assumed to have relation to some object. This is then confirmed by the conclusion of the P-argument at B137, which says that an object is nothing but 'that in the concept of which the manifold of a given intuition is *united*', that is, nothing but a *function* of objectivity or a rule under which something can first be considered an object.[13]

All this still needs a good deal of clarifying, but it is already becoming clear that the identity of self does not concern the presumed existential unity of all of one's (possible) representations, including ones that one has (or has had, or will have) but to which one does not occurrently attend by apperceiving them in the transcendental way, namely by synthesising them, and which thus do not on that account have objective validity for one (objective in the sense of these representations genuinely being *something* 'for me'). Nor does it concern an original combination of all one's possible thoughts or representations, which putatively make up the thinking self's unity or co-presence that is *prior to* a priori synthesis as an activity of the subject, as Henrich (1976: 58–9, 63, 65–6) and recently Wunderlich (2005: 215)[14] have suggested. Contrary to what Guyer believes, this indicates—as will become clearer in the following—a claim to *conditional* necessity regarding the self-identity underpinning *some* of one's possible representations (viz. '*my* representations' 'in a certain intuition' [B132]) and not an unconditional, *existential* claim regarding the unity of *any* or *all* of one's possible representations (namely any arbitrary array of perceptions one happens to have, may have and/or might have had).[15]

---

[13] This refers to the 'same function' of which Kant speaks in the crucial *Leitfaden* passage (A79/B104–5) (see again Chapter 5). The object is thus the correlate of the original thinking self—transcendental apperception as original synthesis of one's representations—in that its 'identity of the function' of synthesis (A108) is at the same time that which establishes the unity of the manifold of the intuition of an object.

[14] Wunderlich thinks that the 'original combination' of the first paragraph of § 16 is the analytic unity of apperception, not the synthetic one. He writes: 'Alle möglichen Vorstellungen eines Subjekts sind in einem allgemeinen Selbstbewußtsein dadurch ursprünglich verbunden, daß sie durchgängig von diesem Subjekt mit „Ich denke" begleitet werden können. Entgegen dem naheliegenden Anschein [...] bezeichnet die ursprüngliche Verbindung daher gerade nicht die Synthesis zwischen den Vorstellungen durch Kategorien. Dafür spricht auch, daß das, was sich im zweiten Absatz von § 16 aus der ursprünglichen Verbindung „folgern" lassen soll, die Notwendigkeit einer Synthesis ist; und eben daher kann die ursprüngliche Verbindung keine synthetische sein [...]' (2005: 215). This seems mistaken to me if only for the fact that the original combination is surely the original-*synthetic* unity of apperception of which the heading of § 16 speaks.

[15] Cf. Guyer (1987: 132, 137, 140, 144); see also Guyer (1987: 123ff, 1992: 139ff., 143). See further again Chapter 4, Section 5. Notice that in the A-Deduction Kant generally still argues that *all pos-*

6.3 The 'I think'-Proposition: The Analyticity of Apperception

Consequently, Kant's argument regarding the identity of self-consciousness, as a function of synthesis among one's *own* representations, must be seen as effectively yielding a properly analytic proposition, as Kant himself observes at B135 and again at B138, and not a synthetic proposition as Guyer asserts (although that is what Kant, for some context-dependent reason, says in the A-Deduction at A117n.[16]). This view of the identity of apperception comports with my thesis that there exists a rigorous coextensivity between the analytic unity of consciousness and the synthetic unity of apperception, which just means that the 'thoroughgoing identity of self-consciousness', the logical truth of which is expressed by the analyticity or sameness of representations that are apperceived, is dependent on and can only be thought by means of an underlying necessary (and therefore a priori) synthesis (B135). Kant writes:

> Thus all manifold of intuition has a necessary relation to the 'I think' *in the same subject in which this manifold is to be encountered*. (B132, emphasis added)

The identity of the self relates to '*this* manifold', which is to be found in the correlate subject, so that the relation between manifold and subject is analytic, for it is the intimate relation between, on the one hand, 'all my representations', my representations in a given manifold that I take *as* same, and, on the other hand, the ground of this *sameness*, namely the identical self that I am with regard to *these* representations in '*this* manifold'. That which constitutes this analyticity is a *function* of identity, namely the principle of apperception or synthesis. It is this function which first establishes the identity of the self with regard to her own representations (for the self, not noumenally). Consider for example a notorious passage at A108, where Kant says that

> the mind could not possibly think of the identity of itself in the manifoldness of its representations, and indeed think this *a priori*, if it did not have before its eyes the identity of its

---

sible representations are subject to the condition of apperception, suggesting indeed an existential claim (see for example at A113, 116). It is therefore understandable based on the apparent evidence of the A-Deduction that Quassim Cassam, among so many others, should think that Kant holds the belief that it is impossible that 'appearances should be apprehended otherwise than under conditions of the unity of apperception' (1987: 370). There is, however, another way of reading the 'all possible' claim that Kant makes in the A-Deduction. See further below Section 6.4.

16 Guyer (1987: 134, 136 ff., 139 ff.) has called attention to this apparent contradiction. For a possible solution, see Allison (2004: 165–7).

action [*die Identität seiner Handlung vor Augen haben*],[17] which subjects all synthesis of apprehension [...] to a transcendental unity [...].[18]

The identity of the thinking self is reciprocal with a consciousness of the identity of the act of unification among her representations, meaning that the identity of the thinking self (for the self) is first established by virtue of the unifying act. A passage from the *Lectures on Metaphysics* can throw light on this idea:

> Understanding is the faculty for bringing various representations under a rule. It rests on apperception. (It is the faculty for determining the particular by the general. With the higher cognitive power the cognitive faculty is considered not in relation to intuition, but rather to the unity of consciousness. This is the representation of one's representations and therefore is also called apperception. *Without the consciousness of the sameness of a representation in many representations, no general rule would be possible.* For a rule is a necessary unity of the consciousness of a manifold of representations, relation of the manifold of representations to one consciousness.) But how are concepts possible through apperception? *In that I represent to myself the identity of my apperception in many representations.* The concept is a common perception <*perceptio communis*>, e. g., the concept of body. (*Met-Mron*, AA 29: 889 [LM: 257], emphasis added)

This passage contains much information, not all of which is relevant for present purposes. Apperception is here linked to the identity that 'I represent to myself', which is a 'consciousness of the sameness of a representation in many representations', enabling us to form concepts out of our various representations in an intuition. In other words, the consciousness of an identical characteristic in the manifold representations provides a 'general rule' by means of which the

---

17 *Vor Augen haben* must be read in terms of *vor Augen führen/legen*, which means *deutlich machen* or *vor sich klarmachen* ('explicate', 'clarify'), or also *anzeigen* ('demonstrate'). Cf. B575/A547, B20, A150/B189, B202, A13.

18 As is well known, this passage has had the special interest of Henrich (1976: 64) in his philosophically rich but often also rather enigmatic account of the Transcendental Deduction. Henrich (1976: 102) asserts regarding A108 that here Kant aims at the derivation of a priori rules based on the identity of the subject, which must be known a priori, and that self-consciousness can be established only in relation to these a priori rules. Importantly, however, as Henrich subsequently notes, in this passage Kant uses the concept of 'identity' ambiguously: 'Der zu interpretierende Text [A108] schreitet aber ganz unvermittelt von der Identität des Subjektes zu der Identität einer Handlung fort. [...] In Kants Text findet sich kein Hinweis auf ein Argument, mittels dessen ein Zusammenhang zwischen dem Bewußtsein der Identität des Ich und dem Bewußtsein von Regeln als notwendig einsichtig gemacht werden konnte. [...] Das Argument selbst hatte aus der Ich-Identität ein Wissen apriori von der Synthesis und aus ihm wiederum die Folgerung zu gewinnen, daß diese Synthesis als geregelte gewußt werden muß. Erst danach kann, wenn überhaupt, davon die Rede sein, daß diese Regeln aus einer Handlung hervorgehen, der Identität zuzusprechen ist' (1976: 103).

manifold can be regarded as unified and conceptualised. As at A108, the identity of the mind (for the self) *is* the identity of the consciousness of the various representations in an intuition being brought under a general rule by means of an act of apperception. Representations are united, by what constitutes their sameness in respect of their unity, only to the extent that an act of unification has taken place. At the same time, there is no identical mind (for some self) other than by virtue of such an act of unification among one's various representations. The identity of a self is not a primordial *fact*, but first established *in* the act of apperception, and thus representations do not 'belong' to this identical self as a matter of course but belong to the identical self only in order to yield a rule-governed cognition.

Yet in Guyer's defence one may want to insist that Kant clearly asserts that

> the manifold representations that are given in a certain intuition would not *all together* [*insgesammt*] be *my* representations if they did not all together [*insgesammt*] belong [*gehörten*] to a self-consciousness. (B132, emphasis added; notice that the indexical 'my' is in spaced type in the original)

On a cursory reading of this passage, Kant appears indeed to be saying that if representations did not all *belong* to self-consciousness, they could not be considered my representations and a fortiori I could not be conscious of them.[19] Critically, based on this passage, one might be inclined to subscribe to the (quasi-)Cartesian reading that Guyer imposes on it; that is, one might want to argue that Kant espouses the dogmatic view that there is a presupposed thoroughgoing identity *throughout* my representative states (ostensibly borne out by the expression *durchgängig mir angehören* [B132–3][20]) of which a fortiori there is a priori knowledge. This primordial identity is then supposedly necessarily referred to as the element of sameness *whenever* one is conscious of or, in some way, attending to one's mental states. What is more, the passage might be interpreted in such a way that it is taken to mean that 'all my representations' whatever *really belong* (in the possessive sense) to my numerically identical self, which would be tantamount indeed to an intemperate claim to absolute necessity regarding the

---

19 Notice however that in the original it reads, not my self-consciousness, but *einem Selbstbewußtsein*, with an unusual indefinite article, indicating that it concerns a unitary self-consciousness to which my representations must belong in order to count as 'my representations'. Kemp Smith's rendering of *einem Selbstbewußtsein* as 'one self-consciousness' is therefore apt.
20 Kemp Smith's translation of *durchgängig* as 'all without exception' is telling in this regard.

unity of one's mental states regardless of *my* whether or no attending to them.²¹ Consider also the following passage from the A-Deduction:

> All possible appearances belong, as representations, to the whole possible self-consciousness. But from this, as a transcendental representation, numerical identity is inseparable, and certain *a priori*, because nothing can come into cognition except by means of this original apperception. Now since this identity must necessarily enter into [*hineinkommen*] the synthesis of all the manifold of appearances insofar as they are to become empirical cognition, the appearances are thus subject to *a priori* conditions with which their synthesis (of apprehension) must be in thoroughgoing accord. (A113)

The first two sentences of this passage appear to suggest indeed that representations, or appearances, do belong originally to self-consciousness, from which 'numerical identity is inseparable' and of which we can be 'certain *a priori*'. Crucially, it seems that Kant indeed means that the certainty of our numerical identity with regard to all possible appearances is *prior* to the synthesis of the manifold so that a cognition can come from this. Secondly, and this seems to confirm Guyer's (and also Henrich's) reading, it appears that this synthesis must subsequently be seen to be in accord with the a priori conditions to which it is subject, presumably the original apperception of one's numerical identity.

The clearest evidence for Guyer's reading can probably be found at A116. There, Kant writes:

> We are conscious *a priori* of the thoroughgoing identity of ourselves with regard to *all representations* that can ever belong to our cognition, *as a necessary condition of the possibility of all representations* (since the latter represent something in me only insofar as they belong with all the others to one consciousness, hence they must at least be capable of being connected in it). This principle holds *a priori*, and can be called *the transcendental principle of the unity* of *all the manifold* of our representations (thus also in intuition). (emphasis added)

Kant here appears to say that all representations of which we *can* become conscious are related to the thoroughgoing identity of ourselves, and even that the 'possibility of all representations' depends on their being united in one consciousness, that is, all representations must *be* such as to be amenable to being connected in accordance with the '*transcendental principle of the unity of all the manifold* of our representations' (emphasis added). (But notice the qualifying relative clause in the first sentence of the quote 'that can ever belong to our cognition [*die zu unserem Erkenntnis jemals gehören können*]', which sug-

---

21 See also Guyer (1980: 208ff.).

gests that it only concerns representations that are epistemically relevant which must conform to the transcendental principle of unity.) Or also consider A122, where Kant says that

> *all appearances whatever* must come into the mind or be apprehended in such a way that they are in agreement with the unity of apperception, which would be impossible without synthetic unity in their connection [...]. (emphasis added)

This suggests that the way in which representations or appearances originate empirically in the mind must already be such that they agree with the unity of apperception, denying the possibility that representations or appearances could ever be present in the mind without being connected in accordance with the unity of apperception.²²

Apart from this ostensible evidence from the A-Deduction, which seems to support his reading of apperception, Guyer's interpretation is more interesting philosophically as well as interpretatively than I have perhaps made it out to be so far.²³ There is a sense in which he is right to emphasise the *a priori synthesis* of all representations that belong to my *identical* self of which I have a priori knowledge (in some sense), regardless of any *actual* act of apprehending my representations. However, in contrast to what Guyer believes, this can be brought into line with reading apperception as an *analytical* principle. I want to focus on the meaning of 'thoroughgoing identity' (*durchgängige Identität*) in relation to the sense of 'belonging to the unity of self-consciousness' out of which arises the possibility of a priori knowledge.²⁴ These notions that Kant uses in § 16 seem to hint at an idea of the thoroughgoing determination (*durchgängige Bestimmung*) of the thinking self as an individual, which can only be a putative noumenal self, and of which as such I cannot have discursive knowledge without an added empirical intuition, but of which I have at least *some* a priori knowledge. This concerns the a priori knowledge that I have of myself as agent of thought to

---

22 However, in the same context, at A120 Kant writes that 'since every appearance contains a manifold, thus different perceptions by themselves are encountered dispersed and separate in the mind, a combination of them, *which they cannot have in sense itself*, is therefore necessary' (emphasis added). This clearly shows that the manifold in inner sense is not connected as a matter of course, and hence suggests that the strong synthetic reading of apperception is not licensed by the text.
23 Cf. concerning these passages and others also Rosefeldt (2000: 128–35).
24 Hoppe (1983: 122–5, 210) interprets the unity of self-consciousness as *durchgängige Mir-Gehörigkeit* of representations in terms of the intemperate claim that the mere possession of one's representations already requires pure self-consciousness. But I argue that the sense of belonging should not be interpreted possessively. See also Schulting (2017a: 161–6, 185n.15).

the effect that when I think I, as thinker, must posit myself as existing, with all my determinations, and that this can ex hypothesi only be done in any *real* act of thought or self-consciousness. This last aspect thus indicates that such a priori knowledge *presupposes* at least one possible instantiation of my 'I think'. I cannot have this knowledge with regard to myself in abstraction from the act of thinking. The positing of oneself as existing is reciprocal with the *act* of thought. Nevertheless, the a priori knowledge that I have of myself as agent of thought concerns all possible instantiations of my 'I think'. What I am suggesting here is that in any act of self-consciousness I, as agent of thought, affirm, as it were, the noumenal self that I am as thinking being and is thoroughly determined in respect of all its *possible* determinations (presumably, all *my* possible *representations*), without however having or gaining complete knowledge (a priori or otherwise) of this synthetic unity of all possible representations that 'throughout' (*durchgängig*) belong to my self.[25]

Or so one could read Kant's claim in the above-quoted passage towards the end of B132 regarding my representations that 'throughout belong to me'. However, even if this were a bona fide reading of Kant's claim here, a distinction must be made between the possible or problematic self, relative to which all her possible representations as determinations are posited, and the actual self which implies an existent, actual thinking 'I', whereby this self posits herself absolutely together with all her determinations. The thoroughgoing identity of the self can be determined only 'sensibly' (B430), that is, with regard to a *given* manifold of representation in an empirical intuition, which means that the 'belonging of representations "throughout" to me' must be interpreted in a weaker sense. That this is indeed what Kant appears to hint at will be explored further below in Section 6.4.

6.3.1 The Austere Reading of Apperception

First, however, I want to direct attention to the *analyticity* of the principle of apperception, concentrating on Kant's arguments in the passage at AA 3: 108.19– 109.12, which starts with the familiar 'I think'-proposition: 'The *I think* must *be able* to accompany all my representations' (B132). Many commentators take this proposition, with which Kant launches the P-argument in the B-Deduction,

---

[25] For one thing, I could not determine whether or not the class of all possible *determinations* of my noumenal self has the same extension as the class of all my possible *representations*. It is not a matter of course that my noumenal self is exhausted by mental properties.

6.3 The 'I think'-Proposition: The Analyticity of Apperception

to express the analytic principle PS. Call PS the definition for self-ascription or apperception, which explains the possibility of subjective 'experience' or representation:

{PS=Principle of Self-ascription}: (∃z)(z is a thinker at time t) ⟶ {(∀x)(x is a representation ∧ x is being represented at t) ⟶ □ [(∃y)(y is a thinker 'I' ∧ x is self-ascribed or at least self-ascribable under certain conceptual constraints by y)]}

There are grounds for thus reformulating the 'I think'-proposition in Kant's text. For Kant himself states regarding the possibility of self-ascription of representations:

> This last proposition [viz. that unity of consciousness is only possible through synthesis, D.S.] is [...] itself analytic [...] for it says nothing more than that all *my* representations in any given intuition must stand under the condition, under which alone I can ascribe [*rechnen zu*] them to the identical self as *my* representations, and thus can grasp them together [*zusammenfassen*] as synthetically combined in one apperception through the general expression *I think*. (B138 [AA 3: 112.13–19], trans. slightly modified)

Not surprisingly, Kant's reference to an earlier section in the text ('this last proposition') is ignored by commentators who stress the analyticity of PS. Strawsonians, who insist on the analytic nature of the principle, namely fail to assess Kant's assertion, earlier at B135, that

> this principle of the necessary unity of apperception is, to be sure, itself identical, thus an analytical proposition, which *explains* [*erklärt*] as necessary a synthesis of the manifold given in an intuition, without which that thoroughgoing identity of self-consciousness could not be thought. (B135 [AA 3: 109.19–23], emphasis added and trans. emended)[26]

A good example of the difficulties that the Strawsonian runs up against in regard to Kant's analyticity claim as a direct result of this failure of assessment, is provided by Cassam's (1987: 375 ff.) reflections on this score.

PS is routinely taken to explain a de dicto necessity: I must be able to ascribe to myself any representation that I have, I being the subject of any of a series of representations that I ascribe to myself, for which certain conceptual conditions for unification should be met.[27] By implication, de facto self-ascription establishes, *a posteriori*, a synthetic existential unity of all representations so ascribed as belonging to the unity of consciousness; however, nothing in the way of *a pri-*

---

[26] Notice that for Kant the notions of necessity and apriority are inseparably linked (cf. B4).
[27] Cf. A122 (AA 4: 90.18–20).

ori synthesis seems thereby required.²⁸ Presumably, the analyticity of PS has to do with self-ascription being criterionless, that is, immune to error through misidentification: one knows and cannot fail to know the conditions under which one ascribes one's representations to oneself.²⁹ Contrary to the application of concepts to objects, presumably regarding one's own representations no identificatory criteria are required that first enable their self-ascription and no possibility of error exists: the concept of self applies to one entity and one entity only, namely the self that I am when ascribing my representations to myself. That is to say, the extension of the concept of 'self' consists of just one possible *particular* tokening at any one time at which the concept is instantiated by some self who is self-consciously aware of her own representations.³⁰ In any case of representing, I know, *by way of* self-ascribing any representation that I have, that I am the one representing and that the representation 'belongs' to me. As it appears, the analyticity of PS would thus concern the conceptually trivial truth that the ability to conceive of one's representations as one's own is reciprocal with the capacity to employ the indexical 'I' in all cases of such conceiving. This is then taken to mean that there is an analytic, conceptual relation between a representation and the agent of representation, which is the self-ascribing representer. Guyer (1980: 209) puts it quite explicitly by contending that Kant holds that '[w]hatever is to count as a representation at all must be fit for self-ascription'.³¹ He continues:

> [The 'I think'-proposition] asserts [...] that I cannot have a representation which is not subject to these conditions [i.e. the conditions for self-ascription, D.S.]. To put it bluntly, Kant asserts that I cannot have a representation which I cannot recognize as my own.³²

---

28 According to Paul Guyer, the notion of apperception, as a consciousness of one's self-consciousness, can only be retained once freed from the 'encumbrance of *a priori* synthesis' (1980: 212). In other words, on the austere analytic reading of the principle presumably expounded by Kant at B138, any synthetic unity that would be involved can only be *a posteriori*, namely a unity of all *de facto* ascribed representations, not of all possible (i.e. past, present and future) representations (cf. Strawson 1968: 96). At any rate, this gainsays Kant's view, also expressed in the omitted passage in the above quotation from B138, that the synthetic unity at issue is an *a priori* unity that is the very *ground* of any analytic unity of consciousness (see B135; cf. B134 [AA 3: 110.9–11], where Kant speaks of 'synthetic unity of the manifold of intuitions, as given *a priori*' being 'the ground of the identity of apperception itself').
29 Cf. Strawson (1968: 92–3, 98, 165).
30 Cf. Rosefeldt (2000: 20, 21–2).
31 Strawson (1968: 101, 114, 117) speaks similarly of any representation's *potentiality* for self-ascription.
32 Notice that Guyer is critical of this view that he attributes to Kant. Also Heiner Klemme thinks that the unity and identity of the subject are 'Kriterien dafür daß Vorstellungen von

On this account, it seems that not only are the conditions for representation or representing (that is, for *having* representations) and the logical conditions for self-ascription of representations conflated, but also the conditions for representing and *self-consciousness* are conflated given that, as Strawson (1968: 108) asserts, transcendental self-consciousness is the a priori form or condition of self-ascription. A representer could thus not *be* otherwise than an at least potential self-conscious representer. I believe that this view of the analyticity of the apperception principle is flawed, if only for the fact that it provides no ground for the assumption that any agent of representation is eo ipso, even if only potentially, a self-conscious subject or that the subject who envisages her own future states of affairs has complete knowledge of future states of affairs as involving herself.[33] Notice furthermore that Strawson (1968: 92) claims that experiences are necessarily unifiable in that they must satisfy the conditions of belonging to a single consciousness. This is a rather different claim from the one about the criterionless nature of self-ascription. It seems that Strawson confuses two different arguments: one concerning the logical conditions governing the self-ascribability of one's *own* representations and another for the necessary unifiability of representations *tout court*, only the former of which would prima facie amount to a self-evident conceptual truth, namely the tautology that Strawson considers to be the nub of Kant's premise.

To illustrate the austere conception of apperception as a condition for representation in terms of PS, which dispenses with *a priori* synthesis, consider Malte Hossenfelder's (1978) interpretation of the 'I think'-proposition. Having noted that there are ostensible intrinsic problems with Kant's appeal to *a priori* synthesis and assuming that the principle of self-consciousness is a tautological principle as previously defined (PS), Hossenfelder (1978: 100 – 1) attempts to cast light on the analyticity of the principle by suggesting that we substitute 'to represent' for the verb 'to think' in Kant's proposition

---

einem Subjekt "gehabt" werden können' (1996: 186). But see Klemme (1996: 188), where he distinguishes between two senses of *haben*.

33 Not all future representative states *need* be ones that I *self-consciously* represent, lest the conceptual condition for self-ascription be seen to concern an ontological necessity, implying a necessary coexistence of representer and self-conscious agent (cf. Ameriks 2000b: 249). Therefore, I think that Arnulf Deppermann is mistaken when he observes: 'Es fragt sich [...], ob die Rede von Vorstellungen in einem Subjekt, die nicht notwendigerweise Vorstellungen für ein Subjekt sind, sinnvoll ist. Obwohl Kant diese Sprachregelung selbst benutzt (B132), scheint es mir in semantischer Hinsicht problematisch zu sein, *einen Inhaber mentaler Zustände als Subjekt dieser Zustände zu bezeichnen, wenn er nicht als Denker dieser Zustände konzipiert wird*' (2001: 137n.23, emphasis added).

> The: *I think* must *be able* to accompany all my representations.

The proposition would then read

> The: *I represent* must *be able* to accompany all my representations.

Only in this way, Hossenfelder argues, can the analytic character of PS become explicit, for quite clearly its denial logically entails a contradiction. The premise of Kant's argument is then tantamount to nothing more than the unpacking of what is already contained in the concept of 'representation'. Hossenfelder thus reduces apperception to a conceptual principle of *representation simpliciter*. We can translate Hossenfelder's substitution reading of PS as:

> {PS'}: $(\exists z)(z$ is a representer at time $t) \longrightarrow \{(\forall x)(x$ is a representation $\wedge\ x$ is being represented at $t) \longrightarrow \Box\ [(\exists y)(y$ is a representer 'I' $\wedge\ x$ is self-ascribed or at least self-ascribable by $y)]\}$

However, there is no reason to believe that Kant himself regards the principle of self-consciousness as simply a principle of *representation*, so that the analytic (conceptual) relation obtains between represented and representer. Notice that the sentence at B131–2 (AA 3: 108.20–1), after the actual 'I think'-proposition, continues: '…for otherwise something would be represented in me that could not be thought at all', which would make no sense on Hossenfelder's substitution proposal. Kant's suggestion is rather that if I did not accompany my representations something could still be represented (in me) but I would not thereby *think* it, which is trivially true, but not in Hossenfelder's sense. But even while disregarding this point, it does not seem true to hold that the said conceptual connection is eo ipso substitutable, in all possible cases, for the relation between a representation and a *self* who self-ascribes her representations to her identical self. First, a representer could just *be* representing without *self-ascribing* representations at all—this would amount to first-order representing without a second-order *representing* of one's representing by virtue of the self-ascription of representations to one's identical self (or to a perceiving without apperceiving).[34] More intriguingly, a representer could be representing representations, and indeed ascribing representations to herself (through a self-reference of sorts), without however thereby self-ascribing them to her self in the strict sense, by which I mean the *same* self (de re) to which she also ascribes other representations (over time). This would undercut the analyticity of the relation between the representations ascribed and the identity of the self-ascribing self. It is possible even that

---

34 Cf. *Anthr* § 5, AA 7: 135.

a representer could effectively (de re) ascribe representations to 'others' when in fact she *believes* that she is ascribing them to herself (de dicto).³⁵ (This involves problems concerning the metaphysical status of the identical self to which one ascribes representations, which I must leave aside for present purposes.)³⁶

6.3.2 A Formal Analysis

If we look at the possible cases of instantiation of the 'I think', then it becomes clear that not *all possible* representations are *necessarily* accompanied by an 'I think', nor that it is the case that all possible representations necessarily entail the transcendental unity of apperception, that is, are necessarily possibly accompanied by an 'I think'; nor that all of them really belong to the thoroughgoing identity of *my* self-consciousness, in the possessive sense.³⁷ This can be shown in a breakdown of the 'I think'-proposition into its possible logical modalities P. Assuming that the 'I think' is existentially instantiated at least once, consider the necessary possibility P1:³⁸

---

35 Cf. e.g. A363 (AA 4: 228.32–229.4) and A363–4n. (AA 4: 229).
36 I believe that the substitution by some of de se modality for the distinction of de dicto/de re in the case of self-consciousness glosses over the problems involved in attempts to determine the ontological status of the self underlying apperceptive self-consciousness and is therefore wholly stipulative. For an authoritative account of Kant's metaphysics of the self, see Ameriks (2000a). See also Chapter 7, this volume.
37 This latter claim needs to be qualified though, as the sense of Kant's term 'gehören' is still in need of clarification. See Section 6.4.
38 Note that here an analysis, *ad oculos reflexionis*, of the possible cases of satisfaction of the instantiation of the 'I think'-proposition in terms of its necessary logical purport is concerned, given that the 'I think' is existentially instantiated at least once. It is not suggested here that the *existential necessity* of the instantiation of the 'I think' is implied or that 'everything that thinks, exists' (B422n.), although Kant is committed to the *fact* of discursive thought, implying an existing 'I think', which acts as the operative premise of the P-argument, and that thus the 'I think' is taken to be instantiated at least once (cf. B418, 423n.; see further below Section 6.4). Nor is it suggested that the necessity of an actual occurrence of empirical consciousness is at issue (cf. Reich 1992: 27), even though Kant says elsewhere that the proposition itself, though not the representation 'I', is empirical (B420, 423n., 428). By this Kant must be taken to mean that the existence *implied* in the *cogito* is necessarily (for us) in time, viz. sensibly determined, and so reveals the requirement that a sensible manifold in inner sense is given a posteriori to thought for the subject of thinking to be determined as existing (cf. B144ff., B429; see also Watkins 2005: 280–1). What is my concern here, however, is to tease out the *logically* necessary possibilities and impossibilities for all possible cases in which the 'I think' is and is not existentially instantiated.

P1: *the 'I think' accompanies all my representations;*

If P1, then ex hypothesi it must also be possible that

P2: *the 'I think' does not accompany all my representations*

and/or it must be possible that

P3: *the 'I think' does not accompany any representations that happen to occur and are so occurrent in the mind at any time t at which the 'I think' is not instantiated*

and/or it must be possible that

P4: *the 'I think' does not accompany any representations that happen to occur and are so occurrent in the mind at any time t at which the 'I think' is not instantiated, and that are also interminably barred from being able to be so accompanied, i.e. such representations as evanesce immediately after having been prompted and which leave no significant traces for possible retention and 'taking up' by an act of apperception (some representations may simply not be able to be retained or retrieved);*

P2 is obviously spurious, for it is logically inconsistent for me, as the subject of thought, to assert that 'I' am thinking (de facto)—or to assent, while thinking, to the proposition 'I am thinking'—and yet *not* to accompany my representations that I am *thereby* thinking. In other words, P2 amounts to a contradiction. The possessive pronoun 'my' in the predicate 'all my representations' refers rigidly.[39] Those representations are *my* representations that *I* accompany as such by *actually* thinking them.[40] This is shown by P1. P1 is analytically true: the totality of *my* representations that are occurrent share the same common mark 'I think', just in case I am accompanying them (as *my* representations 'all together' (*insgesammt*) in 'a certain intuition', as Kant puts it at B132 [AA 3: 109.5–6]) by means of the act of thinking precisely *when* I am in the business of thinking (representing in a particular way). '[A]ll *my* representations in any given intuition' (B138) analytically relate to the identity of the 'I think', for all its possible token-

---

[39] Cf. Rosefeldt (2000: 98–9).
[40] Some commentators (whose reading I labelled NER and NER' in Schulting 2012a) appear to argue that even when P1 holds P2 is still possible, namely when the possibility of reflective consciousness (an 'I think' reflecting on her states) is at any rate necessarily presupposed (which accounts for the modal verb 'must' in the proposition) but not *actually* instantiated (which ostensibly accounts for the verb phrase 'be able'). This would suggest that 'I think'-consciousness is indeed some psychological reflection on one's first-order states. But this construal shows a misunderstanding of the modality of the proposition.

ings. Or put differently still, 'in all the manifold of which I am conscious I am identical with myself' (B408, Kemp Smith).

The a priori knowledge that I have of my identity applies only to the analytic principle that for all possible tokenings of the 'I think', all my representations analytically relate to the identity of the accompanying 'I think' (cf. B408). No a priori knowledge however is possible of the putative *synthetic* unity of all my representations for *all possible* tokenings of my 'I think', although I do know a priori that for *any given* tokening of my 'I think', all representations accompanied by me must be synthesised. Knowledge of the synthetic unity of all my representations is possible only on condition of a manifold of representations in an *empirical intuition being given* for unification. By contrast, Dieter Henrich argues, in his well-known book on the Deduction, that

> 1) the '*unbestimmten* Menge *möglicher* Gedanken [...], die unsere Gedanken sind oder sein können' (emphasis added) and are thought by an identical 'I' constitutes the original-synthetic unity of apperception,

and further that

> 2) the 'Verbindung' of these thoughts is not an 'Aktivität [...] die etwa vom Subjekt ausgeführt werden müßte', but 'bezeichnet hier nichts als den Zustand der Zugehörigkeit' (1976: 59; cf. 1976: 63–4).

For Henrich, activity is accorded only to a *reflexive* 'I', which is conditioned on contingent circumstances (1976: 60). This suggests that the original-synthetic unity of apperception must be read in terms of a primordial self thoroughly determined with regard to *all her possible thoughts* in contrast to, and apparently independent of, an active 'I' reflexively accompanying her thoughts. To this end, Henrich makes a distinction between the self's singularity, which concerns *merely* the unity of all her representations, and her numerical identity. I believe this interpretation of apperception is mistaken as it, first, suggests—as Guyer (1980: 208) puts it—an 'advance guarantee' of the synthetic unity of all of a subject's thoughts, which makes it hard to understand why Kant insists on the *active* role of the thinking self in the unification of her representations, and secondly, it assumes a (more than formal) distinction between, on the one hand, the 'original-synthetic unity of apperception' and, on the other, the accompanying 'I think' as an *act* of apperception. The distinction that Henrich proposes is not warranted by Kant's text in § 16 and e.g. at A108, where Kant suggests the contemporaneity of synthetic unity in the manifold of representations and the identity of a *function* or *act*.

P1 constitutes the singularity of the 'I think' that is identical with itself in all the representations that are accompanied by it.[41] However, although it would seem that I can think only one thought at a time, the nature of discursive thought is such that every *singular* thought, which is accompanied by an 'I think', consists of *several* representations taken together and thus thought simultaneously as same qua their being subordinated under one common denominator or 'concept' (the 'I think' [cf. A341/B399]). For discursive minds such as ours, unity always implies multiplicity, which in turn entails synthesis *to the extent* that one's various representations are identical or equal or have something in common, namely to be related to the identical 'I think' (that is, only analytically united representations must also be synthetically united). This will be explicated later in more detail.

The determiner 'all' in the predicate 'all my representations' creates an ambiguity, for the proposition could, superficially, be construed as asserting that the 'I think' does not actually accompany *all*, but only *some* of my representations, which could lead one to presume that P2 is not strictly speaking false. This is indeed the route that most interpreters take. I argue that this view is mistaken and runs into exegetical difficulties in Chapter 9. From a systemic point of view, I believe it is logically nonsensical to assert, from a first-person perspective, that while I am thinking, I am only thinking *some* of *my* representations, unless I assume a possessive reading of my unity of consciousness as putatively consisting of all of the representations I can possibly have; of course, I *could* be accompanying my representations in future, but I cannot be certain *that* I will, as I could cease to exist at any point in time.

In the deduction of the categories of quantity (Chapter 9), it will become clear that the predicate 'all my representations' is a single complex representation, which *as such*, and *only* as such, is accompanied (actually) by the 'I think' as a common representation contained in *various* representations, which *as such*, that is, as in a *unified* compound, it accompanies (cf. B137 and B133 ff. note; see also *Met-Mron*, AA 29: 889, quoted earlier in this chapter). Again, this does not mean that in future I could not accompany representations that are mine (or indeed in the past could not have accompanied representations that were mine). But what it does mean is that I can know that representations are mine only when I *actually* accompany them in a thinking manner. The only *a priori* knowledge of my future thinking self that I have is the knowledge that *if* I *actually* ac-

---

[41] Hence, Kant calls it the 'numerical unity of apperception' (A107, 113; cf. B402, 407). Kant seems to confuse numerical identity with numerical unity, but one should note that here the analytic identity of the 'I think' with all the representations that it accompanies and which contain it as analytic unitary ground, is concerned, hence numerical *unity* of apperception.

company my representations, then they will indeed be mine (in the sense of being recognised by me to be mine). The same holds for the past: I know a priori that for all representations at any time in the past to have been recognised by me to be mine, an act of apperceptive accompaniment would have taken place, but I do not know for certain whether or not I in fact had then recognised representations to be mine so that the 'I think' had indeed been instantiated at that point in time in the past. The knowledge that I have of my past representations as being mine is therefore quite meagre.

With P3 the case of a representer R representing any arbitrary occurrent representations x,y,z reflects the circumstance that P1 is not actualised. In that case, the representer R would still be a representer R of x,y,z, even if not aware of herself (*stricto sensu*) as in the business of representing and hence being *self*-aware in the strict sense of doing so. R does not accompany her representations in the transcendental way, but merely in the empirical way by just *having* them in any arbitrary mode peculiar to her occurrent physio-psychological stance at any time t. Strictly speaking, R does not *think*. Furthermore, P3 leaves open whether representations are in future apperceived by an 'I think'. It might or might not happen.

P4 is a real Lockean possibility.[42] Although at first sight Kant does not venture an opinion on the possibilities P3 and P4, regarding which it is further open to question if they are anything more than merely formally distinguishable, these are surely logically inferable from the 'I think'-proposition. This is confirmed by some of Kant's assertions in the text of the Deduction. P3/4-representations are representations, which, as Kant puts it, are 'nothing for me' (B132), which is consistent with the rigid reference of the possessive determiner 'my' of P1-representations.[43] Direct textual grounds in §§ 16–17 itself can further be found for exam-

---

42 See e.g. Locke's *Essay*, where he considers the following objection: '[S]uppose I wholly lose the memory of some parts of my Life, beyond a possibility of retrieving them, so that perhaps I shall never be conscious of them again' (Book II, Ch. xxvii, § 20). Locke's argument here is of course that despite this being a real possibility it does not affect *personal identity* (§ 25.15–20), because such identity consists for Locke, much in the same way as for Kant, in nothing but consciousness as the 'reflex act of perception' (§ 13) of one's action, viz. the consciousness that accompanies all ideas that are *present* to one (which is the Lockean equivalent of Kant's P1). What I here want to stress is the fact that, for Locke and I want to argue for Kant as well, there is a real possibility of losing one's memory, so that, in Kant's case at least, the representations that I *had* I can no longer retrieve and so cannot currently apperceive.

43 Notice that, significantly, at A116 Kant speaks of 'all possible representations' without the indexical 'my'. See also A111, where Kant speaks of 'all possible appearances', which stand in a relation to apperception; also at A113 Kant says that 'all possible appearances belong, as representations, to the entire possible self-consciousness'. See further below Section 6.4.

ple at B133 (AA 3: 109.16–20)[44] and B134 (AA 3: 110.7–9).[45] Indirect grounds are provided at B137 (AA 3: 111.12–15), from which it is clear that given representations that have not been *combined* by the understanding 'in one consciousness' do 'not have in common the act of apperception, *I think*, and [are] thereby [...] not [...] grasped together in one self-consciousness [*einem Selbstbewußtsein*]' (trans. emended). Synthesis (or combination) is on a par with the common mark 'I think' being actually attributed to the manifold of representations as an integral representative compound (I discuss the aspect of synthesis in detail in Chapter 7). Put otherwise, synthesis is contemporaneous with the analyticity of the 'I think' as partial representation contained in the manifold of representations that are accompanied by the thinking 'I' (hence the parity of the synthetic and analytic unities of apperception, which I have called Rigorous Coextensivity).[46]

Therefore, only synthesised representations, as together forming a synthetic compound, show up the common mark 'I think'. Kant says, at B133, that 'this thoroughgoing identity of the apperception of a manifold given in intuition contains a synthesis of the representations, and is possible only through the consciousness of this synthesis' or 'the *analytical* unity of apperception is only possible under the presupposition of some *synthetic* one'. Those that do not exhibit the partial representation 'I think', namely P3/P4-representations, have eo ipso not been synthesised and are not *my* representations strictly speaking and hence do not 'belong', all together, to my thoroughgoing identity.[47] This is not

---

44 Cf. e.g. R5923, AA 18: 386.
45 Here, Kant does not just provide a hypothetical counterexample, but hints at a genuine (real) possibility on account of which, however, no *unitary cognition* would follow.
46 Cf. Kant's letter to J. S. Beck of 1 July 1794: 'The grasping [*Auffassung*] (apprehensio) of the given manifold [*des Manigfaltigen Gegebenen*] and its reception [*Aufnehmung*] in the unity of consciousness (apperceptio) is the same sort of thing as [*ist nun mit* [...] *Einerley*] the representation of a composite (that is, it is only possible through composition), if the synthesis of my representation in the grasping of it, and its analysis insofar as it is a concept, yield one and the same representation (reciprocally bring forth one another)' (*Corr*, AA 11: 515).
47 Therefore, Kant speaks of 'all my representations', not 'each of my representations'. He does however speak of 'each representation' at B133, namely when it is the case that the 'empirical consciousness' which 'accompanies' representations severally is not related to the identity of the subject (note the 'empirical consciousness' that accompanies several representations, which eo ipso cannot be taken to be the 'I think', which is not an empirical representation or consciousness [B404/A345–6; A381], as so many commentators take for granted [see, among others, Klemme 1996: 193 and Wunderlich 2005: 214–15]). Consequently, such representations that are accompanied severally are not strictly speaking part of the compound of 'all my representations' which are de facto accompanied by transcendental consciousness, in all possible cases of such accompaniment; these discrete representations, which—not being apperceptively accompanied—are not mine in a de dicto sense (they are not *said* by me to be mine), could even

6.3 The 'I think'-Proposition: The Analyticity of Apperception

to say that such representations do not *exist* (in any arbitrary co-presence in the mind, being discretely given to it), or could not be consciously apprehended in any subcognitive sense (by means of empirical apperception).[48] What it does mean is that I just do not, in the transcendentally accompanying kind of way, think of them as mine. They are merely represented in any arbitrary order and combination without being synthesised such that I reflexively think of them as my representations as together constituting one identical thought (as *insgesammt meine Vorstellungen* [B132]).[49]

Most commentators are committed to a reading that has Kant deny, if not the actualisation of P3, then certainly the possibility that representations are not even *potentially* accompanied by an 'I think'; they must repudiate P4.[50] This reading takes Kant to make a claim regarding the susceptibility of all of one's perceptions (including ones that have not, or not as yet, been taken together synthetically) to the unity of apperception, so that no perception or representation is at any rate precluded from *potentially* being accompanied by an 'I think'.[51] I be-

---

not be mine in a de re sense (possibly, they *are not* mine). See further Chapter 9 on the distinction between 'each' and 'all'.

48 Such a co-presence would in fact be a succession of unrelated 'now's' (cf. Brook 1994: 125).

49 Cf. Henrich, who writes: 'So viele Gedanken möglich sind, so viele müssen auch als eines Subjektes Gedanken bewußt gemacht werden können. Die Singularität des Subjektes ist also insofern wirksames Einheitsprinzip, als sie von der Synthesis alle solche Gedanken ausschließt, die nicht in einen Zusammenhang gebracht werden können, in Beziehung auf den das Subjekt sich seiner als eines einziges Subjektes bewußt werden kann. Viele Vorstellungen mögen deshalb nicht zu möglichen Gedanken des Subjektes werden können' (1976: 66).

50 See e.g. Keller (1998), who asserts that 'any connection that might hold between individual representations in a particular consciousness must be such that it is consistent with the unifiability of those representations in self-consciousness' (1998: 57). Keller claims that Kant argues 'that, if something in me is to be represented by anyone, it must be represented by me' and that '[f]rom this, he concludes that, if I cannot think a representation in me, then no one else can either' (1998: 66); or also that '[i]f a representation is mine in principle, I must be able to recognize it as such, even if a representation can be mine without my being conscious at that time that it is mine' (1998: 67). These claims are far too strong. See further Schulting (2012a), where I canvass various construals of transcendental apperception in the literature.

51 See for example the claim made by Allison that 'room is left in the Kantian scheme for intuitions that are not brought under the categories (*though not for those that cannot be brought*)' (Allison 2001: 191, emphasis added). This view, which holds that the principle of apperception implies that it must be *possible* that the 'I think' accompanies all my representations, 'not that it actually does so on every occasion' (Allison 2001: 191), creates a problem as to how the difference between, on the one hand, apperception as the necessary precondition for the entire class of one's representations and, on the other, the condition for its satisfaction in regard to a subclass of representations can be accounted for. I note that Allison's view, which does not account for this difference, is symptomatic of the standard reading of transcendental apperception.

lieve there is no reasonable ground, intrinsic to the apperception proposition, for such a reading, for it is based on a strongly metaphysical assumption that goes beyond what is implied in the merely analytical representation 'I think' and its a priori constraints and, contrary to Guyer, I also believe that Kant is not committed to it. *There is nothing about representations that predisposes them to being thought* (in the strict sense). The claim is rather that *thought's* disposition is such that logically, by virtue of itself, thought is capable of thinking thoughts that comprise, in a unitary representation (the 'I think'), various representations that are given to it. The *explanandum* is the capacity of discursive thought, that is, the right kind of complex representation; the *explanandum* is *not* representation *simpliciter*.

To return to the formal schema of the 'I think', what can further be said about P4? It is possible that, psychologically speaking, some representations that happen to occur at some point in time cannot be retrieved or recalled so as to be apperceived, because (a) being the fleeting representations that they are such P4-representations evanesce immediately or shortly after having been prompted and leave no significant index or traces that are 'struck again' *when we have memories*, as Kant at one point is reported to have said in discussing Descartes' and Bonnet's views,[52] or (b) the perceptions that were had were not distinct enough to be recognised and thus to be retained for conceptualisation (and a fortiori to be *apperceived*). This is not to say that the representer of those perceptions was not the representer, whoever it was. In the case of P4, what I am unable to determine, and cannot infer from actual memory[53] since the psychological flow of perceptions solely extends forwards, is (1) whether or not previously, on the occasion of their being prompted, *I* was the actual subject of thought representing *those* representations that were being prompted at that point in time, in which case these representations would at the very least have to have been conscious representations accompanied by a 'same-sounding I' (A363)[54] and thus would have been accompanied by my 'I think', or (2) that in-

---

52 See *Met-Mron*, AA 29: 908 (LM: 274).
53 Cf. B239/A194: '[N]o appearance goes back from the following point of time to the preceding one.' For a more detailed Kantian account of why memory cannot play a cognitive role, see Ameriks (2000a: 164 ff.).
54 This involves the issue of the paralogistic inference from a formal-logical unity of thought to numerical identity of the self over time (see A362–4). Cf. Ameriks (2000a: 134–6) and Rosefeldt (2000: 104–5). What is crucial in this regard is that Kant emphasises that the 'same-sounding I' 'keeps in view', even if the underlying subject were replaced, implying that the formal unity of the 'I' does not correspond to a person's collective empirical representations (let alone to her substantial identity), but merely to an instance of synthetic thought (judgement) *directed at* a 'certain' compound of 'successively' apprehended empirical representations. With respect to psy-

6.3 The 'I think'-Proposition: The Analyticity of Apperception — 149

deed *I* was not duly responding, in the appropriate reflective manner, to the representations that I (*sensu lato*) had at that time but was merely giving free rein to my reproductive imagination. (To speak here of an 'I' in the strict sense of transcendental consciousness is not apposite.)⁵⁵

It is common for commentators to argue that Kant wants to exclude the possibility of a mere 'swarm of appearances [...] fill[ing] up our soul' (A111) without such appearances, potentially if not actually, being connected into a unity of consciousness. However, it is important to keep in mind that Kant's argument for the unity of consciousness involves a claim about problematic or conditional necessity. As he writes at A110, 'all appearances, *insofar as objects are to be given to us through them*, must stand under *a priori* rules of their synthetic unity' (emphasis added). The subordinate clause here must be read as a limiting condition. Similarly, when Kant argues that if there were no objective ground for the associability of our perceptions, then 'a multitude of perceptions and even an entire sensibility would be possible in which much empirical consciousness would be encountered in my mind, but separated, and without belonging to *one* consciousness of myself, which, however, is impossible' (A122), he does not mean to imply that it is impossible that some perceptions are indeed not connected into 'one consciousness of myself'. What he means to deny is the possibility that *all* of my perceptions lack such unity, which would a fortiori mean that I would have no cognitions at all, which in turn conflicts with a common sense view of objective experience as de facto given (the premise of the R-argument). Likewise, when Kant argues that without the unification into one consciousness I would be 'as multicolored, diverse a self [viz. a self that cannot properly be represented as numerically identical] as I [would] have representations' (B134 [AA 3: 110.7–9]), Kant does not deny the real possibility of a disparate psychological self, presumably because he is out to prove a numerically identical self over

---

chological continuity or perdurance of 'empirical consciousness in time', consider also *Met-Dohna*, AA 28: 683 (LM: 384).

55 It is not clear whether Kant complies with this proviso at all times. It seems that occasionally Kant hints at merely subjectively valid perceptions (e.g. judgements of perception) as also being forms of *thought*, which carry an 'I' (cf. *Prol* § 22, AA 4: 304–5). Apparently, such perceptions show as much *logical* unity as objectively valid judgements, or cognitions strictly speaking. At the same time, Kant maintains that subjectively valid statements (judgements of perception) with regard to my sensible states only relate to my *present* state of perception (*Prol* § 19, AA 4: 299). In other words, in such statements there would not be an identity 'throughout' (B132) between the various sensations or perceptions that I have, for they would not have been synthesised; and so, strictly speaking, no logical 'I think', in terms of 'the form of apperception, on which every experience depends and which precedes it' (A354), would accompany these sensations as such.

time, or a self-substance.[56] What Kant does want to underscore is that *if* there is to be a synthetic unity of representations, and thus a self *represented* as numerically identical, then a formal act of apperception is required which takes representations synthetically together and establishes the unity of consciousness. And since cognition requires a numerically identical self with regard to a given manifold in intuition, *this* manifold of representations must be regarded as subject to a unifying act of apperception.

6.3.3 Rigorous Coextensivity

A further observation is in order regarding the analyticity of the 'I think'-proposition and the relation between the analytic and synthetic unities of apperception. Certain commentators make it appear as if a distinction could be made between the satisfaction of the apperception principle, which requires synthesis, and an actual instantiation of the 'I think' as a reflection from the side of the thinking subject, which would be contingent on certain additional empirical conditions. For example, Allison states with regard to the 'I think' proposition, that

> this principle affirms only the necessity of the possibility of attaching the 'I think', not the necessity of actually doing so [...] it does not affirm that I must actually perform a reflective act in order to represent (think) anything. (1983: 137)[57]

I believe this reading is unwarranted. Such a reading would belie the rigorous coextensivity that I have argued underlies Kant's reasoning in point of the identity of discursive thought (see above Chapter 5). If the apperception principle is satisfied, then the 'I think' *actually* accompanies the manifold of my representations, even if this means that I am not *explicitly* empirically conscious of my combinatory act of apperceiving (we do not 'watch the synthesis', to quote Patricia Kitcher's [1990: 111, 126–7] well-known turn of phrase).[58] Certainly, at first

---

[56] In fact, Kant even asserts, at A364, that 'we can never make out whether this I (a mere thought) does not flow as well as all the other thoughts that are linked to one another through it'. The 'I think' is only persistent 'in the whole of the time of which we are conscious'. Hoppe (1983: 132–3, 217) precisely believes that Kant is out to deny the real possibility of a disparate self. Hoppe seems to think that Kant believes that for a concrete subject even to *be* a *psychological* subject she would have to be a self-conscious subject being conscious of her numerical identity.

[57] This view also appears to inform certain Fichtean readings of Kant (see e.g. Neuhouser 1990: 93, 97).

[58] More recently, Kitcher (2006: 194–5) appears to acknowledge an (at least) implicit awareness of synthesising activity.

blush Kant himself seems to be saying something along the lines suggested by the reading I reject. He writes at B134:

> The thought that these representations given in intuition all together belong *to me* means, accordingly, the same as that I unite them in a self-consciousness,[59] *or at least can unite them therein, and although it* [i.e. the thought, D.S.][60] *is itself not yet the consciousness of the synthesis of the representations, it still presupposes the possibility of the latter*, i.e., only because I can comprehend their manifold in a consciousness do I call them all together *my* representations. (AA 3: 110.3–5, emphasis added)

The clause 'or at least can unite them therein [*oder kann sie wenigstens darin vereinigen*]' seems crucial. It could be seen as evidence for the reading that is dismissed here. That is to say, Kant's words might be glossed as if implying only the *possibility* of being united in the analytic unity of consciousness for all synthesised representations, thus suggesting that the analytic unity is potentially de facto distinct from, or posterior to, my synthesised representations and that therefore the conditions for such analytic unity are 'not *yet*', as Kant says, satisfied upon the synthesis having occurred.[61] The thought that the representations in intuition belong to me and thus are to be considered unified in one self-consciousness is not *yet* consciousness of this synthesis, even though self-consciousness is not *possible* without the condition of synthesis being satisfied. In other words, one could infer from this that consciousness of synthesised manifolds can occur *without already* an explicit reflection (self-consciousness) accompanying my thus being (implicitly) conscious of it. On such a reading, 'yet' (*noch*) is interpreted temporally.

However, if this were indeed what Kant means, then it would contravene his belief that analytic unity of consciousness and synthesis are contemporaneous. At A108 he writes:

---

59 In the original text it says *einem Selbstbewußtsein*.
60 The original text has *er*, so refers to *der Gedanke*.
61 Paradoxically, whereas some commentators make it appear as if 'I think'-accompaniment were an *additional* feature to one's representations being synthesised, others hold, conversely, that discrete consciousnesses are *always already* analytically united and so formally imply the 'I think', even if *not yet* synthesised in the transcendental way (cf. Baum 1986: 97 ff., esp. 97n.; Wunderlich 2005: 174 ff.). In fact there is no paradox. Although the latter view seems to comport better with Kant's text here at B134, both views stem from the same failure to appreciate the rigorous coextensivity between the analytic unity of consciousness and synthetic unity of apperception.

> Thus the original and necessary consciousness of the identity of oneself is *at the same time* [*zugleich*] a consciousness of an equally necessary unity of the synthesis of all appearances in accordance with concepts. (emphasis added)

Consider also a passage earlier on, preceding the above-quoted passage at B134, where Kant writes that 'the act of pure apperception' (which *is* the 'I think'—see B137 and B401) is

> that self-consciousness which, in that [*indem*][62] it produces the representation *I think*, which must be able to accompany all others and which in all consciousness is one and the same, cannot be accompanied by any further representation. (B132, trans. modified)

Based on what Kant says here, it is evident not only that pure apperception is necessary for 'I think'-accompaniment but also that the synthetic act of apperception is the sufficient ground of the possibility

> for me to represent the *identity of the consciousness in these representations* itself, i.e., the *analytical* unity of apperception is only possible under the presupposition of some *synthetic* one. (B133 [AA 3: 109.22–5])

The analytical unity of consciousness comes about precisely in the act of adding one representation to the other, namely precisely *through* synthesis. Indeed, as Kant writes a bit earlier,

> this thoroughgoing identity of the apperception [...] is possible only *through* [*durch*] the consciousness of this synthesis. (AA 3: 109.13–15, emphasis added)

The relation to the identity of self-consciousness comes about, Kant says, 'by my *adding* one representation to the other and being conscious of their synthesis' (B133; cf. A103). In other words, the analytic unity that constitutes thoroughgoing identity of consciousness comes about *in the very apperceptive act of synthesising* the manifold of representations in a given intuition and *cannot fail* to come about in that very act. More precisely, analytic unity of consciousness in regard to my representations obtains *if and only if* representations have been synthetically combined under one representation (the 'I think'). By the bi-conditional implied in the principle that 'the *analytical* unity of apperception is only possible

---

[62] The German *indem* is better translated as 'in that' instead of 'because' (Guyer/Wood), for the clause explains that the production of the 'I think' is the very constitution of transcendental self-consciousness. The *indem* designates the contemporaneity of the production of the 'I think' and self-consciousness. Kemp Smith's 'while generating' captures the purport of the passage perfectly. See further below Section 6.4.

under the presupposition of some *synthetic* one' (B133) Kant means that the act of apperceiving the manifold of representations by virtue of synthesising them, viz. the synthetic unity of apperception, is contemporaneous with the analytic unity or awareness of identity among one's representations. To put it very bluntly, as Heidegger (1993: 319) does, 'das "Ich denke" besagt: Ich verbinde'. Synthesis is a logically 'antecedently [...] conceived' (B133n.) condition of the analytic unity of self-consciousness, the 'I think'. That is, a priori synthesis is both a necessary and sufficient condition for the representation of the analytical identity of self-consciousness. No analytic unity of the self obtains without a prior synthesis, but also no a priori synthesis fails to result in an analytic unity of apperception, since regarding my representations as thoroughly belonging to me 'means [...] the same as that I unite them in a self-consciousness' (B134). Therefore, rigorous coextensivity obtains between the synthetic and analytic unities of consciousness.

The interpretative problem in regard to the earlier quoted passage at B134 dissolves if we read it as saying that the thought of the unifiedness of representations in a self-consciousness cannot *literally* be the consciousness of the act of synthesising or 'adding' one representation to the other in terms of a psychological mental act taking place over time (that is, I consciously apprehend first representation A, then representation B, and so on). In other words, there is no actual (empirical) consciousness of synthesising activity (so no 'synthesis-watching').[63] Thus, the phrase should be interpreted as saying that despite the fact that we are not capable of being literally conscious of the synthesis, analytic unity of self-consciousness must be seen as presupposing synthesis as its under-

---

63 This might be taken as contrary to what Allison believes, who maintains that 'apperception involves an actual consciousness of this act' (1983: 272), although he also says that the consciousness is not psychological but epistemic (1983: 273) (see also Allison 1996: 62; cf. Allison 1996: 76). Allison also says, with reference to B419, that apperception is 'something real', a 'real mode of self-consciousness' (1983: 273). Cf. R5661, AA 18: 319.9 – 11; 319.32 – 5. In the *Critique*, Kant also appears to refer to apperception as an 'inner perception' (B401/A343) and as 'a unity of the action of which [the understanding] is conscious as such even without sensibility' (B153), thus of which one has consciousness of some sort. See also A115, where remarkably Kant refers to apperception as 'an *empirical* consciousness of the identity of these reproductive representations with the appearances' (emphasis added). However, in *Leningrad Fragment I* ('On inner sense'), Kant says that 'the proposition "I am" is not an experiential proposition' (Brandt & Stark 1987: 18 – 21 [NF: 364 – 6]). In R5661 ('Answer to the question: Is it an experience that we think?'), Kant maintains that 'the consciousness of instituting an experience or also of thinking in general is a *transcendental consciousness, not experience*' (AA 18: 318 – 19), and that 'consciousness is nothing empirical', by which he means 'transcendental consciousness' (AA 18: 319 [NF: 289 – 90]).

lying *logical* ground. In other words, though we are not empirically aware of the synthesis, let alone of the synthesised representations severally, we must assume that it is the necessary ground of the analytic unity of consciousness. Consider also a passage earlier at B132ff., where Kant writes:

> For the manifold representations that are given in a certain intuition would not all together be *my* representations if they did not all together belong to a unitary self-consciousness [*einem Selbstbewußtsein*]; i.e., as my representations (*even if I am not conscious of them as such*) they must yet necessarily be in accord with the condition under which alone they *can* stand together in a universal self-consciousness, because otherwise they would not throughout belong to me. (AA 3: 109.5–11, trans. modified and emphasis added)

The adverbial clause in parentheses 'even if I am not conscious of them as such' refers to the obscurity of the several representations that are taken together in one consciousness and thus constitute 'all my consciousness'.[64] Robert Pippin (1997: 41, 43) uses this passage as support for his reading of apperception in terms of an implicit reflexivity or an adverbial act of implicit *self-consciousness* in any course of experience (which, presumably, may become an explicit reflection).[65] However, neither the B134 passage nor the passage under consideration here indicate the implicitness of the allegedly reflective act of the 'I think', or, self-consciousness, in terms of a possible second-order reflection but rather the implicitness of the synthesis of my representations, the satisfaction of which is warranted by a de facto accompaniment of an 'I think' as the unitary representation required for any synthesis.

6.4 Deriving the Categories of Modality

Having surveyed a series of arguments and possible interpretations of claims advanced by Kant in § 16 specifically relating to the identity of the thinking self, let us now consider, more explicitly, the derivation of the first set of categories from the principle of apperception, namely the categories of modality. Inevitably, I

---

[64] Cf. A103, where Kant speaks of a weak consciousness, which is only noticeable 'in the effect, but not in the act itself'. It concerns an indirect consciousness of the synthesis. Interestingly, Kitcher (1999: 368, 346ff., 372ff.) speaks, in a similar respect, of Kant's commitment to a conception of self-consciousness as a Leibnizian-type obscure consciousness. In Chapter 8, I argue that transcendental apperception has an intensive magnitude of 0, and thus does not amount to empirical consciousness, but is rather the 'negation' of empirical consciousness, by means of which its determination is made possible.
[65] See my account of Pippin's views in this regard in Schulting (2017a), ch. 3.

cover some of the ground I have traversed in the previous sections. I contend that Kant's argument regarding 'the thoroughgoing identity' of apperception, or what he also calls 'the *analytical* unity of apperception' (B133), expressed by the '*I think*'-proposition, which states that the '*I think* must *be able* to accompany all my representations' (B131), concerns the derivation of the categories of modality. In their 'merely logical significance' in abstraction from their empirical use for the cognition of objects of experience the categories of modality 'analytically express the form of *thinking*' (A219/B267),[66] which however does not mean they just concern *logical* conditions. The categories are the *transcendental* conditions of subjective thought as much as of an object in general, of which logical possibility is one, fundamental, condition. By claiming that the categories are derivable *from* apperception, I could be taken to be claiming that apperception is somehow a properly basic *self-standing* principle, which functions as a first premise from which the process of deduction would proceed.[67] However, Kant could not allow such a self-standing *principle* in the proof of the legitimate 'application' of the categories, as it would invite an infinite regress in the explanation of their a priori source. The first, implicit, premise of the P-argument, starting in § 16, is instead merely the given *fact* of discursive thought or the understanding or apperception itself, that is, some 'I' that is the subject or agent of some arbitrary thought, a 'simple' 'I' that thinks.[68] This fact is *expressed* by the first category,

---

[66] This is similar to the way that the modality of judgement adds nothing to the content of a judgement but 'concerns only the value of the copula in relation to thinking in general' (A74/B99–100). The ontological aspect of this relation is significant. The copula is the way that being is manifested in judgement in terms of an objectively valid relation (cf. B141–2). For this latter aspect, see Chapter 10.

[67] There is some controversy in the literature over whether Kant must indeed be taken to mean a deduction '*from* a principle' (*aus dem Grundsatze* [B142]) and not just a proof 'in accordance with' (*nach einem Princip* [A67/B92] or *vermittelst einer Idee* [A64/B89]), which is then not a deduction in the standard sense. See Wolff (1995: 182–4) for an illuminating discussion. From A300/B357, where Kant gives a definition of syllogistic reasoning, it is clear that the standard notion of 'syllogism [as] a form of derivation of a cognition from a principle [*aus einem Princip*]' does not conflict with cognition 'according to a principle [*nach einem Princip*]', which occurs in the following sentence of Kant's text. I concur with Wolff's explanation.

[68] In the context of the analysis of the Deduction, however, the 'I think' of apperception emerges, so to speak, from the transcendental reflection, in the preceding section (§ 15), on the need for a 'higher unity'. I discuss this element a bit more in Chapter 10. Note that the 'simple representation' of an 'I' that thinks, and is itself a 'purely intellectual' representation (B423n.), does not imply that the thought that is thought is itself a *representation*, a sensation, say. It is a discursive, *cognitive* thought, a 'concept', not an 'intuition' (cf. A68/B93), which is 'accompanied' by the 'wholly empty representation *I*' which 'thinks' this thought. This 'I' is a 'transcendental subject of thoughts=x, which is recognized only through the thoughts that are its predicates'

with which the derivation of the pure concepts of the understanding starts out, namely 'actuality' or 'existence', *from* which the subsequent premises of the P-argument are inferred. The 'I think' expresses an 'I am' or 'I exist' (B157, B422n.).

At A355, when comparing the 'I am' with Descartes' *cogito ergo sum*,[69] Kant states that '*I am simple* signifies no more than that this representation *I* encompasses not the least manifoldness within itself, and that it is an absolute (though merely logical) unity'. Kant makes it clear that the 'formal proposition of apperception, *I think*' (A354) is a simple representation, 'a mere Something' even, that does not translate into 'a cognition of the simplicity of the subject itself, since its properties are entirely abstracted from' (A355). However, this does not mean that the 'I think' refers to an impersonal something, although Kant does make it seem that way. See for example the well-known phrase at B404/A346: 'Through this I, or He, or It (the thing), which thinks, nothing further is represented than a transcendental subject of thoughts=x'. Also, 'the consciousness in itself is not even a representation distinguishing a particular object, but rather a form of representation in general' (B404/A346). Nevertheless, the 'I think' is a representation through which '*I* think anything' (B404/A346, emphasis added); it is not something impersonal that does the thinking. Although it is a general, simple, logical representation, the 'I think' is a representation that *I* employ when *I* am thinking, and so it immediately refers to myself as the agent of thought. Kant says: '[I]n the consciousness of myself in mere thinking I am the *being itself*, about which, however, nothing yet is thereby given to me for thinking' (B429).[70] This indicates the immediate evidence of *my* existence as a given (B157n.).

If we look at the metaphysical concept of 'actuality' or 'existence' to which Kant frequently refers in his *Lectures on Metaphysics*, we can get a clearer view of the way in which in thought itself an existence or actuality is expressed, from which the P-argument takes off. Already well before the *Critique* (A598/B626), Kant argued in *Beweisgrund* that 'existence' is not a real predicate (AA 2: 72–3). Existence does not add to all the determinations or properties of some thing, when this thing is posited as existing. Existence is the absolute positing of a thing, with all its determinations (*Met-L₂*, AA 28: 554),[71] or '[a]ctuality is absolute positing <*positio absoluta*>' (*Met-Mron*, AA 29: 822 [LM: 175]). All three categories of modality are 'concepts by which a thing is posited with all predicates'

(A345–6/B404). It is the logical 'I' of the 'sheer spontaneity of combining the manifold' of one's representations (B428).

[69] In the *Meditations* this is actually 'ego sum, ego existo' (AT VII: 25).

[70] See further Schulting (2017a), ch. 9 for references to the secondary literature about the relation between the 'I think' and an underlying noumenal self.

[71] Cf. R5759: 'Everything that exists is thoroughly determined' (AA 18: 346 [NF: 297]).

(*Met-Mron*, AA 29: 821 [LM: 175]). In addition to absolute positing, Kant also talks about relative positing. Kant writes in *Beweisgrund* that

> something can be thought as posited merely relatively, or, to express the matter better, it can be thought merely as the relation (*respectus logicus*) of something as a characteristic mark of a thing. In this case, being, that is to say, the positing of this relation, is nothing other than the copula in a judgement. (AA 2: 73 [TPha: 119])

For Kant, 'positing' is 'being':

> The concept of positing or setting [*Position oder Setzung*] is perfectly simple: it is identical with the concept of being in general. (*Beweisgrund*, AA 2: 73 [TPha: 119])

This concerns Being in the emphatic sense. The absolute positing of the being that I am that is implied in my thinking is a positing of my being with all its properties and so as thoroughly determined as a thing in itself, although I have no knowledge of these properties since my existence could be determined only 'sensibly' (B430), namely in possible experience, for which 'I am also given to myself in intuition' (B157). The actual being that I am, as a thinking being, does not contain more predicates than my logically possible self; the difference lies in the types of positing involved in being merely a possible thinking self and being an actual thinking self. '[I]n possibility these predicates [of my thinking self] were posited only in thoughts, relatively' (*Met-L*$_2$, AA 28: 554 [LM: 319–20]).[72] This evidently applies to existential judgements, which is the context of the discussion in *Beweisgrund*, but it also holds of the way that thoughts as predicates of the 'I' relate to this 'I' (cf. B404/A346). I can think the complete set of all my possible thoughts problematically, that is, insofar as I know what it means to use the indexical 'I' in all possible cases of it being instantiated, so purely look at the *formal* or conceptual relation between my thoughts and the 'I think' that accompanies them. But I do not know beforehand if and when the 'I' will be instantiated for any representation accompanied (other than now[73]). That is, I cannot really determine my own thinking self as a *real* self, for it would mean that I would have to be omniscient to effectively know all my *possible* representations that completely determine my thinking self *and* know all possible instantiations of my thinking self as accompanying those representations.[74] Still, in my actual

---

72 Cf. R5772 (1780s), AA 18: 349.
73 That is to say, in *having* this purely formal thought, which presupposes at any rate the *datum* of that thought, and so the instantiation of the 'I think' as the agent of that thought.
74 The categories of modality do not apply to noumena, as reported in the *Mrongovius* lectures: 'Possibility, actuality, necessity are not concepts of things in themselves; rather possibility al-

accompanying my representations I do posit myself absolutely in that I am immediately conscious of my existence (A355; B157n.), and thus posit myself with all my representations. To this extent, I am, as thinking self, not merely logically possible, but also really possible, that is, actual (cf. Bxxvi n.).[75] The set of 'all my representations' that I am able to actually *determine* is the set of representations that I accompany now, but nonetheless the 'I' that I posit absolutely, as really existing, is the thinking self *with all* possible representations, even though I cannot *determine* the complete set of all possible representations.[76] It is in this sense that my actual thinking self that is posited absolutely is the *same* self as my possible (problematically conceived) thinking self, relative to which all my representations are posited (cf. *Met-Volck*, AA 28: 410, 412). An actual 'I think' accompanying 'all my representations' must be in accordance with the logical possibility of the 'I think' accompanying 'all my representations' *in all its possible instantiations*.

The actual instantiation of an 'I think' thus implies the possible self with all my possible representations (*ab esse ad posse valet consequentia*). However, the converse does not hold: the possible 'I' accompanying all my representations does not entail that there *is* an actual 'I think' accompanying all my representations, in accord with the rule *a posse ad esse non valet consequentia* (however, *a non posse ad non esse valet consequentia*) (*Met-L₂*, AA 28: 555). Nevertheless, the class of all *possible* representations accompanied by an 'I think' (*C*) is not greater than the class of all actual representations accompanied by *C*. In *Metaphysik Volckmann*, Kant writes:

---

ready presupposes the thing with all its predicates, and is the comparison of the thing with the laws of thinking, whether it can be thought or not. [...]' (*Met-Mron*, AA 29: 822 [LM: 175]). Notice, however, that Kant here takes the modal categories for granted and considers how they apply to objects of experience or knowledge. In our case, we attempt to look at how the modal categories are implied in discursive thought at all, in which case we do not look at how *a thing is compared with* the laws of thinking, but at the nature of the laws of thinking themselves.

75 R6290 (1783–84): 'That something is actual because it is possible in accordance with a general concept does not follow. But that something is actual because it is thoroughly determined by its concept among all that is possible and distinguished as one from all that is possible means the same as that it is not merely a general concept, but the representation of a particular thing through concepts thoroughly determined in relation to everything possible' (AA 18: 558 [NF: 353]).

76 R5710: 'Everything that exists is thoroughly determined; but it is not this thoroughgoing determination that constitutes the concept of existence, rather that a thing is posited absolutely and not merely in relation to its concept' (AA 18: 332 [NF: 294]).

> In the actual nothing more can be thought than in the merely possible, for if the actual were to contain more than the possible which I thought earlier, then the actual would not be the same possible but something else. (*Met-Volck*, AA 28: 413, trans. mine)

By conversion, the possible cannot contain *more* than the actual for the *same* thing. It is of course not necessary that all possible representations become actual, but that does not mean that the possible exceeds the actual; this is different from saying that there are all sorts of possible entities that are not or could not be actual, since we can think up all sorts of *entia imaginaria* (cf. *Met-L$_2$*, AA 28: 555).[77]

Guyer's (1980: 208) claim that there is a priori knowledge of the synthetic unity of all my representations as an 'advance guarantee' can be modified in such a way that one reads it as saying that the thoroughgoing determined totality of the set of all possible representations (cf. A116) is an advance guarantee that any actual instantiation of C accompanying all my representations (c) must be regarded as a priori 'unified' with all other possible instantiations of C accompanying c, but *not* an advance guarantee that there necessarily *is* an actual instantiation of C, nor that *all* representations regardless must be regarded as a priori 'unified' with all other possible instantiations of C (the class of *all* possible representations is much greater than the class of all *my* possible representations), or indeed *that* there necessarily is representing going on.

The Kantian reason for denying the possibility of determining an original *synthetic* a priori unity of all possible representations is that I cannot, other than perhaps 'sensibly' (B430), thoroughly determine my existence. To cognise the real possibility of my existence means that (1) my existence must be posited and (2) an empirical intuition must be given to my thought to be able to *determine* my existence (cf. A601/B629, B157n.); and since my existence can only be posited through an actual 'I think', an actual 'I think' thinking its representations (all my representations) must be instantiated. I cannot know the *metaphysical* possibility of my existence.[78] I therefore do not believe one can interpret Kant's arguments in the first half of §16 (AA 3: 108.19–109.12), where Kant speaks of the *transcendental* unity of self-consciousness, in such a way that an *original* combination of all of a self's (possible) representations is concerned

---

[77] Cf. A230–1/B283. Kant here specifically contemplates the possibility of other forms of experience, 'the possibility of things extend[ing] further than experience can reach' or also 'whether my perceptions could belong to more than one possible experience' (A230/B283), which he denies for all that can be experienced must be connected in accord with the rules of empirical experience. See also A234–5/B287n.

[78] Cf. *Met-Mron*, AA 29: 811–12: 'Metaphysical possibility is where the matter in and for itself is possible without relation to my thoughts' (LM: 166).

here, which would be *prior to* the synthesis in virtue of the activity of a self (Wunderlich 2005: 215; Henrich 1976: 58 – 9).[79] The title 'transcendental' makes it clear that it concerns a unity that is dependent on an a priori 'original' subjective *act*, 'an act of *spontaneity*', that 'produces the representation *I think*, which must be able to accompany all others and which in all consciousness is one and the same' (B132).

This last quote might still be read as if indeed a primordial unity of *all possible* representations were concerned that *precedes* the act of accompaniment by the 'I think'. But, first, this would make it unintelligible why the 'I think' is a representation no 'further representation' than which can be regarded as more original. The grammatical structure of the complex sentence at B132 is such that 'self-consciousness' is itself the representation that 'cannot be accompanied by any further representation'. Kant writes there:

> Ich nenne sie die reine Apperception, um sie von der empirischen zu unterscheiden, oder auch die ursprüngliche Apperception, **[EC1]** weil sie dasjenige Selbstbewußtsein ist, **[EC2]** was, **[EC3]** in dem es die Vorstellung: Ich denke, hervorbringt, **[EC4]** die alle andere muß begleiten können und in allem Bewußtsein ein und dasselbe ist, von keiner weiter begleitet werden kann. (AA 3: 108.28 – 109.2)

If we look at the dependent clause 'weil sie dasjenige Selbstbewußtsein ist' **[EC1]**, we notice that the infinitive form of the participle 'begleitet' in the embedded relative clause 'was ... von keiner weiter begleitet werden kann' **[EC2]** that goes with the subject 'dasjenige Selbstbewußtsein' (and of which **[EC1]** is the matrix clause) is also used in the embedded relative clause 'die ... ist' that goes with the subject 'die Vorstellung: Ich denke' **[EC4]** (of which 'in dem ... hervorbringt' **[EC3]** is the matrix clause). The sense of the notion of 'accompanying' that Kant means here is precisely that whatever does the 'accompanying' is the vehicle of all representations without itself being accompanied by any further representation. This strongly suggests that the original self-consciousness (the self of the subject noun of **[EC1]**) here *is* the self of the 'I think' (the object noun of **[EC3]**). This is further confirmed by Kant's use of the connective *indem*.

---

[79] It seems Wunderlich and Henrich believe that the transcendental unity of self-consciousness is merely an *analytic* unity, but that does not make sense given that it concerns a *transcendental* unity from which *cognition* should be able to arise. Although in B132, the first paragraph of § 16, synthesis is not yet mentioned, it is clear from the first sentence of the next paragraph (starting in B133) that synthesis must be seen as implicitly contained in the transcendental unity of consciousness. B133 subsequently makes it clear that synthesis is analytically implied in the identity of transcendental self-consciousness.

6.4 Deriving the Categories of Modality — 161

Moreover, secondly, the context makes it clear that there is a reciprocal relation between a *given* manifold in 'a certain intuition' (B132 [AA 3: 109.5 – 6]) and the subject that 'produces the representation *I think*' (B132 [AA 3: 108.30 – 109.1]). This points to the necessity of an actual instantiation of the 'I think', an existing 'I' that thinks, in order for all its (my) representations to be actually accompanied. The original self-consciousness of transcendental apperception and the 'I think' are equiprimordial, and given that a given manifold in a 'certain' intuition is required for the actual instantiation of an 'I think', the original self-consciousness, or the 'transcendental unity of self-consciousness', *exists* (actually) only when 'caused' to exist by a synthetic act of the thinking subject, which posits its existence absolutely with all its determinations (the element of causality will be the topic of Chapter 7). The cause of existence is not external to the subject but contemporaneous with the act of synthesis, which is also suggested by Kant's assertion that 'I exist as an intelligence that is merely conscious of its faculty for combination' (B158). Also, at B134, Kant states that the 'thought that these representations given in intuition all together belong *to me* means [...] the same as that I unite them in a self-consciousness', confirming that the belonging together of my representations is reciprocal with my unifying them, meaning that the 'belonging together' is dependent on an *act* of the thinking self.

Hence, the 'transcendental unity of self-consciousness' cannot be seen to be equivalent to the unity of all *possible* representations accompanied by C, presumably a substantial thinking 'thing' (a *res cogitans*) that *precedes* the transcendental self, which is merely a 'logical unity of every thought' (A398). Such a thinking 'thing' could not be determined, as it would involve a synthetic 'extended cognition' (A398). The transcendental unity of self-consciousness is just the a priori *formal* unity of all representations that are accompanied by an *actual* 'I think' to which is given a manifold of representations 'in a certain intuition', for all possible tokenings of the 'I think'. The 'transcendental unity of self-consciousness' is equiprimordial with an *actual* 'I think' accompanying all of its representations (all my representations). In other words, there would be no transcendental unity of self-consciousness if there were not at least one instance of an *actual* 'I think' thinking its representations, for the transcendental unity of self-consciousness has no metaphysical or ontological status independently of an actual 'I think' and is merely a 'logical unity of the subject' of thought (cf. A355 – 6).

What about the contradictory or negative counterpart of the category possibility, that is, 'impossibility'? Impossibility follows from the fact that the 'I think' accompanies all *my* representations and not any arbitrary representation r (P3/4-representations). The rigid relation between the 'I' and 'my representations' implies that strictly speaking *I* cannot *think r* as such, for I can only think my own representations. Now whatever I am not able to accompany, I do not accompany (*ab non posse ad non esse valet consequentia*) although *r* could still be going on in some mind. But *r* would be *nothing for me*, as thinker (hence Kant's phrase 'the representation [...] would be nothing for me' [B132]). So the contradictory of the category of existence of the 'I think' (not: of any arbitrary representation), 'non-existence', is entailed by the impossibility of thinkingly accompanying any arbitrary representation *r*. I cannot assert however that the failure of an instantiation of the 'I think' at time *t* entails the impossibility of the instantiation of the 'I think' at any time other than time *t* (*ab non esse ad non posse non valet consequentia*).

Kant says that if a representation would not be thought by me, it would mean

> as much as to say that the representation would *either* [1] *be impossible or else* [2] at least would *be nothing for me*. (B132, emphasis added)

The first disjunct [1] is often ignored in commentary. What could Kant mean by a representation which it is impossible to think? Perhaps the representation is logically impossible, hence cannot exist and therefore I cannot think it. But this seems too trivial, for an intrinsically inconceivable representation is ipso facto unthinkable. I believe Kant means something different here, also because he says that a representation is concerned that 'would be represented in me' but 'could not be thought at all', implying that the representation does exist, thus excluding the trivial reading of mere inconceivability. What Kant means here is this: it points to the circumstance that if, for any tokening of the 'I think', I were not to accompany a representation that is mine *stricto sensu* (that is, in the sense of belonging to the set of all possible determinations of my thoroughgoing identity), there would arise a contradiction with regard to the identity between the set of possible representations that are mine *stricto sensu* and the set of actual representations that are mine *stricto sensu*, and so the representation that cannot be accompanied by my thought must be impossible in the sense that the representation does in fact not belong to my thoroughgoing identity as a thinking agent for all possible tokenings of my 'I think'; that is, it does not belong to the set of all my possible representations, and so it cannot possibly be thought by me. And what it is impossible to think cannot be thought de facto either. If any possible representation is mine *stricto sensu*, then it is impossible that that representation is represented and I do *not* accompany it as mine for any possible tokening of the 'I think'. So if I do *not* accompany a particular representation, some arbitrary representation *r* that is occurrent at time *t*, then *that* representation is not mine—neither as an actual representation, which seems obvious, but nor as a possible representation, for the only possible representations that I can actually accompany are the representations that belong to the set of *my* possible representations (not to be confused with an existential unity of representations) and not any of the representations that are yours, hers or *x*'s. The only representations that I ever accompany are my own. This is what Kant means by saying that if it were the case that some representation would not be able to be thought by me, it would be impossible, for it would be impossible for that representation to be one of the set of *my* possible representations that I am capable of thinking. This reading is confirmed by the second disjunct.

The second disjunct **[2]** qualifies the first (indicated by the words 'at least [*wenigstens*]') by acknowledging the possibility that a representation is not impossible per se (it could be actualised by someone else's thinking it) but just is not a representation that belongs to my thoroughgoing identity and so could a fortiori not be actualised by me by thinking it. The second disjunct thus qualifies the first in the sense that impossibility does not eo ipso imply general inconceivability and thus non-existence per se, but rather non-existence before the 'I'. Kant wants to make sure that he is not making any existence claims regarding the presence of representations in someone's mind. There could be representations present *in* me (my brain) that could also be actualised, that is, actually represented, without these representations being *my* representations in the sense of being actually accompanied by my 'I think'. These representations do not belong to my identity as a thinking agent (an 'I think'), regardless of whether it concerns my possible or actual thoughts. They just exist in some mind. So Kant makes a subtle distinction here between, on the one hand, a representation's impossibility in terms of not belonging to my thoroughgoing identity (which eo ipso precludes it from being *thought* by me) and the existence per se of a representation, on the other.

This yields the following premises for the derivation of the first two categories of modality:

> D1. The fact of discursive thought indicates the *act* of thought or thought's actuality or *existence*, viz. the fact that *I am* the actual subject of my thought whenever I think, meaning that representations that are occurrently thought and accompanied by the identical representation 'I think' exist before the 'I'.
>
> D2. The act of thought presupposes a *possible* 'I think' accompanying all my possible representations, and hence the *possibility* of thinkingly accompanying 'all my representations', which are analytically related to the identical representation 'I' for all representations so accompanied.
>
> D3. The possibility of thinkingly accompanying 'all my representations' analytically implies the *impossibility* of thinkingly accompanying (but not of representing) representations other than 'all my representations' inasmuch as such representations that are other than 'all my

representations' are not analytically related to an identical representation 'I' and so do not belong to the unity of all my possible representations.

D4. The non-actuality or *non-existence* of 'I think'-thought is entailed by representations that are not contained in the unity of all my possible representations, meaning that such representations that do not belong to the unity of all of my possible representations do not exist *before* the 'I' (they are 'nothing for me', though they could exist 'per se').

These results show that

D5. The category of 'existence (/non-existence)' pertains to the identity of discursive thought and hence is analytically derivable from it.

D6. The category of 'possibility (/impossibility)' pertains to the identity of discursive thought and hence is analytically derivable from it.

Now what about the third category of modality, the category of 'necessity'? In a letter to Johann Schultz, of 17 February 1784, Kant writes that

[f]or although the third category does certainly arise out of a uniting of the first and second, it does not arise out of their mere conjunction but rather out of a *connection whose possibility itself constitutes a concept*, and this concept is a particular category. [...] I find that just as a syllogism shows in its conclusion something more than the operations of the understanding and judgment required by the premises, viz., *a further particular operation belonging specifically to reason*, so too, the third category is a particular, to some extent original, concept. (*Corr*, AA 10: 366–7)

In the *Critique,* Kant is somewhat cryptic as to the need for a trichotomy. He just says that

the third category always arises from the combination of the first two in its class

and that

the combination of the first and second in order to bring forth the third concept requires a special act of the understanding, which is not identical with that act performed in the first and second. (B110–11)

But this could be interpreted in the way that Schultz suggested in his letter to Kant, namely that since every third category is derivable from the other two preceding concepts, the 'third category in each group should be eliminated [...] since I take "category" to mean simply a basic concept that is not derived from any prior concept' (*Corr*, AA 10: 354). But Kant has a reason for adhering to the trichotomy and not seeing the third category in each group as 'merely derivative' and not itself 'an ancestral concept' (B111). In the Introduction to the *Critique of the Power of Judgement*, Kant provides a clue:

> It has been thought suspicious that my divisions in pure philosophy almost always turn out to be threefold. But that is in the nature of the matter. If a division is to be made *a priori*, then it will either be *analytic*, in accordance with the principle of contradiction, and then it is always twofold (*quodlibet ens est aut A aut non A*). Or it is *synthetic*; and if in this case it is to be derived from *concepts a priori* (not, as in mathematics, from the *a priori* intuition corresponding to the concept), then, in accordance with what is requisite for synthetic unity in general, namely (1) a condition, (2) something conditioned, (3) the concept that arises from the unification of the conditioned with its condition, the division must necessarily be a trichotomy. (CJ, AA 5: 197n.)[80]

Somewhat earlier, in a *Reflexion* contemporaneous with the *Critique of Pure Reason* (1783–84), this exhaustive philosophical trichotomy is confirmed:

> For this reason there are three logical functions under a certain title, hence also three categories: because two of them demonstrate the unity of consciousness in two *oppositis*, while the third in turn combines the consciousness of the two. Further kinds of unity of consciousness cannot be conceived. For if *a* is a consciousness that connects a manifold, and *b* is another which connects in the opposite way, then *c* is the connection of *a* and *b*. (R5854, AA 18: 370 [NF: 300])

If we look at the passage in the *Critique of the Power of Judgement*, the conditioned here, in the case of the categories of modality, would be the existence, or absolute position, or instantiation, of the 'I think'; the condition would be the logical possibility of the set of all my representations relative to the possible 'I think', that is, the analytical rule that all my representations are accompanied by the same 'I think', the common representation that is shared by them.[81] The conceiving of the relation between the condition and conditioned yields the third category of modality: necessity. The *unification* of the *relata*, condition and conditioned, is not reducible to either of the *relata*, so it amounts to a *sui generis* concept. That is to say, if the 'I think' 'exists', is posited absolutely, or is instantiated, that is, there is a given discursive thought by some thinker, then necessarily the 'I think' is posited in accordance with the rule that all my representations are posited relative to the 'I think', thus presupposing this analytical rule as a condition for the act of thought. This trichotomous relation eo ipso means that

---

[80] Cf. Wolff (1995: 160–4).
[81] Cf. R4298 (1770s), where Kant defines 'possibility' as 'agreement [...] with a rule', actuality as 'simply being posited [*Position schlechthin*]' and necessity as 'being posited in accordance with a rule [*Position nach einer Regel*]' (AA 17: 499 [NF: 126]).

I have no insight into the *absolute* necessity (the metaphysical possibility or *Realnotwendigkeit*[82]) of my thinking self: I do not know *if* or *when* the 'I think' will be next instantiated, and have no determinative insight into the complete set of all my possible representations, or, of all of the possible instantiations of the 'I think'. In other words, there is no a priori knowledge, or knowledge *sans phrase*, of the unity of all my possible (past, present, future) representations.

The necessity involved here is a hypothetical necessity,[83] which means a necessity that is an 'actuality insofar as it can be cognised *a priori*' 'in some respect <*secundum quid*>' (*Met-L₂*, AA 28: 557 [LM: 322]), or that which is 'being posited in accordance with a rule' (R4298, AA 17: 499 [NF: 126]). That is to say, I know that, necessarily, if the 'I think' is instantiated, then the 'I think' accompanies all my representations, which is the rule of the logical possibility of thought that must be satisfied for an instantiation of an act of thought.[84] Absolute necessity would be actuality insofar as it can be cognised a priori *simpliciter*. Absolute necessity would then be the *same* as actuality *tout court*, and hence the same as an a priori *determination* of—in the case of the thinking self—the existential unity of all my *possible* representations. As a discursive thinker, not being omniscient, I have no ability to determine absolute, unconditioned necessity, which 'for human reason [is] the true abyss' (A613/B641).[85]

The contradictory of the category 'necessity' is 'contingency', meaning that for any representations for which the rule of the logical possibility of thought, namely that the 'I think' is the common representation of all my representations, is not satisfied it holds that it is entirely *contingent* that they are accompanied by a possible 'I think'. This points to P3-representations which do not exist before the 'I' and have *as such* no epistemic relevance[86]—they might or might not be taken up by an apperceiving 'I'.[87] This now yields the following results:

> D7. Necessarily, if the 'I think' exists, then the rule that all my representations are accompanied by the 'I think' is satisfied.

---

82 *Met-Volck*, AA 28: 418.
83 Cf. Heimsoeth (1956: 30–1) on the Leibnizian-Wolffian background of the term.
84 Interestingly, in the *Reflexion* just quoted (R4298,) Kant elaborates on the categories of possibility, actuality and necessity: 'The first is thought, without being given. The second is given, without being thought. The third is given insofar as it is thought' (AA 17: 500 [NF: 126]).
85 Cf. *Met-Volck*, AA 28: 417; R3717, AA 17: 260–2; R4007, AA 17: 383. For further references, see Motta (2007: 98–9, 130 ff.).
86 Cf. Kant's letter to Herz of 26 May 1789. Kant here maintains in regard to sense data that do not comply with the conditions under which I can know that I have them that 'consequently *for me, as knowing being*, they would be absolutely nothing' (*Corr*, AA 11:52.7–8, emphasis added).
87 See further my response to Quarfood (2014) in Schulting (2017a), ch. 2.

6.4 Deriving the Categories of Modality — 167

D8. It is contingent that for representations for which the rule that all my representations are accompanied by the 'I think' is not satisfied, the 'I think' is in fact instantiated.

These last results show that

D9. The category 'necessity (/contingency)' pertains to the identity of discursive thought and hence is analytically derivable from it.

This threefold modality ('possibility', 'actuality', 'necessity') is the quintessence of the operative premise of the progressive argument, namely the proposition 'The *I think* must *be able* to accompany all my representations', from which certain other necessary underlying characteristics of thought are logically inferable, as will be shown in subsequent chapters.

7 Apperception and the Categories of Relation

7.1 Introduction

In this chapter, I undertake a reconstruction of the derivation of the categories of relation, namely 'substance', 'cause' and 'community', from the principle of apperception. I explain that self-activity or spontaneity lies at the heart of Kant's understanding of the ground of thinking as such and hence accounts for the category of substance, which in turn must be seen in terms of a self-initiating causality that has no further causal antecedents (spontaneity as a freestanding principle), thus accounting for the category of 'cause–effect'. This relates to the function of synthesis, which is that on which any analytic unity of consciousness, that is, the analytic unity of apperception—which it has been explained in Chapter 6 issues from the modality of thought itself—is necessarily dependent. The 'pure, original, unchanging consciousness' of transcendental apperception, which points to the subject as substance, fundamentally rests on a function of self-initiating or spontaneous causality. In explicating these necessary features of thought, I consider Kant's arguments in § 15 regarding self-activity as the ground for a unified complex thought that is based on a combination of representations. This, then, leads me to discuss the third 'moment' of relation, namely the 'reciprocity between agent and patient' or 'community'. This third 'moment' comprises the first two 'moments' of relation together and accounts for the relational constituent elements of discursive thought.

In Section 7.2, I consider 'substance'. In Section 7.3, I consider 'causality'. In Section 7.4, I consider 'community' by looking at Kant's arguments in § 15 of the B-Deduction concerning 'combination' and 'self-activity'. In Section 7.5, I add to the D-argument the premises that constitute the argument showing that the categories of relation are derivable from the principle of apperception.

7.2 'Substance'

The categories of relation are routinely seen by commentators as the central and most important categories. Kant himself often gives this impression too: 'the category of substance [is] the most preeminent' and 'thus the basis of all other cognition' (*Met-Mron*, AA 29: 769–70 [LM: 177–8]). Of all the synthetic principles, the Analogies, which belong to the dynamical principles, and delineate the categories of relation with respect to the 'three *modi* of time [...] *persistence, succession, and simultaneity*', that is, the 'three rules of all temporal relations of appearances' (B219/A177), are given the most attention in the literature. Also the Paralogisms highlight the centrality of the category of 'substance'. I am here not concerned with Kant's arguments in the Analogies as such, nor with the purpose of the Paralogisms per se, but want merely to tease out any hints of the connection between the subject of thinking, apperception, and the categories of relation, specifically 'substance' in the case of the Paralogisms.

Also some *Reflexionen* and lecture notes from around the period of the *Critique* reflect Kant's concern with formulating the categories of relation, although most of these (bar one that I consider below) are not very informative about a possible connection with apperception. Of course, we should also be careful not to attach too much value to notes that were not written by Kant himself. Nevertheless, some of the lecture notes are a good source for basic definitions, which will be helpful for understanding Kant's reasoning regarding the connection between the categories of relation and apperception. For example in the *Lectures on Metaphysics*, 'substance' is defined as '[t]hat which cannot exist otherwise than as subject' (*Met-Mron*, AA 29: 769 [LM: 177]) or as '[t]hat which exists without being the determination of another' (*Met-Mron*, AA 29: 770 [LM: 178]),[1] whereas an 'accident' is 'what cannot exist otherwise than as predicate' (*Met-Mron*, AA 29: 769 [LM: 177]) or 'that which exists only as determination' (*Met-Mron*, AA 29: 770 [LM: 178]); that is, '[a]ccidents are mere modes <modi> of the existence of substance and these cannot be apart from that substance; for they exist as predicates and these cannot be apart from the subject' (*Met-Mron*, AA 29: 769 [LM: 177]). In the First Analogy, Kant formulates the definition for 'accident' thus:

> The determinations of a substance that are nothing other than particular ways for it to exist are called *accidents*. They are always real, since they concern the existence of the substance (negations are merely determinations that express the non-being of something in the substance). (B229/A186)

Regarding the relation between substance and accident, Kant writes:

> If we leave aside all accidents then substance remains, this is the pure subject in which everything *inheres or the substantial*. (*Met-Mron*, AA 29: 770–1 [LM: 179], emphasis added)[2]

However, strictly speaking the substantial is the subject *in abstraction from* its accidents and 'in which no accidents inhere' (*Met-Mron*, AA 29: 771 [LM: 179]), and which can never be known, whereas the *substance with accidents* is *related*

---

1 Cf. B149.
2 Cf. *Prol* § 46, AA 4: 333–4.

to the substantial, which is the 'pure subject'.[3] In the First Analogy, Kant says the following about the relation between accident and substance:

> Now if one ascribes a particular existence to this real in substance [...], then this existence is called 'inherence', in contrast to the existence of the substance, which is called 'subsistence'. (A186–7/B230)

Furthermore, in the *Lectures on Metaphysics*, Kant says that

> [w]ith a substance we can have two relations <*respectus*>: in relation to accidents <*respectu accidentium*> it has power insofar as it is the ground of their inherence; and in relation to the first subject without any accidents, that is the substantial. (*Met-Mron* AA 29: 770 [LM: 178])

This introduces the notion of 'power', which points to the other category of relation, causality, which I address in Section 7.3 below. On the other hand, in another lecture note, it is said that '[t]he relation of the accidents to the substance is not the relation of the cause to the effect' (*Met-L₂*, AA 28: 563 [LM: 327]). Interestingly, Kant says that '[p]ower is thus not a new accident, but rather the accidents <*accidentia*> are effects produced by the power' (*Met-Mron* AA 29: 770 [LM: 178]), that is, by the substance. Power is the relation of the substance to the accidents, 'insofar as it contains the ground of their actuality' (*Met-Mron* AA 29: 771 [LM: 179]). Importantly, substance *is* not power, but *has* power (*Met-Mron* AA 29: 771).

But how does substance relate to the thinking self (apperception)? In the *Lectures* passage already adumbrated above, Kant is reported as having said:

> I cannot say that the faculty of thinking within us is the substance itself—the faculty belongs to it—nor even [that] an accident of the thoughts is the accident. We thus have something that is not substance, yet also not accident. What then is the faculty of thinking? The relation of the soul to thought insofar as it contains the ground of its actuality. We have absolutely no acquaintance with the substantial, i.e., the subject, in which no accidents inhere, which must be necessarily distinguished from the accident, for if I cancel all positive predicates then I have no predicates and cannot think anything at all. (*Met-Mron*, AA 29: 771 [LM: 179])

This appears to suggest that 'the faculty of thinking' is, not 'substance itself', but the substantial, this latter signifying 'the concept of a subsisting object in general, insofar as one thinks in it merely the transcendental subject without any predicates' (B441/A414; cf. *Prol* § 46, AA 4: 333–4). Discursive thinking is always

---

[3] In the *Met-Herder* Kant still thinks that the '*Substantiale* enthält den letzten Realgrund von allen inhaerirenden Accidenzen' (AA 28: 845).

thinking through predicates. If we think these away, we are left with that which underlies these predicates, namely, the substantial, which can thus a fortiori not be thought and, as 'absolute subject must therefore always be absent' (*Prol* § 46, AA 4: 333). This calls to mind the unavoidable circle of the 'I think' of which Kant speaks in the Paralogisms (B404/A346). The 'substantial' cannot be thought, since it is that which is always already presupposed in whichever thoughts we have, and is 'only a designation of the object of inner sense insofar as we do not further cognise it through any predicate'; it is 'the referring of inner appearances to their unknown subject' (*Prol* § 46, AA 4: 334). However, unlike what is stated in the above quotation from the Mrongovius lecture notes, in the *Prolegomena* Kant does claim that the 'thinking self (the soul), as the ultimate subject of thinking, which cannot itself be represented as the predicate of another thing, *may now indeed be called substance*', even though it 'remains completely empty and without any consequences, if persistence [...] cannot be proven of it', which can be done 'only for the purposes of experience' (*Prol* § 47, AA 4: 334–5 [TPhb: 126], emphasis added).[4] I shall come to this in Section 7.2.1.

In the *Duisburg Nachlass* (1774–75), Kant explicitly relates the categories of relation to apperception. In R4674, Kant notes the following:

> Apperception is the consciousness of thinking, i.e., of the representations as they are placed in the mind. Here there are three exponents: 1. the relation to the subject, 2. the relation of succession among one another, 3. of composition. The determination of *a* in these *momentis* of apperception is subsumption under one of these *actibus* of thinking; one cognizes it as determinable in itself and thus objective, namely the concept *a*, if one brings it under one of these general actions of thinking, by means of which it comes under a rule. [...]. (AA 17: 647 [NF: 160–1])

In R4676, Kant writes similarly:

> If something is apprehended, it is taken up in the function of apperception. I am, I think, thoughts are in me. These are all relations, which to be sure do not provide rules of appearance, but which make it such that all appearance is to be represented as contained under a rule. The I constitutes the substratum for a rule in general, and apprehension relates every appearance to it. / For the origination of a rule three elements are required: 1. *x*, as the *datum* for a rule (object of sensibility or rather sensible real representation). 2. *a*, the *aptitudo* for a rule or the condition, through which it is in general related to a rule. 3. *b*, the exponent of the rule. / Now if a norm for the rule of appearances in general or of experiences is to arise—e. g., everything existent is in substance—then *x* is sensation in general as the *specif*[*ication*] of reality. By being represented as reality it becomes the material of a rule or sensation becomes capable of a rule, and *a* is only a function of the apprehension of

---

4 All translations from the *Prolegomena* in this paragraph are from the Cambridge edition.

appearance as given in general. Now since everything must be given in time, which therefore comprehends everything in itself, thus *b* is [*crossed out:* a function] an *actus* of apperception, namely the consciousness of the subject which apperceives [itself] as that which is given in the whole of time is necessarily connected with it, for otherwise the sensation would not be represented as belonging to me. (AA 17: 656 [NF: 166])

I am not here concerned with the meaning of these passages, which seem to contain in a nutshell central arguments of the Transcendental Deduction. I concur with Kitcher (2011: 93), who takes issue with Carl (1989a, b) on the interpretation of these passages, and believes that the 'hint about apperception in the early Reflection [R4631] and the explicit discussion of it in the *Duisburg Nachlaß* [is] part of the exploration of the necessary conditions for empirical cognition' and need not be seen as vulnerable to Kant's later criticisms of rationalist readings of apperception. By contrast, Carl thinks that these notes are reflective of an abortive attempt by Kant to base the deduction of the categories on an 'ontological' analysis of self-consciousness, a strategy he apparently abandoned after having discovered the paralogisms of reasoning later in the 1770s.[5] However, I do not see any immediate reason to regard Kant's connection of the categories (here, the categories of relation in particular) with apperception as a failure. I agree with Kitcher that the claim that '[i]n thinking cognizers are conscious of representations as set in the mind according to three exponents: relation to the subject, relation of following, and relation to the whole' is not ontological, for in these passages Kant does not at all suggest 'that the representations of which the subject is conscious must belong with others to a subject-substance' (2011: 122). In other words, as Kitcher rightly suggests, what Kant says in the *Duisburg Nachlass* is compatible with the criticisms of rationalist ontological views of the self that Kant presented in the Paralogisms when he published the *Critique* some six years later. Leaving aside an assessment of the merits of the *Duisburg* arguments, let us examine more closely what Kant has to say on the connection between substance and apperception in the Paralogisms.

7.2.1 Substance and the 'I Think' in the First Paralogism

In the First Paralogism, Kant criticises the rationalist view that since I am 'the *absolute subject* of all my possible judgements' and 'this representation of Myself cannot be used as the predicate of any other thing' (A348) the 'I' as thinking being must be considered a substance. The use of 'absolute' in the phrase 'I

---

5 See e.g. Carl (1989b: 16).

am the *absolute subject* of all my possible judgments' might strike as odd. Ameriks rightly stresses that here Kant means that the

> 'I' as a formal representation really is the representation of an 'absolute subject' of all my thoughts merely in that whatever thoughts are had, they necessarily can be prefaced by the phrase, 'I think'. (2000a: 69)

Kant does not imply this to 'mean that I am truly the absolute subject of my thoughts as a substantial mental being'. As Ameriks notes, I am a mental being, but there is a metaphysical possibility that 'what I take to be a substantial soul is ultimately a set of (individually) non-mental beings', in which case 'the real subject could be these things' and the 'I (as the thinking personality that I take myself to be) would really be an accident or resultant of those beings, and so but a prima-facie or relative and not absolute subject' (2000a: 69). What Kant means by the 'absolute subject' is the substantial (the 'I' *without* its predicates), which as 'absolute subject must [...] always be absent' (*Prol* § 46, AA 4: 333 [TPhb: 125]). He also calls the 'I' 'the ultimate subject of thinking' (*Prol* § 47, AA 4: 334 [TPhb: 126]).

That the 'I' that thinks is always a *subject* and never the predicate is true because the 'I think' is always that which accompanies thoughts or predicates and is never itself a predicate of something else; hence the fact that the 'I think' is original (B132). In fact, that the 'I' that thinks is always a subject and never a predicate 'is an apodictic and even an *identical proposition*' (B407). But that the 'I' is always a subject of thought and can never be used as a predicate does not eo ipso mean, Kant says, that the 'I' *is* a substance (de re) or indeed that it could not be a property of another thing (cf. A359). Kant accuses the rationalist of an ambiguity in the use of the term 'subject' in the major and minor premises of the syllogism that putatively shows that I, as a thinking being, am a substance (A348, B410–11). It is clear that the subject that *I* am as the subject of my thoughts is a consideration of the 'I' 'relative only to thinking and the unity of consciousness, but not at the same time in relation to the intuition through which it is given as an object for thinking' (B411). The subject that I *am* is therefore not a substance, namely what something that subsists for itself, and is not just a thought or unity of consciousness but genuinely a thing, would be. Only if we have an intuition with which we can prove the objective reality of the concept of a substance are we licensed to say that we cognise a real substance. However, since 'we have in inner intuition nothing at all that persists, for the I is only the consciousness of my thinking[,] [...] we also lack the necessary condition for applying the concept of substance, i.e., of a subject subsisting for itself, to itself as a thinking being' (B412–13). We have therefore no means to determine the 'I' of thought as a real substance.

But does this mean that the *concept* 'substance' (and the other categories) is not in some intimate way connected with the principle of apperception, the principle of thinking itself, even though it does not allow one to infer from the mere use of the 'I' that the 'I' is a thing that subsists? At B401/A343, Kant says about 'the mere apperception "*I think*", by which even transcendental concepts are made possible[:] what we assert in them is "I think substance, cause", etc.' (trans. Kemp Smith). These transcendental concepts are of course the categories, and Kant shows in the Paralogisms that purely from these 'transcendental predicates', on the basis of which a rational psychology purports to infer the substantiality, simplicity, numerical identity and the existence of the soul, no real knowledge can be gained of the nature of the 'I' of thinking as a thing. In a well-known phrase, Kant puts it thus:

> Through this I or he or it (the thing) which thinks, nothing further is represented than a transcendental subject of the thoughts=*X*. It is known only through the thoughts which are its predicates, and of it, apart from them, we cannot have any concept whatsoever, but can only revolve in a perpetual circle, since any judgment upon it has always already made use of its representation. (B404/A346, trans. Kemp Smith)

Now what Kant says here might just be taken to mean that the 'I' of thinking, which accompanies all my thoughts, cannot be determined *qua* 'I' since that would be viciously circular: the 'bare consciousness which accompanies all concepts' cannot itself be 'judged upon' since 'any judgment upon it has already made use of its representation'. This would imply that any assertion of 'I think substance, cause, etc.', which Kant says is implied in the 'I', as we saw above, must not be literally seen as involving those categories. This would a fortiori mean that the categories cannot be derived from the 'I' of apperception, which would undermine the central claim in this book.

I propose to read this somewhat differently. What I take Kant to be suggesting in these passages is not just that the use of the 'I' is presupposed in any judging and that hence any judging of the object status of the 'I' can only be circular, but also that the employment of the representation 'I' carries with it the use of the categories in any judging so that any putative judging about the substance status of any object, including the 'I', presupposes the categories (cf. A401–2). The fact that the categories are implied in the 'mere apperception "*I think*"', as B401/A343 suggests, does not make a difference with regard to how the categories apply to the 'I' as something putatively objectively real or to a real object external to the 'I'. That is to say, the critique in the Paralogisms is clearly intended to undermine the rationalist agenda of arguing for the soul's substantiality, simplicity etc.

purely on the basis of ostensibly merely 'logical' characteristics that Kant tells us do not translate into an objectively determinable thing. But the fact that this is the case does not imply that those 'logical' characteristics are not in fact the categories 'substance', 'cause' etc. that make it possible in the first place to conceive of *possible* objects of knowledge, for which—and this is the linchpin of Kant's argument—a separate empirical intuition is required to make these concepts objectively real. This holds for both objects and the 'I' as subject of thinking. In other words, Kant does not deny that these categories are characteristics of, and thus derivable from, the 'I' of thinking; what he denies is that any *objective* use can be made of them to establish the putative noumenal nature of the 'I'.

This is what Kant means when he asserts that the

> proposition 'I think' (taken problematically) contains the form of each and every judgement of the understanding and accompanies all categories as their vehicle. (B406/A348, trans. Kemp Smith)

The rationalist is not mistaken because he associates the judgement that 'I, as a thinking being, am the *absolute subject* of all my possible judgments' with the category 'substance' (A348), but he is mistaken in assuming that 'substance' must ipso facto be taken to denote a subsisting real *thing*. Kant therefore writes:

> We have shown in the analytical part of the Transcendental Logic that pure categories (and among them also the category of substance) have in themselves no *objective* significance at all unless an intuition is subsumed under them [...]. *Without that they are merely functions of a judgment without content.* (A348–9, emphasis added)

However, without an intuition the categories still have *subjective* significance. Indeed, '[o]f any thing in general I can say that it is a substance, insofar as I distinguish it from mere predicates and determinations of things'. Since 'I' am the subject of my thoughts which as determinations 'inhere' in me, as thinker, and cannot 'myself' (cf. B412n.) be used as a determination of another thing, it is completely legitimate, and in fact unavoidable, to '*regard*' myself as a substance (A349, emphasis added), although such a concept of myself is not 'empirically usable' (Kant suggests that because of that 'the concept of the substantiality of my thinking subject' is not useful at all, so that I might as well 'dispense with it altogether', but one must be reminded that he says this in the context of the rationalist's interest to infer from the pure use of the concept my 'enduring' self, which 'I can by no means infer' [A349]).

The 'I' is thus not 'a standing and abiding *intuition*, in which thoughts (as variable) would change', and it is not a '*real* subject of inherence' (A350, emphasis added). Nevertheless, 'one can quite well allow the proposition *The soul is substance* to be valid, if only one admits that this concept of ours leads no further [...] thus that it signifies a substance only in the idea but not in reality' (A350–1).[6] In the second Paralogism, Kant argues that 'the simplicity of my self (as soul) [...] lies already in every thought itself', because the 'proposition *I am simple* must be regarded as an immediate expression of apperception' (A354–5). One can argue similarly for the substance of the thinking self, that it 'lies already in every thought itself' because in apperceiving I must *regard* myself as a substance in which my thoughts inhere as accidents, regardless of the question of whether or not I am *really* a soul-substance (which is not to say that the question is unimportant, but that it is of a different order). In A398–9, Kant states that the 'the proposition that expresses self-consciousness', the 'I think', is 'the primary subject, i.e., substance, it is simple, etc.', which are, without experience, of course 'nothing more than pure categories', so to say that 'mere apperception ("I") is substance in concept, simple in concept, etc.' is 'indisputably correct' (A400).

The proposition *I am simple* just means that 'this representation *I* encompasses not the least manifoldness within itself, and that it is an absolute (though merely logical) unity' (A355), and not *I exist only as a simple being*. By the same token, one must take the proposition *I am the absolute subject of my thoughts* or *I am substance* to mean *I cannot regard myself other than as the subject of my thoughts*, and not *I exist only as a substantial subject*. Kant confirms this parallelism at A356: just as 'I always think an absolute but logical unity of the subject (simplicity), but I do not cognise the real simplicity of my subject', 'the proposition "I am substance" signifies nothing but the pure category, of which I can make no (empirical) use *in concreto*'. In other words, the 'I think' is a 'simple substance' in the sense that it is 'a substance the representation of which never contains a synthesis of the manifold'. Here, the concept of substance is 'used only as a function of synthesis, without an intuition being subsumed under it, hence without an object; and it is valid only of the condition of our cognition'. The proposition 'I am substance' thus has its validity 'in its pure significance as a merely rational judgment (from pure categories)', notwithstanding the fact that as 'naked concept' (A401) the concept 'substance' 'contains nothing beyond the fact that the thing is to be represented as a subject in itself without in turn being the predicate of another subject' (A401).

---

[6] Cf. *Prol* § 47: 'This thinking self (the soul), as the ultimate subject of thinking, which cannot itself be represented as the predicate of another thing, may now indeed be called substance [...]' (AA 4: 334 [TPhb: 126]).

The concept of substance 'used only as a function of synthesis' (A356) is precisely what in the context of the 'first step' of the B-Deduction is at issue. In the closing paragraphs of the A-Paralogisms, Kant provides some important clues to reading the link between the categories (especially substance) and apperception that I argue is an intimate one. He writes:

> Apperception is itself the ground of the possibility of the categories, which for their part represent nothing other than the synthesis of the manifold of intuition, insofar as that manifold has unity in apperception. Self-consciousness in general is therefore the representation of that which is the condition of all unity, and yet is itself unconditioned. Hence of the thinking I (the soul), which [thus represents] itself [*sich...denkt*] as substance, simple, numerically identical in all time, and the correlate of all existence from which all other existence must be inferred, one can say *not so much* that it cognizes *itself through the categories*, but that it cognizes the categories, and through them all objects, in the absolute unity of apperception, and hence cognizes them *through itself*. (A401–2)

Unlike what the rationalist thinks, the cognising self, the 'determining Self (the thinking)', which is an 'exercise of spontaneity' (B151), is not equivalent to the cognised self (as object), the 'determinable Self (the thinking subject)', qua noumenal substance.[7] The rationalist erroneously takes 'the unity in the synthesis of thoughts for a perceived unity in the subject of these thoughts' (A402). Nevertheless, as Kant points out in the above-quoted passage, the thinking 'I', the 'determining Self', which as we shall see below is the self-activity or spontaneity of the understanding as a form of pure causality, 'cognizes the categories, and through them all objects, in the absolute unity of apperception'. Indeed, the thinking 'I' knows the categories 'through itself' (*durch sich selbst*) (A402). In other words, the categories *are* just the characteristics or functions of thinking itself![8] Through them objects can be known (in combination with an empirical intuition), but obviously not the 'thinking I' itself *qua* object, as this would effectively come down to the categories determining *themselves*, which is viciously circular. Kant writes at B422:

> Thus the subject of the categories cannot, by thinking them, obtain a concept of itself as an object of the categories; for in order to think them, it must take its pure self-consciousness, which is just what is to be explained, as its ground.

This circular reasoning, which amounts to a hypostatisation of apperception itself by surreptitiously employing a transcendental concept empirically in order

---

7 Cf. B407.
8 Cf. *Prol* § 39, AA 4: 324.

to determine the subject of thought as an object, is the mistake that ensnares the rationalist. The rationalist view that I, as thinking agent, must *regard* myself as substance remains nonetheless perfectly valid.

7.2.2 Substance in the Transcendental Deduction

At A182, at the start of the argument of the First Analogy in its A-version, Kant states that substance is that which *persists*, while that which can change is its mere determination. He then writes:

> Our *apprehension* of the manifold of appearance is always successive, and is therefore always changing. We can therefore never determine from this alone whether this manifold, as object of experience, is simultaneous or successive, if something does not ground it *which always exists*, i.e., something *lasting* and *persisting*, of which all change and simultaneity are nothing but so many ways (*modi* of time) in which that which persists exists. (B225–6/A182)

I am here not concerned with the argument of the First Analogy per se, which involves the necessary determination of the manifold of appearances in time. But we can see a clear connection with the argument of the Transcendental Deduction that the manifold of representations itself is 'always changing', 'forever variable', and cannot by itself be regarded as already having that unity required for the determination of the manifold as either 'simultaneous or successive', which is the concern of the Second Analogy. The manifold representations are mere 'determinations' of inner sense without containing that unity that relates them to an identical subject. The representations are in constant change and do not persist. In the A-Deduction, Kant writes:

> The consciousness of oneself in accordance with the determinations of our state in internal perception is merely empirical, forever variable; it can provide no standing or abiding self in this stream of inner appearances, and is customarily called *inner sense* or *empirical apperception*. That which should *necessarily* be represented as numerically identical cannot be thought of as such through empirical data. (A107)

For the manifold of representations in inner sense to '*necessarily* be represented as numerically identical', and to be (relatively) 'lasting' or held together in a unity, a 'standing or abiding self' must be presupposed that provides the representations the ground for a numerically identical relation among them or a unity. According to Kant, it is the transcendental apperception that is the 'pure, original, unchanging consciousness' (A107)—the 'I' that 'remains' (*Met-Mron*, AA 29: 878 [LM: 248])—that provides the required unity among the changing representations in inner sense. At A123, Kant states that 'the standing and lasting I (of pure apperception) constitutes the correlate of all of our representations, so far as it is merely possible to become conscious of them'. As Kant argues just prior to this passage, at A122, it is this 'standing and lasting I' of transcendental apperception that is the 'objective ground', or 'affinity',[9] that makes it possible to regard one's representations as belonging to '*one* consciousness', as being determinations of a self, indeed accidents of something that subsists, viz. a substance.

This 'standing and lasting I', which relatively subsists and in which my determinations inhere by 'originally' belonging to it, is of course not an absolute self-substance in the strong noumenal sense, as we have seen Kant clearly deny in the First Paralogism. But I want to claim that the notion of pure apperception as 'the standing and lasting I', required for the unity of representations, is in fact the very *notion* of a substance as 'something' that persists (relatively) throughout my mental states and so always already precedes any consideration of the putative underlying substantial nature of the 'I'. In other words, the notion of a standing and lasting 'I' is *conceptually* more primordial than a noumenal substance. The concept of 'substance' as that which is always subject and never predicate of another thing is conveyed by the very notion of the 'I think' that 'must *be able* to accompany all my representations' but itself 'cannot be accompanied by any further representation' (B131–2).[10] However, the representations that are the accidents of this ultimate subject of thinking, the 'I', belong to the 'I'—or what Kant calls the '*transcendental* unity of self-consciousness' (B132)—if and only if they have been taken together as belonging to it. Representations do not inhere as accidents in the 'ultimate subject' (*Prol* § 47, AA 4: 334) as a matter of course, as if they existentially belonged to some putative absolutely subsisting substance. Kant's view that 'the standing and lasting I' is the 'correlate of all of our representations' (A123) means that the 'I' or apperception as substance, in terms of an 'ultimate subject', is the *concept* of a relation between something that subsists and what inheres in it that is required for one's representations to belong together as inhering in the same unitary self. The sense in which representations belong to the unitary self, which is by itself nothing but an empty formal 'I', the 'poorest representation of all' (B408), is not as if they

---

9 On 'affinity' in relation to apperception, see Schulting (2009b).
10 Cf. again *Prol* § 47, AA 4: 334. Heimsoeth (1956: 73) points out the close relation that, for Kant, exists between the soul or the 'I' and the concept of substance, most notably articulated in a *Reflexion* from 1769 (R3921): 'The idea of substance actually comes from the *repraesentatione sui ipsius* [representation of oneself], insofar as we represent that something is separate from us, and predicates cannot be thought without a subject and without an ultimate subject; the constant predicates together are then called the subject' (AA 17: 346 [NF: 95]).

belonged together in an existential unity. There is no primordial 'I' nor a fortiori a primordially belonging to such an 'I'. The belonging is the result of an act that unifies the representations by virtue of their being accompanied by the original representation 'I think'. This act of unification and the belonging of representations to a unity is reciprocal. That is, the identity of the 'I', as a substance in which thoughts inhere as accidents, is an 'identity of the function', as Kant puts it at A108, that first takes or puts various representations together in a unity. This makes the concept of substance a relational concept and at the same time connects it to that other crucial concept of relation: causality.

7.3 'Causality'

In the *Lectures on Metaphysics*, the concept of 'cause' is described as

> [t]hat which contains the ground of the existence of something.

Furthermore it is said that

> [w]hat can exist only as effect <*causatum*> is a thing derived from another or dependent <*ens ab alio sive dependens*>. (*Met-Mron*, AA 29: 843 [LM: 200])

The relation between cause and effect is in principle a relation of ground and consequence, whose relation is characterised by Kant in terms of 'connection <*nexus*>' (*Met-Mron*, AA 29: 807 [LM: 160]). Now ground is 'that through which I posit something', something A, say, and consequence is 'that which is posited', something B, and

> those things are joined of which it is the case that when one has been posited, the other is posited <*connexa sunt, quorum uno posito ponitur aliud*>. (*Met-Mron*, AA 29: 807–8 [LM: 161–2])

However, Kant makes a distinction between logical and real connection, or equivalently, real opposition, which is synthetic, and logical opposition, which is analytic. In a real *nexus*, 'the consequence is really distinguished from the ground', in which there is thus 'no connection <*nexus*> [merely] according to the rule of identity'. On the other hand, logical opposition means that '[t]hings are logically different when they are really one, but in a hidden way'; in this case, 'the connection <*nexus*> of the ground and consequence is analytic according to the rule of identity' (*Met-Mron*, AA 29: 810 [LM: 164]). Evidently, the relation cause–effect plays an important role in Kant's account of the possibility of a connection of ground and consequence that is not just based on the conceptual rule of identity, but tantamount to a real connection of existing things (appearances), an argument central to the account of the Second Analogy. But how is such a relation established in the first place, that is, conceptually?

At B249–50/A204–5, Kant makes two pivotal observations:

> [1] This causality leads to the concept of action, this to the concept of force, and thereby to the concept of substance.[11]
>
> [2] Where there is action, consequently activity and force, there is also substance, and in this alone must the seat of this fruitful source of appearances be sought.[12]

But, Kant asks,

> How will one infer directly from the action to the *persistence* of that which acts, which is yet such an essential and singular characteristic of the substance (*phaenomenon*)?

Answer:

> Action already signifies the relation of the subject of causality to the effect.

Kant reasons that

> according to the principle of causality actions are always the primary ground of all change of appearances, and therefore cannot lie in a subject that itself changes, since otherwise further actions and another subject, which determines this change, would be required. (B250/A205)

Action, as 'primary ground' of change, must therefore be the action of a subsisting substance, and cannot be dependent on something else but must be an original act. That there must be a substance can thus be inferred or proven from the fact that there is action and that actions are the primary grounds of change, as Kant maintains.[13] However, in the Critical view, the sense of substance meant is

---

11 Cf. R5290: 'The relation of a substance to the *accidens* is mere *actio. Vis...*' (AA 18: 144 [NF: 225]). See also R5650: 'Substance is the ultimate subject of reality. Its relation to the existence of this is called force, and it is this alone through which the existence of substance is indicated and in which its existence even exists. [...] The constitution of something as an absolute subject that does not inhere in anything else signifies a force that does not consist in a multiplicity of reciprocally determining forces, but rather consists in a degree' (AA 18: 298–301 [NF: 278–80]).
12 Cf. R4056, AA 17: 400; R5650, AA 18: 298–301. See further Heimsoeth (1956: 71–3).
13 Cf. R4679, AA 17: 663.

not separable from the action itself. Therefore, Kant can argue that there is action '*because* the subject subsists' (emphasis added).[14] Action is not only the action of a subject that is subsistent, hence of a substance, but the subject itself *is* the act that is the act of causality; hence, there is action because there is a subsisting substance. The subject is the original act of synthesis, the original synthetic unity of apperception, which is that action which lies in a persisting subject (substance), more original than which there is no subject or act.

Eric Watkins (2005: 272–82) has rightly emphasised the connection between Kant's model of causality and his notion of an awareness of synthesis, indeed of the self which 'can become aware of its identity not directly as an object of consciousness, but rather indirectly as the subject of activities of which we can be conscious' (2005: 278).[15] Watkins says about 'these activities' that they 'would seem to be instances of a particular kind of activity, namely an activity whereby a connection between representations is brought about as its effect' (2005: 278–9). Watkins also, rightly, points out that Kant 'states quite clearly that apperception *produces* [the] "I think", which is obviously an activity of the self' and that 'the effect' of this self-activity is 'determinate insofar as the particular kind of connection required by self-consciousness, namely a connection represented by the categories, *determines* our representations of an object' (2005: 279). While, as Watkins asserts, 'determinacy is the result, product, or effect of these synthetic activities, the synthetic activities cannot themselves be determinate' (2005: 279). Self-consciousness itself thus shows up a relation of cause and effect, where the activity of the self is the cause of determinacy as effect, and itself does not rest on a more original determination. Self-consciousness is essentially 'self-activity' (B130), or spontaneity.

7.3.1 Spontaneity as Action of the Understanding or 'Self-Activity'

At B428, Kant associates the thinking 'I' with the 'sheer spontaneity of combining the manifold of a merely possible intuition'. Similarly, in the Refutation of Idealism, Kant states that '[t]he consciousness of myself in the representation *I* is no intuition at all, but a merely *intellectual* representation of the self-activity

---

[14] *Met-Mron*, AA 29: 773: 'Every substance acts, because the subject subsists. The predicates inhere in each substance, the accidents [...] cannot exist other than in the substance, thus it contains the ground of something which belongs to existence, thus it acts' (LM: 180).
[15] Watkins believes that Kant thus attempts to resolve the Humean dilemma that 'either we can know the self directly through an impression [...] or we cannot know it at all' (2005: 277). Regarding the awareness of synthesis, see also Allison (1983: 272–3, 1996: 62).

of a thinking subject' (B278). Spontaneity and self-activity are terms that convey the same idea. At A51/B75, Kant calls the spontaneity of the power of representation the 'faculty for bringing forth representations itself [*selbst hervorzubringen*]'. There is an intricate relation between the self-activity of the thinking self and the intellectual capacity to 'self-produce' representations. In the *Groundwork*, Kant speaks of the 'self-activity' of the understanding, which 'does not, like sense, contain merely representations that arise when we are *affected* by things (and are thus passive)' but 'can produce from its activity' concepts that 'serve [...] *to bring sensible representations under rules* and thereby to unite them in one consciousness, without which use of sensibility it would think nothing at all' (AA 4: 452). This way of seeing the act of the understanding as 'producing from its activity' concepts that serve to bring representations under rules is consistent with Kant portraying spontaneity in terms of 'self-activity from an inner principle' (*Met-L₁*, AA 28: 267; cf. AA 28: 267–9, 275, 285).

In the Transcendental Deduction, Kant furthermore contrasts what is merely given in our *faculty* of representation (*Vorstellungsvermögen*, B129) with the act of spontaneity of the *power* of representation (*Vorstellungskraft*, B130), which is responsible for the combinatory activity (see below Section 7.4). The spontaneity of discursive understanding is dependent on the receptivity of representations which it brings under rules that are, as it were, produced from the understanding's self-activity. This constitutes the difference with an intuitive understanding, which would not need to produce concepts, as analytical rules for bringing representations into a synthetic unity, but produces the manifold as a whole already unified.[16] Such a self-consciousness 'through whose representation the objects of this representation would at the same time exist, would not require a special act of the synthesis of the manifold for the unity of consciousness' (B138–9).

With this arises the question of the extent to which the spontaneity of the discursive understanding is an *absolute* spontaneity of actions (*spontaneitatem absolutam actionum*; *Met-L₁*, AA 28: 269). Kant says of the 'I think' that it concerns an inner perception (B401/A343), a consciousness of 'its faculty for combination' (B158), just as Watkins says (see above), which might suggest that I am aware of myself as an absolute spontaneity *tout court* (*spontaneitas absoluta vel simpliciter talis*) and not a spontaneity *secundum quid talis*, which Kant associates with a *spontaneitas automatica* or the notorious 'turnspit' (CPrR, AA 5: 97). This is obviously important for the practical context, where Kant wants to make it clear that the causality of our action is completely independent of external influences. But it is not prima facie clear whether in the theoretical context the

---

16 Cf. Quarfood (2011).

spontaneity of cognition concerns an absolute spontaneity or merely a relative spontaneity (*spontaneitas secundum quid*), namely relative to a necessarily given manifold of representations that the combinatory activity of the discursive understanding requires.[17] Spontaneity is not just *conceptually* contrasted with receptivity, the way that representations are first received in the mind (A50/B74), so that receptivity is merely a neutral foil for spontaneity. On the contrary, receptivity is a fundamental aspect of discursive thought, which together with spontaneity enables knowledge. The spontaneity of cognition is the understanding determining the manifold, rather than being the determinable, which is the manifold given to it (B150–2). The spontaneity of the determinative understanding is uncaused, that is, itself not further determinable as to its cause, but is also a spontaneously determining cause only *relative to* the receptivity in empirical intuition and therefore it cannot be absolutely determining. This limiting condition seems confirmed by what Kant says in passage in the B-Paralogisms with regard to the proposition 'I think' itself: to the extent that it concerns an actual existing subject, the 'I think' presupposes inner sense, that is, a given manifold of representations that are determined by the thinking self to belong to herself in that she accompanies the manifold. Kant writes:

> Thus in this proposition there is *already no longer merely* spontaneity of thinking, *but also* receptivity of intuition, i.e., the thinking of my self applied to the empirical intuition of the very same subject. (B429–30, emphasis added)

Kant points out that 'the thinking self must [...] seek the conditions of the use of its logical functions for categories of substance, cause, etc.' in empirical intuition for the possibility of determining an object (either inner or outer). This means that empirical intuition is a necessary constraint on the spontaneity of the understanding. Hence, the spontaneity of the understanding cannot be absolute, that is, a *spontaneitas simpliciter talis*.

In a note to B157–8, Kant appears to confirm that this is indeed the way that the spontaneity of the understanding must be interpreted. What Kant says here is that though I am aware of the spontaneity of the '*determining* in me' (*Bestimmende in mir*), this 'determining' self is not *given to me* by means of some sort of self-intuition,[18] in the way that the *empirical manifold is given to* the determin-

---

[17] Allison (1996: 57, 62–4) believes that also in the theoretical context absolute spontaneity is concerned. See also Pippin (1997). For more discussion, see Schulting (2017a: 124–31).
[18] Cf. B429: '[I]n the consciousness of myself in mere thinking I am the *being itself*, about which, however, nothing yet is thereby given to me for thinking.' Cf. Heidemann (1958),

ing self, which determines it sensibly. The spontaneously determining self is merely a logical function, operated by an epistemic agent (a subject), that has determining power only relative to a given manifold in empirical intuition.[19]

Nevertheless, Kant's phrase '[...] self-intuition, which would give the *determining* in me, of the spontaneity of which alone I am conscious' does suggest that I am indeed conscious of the spontaneity of the determining self even if I have no conscious access, through some sort of self-intuition, to the determining self as such.[20] It is not prima facie clear whether Kant indeed here means that in the determining act of synthesis I am aware of the spontaneity of the absolute self, hence of absolute spontaneity.[21] I think it is appropriate to uphold a distinction between relative and absolute spontaneity given Kant's discussion of spontaneity in the noumenal context, relevant for his notion of freedom, where reason always seeks 'an *absolute* causal *spontaneity* beginning *from itself*' (A446/B474), a cause that is uncaused by the causal chain of natural mechanisms (cf. A533/B561; A445ff./B473ff.). Kant's view of transcendental freedom as a self-determining cause outside the 'continuous natural chain' (CPrR, AA 5: 95) plays a crucial role in the way we must conceive of ourselves as rational agents, who rather than possessing the relative spontaneity of a 'turnspit' (CPrR, AA 5: 97)—where freedom would consist merely in the subjective representation of the '*mechanism* of nature', a kind of '*automaton* [...] *spirituale*' (CPrR, AA 5: 97)— must be seen as possessing of 'absolute spontaneity' to freely will an action

---

ch. 10, in which she addresses the topic of 'spontaneity and noumenal existence'. See also Schulting (2017a), ch. 9 and Schulting (2017c).

19 This would also be consistent with Kant's statement that '[t]hrough this I, or He, or It (the thing), which thinks, *nothing further is represented than a transcendental subject of thoughts=x*, which is recognized only through the thoughts that are its predicates, and about which, in abstraction, we can never have even the least concept' (B404/A346, emphasis added).

20 Cf. Pippin (1997: 34). Pippin also points to B574–5/A546–7, where Kant contrasts knowledge through the senses with knowledge of oneself 'through pure apperception', which is the knowledge that one has 'in actions and inner determinations which cannot be accounted at all among impressions of sense'. Kant even associates this with the fact that 'the human being' is 'one part phenomenon, but in another part, namely in regard to certain faculties, he is a merely intelligible object because the actions of this object cannot at all be ascribed to the receptivity of sensibility', these faculties being 'understanding and reason', although, as Kant concludes rather cryptically and surprisingly, the former of these is said to make an 'empirical use of its own concepts (even the pure ones)'. Note that Pippin does not think that Kant's emphasis on absolute spontaneity implies a noumenal subject, but just indicates the *non*-phenomenal nature of spontaneity, irreducible to causal series of sense determinations. Pippin (1997: 39) links spontaneity to what he calls the 'ineliminably reflexive' aspect of apperception. See Schulting (2017a: 124–31) for more discussion.

21 Cf. *Met-L₁*, AA 28: 267–70.

(CPrR, AA 5: 48). In the latter case, the agent possesses the capacity of 'pure self-activity' (*Selbstthätigkeit*) of *reason,* by means of which he 'distinguishes himself from all other things, *even from himself insofar as he is affected by objects*' (*Groundwork,* AA 4: 452, emphasis added).

This must be seen in sharp contrast to the self-activity of the *understanding,* which 'though [...] does not, like sense, contain merely representations that arise when we are affected by things (and are thus passive), yet [...] can produce from its activity no other concepts than those which serve merely *to bring sensible representations under rules*' (*Groundwork,* AA 4: 452). Here, self-activity rests on the function of combination that the understanding must operate in order for a given manifold of representations to have a synthetic structure, which is 'not given through objects' (B130). Self-activity in this sense is thus merely relative to the need for combination of the sensible manifold in receptivity that the manifold itself does not contain. Reason, on the other hand, shows itself to be 'a spontaneity so pure that it thereby goes *far beyond* anything that sensibility can ever afford it' (*Groundwork,* AA 4: 452, emphasis added), implying that it is also far elevated above the spontaneity of the understanding. Kant thus appears to discriminate between the spontaneity involved in the act of understanding, which is linked to receptivity, and the absolute spontaneity of reason, which is far removed from it.

In the next section, I elaborate on the nature of the spontaneity of the act of the self that produces or 'causes' a connection among its representations, which results in a determinate representation that has 'objective validity'. In this way the necessary interaction of the spontaneity of the understanding with the manifold in intuition is reinforced, pointing to the category of 'community'.

7.4 Combination, Synthetic Unity, and 'Community'

In the introductory section of the B-Deduction, § 15 (B129–31), Kant makes the following remarkable observations:

> **[a1]** [A]ll combination [*Verbindung*], whether we are conscious of it or not, whether it is a combination of the manifold of intuition or of several concepts, and in the first case either of sensible or non-sensible intuition, is an action of the understanding, which we would designate with the general title *synthesis* [...]. (B130)

> **[b]** [I]n addition to the concept of the manifold and of its synthesis, the concept of combination also carries with it [*führt* (...) *bei sich*] the concept of the unity of the manifold. Combination is the representation of the *synthetic* unity of the manifold. The representation of this unity cannot, therefore, arise from the combination; rather, by being added to the representation of the manifold, it first makes the concept of combination possible. (B130–1)

7.4 Combination, Synthetic Unity, and 'Community' — 187

The first observation **[a1]** appears simply to articulate the idea that the understanding is responsible for any kind of connection of any arbitrary manifold of representations.[22] That this is in fact not the case, will be pointed out below. What Kant means to say in the second passage from B130–1 **[b]** is not immediately clear. At first sight, Kant seems to say that connection first originates from the unity of the manifold and that therefore unity is more original than connection or combination. But Kant also claims, confusingly, that in that the unity is 'added [*hinzukommt*] to the representation of the manifold, it first makes the concept of combination possible' (B131). This implies that combination cannot be regarded as a kind of a posteriori apprehending of an already *given* synthetic unity. Indeed, Kant says that combination 'can never come to us through the senses, and therefore cannot already be contained in the pure form of sensible intuition' (B129).[23] The unity from which combination, or synthesis, is then said to originate cannot simply be any unity merely encountered in the manifold. Both unity and combination must thus be a priori, and given this unity must thus be added to the manifold so that a combination can arise.

But what exactly is the relation between, on the one hand, the unity that is *added to* the manifold, and thus makes combination possible and, on the other hand, the combination that arises from this unity? If Kant speaks of 'adding' a representation of unity to a representation of the manifold to get a combination, are we to understand by this that we literally first have a representation of the manifold, which is subsequently followed up by a representation of unity? Now, according to the text, unity is the condition of possibility of synthesis or combination. However, one might rejoin that in passage **[b]** Kant also says that synthesis (combination) is the *representation* of synthetic unity. This is rather odd, since, as it appears, the combination or synthesis is the representation of the very unity that *first brings forth* synthesis. There appears to be no other way

---

[22] Cf. B164, where Kant speaks of the connectivity of the law of nature; appearances as such, '[a]s mere representations [...] stand under no law of connection at all except that which the connecting faculty prescribes'. Nevertheless, Kant recognises various types of connection or *Verknüpfung*. Kant even uses the term synthesis for mere reproductive connections, which have no relation to the understanding. See e.g. B152, where he uses the term to describe merely reproductive connections; cf. A198/B243; also the term *Verbindung*, used here in § 15, appears not to be exclusively reserved for the specific synthetic activity of the understanding. See also Klemme (1996: 196–8).

[23] Cf. B233: '[C]onnection [*Verknüpfung*] is not the work of mere sense and intuition, but is here rather the product of a synthetic faculty of the imagination, which determines inner sense with regard to temporal relations.'

than to conclude that Kant's argument is viciously circular.[24] As I shall argue below, a solution to this conundrum is that combination and unity must be seen as equiprimordial. They mutually produce each other.

However, if **[a1]** is to be understood in such a way that the understanding must be held responsible for literally every kind of combination or connection in the manifold, then this would appear to conflict with **[b]** (which we read as showing combination and unity to be equiprimordial) unless the manifold of representation to which the combination enabling unity is added is itself fully chaotic, a 'swarm of appearances' (*Gewühle von Erscheinungen*) (A111), 'a chaos, a blooming, buzzing confusion', as Hoke Robinson (1988: 172)—referring to William James—puts it.[25] However, I do not think this is necessarily the case. A manifold that is not combined by the understanding can nonetheless display some form of connectedness. Not every type of combination is necessarily one performed by the understanding. That is, a de facto connectedness of representations always already obtains in terms of their contiguity in the way that representations are prompted to occur in the mind (e. g. their affinity as mental states) and are necessarily had by an arbitrary representer. In this regard, Hansgeorg Hoppe (1991: 51–2) speaks appropriately of 'merely contingent co-occurrences' (*bloß zufälligen Kookkurrenzen*) in contrast to a rule-governed pattern of events, which requires categorial synthesis. In respect of the 'swarm' Hoppe says that it signifies 'a categorial disorder, which can exist even when our representations are factually well-ordered and orderly connected'. Secondly, Kant is clearly concerned with arguing for the possibility of object reference, not with arguing for the possibility of any arbitrary psychological makeup or co-occurrence of one's mental states. This is clear from the same passage in which it is claimed that all combination is due to the understanding. Kant completes the sentence started in **[a1]** thus:

> **[a2]** [...] in order at the same time to draw attention to the fact that we can *represent nothing as combined in the object* without having previously combined it ourselves, and that among all representations *combination* is the only one that is not given through objects but can be

---

[24] See also Thöle (1991: 250). Thöle suggests that the problem here is due to an oversight on Kant's part and that *Verbindung* should be replaced with *Mannigfaltiges*, so that the meaning of the sentence becomes immediately clear as saying that the combination does not arise from the manifold, but is first established by a unity being added to it.

[25] Cf. per contra Kant in the *Met-Dohna*: 'Perceptions and *their* connection do not yet constitute *experience*' (AA 28: 673 [LM: 374], emphasis added). A non-orderly connection is mostly referred to by Kant as aggregate in contrast to a unity (see e. g. *Met-Mron*, AA 29: 795 [LM: 150]; cf. A170/B212). However, at B195/A156 Kant calls an unsynthesised unity of appearances a 'rhapsody of perceptions', reinforcing the suggestion of a 'swarm'.

executed only by the subject itself, since it is an act of its self-activity. (B130, emphasis added)[26]

As a prelude to the argument of § 17, Kant here gives us already a clue as to what the referent of the synthesised manifold amounts to, namely the concept of an 'object'.[27] Notice also the implicit conditional in the phrase 'we can represent nothing as combined in the object without having previously combined it ourselves'. It is through an act of synthesis, and through this act alone, that unites one's representations that we 'posit an object for these representations, or ascribe to their subjective reality, as modifications, some sort of objective reality' (B242/A197). As to the apparent claim that any type of connection is meant by Kant's claim that 'all combination [...] is an action of the understanding', it is evident, given the purport of the argument here in § 15, that 'all combination' does not include any mere empirical co-presence of mental states and their putative material affinity. If it did, Kant would be arguing, contradictorily, both that the empirical co-presence already constitutes object-reference, given that the argument about combination is directed at the possibility of the cognition of an object, *and* that such object-reference is not yet 'given through objects'—that is, in the manifold of representations itself—and thus requires an additional act.

Hoppe (1983: 138) makes a useful distinction between, on the one hand, a 'factual connection of representations' (*faktischer Vorstellungszusammenhang*), which correlates with the 'dispersion [*Zerstreutheit*] of a mere empirical consciousness that is not synthetically united' and, on the other, an 'objective context of meaning' (*gegenständlichen Sinn-Zusammenhang*), which is produced by an act of self-activity (the unity of apperception).[28] This contrast is important for an understanding of Reciprocity, which concerns the intimate relation between self-consciousness and the concept of an object in general (see Chapter 4). The objections raised against Reciprocity are largely the result of an inflated reading of Kant's claim about synthesis (combination) and its scope, as well as a psychologistic reading of transcendental self-consciousness.

But it is also odd that one would raise precisely this objection as if Kant were naïve enough plainly to assume a necessary link between, on the one hand, the psychological (or physiological, for that matter) constitution of one's mental

---

26 Cf. B134–5.
27 This reinforces the idea (discussed in Chapter 4) of the Transcendental Deduction as, in one sense, being a regressive argument. That is to say, the operative premise of the P-argument, starting in § 16, is implicitly premised on the argument from § 15 for object-intentionality. The P-argument is embedded within the context of the overall R-argument. See further Chapter 10.
28 See also Hoppe (1983: 113–19) on B129.

states and their material affinity, corresponding to what Kant labels a subjective unity of consciousness (B139–40), and, on the other, an objectively valid combination of representations (which is an objective unity of consciousness). The problem that no such link can be assumed to obtain as a matter of course is precisely what crucially informs Kant's transcendental proof for the legitimation of objective experience as necessarily connected experience, since no such necessary connection, and so no such objective unity, is already given with the subjectively (psychologically) arranged representations themselves.[29]

Let me get back to passage **[b]**. How should we understand the relation between synthesis and synthetic unity? How can synthetic unity be the enabling ground of synthesis if synthesis is also the representation of synthetic unity? At this point, it becomes clear why the third category of relation is necessarily involved, namely 'community' (or 'reciprocity between agent and patient' [A80/B106]). As with the categories of modality, where necessity is the relation between, or unification of, possibility and actuality as condition and conditioned respectively, 'community' effectively is the relation of both the concepts 'substance' and 'cause'. The difference here, with the categories of relation, is that the concept of 'community' or 'mutual interaction' is necessary, as an independent category, to show that 'substance' and 'cause' are *reciprocally* conditioned: they are both condition and conditioned. 'Cause' or, more precisely, 'cause–effect' is the condition of substance, while simultaneously 'substance' is the condition of 'cause–effect'. How should we understand this?

The concept of 'cause–effect' already is a condition–conditioned relation (as we saw earlier, the cause–effect relation rests on, or is in principle, a ground–consequence relation), so that the relation between *this* relation and *its* ground, namely the ground of its causality, substance, amounts to a *reciprocally* conditioning relation, which concerns the causality of causality, as it were. Synthesis as act (the causality of self-activity) is the power of the 'I' of apperception, which as substance is the ground of, or self-actively 'produces', the synthetic unity among the representations; synthetic unity among the manifold representations is the consequence, 'effect', or 'product' of such an act of synthesis (apperception). This accounts for both the concepts of 'substance' and 'cause', since they are inextricably connected as two sides of the same coin: on the one hand, synthesis as 'producing' act or spontaneous power of representation (*Vorstellungskraft*) (B130) of the apperceptive 'I' as substance and, on the other, syn-

---

[29] Cf. A89–90/B122–3. This passage is extensively discussed in Schulting (2015b, 2017a: 226–40).

thesis as 'product' (*causatum*),³⁰ namely as 'synthetic unity of the manifold'. No synthetic unity of the manifold exists without an act of synthesis having taken place, but equally no act of synthesis fails to result in a synthetic unity of representations, for that is precisely what an act of synthesis does: it produces a synthetic unity of representations. The notion of a producing 'I', as substance, and the synthetic unity of connected representations, as the 'I's product, as it were, is what is behind the 'principle of simultaneity' (B256/A211) as the key notion in the Third Analogy. But does Kant not say that the unity has to be 'added to the representation of the manifold'?³¹ Does this not suggest a distinction between the unity of the manifold and the act of synthesis? No, for (1) the representation of unity is 'added' to the manifold as such, since unity is not already given in the manifold as such; and (2) the representation of unity 'being added to the representation of the manifold' is coextensive with making 'the concept of combination [first] possible'.

Hoppe (1983) disputes the intimate relation between the synthetic unity of the manifold and the unitary act of synthesis. Referring to the **[b]**-passage, Hoppe (1983: 121–2) argues that the unity, and not the unification as act (cf. Kant's observation at AA 3: 107.26 that the action at issue is 'originally unitary [*einig*]') is what is decisive for the synthesis of representations. On Hoppe's reading, it is the unity of an a priori self-consciousness, interpreted as somehow given antecedently to the synthesis, not the unity of action (the act of synthesis) that underwrites the possibility of synthesis and is thus its ground. The unity at issue here is the original unity which, presumably, precedes all categorial determination, and which Hoppe associates with the 'original-synthetic unity of apperception' (see again above Section 6.3).³² Presumably, in this way Hoppe hopes to be able to avoid the circular reasoning that would otherwise seem to result. Although Hoppe is right to identify synthetic unity as the unity of self-consciousness and indeed with the 'original-synthetic unity of apperception', he does not seem to capture the extent to which this unity (which is the transcendental unity of self-consciousness, or the 'I' of the 'I think'), in the very act of its being added (*hinzukommen*)—the sense of which Hoppe cannot really fathom—is produced as the ground of synthesis and so is crucially equiprimordial with the act of synthesis. This is not just trivially circular. The original synthetic unity of apperception is not just an original *unity*, it is also an original *act*. Hoppe misses

---

30 *Met-L₂*, AA 28: 571.
31 Note though that the verb in German is intransitive: *hinzukommen*, hence there is no suggestion that a subject must literally add, or indeed impose, a unity on the manifold.
32 Cf. Henrich (1976) and Wunderlich (2005: 215).

the crucial reciprocal relation between synthesis as synthetic unity and synthesis as act.

Thus, substance is the ground of the causal act of synthesis, of the causality that 'causes' or produces the synthetic *unity*. At the same time, there *is* only a substance insofar as there is an act of synthesis, namely a causality that produces the synthetic unity among representations. This effectively comes down to causality *itself* being the ground of substance as the agent of synthesis. This argument resurfaces in the central text of the first half of the B-Deduction, in § 16. At B134, Kant asserts that

> [s]ynthetic unity of the manifold of intuitions, as given *a priori*, is thus the **ground** of the identity of apperception itself, which precedes *a priori* all *my* determinate thinking. (boldface added)

In other words, the synthetic unity of the manifold is the condition of the act of apperception, that is, of the *analytic* principle of the 'I think' accompanying all its (my) representations as its (my) *selfsame* representations that inhere in the subsisting 'I' of apperception. However, at the same time it is transcendental apperception itself, the 'I think' which accompanies all my representations, and a more original representation than which there is no other (that is, it is *substance*), that *causes* this synthetic unity. Despite what Kant might be taken to say in the above-quoted passage at B134—namely, 'synthetic unity of the manifold of intuitions, as given *a priori*'—the synthetic unity is not simply given (so that it could be found), but the manifold of intuitions is given a priori in the sense that receptivity of representations is necessary for representations being able to be combined. The synthetic unity must in fact be 'added' to the given manifold, which the higher unity of the 'I think', that is, the self-consciousness that 'produces the representation *I think*' (B132), achieves in 'causing' it in the manifold. Apperception, the act of synthesis, itself is substance, cause, and community, of which the latter expresses the fact that apperception is both the *act* of synthesis, as a causality of causality, and the original-synthetic unity of apperception, as substance, that is rigorously coextensive with the synthetic unity of the manifold in intuition.

In the Third Analogy of Experience, Kant speaks significantly of a 'community (*communio*) of apperception' (A214/B261). Watkins (2011: 51) portrays this in terms of 'a subjective community that representations have by virtue of being associated with each other in a mind'. Watkins believes that Kant introduces this term for the reason that 'it allows him to extend the scope of a claim made earlier', that is, in the Transcendental Deduction (Watkins refers to B140) and in the Second Analogy, 'that the subjective order (of our representations) depends on the objective order (of the states of objects)'. In the subjective unity there is no *commercium* between the representations. Kant, Watkins writes,

> wants to state here [i.e., in the Third Analogy, D.S.] that if representations associated in a mind are supposed to represent objective reality, then there must be not only causality but also specifically *commercium* (dynamical mutual interaction) between the objects they represent. For we would otherwise have no reason not to ascribe the succession that occurs in all of our representations to the states of the objects they represent, even if those states happen to be simultaneous. (2011: 51)

I agree with Watkins's last point. However, we must bear in mind that the objective order of objects, on which the order of successive perceptions depends, is not *given* but rests on the way that the objects are '*represented* as being connected by existing simultaneously' (A214/B261, emphasis added). The ground of their community is therefore the community of *apperception* itself, not any given *commercium* among objects themselves, as I have explained in the preceding paragraphs. The community of apperception, as the mutually conditioning relation between the act of synthesis and the synthetic unity of the manifold of intuitions, in short, the *category* of 'community', is the basis on which the *commercium* of objects can be established. This is the reason why Kant calls the transcendental unity of self-consciousness an *objective* unity of consciousness as differentiated from a merely subjective unity of consciousness that reflects the material affinity of mental states (which ultimately derive a posteriori from the objective order of states of objects [cf. B140]). The category of 'community' is of course, as with the other relational categories, especially significant in the context of the analytic of the principles of spatiotemporal experience (namely in regard to the determination of numerically identical objects and events over time and in space). But these would not have the application they have if they did not formally hold also of the mode of thinking *in general* as the necessary and formally sufficient condition of any experience, spatiotemporal or other, inasmuch as thought itself, as a synthetic function for any determinate combination of representations, is a transcendental unity of reciprocal constituents as the principle which holds the constituents together (cf. R4417, AA 17: 538).[33]

---

[33] See further Longuenesse (2005), ch. 7, and Watkins (2011) on aspects of the concept of 'community' in relation to disjunctive judgement, the Third Analogy and MFNS. See especially Edwards (2000) for an extensive account of the role of community in Kant's philosophy of nature. See Heimsoeth (1956: 85 ff.) on the primordial metaphysical sense of the concept of 'community', in particular in regard to body–soul interaction.

7.5 Deriving the Categories of Relation: Summary

Having expounded the arguments for deriving the categories of relation from the unity of apperception, this gives us the following additional premises of the D-argument:

> D10. The notion of pure apperception as 'the standing and lasting I', required for the unity of representations, is that which subsists throughout (the apprehension of) my mental states, which inhere in me in that they are apperceived by me as my thoughts.
>
> D11. The subsisting 'I' is the original synthetic unity of apperception, which is that action which is the power of the self-active subject and spontaneously produces a synthetic unity among the manifold of representations.

These results show that

> D12. The category of 'substance' pertains to the identity of discursive thought and hence is analytically derivable from it.
>
> D13. The category of 'cause–effect' pertains to the identity of discursive thought and hence is analytically derivable from it.

However, as we have seen, the categories of 'substance' and 'cause–effect' are not merely unilaterally connected. The very same subject that is the substance in which inhere her thoughts has the power to cause a synthetically necessary relation of representations. Substance and cause–effect are bilaterally related, or in other words,

> D14. Substance and cause–effect mutually condition each other in that apperception is both the act of synthesis as an act of original self-activity which produces synthetic unity in the manifold of intuitions and that which is grounded on the synthetic unity to first constitute the identity of the function of combining representations into one cognition.

One can conclude that 'community' (reciprocal interaction) is a necessary independent category of relation. Therefore,

> D15. The category of 'community' pertains to the identity of discursive thought and hence is analytically derivable from it.

8 Apperception and the Categories of Quality

8.1 Introduction

In this chapter, I argue for the derivation of the categories of quality from apperception. As Daniel Warren (2001: 16) has hinted, the link between these categories, which are 'reality', 'negation', and 'limitation', and apperception or self-consciousness might seem slight. Especially the category of 'negation' appears out of place, as it suggests a purely *logical* aspect of a proposition and does not seem to have to do anything with the apparently *ontological* category of 'reality'. However, in the Metaphysical Deduction Kant explicitly claims a correspondence between the negative quality of a judgement in general and the category of 'negation'. The close link between 'reality', as 'pure category', and the affirmative function of judgement is for example asserted at A246: '[R]eality [is] that which can be thought only through an affirmative judgement.' By implication, 'negation' then indeed seems just that which can be thought only through a negative judgement, or to put it in the way that Kant defines the categories, as Longuenesse (1998: 294) suggests: 'negation' is the concept 'of an object in general, by means of which the intuition of this object is regarded as determined *in respect of the logical function of negation in a judgement*' and so also for reality.[1] But this way of seeing the relation between the categories and judgement seems rather contrived: surely the transcendental category of negation cannot be equated with *negative judgements* only, as much as the category of reality cannot be taken not also to play a constitutive role in *negative* judgements.[2] It is also not immediately clear what role 'limitation' might play, let alone how it could be seen as having its 'seat' in pure understanding, that is, in apperception.[3]

In Section 8.2, I look at material in the Schematism and the Anticipations of Perceptions, where Kant explicitly addresses the categories of quality in the context of the principles of experience. In particular, I discuss the notion of 'sensa-

---

[1] See Longuenesse (1998: 293) where she writes that 'in elaborating his view on the categories of quality, Kant relies on a generally accepted correspondence between ontological determinations (reality and negation) and forms of predication (affirmation and negation in judgment). But he transforms the meaning of this correspondence by making the latter the origin of the former, and by claiming further that logical forms give rise to ontological determinations only if they are related to a sensible given.'
[2] Longuenesse (1998: 303) indeed points out that 'cognizing a *negation* depends on cognizing the corresponding *reality*'. But note that cognising a negation is not the same as applying the category 'negation'.
[3] See the account of Longuenesse (1998: 292ff.).

tion' as intrinsically characterised by a certain degree of reality, which makes up the intensive magnitude of any appearance, in contrast to the extensive magnitude of an intuition as a spatiotemporal perception. In Section 8.3, I link the discussion about reality and sensation to consciousness (and hence apperception), by showing that since representations always have some degree of sensible intensity they must therefore always be conscious to some degree, and argue that first-order consciousness as such is not dependent on transcendental apperception. In Section 8.4, I elaborate on the question of how transcendental apperception as the *form* of consciousness must be seen as correlative with the category of 'negation' and how this results in a 'limitation' of empirical consciousness as something real. My discussion of the categories of quality is really only concerned with the extent to which they can be seen as derivable from apperception. I do not address the historical background of these categories, neither in Kant's immediate predecessors nor in Kant's own pre-Critical work, for example the role of 'negation' in his work *Attempt to Introduce the Concept of Negative Magnitude into Philosophy* from 1763 or the important discussion in the transcendental Ideal in the *Critique* concerning the validity of the concept of the *ens realissimum*.[4] In Section 8.5, I add to the D-argument the premises that constitute the arguments showing that the categories of quality are derivable from the principle of apperception.

8.2 Sensation and the Categories of Quality

As we have seen in Chapter 6, the 'actuality' of thought is one of the modalities of discursive thought. 'Actuality' is the name Kant gives to the category in some of the *Lectures on Metaphysics*, but in the *Critique* and *Prolegomena* he labels it 'existence'. It has often puzzled commentators that Kant also has a separate category for 'reality', in German *Realität*. This latter term should not be confused with the German term for 'actuality': *Wirklichkeit*.

Anneliese Maier (1930: 45) describes 'reality' as *die Position schlechthin*. She relates this to a passage in the Schematism (B182/A143), which I quote below.

---

[4] See Heimsoeth (1956: 51–67), Maier (1930), Schulting (2015a, 2017a), and Warren (2001). See also Longuenesse (1998: 292ff.). Both Maier and Warren are invaluable contributions to the sparse literature that there is on Kant's categories of quality. In this chapter, I am concerned neither with Maier's attempt to argue for a third a priori form of sensibility (in addition to space and time) nor with Warren's account of reality in relation to space and time. Both Longuenesse and Warren provide extensive accounts of the relevance of the categories of quality for Kant's philosophy of nature.

8.2 Sensation and the Categories of Quality — 197

This might be confusing, as I used this terminology, in Chapter 6, to describe the categories of modality, where 'existence' is *absolute position* or *Position schlechthin* (cf. Heimsoeth 1956: 27). However, Kant uses the term *Position* both in relation to the category of reality and the categories of modality. For example, in R5582 (AA 18: 239) he identifies *realitaet* with *absoluten position*. Likewise, in R4796 (AA 17: 731) *realitaet* is identified with *transscendentale position*. On the other hand, in R4298 (AA 17: 499), *Position schlechthin* is the definition for *Wirklichkeit* (actuality or existence). The same Kant says in R5557:

> Moglichkeit, wirklichkeit und Nothwendigkeit sind nicht determinationen, sondern modalitaet der position des Dinges mit seinen Praedicaten. (AA 18: 232)

A useful way to distinguish the two categories might be to reserve *Position* for 'actuality' (*Wirklichkeit*) and what in his account of *realitas noumenon* in the transcendental Ideal Kant calls 'transcendental affirmation' for 'reality', unlike Maier (1930: 53), who regards *transzendentale Position* and *Bejahung* as equivalent—however, she also makes a distinction between *relative* and *absolute Position*, whereby only the latter concerns actuality (*Wirklichkeit*) (1930: 75n.1). Maier stresses that the Being which the concept of reality points to (B182/A143), is therefore not Being as actuality.[5]

What in normal English usage is thought of as reality is closer to Kant's *Wirklichkeit* than it is to *Realität*. Nevertheless, they are not completely separable: (1) Kant appears sometimes to use the terms interchangeably, and (2) in order for an object to be determined as actual (*wirklich*) it must be 'in connection with perception (sensation, as the matter of the sense)', which corresponds to the 'thing (the real [*Realen*])' (B286/A234; cf. B272–3/A225).[6] The second postulate of empirical thinking states that only '[t]hat which is connected with the material conditions of experience (of sensation) is *actual* [*wirklich*]' (A218/B266). This links actuality to reality, to which sensation corresponds. (Kant defines sensation as the 'effect of an object on the capacity for representation, insofar as we are affected by it' [B34/A20], whereby it makes sense to take 'object' here as the thing in itself, not the appearance.[7] In the *Stufenleiter*, sensation is defined as a 'perception that refers to the subject as a modification of its state' [B376/A320].) What is actual (posited as existing) must thus be (objectively) real. It must be 'affirmed'[8] as real (cf. B336/A280). Nevertheless, actuality and reality

---

5 See also Warren (2001: 3).
6 Cf. R4685, AA 17: 674. Kant here connects reality to *quidditas* (thinghood).
7 Cf. Longuenesse (1998: 300).
8 See Warren (2001: 7 ff.).

are different categories since positing that something is actual (modality) does not eo ipso determine, in time, its (objective) reality in terms of a *categorial measurement* of the intensive magnitude of the empirical intuition that is the 'material condition of experience', that is, it does not determine that the object of intuition has some positive properties.[9] 'Reality' is the category of quality that concerns the intensive magnitude of a representation, that is, the fact that a representation contains an empirical sensation of some degree, which denotes something real.[10] Maier calls it appropriately the *Empfindungskategorie* (1930: 53) or *Intensitätskategorie* (1930: 56). The intensive *quantitas qualitatis* concerns, not the real parts of space and time as extensive magnitudes, where a successive synthesis from the parts to the whole takes place, but what Maier (1930: 70) calls 'imaginary parts', where a successive addition of the plurality filling time is concerned.

In the Deduction itself, at any rate in the first half of the B-Deduction, which only concerns the intellectual aspects of possible knowledge, Kant hardly, if at all, seems to address the categories of quality. It would thus seem difficult to extract much from the text that might serve as evidence of a derivation of the categories of quality from apperception. One ostensible reference to reality is at B150–1 in the second half, and there are a few indirect references when Kant talks about empirical apperception or empirical consciousness, at B139–40, and the important note at A117n. in the A-Deduction, where Kant links absence of consciousness to non-existence. This absence from the Transcendental Deduction is not surprising, however, as the qualitative features of knowledge clearly concern the *empirical content of intuition*, which makes it difficult to address them in abstraction from the latter. Nevertheless, there are some hints as to how we can derive the categories of quality from pure apperception provided elsewhere in the *Critique*, especially in the Schematism and in the Anticipations

---

9 Cf. Maier (1930: 74–5). Maier also quite rightly points out that the sensible material which we apprehend and is determined a priori by means of the category of reality *does not* eo ipso constitute something actual. The givenness of sensations has two aspects: on the one hand, their qualitative intensive quantity and, on the other, the fact that it points to something unknown to us, the thing in itself, but which 'appears' to us in objective experience. The modal category of actuality concerns the latter, whereas the category of reality the former. Both categories have their separate functionality.

10 In R6349, AA 18: 673, Kant identifies reality as having a degree as a category. See also R6338a, where Kant writes: 'Quality is that inner determination of a thing that can become greater or smaller without enlargement or diminution of the thing' (AA 18: 663 [NF: 380]). The examples that Kant gives here are mass and velocity, but also *qualia* must be seen as intensive magnitudes.

of Perception,[11] but also in the Refutation of Mendelssohn's proof in the B-Paralogisms. Kant writes in the Schematism chapter:

> Reality is in the pure concept of the understanding that to which a sensation in general corresponds, that, therefore, the concept of which in itself indicates [*anzeigt*] a being (in time). (B182/A143)

Reality is 'being' (in the German it says *ein Sein*) to which a sensation refers or to which it corresponds. But does Kant mean by this empirical reality or objective reality? Presumably not:

> Since time is only the form of intuition, thus of objects as appearances, *that which corresponds to the sensation in these is the transcendental matter of all objects, as things in themselves* (thinghood [*Sachheit*], reality [*Realität*]). (B182/A143, emphasis mine)

Here, Kant would appear to assert that the Being to which a sensation corresponds is not an empirically real object or empirical reality as such (a being in time), but 'the *transcendental* matter of all objects', that is, things in themselves. This is quite a striking assertion that immediately triggers idealist alarm bells.[12] That indeed Kant might be taken to mean reality in itself can be made out from his account of what must be *transcendentally* (not: empirically) given for the possibility of knowledge of things, namely 'the complete material condition of [the] possibility' of a thing qua thinghood, in the chapter in the *Critique* that deals with the transcendental Ideal (A576/B604).[13] Indeed, '[t]ranscendental matter is the reality or the given <*datum*> for *all* things' (*Met-L₂*, AA 28: 575

---

11 For an account of the Schematism and Anticipations, see Maier (1930) and Warren (2001).
12 For example, Longuenesse (1998: 301) is alarmed by it and notes the conflict with the way that the matter of appearances is said to correspond to sensation in the Transcendental Aesthetic (B34/A20). I do not agree with her 'weak' reading of things in themselves here in the Schematism as *empirical* things in themselves, which prima facie conflicts with her acknowledgment of the affective relation as concerning 'the relation of our receptivity to a thing in itself in the strong sense' (1998: 302). However, this discussion goes beyond the concern of this book.
13 Maier (1930: 54, esp. 54n.2) disputes that there is a direct relation between the 'transcendental matter' of the Schematism passage and the pre-Critical *realitas noumenon*, a metaphysical thing in itself. It concerns 'eigentlich nichts anderes als die hypostasierte "Materie" der Vorstellungen, das Objekt etwa einer (problematischen) nicht-sinnlichen Empfindung und damit ein negatives Noumenon im Sinn der Kritik'. In Maier's view, there is also therefore not a direct connection with the transcendental Ideal. Answering the question whether this is indeed the case for Kant depends on one's interpretation of Kant's notion of things in themselves and the positive role of metaphysics in Kant's Critical philosophy. See also Heimsoeth's (1956: 64–5) observations regarding Maier on this point.

[LM: 339], emphasis added), not just objects of experience. But we can abstract from these metaphysical issues here, as Kant's account in the Transcendental Deduction only concerns the possibility of knowledge of the objects of experience, as what before would be called *realitates phenomena*, and not what makes them things in the first place.[14] Our interest here concerns the categories of quality insofar as they are capable of being schematised to sensible appearances.[15] Towards the end of the section on the transcendental Ideal, Kant provides some insight into how these categories are applicable to 'the thing itself (*in appearance*)' (A581/B609, emphasis added) rather than to the thing in itself *tout court*, that is, the thoroughly determined thing (A576/B604). I discuss this below in Section 8.4.

In the passage immediately following the above-quoted ones, Kant fills in more of the details regarding the categories of quality. He writes that

> every sensation has a degree or magnitude, through which it can more or less fill the same time, i.e., the inner sense in regard to the same representation of an object, until it ceases in nothingness (=0=*negatio*). Hence there is a relation and connection between, or rather a transition from reality to negation, that makes every reality representable as a quantum [...] (B182–3/A143).

We have here the categories of reality and negation, the former pointing to being and the latter to non-being. They concern not the form but the material content of a *representation* of an object, namely its being a sensation, which must have any degree from close to zero upwards. This material, sensible aspect of any representation, by means of which a representation is directly related to the reality of a thing whose representation it is, concerns the intensive magnitude of an intuition of an object (a perception), as Kant argues in the Anticipations of Perceptions (B207).[16] This relates to consciousness, which is the connection with apperception that we are seeking. Kant writes:

---

14 Cf. R4817, AA 17: 737. What is at issue in Kant's metaphysical account of transcendental matter concerns what he calls 'transcendental affirmation, which is a Something [*Etwas*], the concept of which in itself already expresses a being, and hence it is called reality (thinghood), *because through it alone* [...] *are objects Something (things)*' (A574/B602, emphasis added). See further Schulting (2017a), ch. 9.
15 Maier (1930: 53) is right though to suggest that the pure categories go beyond application in sensible experience and thus also relate to *realitas noumenon*.
16 Although sensation is instantaneous and does not rest on a successive synthesis as is the case with homogeneous quanta such as space and time, which are extensive magnitudes, it is still a magnitude, namely an intensive one. But as with space and time, perception is also a 'continuous' or 'flowing' magnitude (B211/A170), for 'between reality in appearance and negation

> Perception is empirical consciousness, i.e., one in which there is at the same time sensation. Appearances, as objects of perception, are not pure (merely formal) intuitions, like space and time (for these cannot be perceived in themselves). They therefore also contain in addition to the intuition the materials for some object in general (through which something existing in space or time is represented), i.e., the real of the sensation, as merely subjective representation, by which one can only be conscious that the subject is affected, and which one relates to an object in general. Now *from the empirical consciousness to the pure consciousness a gradual alteration is possible, where the real in the former entirely disappears, and a merely formal (a priori) consciousness of the manifold in space and time remains.* (B207–8, emphasis added)

In a refutation of Mendelssohn's proof of the persistence of the soul on the basis of the alleged simplicity of the soul, Kant shows that even if it were granted that the soul is simple, and so contains no parts '*outside one another*', it would still be the case that it has a plurality of parts 'inside', as it were, as it would be an intensive magnitude of some infinitesimal degree, so that the soul-substance might be said to disappear 'by a gradual remission (*remissio*) of all its powers' (B413–15). Kant links this discussion of intensive magnitude to consciousness, and points out in a footnote, in which he criticises the standard view which identifies consciousness with clear representation, that 'even in some obscure representations' there must be consciousness.[17]

In the *Lectures on Metaphysics*, the link with apperception is even clearer:

> All reality has degree. There are degrees from sensation to thought, i.e., up to apperception, where I think myself with respect to the understanding. Something can have so little degree that I can scarcely notice it, but nonetheless I am still always conscious of it. There is, properly speaking, no largest and smallest in experience. (*Met-Mron*, AA 29: 834 [LM: 192])

This passage contains some significant clues as to how to approach the question of the necessary qualitative aspect of the representation of an object (or any representation for that matter), which can be indirectly demonstrated by looking at pure apperception in abstraction from empirical intuition, with only the latter being that which is actually characterised by an intensive magnitude. Both in the Mrongovius notes and in the Anticipations, as well as in the Schematism, it is made clear that 'apperception' or 'formal (*a priori*) consciousness' or 'pure consciousness' (B208) equals zero or amounts to negation, that is, 'that the concept of which represents a non-being (in time)' (B182/A143), and that 'empirical

---

there is a continuous nexus of many possible intermediate sensations' (A168/B210; cf. A143/B182–3).
17 See further Wunderlich (2005: 141–2). Cf. Schulting (2015a).

consciousness' must be any degree greater than zero. (Notice that in the Anticipations passage, the contrast is between empirical consciousness and *pure intuition* as that which has zero degree, which makes sense in the context of an account of the mathematical principles of empirical experience.) From this fact it follows that the manifold of representations that is given to apperception or pure, formal consciousness in fact provides the material content of consciousness, namely sensations. The sensations provide the connection to reality. Pure, formal consciousness is itself empty, not just qua the multiplicity of parts of an intuition in terms of extensive magnitude (see Chapter 9), but also qua the multiplicity of degrees of intensive magnitude. Pure consciousness or apperception corresponds to the opposite of reality, a non-being, that is, the negation of reality.[18] Furthermore, since sensation is connected to the real, any determination of the degree of sensation amounts to a determination of the empirical reality of the object of perception, to which the sensation corresponds. But since what is determined as real is that which is represented by a *concept* of reality, in fact 'a pure concept of the understanding' (B182/A143), the real 'does not signify anything except the synthesis in an empirical consciousness in general' (A175–6/B217). *Determination* of the empirical reality points to the third category of quality, limitation, which is 'nothing other than reality combined with negation' (B111).

But before coming back to the categories themselves, I would like to look first at some arguments from the literature concerning the relation between *transcendental* consciousness and *empirical* consciousness as that which points to reality, and point out why it is mistaken to take Kant's position to be that transcendental apperception is the necessary condition of consciousness *tout court*. Subsequently, in Section 8.4 I shall be able to show how the categories of quality, namely 'reality', 'negation', and 'limitation', are in fact derivable from the principle of apperception.

8.3 Sensation, Consciousness, and Apperception

The 'I think' of apperception is closely linked up with, if not identical to, what is called transcendental self-consciousness or the unity thereof (B132 [AA 3: 109.3–4]). At A117n., Kant indicates that the 'mere representation I' is 'transcendental consciousness'. In fact, in the Transcendental Aesthetic, at B68, Kant already identified 'simple [*einfache*] representation of the I' as 'consciousness of

---

18 Notice that this is not *logical* negation, as a quality of judgement.

self [*Bewußtsein seiner Selbst*]' (trans. Kemp Smith).[19] 'I think'-consciousness, transcendental apperception and self-consciousness are, for Kant, thus equivalent. Although Kant suggests that pure apperception is the same 'in all consciousness' (B132), it is not at all implied that consciousness is only first possible under the presupposition of transcendental consciousness. It does not follow from the 'I think'-proposition that unaccompanied representations (which I called P3- or P4-representations in Chapter 6) are eo ipso unconscious representations, for (1) the proposition is not about what conditions must be satisfied for awareness to obtain but about what conditions must be satisfied for a thoroughgoing unity of one's representations to obtain and to have a grasp thereof and (2) if representations are unaccompanied, then there is no cognitively available way to determine their putative unconsciousness, precisely *because* they are unaccompanied by an 'I think' (contrary to what some believe, third-person inferential routes are to no avail either here). In other words, it is analytically true that the absence of consciousness cannot be proved for representations that are *not* accompanied by the 'I think' (that is, apperceived in the transcendental way).[20] Evidently, for transcendental consciousness to be of real cognitive value and to lead to knowledge (*empirische Erkenntnis*), an empirical perception or empirical apperception is required (cf. B140), but this is of course not to say, as is often believed, that, by implication, empirical consciousness or empirical apperception eo ipso entails transcendental apperception.[21] Transcendental self-consciousness is neither a necessary condition nor a sufficient condition of empirical consciousness (although, in the case of possible experience, a perception's conscious intensity *in general* can be a priori anticipated by means of the cate-

---

19 The translation of Guyer/Wood is not precise here; by translating *das Bewußtsein seiner selbst* as 'consciousness of itself' it is suggested that Kant speaks of consciousness *tout court*, rather than self-consciousness. Moreover, the reflexive sense of the German is lost in translation. Kemp Smith is more exact here.
20 Cf. A172/B214; *Prol* § 24: '[T]here is no perception that can show an absolute absence' (AA 4: 307). The fact that 'the entire absence of the real in sensible intuition cannot itself be perceived' (A172/B214) is important for showing that the standard assumption of natural philosophers 'that the *real* in space [...] is *everywhere one and the same*, and can be differentiated only according to its extensive magnitude' (A173/B215)—which leads them to think that only assuming that volume 'is empty in all matter' (ibid.) can explain differences 'in the quantity of various kinds of matter in bodies that have the same volume' (ibid., trans. Kemp Smith)—is 'merely metaphysical' and thus mistaken in Kant's view (A173/B215). These differences can be accounted for because of the differences in intensive magnitude (mass, velocity etc.).
21 However, prima facie evidence to the contrary is provided by certain ambiguous text passages in the A-Deduction (esp. A117n.) and, to a lesser extent, in several notes and letters from Kant. See again Section 6.3.

gory of reality). In fact, and this is one of the reasons why the categories of quality are derivable from the principle of apperception, transcendental consciousness itself is conditioned on the fact that there is *empirical* consciousness, namely *some* reality that is presupposed by the 'I think' of apperception, for any given instantiation of the 'I think'. This is argued by Kant in a well-known note in the B-Paralogisms, in which he writes that the 'I think'-proposition

> expresses an indeterminate empirical intuition, i.e., a perception (*hence it proves that sensation, which consequently belongs to sensibility, grounds this existential proposition*). (B422–3n., emphasis added)

For any amount of empirical consciousness to be *determined* transcendental consciousness is required as its categorially necessary condition, but at the same time transcendental consciousness is not a necessary condition for the emergence or givenness of empirical consciousness, which is a brute fact that must be presupposed.[22]

That transcendental self-consciousness is not a necessary condition of empirical consciousness *tout court*, can already be seen from looking again at the modal structure of the 'I think'-proposition, as was done in Chapter 6. If, in conformity with B132 (AA 3: 108.29–30), where Kant indicates that the 'I think' denotes transcendental *self-consciousness*, we substitute the predicate 'all my (episodes of) consciousness' for 'all my representations', an analogous account can be given of the putative entailment relation between empirical consciousness and transcendental self-consciousness, so that the necessary possibility P1, supposing that the 'I think' is existentially instantiated at least once, reads:

> P1': *the 'I think' accompanies all my (episodes of) consciousness*

if P1', then, ex hypothesi, it must also be possible that

> P2': *the 'I think' does not accompany all my (episodes of) consciousness*

and/or it must be possible that

---

[22] This is however contradicted by what Kant says in a note from around 1790 (R6311): 'If impressions on my inner sense occur, this presupposes that I affect myself (although it is inexplicable to us how this happens), and thus empirical consciousness presupposes transcendental consciousness' (AA 18: 611 [NF: 356]).

P3′: *the 'I think' does not accompany any (episode of) consciousness that happens to occur and is so occurrent at any time t at which the 'I think' is not instantiated*

and/or it must be possible that

P4′: *the 'I think' does not accompany any (episode of) consciousness that happens to occur and is so occurrent at any time t at which the 'I think' is not instantiated, and that is also interminably barred from being able to be so accompanied, e.g. because the intensity of such an episode of consciousness decreases (close) to zero before it can even be retrieved for apperception.*

Conformably to the analysis of P3 and P4, P3′ and P4′ signal the failure of satisfaction of P1′. P3′ and P4′ denote episodes of empirical consciousness nonetheless, but the subject that has these episodes cannot, for some reason, retain them to connect them in a collective unity (see further Chapter 9).[23] P1′ shows up an analytical truth (from which P3′ and P4′ are logically inferable), so that P2′ must be seen as spurious, as it would be contradictory for me to state that 'I am not self-aware of all my consciousness', since there is complete identity between transcendental consciousness or self-consciousness and 'my consciousness' of 'all my representations', that is, all episodes of *my* empirical consciousness analytically relate to the identity of self-consciousness for all possible instantiations of the 'I think' (B135; see also A362ff.).

However, there is no such identity between transcendental consciousness and any arbitrary P3′- or P4′-consciousness, which is constituted of sensations as modifications of *some* subject's state of mind (cf. B376/A320). This is confirmed by a passage at B133 (AA 3: 109.16–20), where it is asserted that 'the empirical consciousness that accompanies different representations is by itself dispersed [and thus amounts to different instances of consciousness, D.S.] and without relation to the identity of the subject [i.e., the identity of the self of which I am conscious when I accompany representations that *would be* identical were I indeed to simultaneously take them together, D.S.]'.[24] Thus, transcenden-

---

[23] Cf. André de Muralt in his classic book on apperception: 'Le sujet peut bien avoir conscience de ses représentations, mais l'une lui échappe au moment de l'appréhension de l'autre. Il se produit ainsi un flot continu d'impressions sensibles qui apparaissent tour à tour dans la conscience pour disparaître ensuite aussi vite qu'elles étaient venues. [...] le sujet n'est pas capable de prendre conscience de son intégrité [...] le sujet n'est pas capable par lui-même de retenir ses différentes représentations et de lutter contre l'anéantissement des diverses consciences empiriques dans le temps fuyant' (de Muralt 1958: 55–6).

[24] Notice that the empirical consciousness that accompanies discrete representations collapses into these representations themselves, for given that they are not related to the identical self that

tal apperception does not indicate a capacity for mere awareness or the having of sensations, namely the different representations accompanied by a dispersed empirical consciousness of which Kant speaks at B133 (P3'- and P4'-awareness). It only provides the rules for unification of 'all my empirical consciousness' in a unitary self-consciousness, namely the 'transcendental unity of self-consciousness' that generates the simple representation 'I think' (B132). In principle, a representer R could thus be aware of stand-alone representations in giving free rein to the play of representations, without having a second-order reflective awareness, by virtue of self-consciousness, *that* she is aware,[25] given that representations are just conscious impingements or impressions, of a certain degree of intensity, on the mind.[26] In such a case, there would only be a subjective unity of consciousness, the constituents of which do not make up an objective unity by being related to the identity of a thinking self, and hence there would not be self-consciousness *stricto sensu*, that is, a 'thoroughgoing identity of self-consciousness' (B135). P4' is more extreme, but one example of P4'-consciousness is provided by Kant himself, namely childhood experience.[27] Furthermore, it should be

would accompany them in a thoroughgoing way the relation between empirical apperception and the discrete representations it accompanies (severally) is psychologically opaque (see further below Section 9.3).

25 Like Brook (1994: 82ff.) I believe that, for Kant, a psychological self can be aware of stand-alone representations, but never that such a self is at the same time also aware of herself as subject of other such-like representations (Brook points to B134 [AA 3: 110.7–9]). However, I do not believe that one is licensed to argue, as Brook seems to do, that, necessarily, such stand-alone representations are nonetheless de facto *that self's* representations, while she is thereby not aware of her identity. To be able to determine that the self's representations, which are not apperceived by the same self, are still *that* self's representations would necessarily invoke the very principle of apperception that is required for identification of one's representations as one's own; by implication, the putative identity of non-apperceived representations and an underlying self to which they belong, cannot be made out in a de re fashion, not from the first-person point of view nor, of course, from a third person's perspective. But perhaps Brook means that stand-alone representations are necessarily *someone*'s representations, so that every representer of course *has* the representations she represents, even if she is not aware of herself as so representing. My point is that such possession of representations can never *as such* be reported or determined other than by 'pulling' these representations into 'I' awareness (*stricto sensu*).

26 I agree with Guyer that representations 'cannot exist except as states of consciousness' (Guyer 1980: 209). Cf. *Met-L₁*, AA 28: 227 (LM: 46), where Kant says that subjective consciousness or psychological consciousness is a 'forcible state'.

27 See *Anthr*, AA 7: 128ff. Here, Kant makes it clear that children do not have conceptual experience and that, as a result, memories of one's childhood do not *really* extend back to it. Interestingly, in the very first section of the *Anthropology* (AA 7: 128) Kant observes that very young children do not employ the first person pronoun while referring to themselves, but refer to them-

observed that there is no *reportable* difference between P3′ and P4′, for their distinction is psychologically opaque.[28]

A persistent assumption in the literature is that transcendental apperception just is the capacity for awareness (see most recently Dickerson 2004: 93ff.). For example, to apperceive means for Collins (1999: 108) to be conscious, or indeed, 'conscious experience is the ultimate product of this mental activity [viz. apperception, DS]', so that '[w]e are not conscious of either the original representations of outer sense or of the application of the mind to them'.[29] Collins is right of course if he means that one is not conscious of the already synthesised representations severally (see again Chapter 6), but that does not mean that synthesis first generates consciousness. In the earlier literature, Robert Paul Wolff (1973: 94, 158–9) also adheres to the standpoint that apperception is the condition of consciousness itself. He claims that it is the 'very heart of the entire Deduction' (1973: 158) that the categories are the necessary conditions of consciousness, indeed of 'any consciousness whatsoever' (1973: 159). Like Collins, Wolff (1973: 158) states, on the basis of a reading of A121–2, that 'we cannot be conscious of an unsynthesized manifold'.[30] In the oft-cited letter to Herz from May 1789 (*Corr*, AA 11: 50.10–23), among other places,[31] Kant makes it clear however that a capacity for awareness is not what he means by transcendental apperception.[32] Transcendental apperception rather concerns a special kind of unified consciousness in terms of a conceptual grasp of objects or objective events. That said, Kant's own frequent use of the general term *Bewußtsein* or *Bewustseyn* for transcendental apperception (see for instance at A103), where he means it to be not just awareness or even a capacity for clarification, can be confusing.

But is it not true that Kant claims that apperception is required for consciousness, even if it does not generate it? What would it mean when I am not explicitly aware of my representations as mine, but am merely *having* representations, in other words, when apperception is not actually instantiated? Would

---

selves by their first name (i.e. via third-person routes). Cf. Castañeda (1990: 152), Ameriks (2000a: 248–9) and Hoppe (1991: 53).

28 See further my comments in Schulting (2017a), ch. 2.
29 See his further remark that the 'transcendental unity is a condition for the possibility of conscious experience' (1999: 137).
30 Cf. Wolff (1973: 148–9, 116). For a critique of Wolff, see Ameriks (1978: 280). See similar observations made by Van Cleve (1999: 97) and a critique of Van Cleve's view of apperception in Ameriks (2003a). See also Kemp Smith (1999: xli-xlii, 222–3).
31 See also Kant's letters addressed to J. S. Beck in the 1790s (*Corr*, AA 11: 314.27ff. and 515.26). But see, by contrast, MFNS, § 98 Remark (AA 4: 542 Anm.), where Kant himself says that apperception is the capacity (*Vermögen*) for consciousness; see also *Met-L₂*, AA 28: 584 (LM: 344).
32 See also La Rocca (2008: 462–3).

my representations then be *conscious* ones or would they literally be unconscious? In general, one would presume that representational states that are not attended to by a second-order act of reflection are conscious states of mind regardless, based on the idea that one must distinguish between first- and second-order consciousness. The absence of second-order consciousness does not logically entail the absence of first-order consciousness. Allison (1983: 153ff.) disputes this, for like the aforementioned Collins and Wolff he thinks that apperception is presupposed for consciousness even of our subjective mental states (that is, states that have no cognitive, objective, value), hence for first-order consciousness.[33] Thus, one could not be conscious even of one's own mental states, more precisely, *be* in a state of consciousness, unless transcendental apperception is instantiated.[34] Allison makes an ostensibly crucial distinction between representations and *conscious* representations. For representation to be conscious a further condition needs to be satisfied, this condition being tantamount to pure or transcendental apperception. But what are representational or mental states, if not themselves episodes of consciousness or states of awareness (of whatever degree of intensity), regardless of issues that have to do with epistemic significance? Kant notices this in the *Anthropology* (§ 5):

> A contradiction appears to lie in the claim *to have representations and still not be conscious of them*; for how could we know that we have them if we are not conscious of them? (AA 7: 135 [*Anthr-C:* 246])[35]

Suppose that subjectively valid perception eo ipso consists in *unconscious* representation. How, then, could representations still be accorded subjective value, as modifications of the mind that, to be sure, have no *objective* significance, but

---

33 See also Allison (1996: 72–4). Cf. Kitcher (1984: 117n.6, 140) and Pippin (1997: 41).
34 Allison (1983: 153) misreads the passage from the letter to Herz of 26 May 1789, *Corr*, AA 11: 52. In my view, Kant does not at all deny here the real possibility of consciousness of 'each individual representation', of sense data; what he denies is a unified consciousness of these sense data as such, which would yield knowledge (of myself or an object). In other words, sense data are *epistemically* irrelevant, even if I would in fact be aware of individual data (the real possibility of which Kant grants). See again Allison (1996: 72–4).
35 The context of this quotation is somewhat different from what I want to suggest here. Kant in fact criticises here Locke's view of 'having *Ideas*, and Perception being the same thing' (*Essay*, II.i.§ 9), that is, the view that representations are by implication conscious states. By contrast, Kant believes 'we can still be *indirectly* conscious of having a representation, even if we are not directly conscious of it' (AA 7: 135 [*Anthr-C:* 246]), suggesting that having the representation itself, which he calls 'obscure', is not tantamount to consciousness. We should however not conclude that for Kant obscurity (as opposed to clarity) equals lack of consciousness (see B414n.) See further below Section 8.3.2. Cf. Schulting (2015a).

which must to a certain extent still be reckoned to amount to consciousness, as Kant writes at B242/A197?[36]

However, one might want to insist (and I take Allison to be insisting on this line of thought) that representing *as such*, that is, representing of which I am not aware by virtue of a second-order act of apperception, cannot be taken to be coextensive with consciousness. This is not as odd as I may make it appear, since presumably Leibniz thought the same: perceptual states need not be conscious or apperceived states.[37] Consciousness, then, is to be considered to be exclusively something of a higher order, governed by the constraints of transcendental apperception. Some conspicuous formulations of Kant himself appear to imply that such a construal is justified.[38] Moreover, at times Kant appears to suggest that for consciousness to occur, whether subjectively valid or objectively real, a combination, more specifically a synthetic act of the imagination, should at least have taken place (see for example B233), suggesting that any lower-level representation must be unconscious. Now even if it were granted that, in general, first-order mental states must be empirically conscious states for them to *be*

---

[36] Cf. again Kant's letter to Herz of 26 May 1789, *Corr*, AA 11: 52.10–15. In spite of Kant's suggestion in the letter that I can be conscious of 'each individual representation' when I merely associate, Allison, reading the passage counterfactually, avers that 'such a unity is [...] not [...] in any sense a *mode* of awareness' (1996: 74).

[37] See Leibniz, *Principes de la nature et de la grâce*, § 4. See Schulting (2015a).

[38] Kant appears to identify empirical consciousness with the transcendental identity of the self at A115–16. Also, at A350 Kant asserts that 'consciousness is the one single thing that makes all representations into thoughts, and in which, therefore, as in the transcendental subject, our perceptions must be encountered'. See also MFNS, § 98 Anm. (AA 4: 542) and *Met-L$_2$*, AA 28: 584 (LM: 344). But see R5923, AA 18: 386 and *Met-L$_1$*, AA 28: 227 (LM: 46–7). For a less moderate conception of consciousness, consider for example a passage in *Met-Mron*, where Kant appears to hold the view that the self of transcendental apperception is indeed the necessary condition of consciousness: 'Consciousness is the principle of the possibility of the understanding, but not of sensibility. [...] The self underlies consciousness and is what is peculiar to spirit' (AA 29: 878 [LM: 247]). Or a few pages further on: 'Inner sense is the consciousness of our representations themselves. (Apperception is the ground of inner sense.)' (AA 29: 882 [LM: 250–1]). By this latter assertion, Kant seems to waver between, on the one hand, granting inner sense some form of consciousness independently of apperceptive consciousness (in conformity, it seems, with the Critical doctrine of the distinction between inner sense and apperception [B153]) and, on the other, propounding the immoderate view that, if it is to amount to conscious representations, inner sense must have its ground in transcendental apperception. Most probably following Baumgarten regarding inner sense, the Critical Kant however clearly distinguishes between inner sense and apperception. And given that Baumgarten regards inner sense as *conscientia strictius dicta* (*Metaphysica*, § 535), it seems justified to infer that Kant did not just conflate *mere* consciousness with apperception, although Baumgarten himself probably means to identify *conscientia strictius dicta* with *self*-consciousness. See further Schulting (2015a).

mental states (existentially), someone reasoning in accordance with Allison's line of thinking could still insist that for such states to be *conscious* states they necessarily *entail* a second-order state (viz. transcendental consciousness).[39] One might then further qualify this requirement by maintaining that such representations must be synthesised, in order to be able to be conscious of them, but that they may not *actually* be accompanied by a reflective 'I think' (see again Chapter 6). In any case, mental states that do not have a relation of entailment to transcendental self-consciousness must be taken, it is argued, to remain hidden in the dark recesses of the mind, indeed they would be, as Kant says in the A-Deduction, 'but a blind play of representations, i.e., less than a dream' (A112).[40]

Let me examine, in the next section, more closely the difference between 'having representations' and 'being conscious *of* representations', which presumably parallels the distinction between sheer representing and consciousness *tout court*. This discussion bears directly on the issue of the nature of the entailment relation between consciousness and transcendental self-consciousness.

8.3.1 First-Order Consciousness and Apperception

I want to dwell on Allison's main point a little longer, that is, the claim that a type difference must be made between 'having representations' (being properties of the mind or mental states) and 'being conscious of having them', which presumably he understands to be the same as a second-order reflexive or apperceptive awareness. Consider an ostensibly similar position advanced by Georg Mohr (1991: 106 ff.), whose detailed view on the matter appears to lend support to Allison's distinction. Mohr reflects on the possible equivalence of 'representation' and 'state of consciousness' (*Bewußtseinszustand*) or 'conscious content' (*Bewußtseinsinhalt*). He believes that these designations are not equivalent. If consciousness were to be taken as equivalent to representation, Mohr reasons, 'having a representation' would indeed imply that one is eo ipso conscious of it. It seems that if representation were equivalent to consciousness this would result in a surreptitious conflation of representing and *apperceiving*, which obviously cannot be true. It is then only appropriate to insist that Kant, as Mohr puts it,

---

[39] See Allison (1996: 76). In a critique of Gurwitsch, Allison appears to identify the conditions for consciousness with the conditions for synthesis, for, as he says, 'the very act of bringing [a preconceptualized manifold] to consciousness would necessarily subject it to determination by means of the categories' (1996: 72).
[40] See L.W. Beck (1978) as the *locus classicus* on this topic.

8.3 Sensation, Consciousness, and Apperception — 211

'has not adopted an equivalence of meaning between "representation" and "conscious content"' (1991: 107).[41]

Several reasons seem to corroborate Mohr's distinction and, hence, to bear out Allison's position on this issue. First, Mohr refers to the *Stufenleiter*, which Kant provides at A320/B376–7, where it seems that Kant holds that representation is not to be equated with consciousness. However, I believe reference to the *Stufenleiter* does not lend undeniable support to Mohr's view, for 'representation' is to be taken as the genus of all possible species of representation (perceptions etc.), and not itself an actual instantiation of it. The passage does not appear to imply the view that a representation in general (that is, without being a representation with consciousness, viz. perception) can *actually* exist as a modification of the mind. As Kant says, 'a *perception* that refers to the subject as a modification of its state is a *sensation*' (B376/A320).[42] This would appear to mean that a *perception* is the *minimally* instantiatable form of representation for a mind such as ours. Thus, since any perception is a 'representation with consciousness', a sensation is eo ipso always conscious, and hence, any *actual* representation, regardless of whether it is objectively or merely subjectively valid, is at least a minimally conscious representation. Given, then, that representations as modifications of the mind must always have a psychological content of some intensity for them to be mentally real, I believe one cannot consistently argue on the basis of the *Stufenleiter* that there can be actual representations that have *no* consciousness attached to them.

The second, systematic reason Mohr adduces is that 'taking up into consciousness [*Aufnahme ins Bewußtsein*] is an additional condition, under which an intuition must stand to first be able to be considered a "conscious representation", a representation "for us"', and further that 'an intuition (sensible representation) therefore does *not already in itself* satisfy the condition of being a conscious representation' (1991: 107). Mohr thus asserts that consciousness *is* the very condition under which a representation can count as a conscious representation, a representation 'for us'. Apparently, Mohr reasons that it would be log-

---

[41] Also Ameriks (2000b: 109) stresses that 'representation' must not be taken to be equivalent to or coextensive with 'consciousness'. I take it that Ameriks does so because he wants to warn against an all too quick identification of consciousness and pure apperception and specifically against Reinholdian speculations regarding the principle of consciousness as a presumed basic ground of cognition (but see Schulting 2016a). Cf. de Muralt (1958: 25), who appears to adopt the Reinholdian view. See further Ameriks (2000b: 238ff.) on what he calls the Strong Apperception Theory (SAT). Overall, I agree with Ameriks's critique of SAT.
[42] Notice however that Mohr differentiates *Bewußtseinsinhalt* explicitly from Kant's technical *Modifikation unseres Gemüts* (Mohr 1991: 107, 107n.2).

ically nonsensical to claim to be consciously representing without the condition for consciousness having been fulfilled. Thus, Mohr rejects the possibility that 'A has no awareness of the fact that it has awareness of X' on the grounds that it entails a contradiction. He notes: 'When A is not aware that X is represented in him, then A is not aware of X' (1991: 115).[43] Mohr appears to mean that having no second-order consciousness *that* one has a representation implies that there can be no first-order consciousness either.[44] If this is what he means, I believe Mohr commits a fallacy here, by assuming that consciousness 'for me' and consciousness 'per se' are equivalent. Presumably, he wants to emphasise that it is trivially true that to be conscious of *x* is not *not to be conscious of x*. But it appears that he understands the notion of consciousness as being already in itself attentive consciousness, that is, consciousness 'before' the subject or the 'I', although elsewhere he carefully separates intransitive from apperceptive consciousness. One should be heedful that the fact that one does not consciously attend to one's representations does not constitute in itself a proof of the unconsciousness of representations which are not attended to.[45]

There is an additional ambiguity in the way Mohr articulates the problem. Mohr is careful not to conflate representing and apperception or inner sense and apperception. Yet, given that he argues that *consciousness* is the additional condition for an intuition to become an intuition 'for us' and given that according to B132 apperception is precisely that condition which makes a representation be 'something for me', apperception and consciousness apparently do coincide for Mohr. But if one heeds the distinction between mere consciousness and attentive consciousness (only this latter consciousness being coextensive with apperception), there is nothing problematic about the hypothesis Mohr sets up at the beginning of his account and works to undermine, namely the hypothesis that a representational state of mind would perforce be a conscious state of mind (of a particular intensity). The difference—to which Mohr is careful to draw our attention in respect of the epistemically relevant additional condition of *apperceptive* consciousness—would then not be a difference between representing (R) and consciousness (C), but between first-order consciousness (C_1) and second-order consciousness, a 'consciousness *that*' ($C_2[C_1R]$). This distinction would correspond with the difference between *having* a representation (a representation being a modification of my mind) and *representing that* one is having a

---

[43] In German the verb 'to be conscious of' or 'to be aware that' is always already reflexive. Mohr's original thus reads: 'Wenn A sich nicht bewußt ist, daß in ihm X vorgestellt wird, dann ist A sich X nicht bewußt.'
[44] Cf. Thöle (1991: 68).
[45] Cf. Sturma (1985: 42).

representation, that is, having a complex representation. In general, when Kant, especially in the A-Deduction, talks about consciousness he means a second-order consciousness, a 'consciousness that…', which introduces an obligatory clause (see A103), not just any first-order consciousness.

The transcendental consciousness which Kant argues is requisite for representational manifolds to be synthesised, is merely formal and has no psychological content. This is a point that has been frequently emphasised by Allison. It is not controversial. However, what is often not so clear is that this formal transcendental consciousness should also not be conflated with the *empirical conditions* for psychological consciousness, which are not at issue in the Transcendental Deduction (see B152). What I am driving at is that nothing in Kant's reasoning with regard to transcendental self-consciousness indicates that unaccompanied or unsynthesised representations must ipso facto be unconscious, presumably because transcendental consciousness is a necessary condition of any consciousness. More boldly, I believe that such representations *cannot* really be unconscious, at least insofar as *sensible* representations are concerned, especially if one heeds Kant's thesis that the 'proper material' (*den eigentlichen Stoff*) of inner sense consists of the representations of outer sense (B67).

As we have seen in Section 8.2, Kant says that a sensation—the material of perception (immediately relating to the existence of something=*x* as that which is not yet determined)—has an intensive magnitude or a degree. In apprehending the sensation at a particular point in time (in abstraction from the extensive magnitude of an appearance), an empirical consciousness with a certain degree of intensity is apprehended (this requires a *synthesis speciosa*).[46] The degree of intensity can increase on a scale from something approximating zero 'until its given measure' or decrease until its magnitude equals zero, which effectively amounts to its negation (A167–8/B209–10, B208). As I read this, regardless of the issue whether the matter it furnishes pertains to a subjectively or an objectively valid representation, any sensation is necessarily (empirically) *consciously* apprehended, as consciousness itself is the measure of intensity.

I should note that this does not alter the fact that the intensity *principle* itself, as part of the system of synthetic principles, must be regarded as a *categorial* principle that is co-constitutive of objective experience (cf. *Prol* § 24). This principle designates the a priori form (the *categories* of quality) under which one can synthesise the *reality* of appearance, the *quale* of sensation qua sensation, into an *objective reality*, namely, the existential content of a determinate ob-

---

[46] See Longuenesse (1998: 298 ff.).

ject.⁴⁷ The property of sensations 'of having a degree' is a priori determinable (A176/B218). However, as is generally the case in Kant's theory of experience, a distinction must be heeded between the transcendental character of the anticipation of the intensity of sensations and the *quid facti* with respect to their reality (as having been affected by the things in themselves). Sensations as such, that is, as the matter of purely sensible apprehension, must be considered to *have* a 'quality', a *quale*, before even what Maier has called the *Intensitätskategorie* can be applied to it by the understanding. By implication, contrary to Allison (1996: 73), we may ascribe to Kant the view that sub-categorial consciousness, 'atomistic consciousness' of qualitative mental percepts, the intensity of which can be such that it is barely noticeable, is a perfectly viable notion and even necessary for any sensation, and hence representation.⁴⁸

8.3.2 Consciousness, Unconsciousness, and Obscurity

At this point we might want to consider a clearer definition of what one understands by 'unconscious': does 'unconscious' indeed mean 'not conscious at all' in the most literal sense, or does it manifest an attempt to express what is conveyed by 'not *purely* conscious' (pure in Kant's sense, that is, transcendentally conscious)? The former definition would seem to be out of keeping with what we have just discussed as well as Kant's enunciations at B414 regarding his position on the possibility of a gradual remission of consciousness. It would also conflict with the classification of types of representation in the *Stufenleiter*

---

47 I do not mean to say that here the subjective, ineffable aspect of sensation, discussed by Kant in the *Critique of the Power of Judgement*, is at issue. What is determinable by the categories of quality is rather the material, sensible matter in general that constitutes the quality of a representation, that is, what 'belongs to *objective* sensation, as perception of an object of sense' (CJ, AA 5: 206). I thank Christian Onof for raising this point.

48 Kant's position in the Anticipations of Perception, as I have construed it, is confirmed by several passages in his *Lectures on Metaphysics*. In addition to the passage from *Met-Mron*, AA 29: 834 (LM: 192), which I quoted at the beginning of this chapter, consider further a passage in *Met-Vigil:* 'It follows now from this, that the real, since it has its ground in sensation, therefore in the object of the senses, could not have its abode in the merely intellectual, therefore the degree of the real can thus be thought neither as greatest <*maximum*> nor as smallest <*minimum*>. On the other hand, it is certain that the modification of the degree of the intensive magnitude of the real quality must be infinite, *even if it can also be unnoticeable*. Therefore between the determinate degree A until 0=zero there must be found an infinite multitude of qualities of the real, *even if in an unnoticeable degree, e.g., knowledge, representations, yes even the consciousness of human beings have many degrees, without one being able to determine the smallest*' (AA 29: 1000 [LM: 468], emphasis added).

(A320/B376–7), as we have seen above. True, in the *Anthropology* (§ 5) Kant talks about 'obscure representations', of which we are 'not directly conscious' (AA 7: 135). While in his critique of Locke's conflation of representation and consciousness he might be taken to believe that obscure representations are unconscious representations, Kant does not specifically use the expression 'unconscious representation' there, although he speaks, somewhat luridly, of 'unconsciousness' as 'a foretaste of death' in another passage of the *Anthropology* (§ 27, AA 7: 166).[49]

'Obscure' does however not denote 'unconscious' in the strict sense. I believe that here in § 5 of the *Anthropology* Kant merely finds fault with Locke's view that in any perceiving I *simultaneously* (ap)perceive that I so perceive, which could be seen as a proto-adverbial view on consciousness (anticipating Pippin's [1997: 39] thesis of apperception as 'ineliminably reflexive', which he presents as an adverbial theory of *Kantian* apperception, although Pippin would object to a straightforward Lockean conflation of representation and reflection). Kant is not saying that there could be actual representations with *no* intensity of consciousness, nor does he say that there could not be conscious representations of which I cannot remember having them. From what the context of the discussion in the *Anthropology* section (§ 5) makes clear, the issue really is whether *each* or *any* perceiving is accompanied (individually) by a higher form of consciousness, that is, transcendental consciousness. Kant negates this question (he follows Leibniz in this). Many perceptions that we have remain unconscious in the sense of not being *directly* accompanied by this higher consciousness.[50] Importantly, this is not to say that unaccompanied representations lack *any* intensity of awareness or are unconscious.

Such a reading is confirmed by what Kant asserts at B414n., to wit, that consciousness does not settle the determination of clarity (as the opposite of obscurity), a belief for which he in fact criticises the 'logicians' (he presumably refers to Meier). Again, Kant here emphasises that even in obscure representations there must be a degree of consciousness (hence the label 'obscure' [*dunkel*], rather than 'unconscious') to be able to make a minimal distinction but which is short of conceptual recognition, or, second-order awareness.[51] Mere consciousness would not be sufficient to make a representation clear, just as much as there must be possible consciousness, as an ability to make distinctions, that does not already belong to the '*higher* cognitive faculty' (*Anthr* § 7, AA 7: 140–1). That amount of consciousness in a representation is concerned that en-

---

49 See also *Anthr-Fried*, AA 25:511. 'Unconsciousness' is the translation of *Ohnmacht*, i.e. *Bewusstlosigkeit*.
50 See also Kitcher (1999: 346ff., esp. 348–9) and La Rocca (2008).
51 See e.g. Wunderlich (2005: 141–2). See also Schulting (2015a).

ables a consciousness of the difference between it and other representations (cf. *Anthr* § 6, AA 7: 137–8). In other words, a difference must be made between 'mere' consciousness and its various grades and 'clear' consciousness, not just between consciousness and unconsciousness—notice however that the clarity of *apperceptive* consciousness might equally not be great, psychologically speaking (see e. g. A103–4) (in fact, I shall be claiming that apperceptive consciousness is merely formal). Moreover, as we saw Kant observe earlier, unconsciousness in the literal sense would be close or perhaps identical to (the instant of) death. Therefore, even a comatose person cannot be said, on a purely physiological level, to be *completely* unconscious, given the graded nature Kant accords to consciousness. Evidently, there is a difference between being in a coma (of whatever type), that is, being in a certain psychological or sensible ('vegetative') state that is utterly unreportable, and the instant when death, that is, *absolute* unconsciousness (cessation of brain electrical activity), actually sets in. It is the difference between being still alive and being technically dead. This suggests that *absolutely* unconscious representations have no correlate in reality because the corresponding sensations would perforce have no reality (since their intensive magnitude would equal zero). Consciousness is thus strictly related to existence (B414), while unconsciousness in the strict sense is equivalent to non-existence, conformably to the intimate relation between the categories of existence and reality.[52]

8.4 Transcendental (Self-)Consciousness, 'Negation', and 'Limitation'

Maier (1930: 55, 61) focuses entirely on the category of 'reality' and sees no role for the categories of 'negation' and 'limitation' (at least not as schematised in experience). She argues with regard to 'negation', the category that indicates zero intensive magnitude:

> There is no lack in the appearance, which could be regarded as the objective correlate of the category of negation. With that also the category lapses—at any rate as synthetic function of our objective thought, i.e. in Kant's language, as schematised category. (1930: 61)

---

[52] In the *Prolegomena*, Kant identifies 'total unconsciousness' with 'psychological darkness'. He reasons that 'complete absence' of consciousness cannot be perceived; any supposed absence of consciousness is in fact a psychological darkness that is a degree of consciousness that is 'merely outweighed by another, stronger one' (*Prol* § 24, AA 4: 307 [TPhb: 100]). There is thus always a sensation, a degree of consciousness, however minimal or immeasurably small.

8.4 Transcendental (Self-)Consciousness, 'Negation', and 'Limitation' — 217

Presumably, Maier reasons that to something which has no reality, that is, has an intensity equal to zero, no category can correspond. According to Maier, '[i]t is only under the condition that the real be regarded as something intensive that it can become an object of experience'. Although 'negation' as pure category can be thought, 'negation in the appearance is [...] merely *realitas evanescens*' (1930: 61).

Warren (2001: 20) seems to suggest something similar, but for a different reason, arguing that 'we regard reality and negation as differing only quantitatively (i.e. only by degree), and as being otherwise homogeneous with one another'. He believes that '[n]egation simply corresponds to one of the values that the intensive magnitude can take on, namely, the value zero'. However, for the reasons that Maier provides, zero cannot *really* be a value that the intensive magnitude takes on, since the absolute zero of consciousness is only a limit concept (Longuenesse 1998: 65n.10). By contrast, Longuenesse (1998: 297) argues that the category of limitation is 'pivotal', '*the* category of quality' in fact. By means of limitation, she points out,

> all possible determinations (realities) of any object as appearance are thought as delimited against the background of all the determinations that do *not* belong to it (negations), all of which, however, belong to the common infinite sphere of the concept 'given in the forms of space and time'. (1998: 297)

I concur with Longuenesse's view to the extent that limitation concerns all possible objects of experience[53] but I am here interested merely in the sense in which the categories of 'negation' and 'limitation' can be considered in abstraction from their application to the experience of an object as appearance. In addition, I shall say something about the role of limitation in the context of the sum total of all empirical reality as the material for possible experience.

I contend that the limit concept of 'negation' is expressed by transcendental consciousness itself, or the transcendental unity of self-consciousness, which determines all the episodes of my consciousness and delimits them from all those episodes of consciousness that do not belong to it. The category of 'negation' is important to be able to determine conscious mental states *as one's own* and as objectively *real*. We should bear in mind that the 'real' 'does not signify anything except the synthesis in an empirical consciousness in general' (A175–6/B217). Kant means that a *determination* of the real (the object as appearance) is possi-

---

[53] See Schulting (2017a), ch. 9, for a critique of Longuenesse's view regarding the different senses of reality and the meaning of the 'material of all possibility' of which Kant speaks in the transcendental Ideal.

ble only to the extent that a synthesis of the sensible material in an empirical consciousness is performed. We do not have immediate access to the 'real' object or subject (i.e. ourselves), neither conceptually nor by means of an empirical intuition, although the latter signifies an immediate *relation* to whatever is real, which is at any rate presupposed as a fact that is implied in thinking itself (cf. B422n.). This determination effectively occurs by virtue of an a priori act of the imagination, as Kant explains in the Schematism (B179/A140). Warren provides the following explanation for the schema of the category of reality:

> [T]he act of imagination whereby we gradually diminish a sensation from a given degree to its vanishing point, or vice versa, is necessary to representing that sensation as a quantity, and in particular, as an intensive quantity. In the course of this synthesis, we regard a series of representations as formed from one another in sequence, merely by means of the operations of augmentation or diminution. (2001: 17)

By contrast, Maier (1930: 57) thinks that Kant argues for an a priori form of the apprehension of sensation, that is a pure form in addition to space and time as a priori forms of intuition, so that sensation itself is the *product* of a subjective apprehension of something that is empirically given, and not a merely 'passive affection' (*Affiziert-werden*). In other words, we must distinguish between the form and matter of sensation, whereby the form of sensation constitutes 'pure apprehension' (1930: 63). On this reading, the category 'reality' would then be 'the form of apprehension of quality' which is 'the subjective and formal ground of the capacity for receiving qualitative representations through sensible impressions'. This form of apprehension is 'in a certain sense the logically first formative function [*Formungsfunktion*], with which we approach the given' (1930: 63).

Notwithstanding the merits of Maier's reading, which is reminiscent of an interpretation offered by Kant's contemporary Johann Heinrich Tieftrunk, who argues that '[e]very sensation as such (as empirical consciousness) has two parts, one subjective, the other objective' (*Corr*, AA 12: 213) (but see below), it would appear that Kant rather argues that it is possible to determine, from an a priori perspective, *that* 'there is something which can be cognized *a priori* in every sensation, as sensation in general (without a particular one being given)' (A167/B209). Sensation itself, that is, any *particular* sensation, is *always* the a posteriori material content of an intuition; it has no a priori side. What *is* a priori is the anticipation of the fact that at least a sensation must be given for a connection to the real to be possible. The anticipation concerns the possible determination of sensation, which given that, unlike space and time, it rests upon an instantaneous rather than successive synthesis of homogeneous quanta, is an intensive rather than extensive magnitude, as we have seen earlier. The determination of the continuous or 'flowing' quanta of sensations (B211/A170) amounts to determining the greater or lesser degree of intensity of each quantum 'that makes every reality *representable* as a quantum' (A143/B183, emphasis added). Kant even speaks of a 'continuous and uniform *generation* [*Erzeugung*]' (A143/B183, emphasis added), which points to the a priori activity of synthesising the 'many possible intermediate sensations' (A168/B210), 'from the sensation that has a certain degree to its disappearance or gradually ascends from negation to its magnitude' (A143/B183).

It might seem from this last quotation that 'negation' is indeed, as Warren noted, one of the possible values that the intensive magnitude can take on. However, as Kant observes in the *Prolegomena*, 'nothing' (*der Null*) as the contrary of reality is 'the complete emptiness of intuition in time' and is the limit of possible degrees between any given degree of intensity and its negation, for example, 'any given degree of light and darkness, any degree of heat and complete cold, any degree of weight and absolute lightness, any degree of the filling of space and completely empty space' (*Prol* § 24, AA 4: 306 – 7 [Cambridge trans. emended]). Negation is not an actually perceivable or determinable degree; *it is rather the condition of determination itself.* In the same section of the *Prolegomena* (§ 24, AA 4: 307), Kant links the analysis of sensations as intensive magnitudes explicitly to consciousness, between which and 'total unconsciousness (psychological darkness) ever smaller degrees occur'. In the Anticipations of Perceptions, Kant reveals that 'pure consciousness' is the correlate of 'negation':

> Now from the empirical consciousness to the pure consciousness a gradual alteration is possible, where the real in the former entirely disappears, and a merely *formal* (*a priori*) consciousness of the manifold in space and time remains. (B208, emphasis added)

From the text, this might prima facie be taken to concern only 'pure intuition' (cf. B347). But given the context (the Anticipations belonging to the mathematical principles of experience), we can extrapolate from this that pure formal consciousness in general, in abstraction from its relation to objects of spatiotemporal experience and thus from pure intuition, is pure apperception or transcendental consciousness.

What is important to note here again is that negation is *not* itself a value on the scale from a given degree to an approximation of zero or vice versa, but instead it is a 'point' or 'instant', a 'boundary' of the continuous quantum of the intensive magnitude, hence of empirical consciousness, by analogy with Kant's claim regarding space and time that '[p]oints and instants are only boundaries, i.e., mere places [*Stellen*] of their limitation' (A169/B211), that is, the limitation of space and time. Empirical consciousness, as consisting of sensations as *quanta continua*, is presupposed as a posteriori given, 'an itself raw and material something', whose 'gradual apprehension' (*gradirte Auffassung*) is a function of apperception, as Tieftrunk writes in his letter to Kant of 5 November 1797 (*Corr*, AA 12: 214). Apperception, then, is purely 'the *determination* of the material (of sensibility)' (*Corr*, AA 12: 215), or indeed a 'boundary' of the continuous quantum of the sensible material. Tieftrunk sees the a priori elements as merely lying in the transcendental act of limitation. Although Tieftrunk insists on not arguing for the a priori deduction of reality per se, as Fichte allegedly does, his account does seem to come close to the Fichtean position. Nevertheless, some of the elements of Tieftrunk's analysis, which he claims reflect the position of the *Critique* (*Corr*, AA 12: 215), are worth considering. Similarly to Maier, Tieftrunk says that '[t]he function of self-consciousness referred to under the title "Quality" consists in positing', which he regards as the act of spontaneity. He claims that the 'function of determination of positing consists [...] in the uniting of positing and non-positing into a *single* concept' and that the 'determined positing is [...] the same as the determination of degree'. He then makes the prima facie mysterious claim that

> just as positing is the original function of apperception, so the determination of degree (gradation, limitation, uniting of positing and non-positing into a *single* concept) is the a priori condition of the unity of positing. (*Corr*, AA 12: 213)

The determination of the degree of the intensive magnitude, which determines the real corresponding to it, is said to rest on the unification in one concept of the positing (=1) and non-positing (=0) of reality.

Tieftrunk thus claims that apperception is the 'condition of the possibility of all empirical consciousness' (*Corr*, AA 12: 213) and that '[a]ll existence [*Dasein*] is therefore based on this original positing, and existence is actually nothing else than this being-posited'. Indeed, according to Tieftrunk, '[w]ithout the original, pure act of spontaneity (of apperception), nothing *is* or exists' (*Corr*, AA 12: 214). With these last statements he seems to take back what he insisted on earlier, namely that he opposed Fichte's a priori deduction of reality *tout court*. This seems too extreme a reading of Kant: existence per se is certainly not *dependent on* apperception and, as I have argued in this chapter, for Kant transcendental apperception is *not* the condition of all empirical consciousness *simpliciter*.[54]

---

[54] Tieftrunk also makes the dubious claim that '*sensation originates* through the influence of apperception on the matter of sensibility, in that it synthesises [*zusammensetzt*] it (by means of the imagination) and raises it in the positing through determining the degree [*auf Gradesbestimmung im Setzen erhebt*]; sensation has two sides: first, something a priori, that is, the determination of degree (determination of the positing of the unity of apperception), and second,

8.4 Transcendental (Self-)Consciousness, 'Negation', and 'Limitation' — 221

Apart from this, the Fichtean sounding language is also clear from the use of such terms as positing and non-positing, but we should be mindful that Kant already uses this terminology, in particular in the context of modality, which I discussed in Chapter 6. As with Maier (see Section 8.2), I am not sure with regard to the use of these terms for the categories of reality. Nevertheless, I contend that the category of 'limitation' is captured in the idea proposed by Tieftrunk that a unity of positing and non-positing is concerned, that is, a unity of reality and negation. As with the other categories, the third moment of the title 'quality' is the unification of the first two moments, reality and negation. Tieftrunk explains this in the following way:

> Now the synthesis of the transcendental consciousness consists in the category of quality in the positing (spontaneity). The positing, however, as function of unity, is only a determinate positing in that in it position and negation are connected into one concept, which is the act of gradation. This is therefore the condition of all positing, of all positedness, of all existence. [...] [N]o perception is possible without positing by virtue of the transcendental apperception. The positing however is, as function of unity, possible only in that the apperception gradually varies [*gradire*], as neither absolute non-positing (=0) nor an infinitely progressing positing (=G) is a possible act for apperception. (*Corr*, AA 12: 215, trans. mine)

Limitation is the *qualitative unity* of consciousness (cf. TD § 15, B131) insofar as transcendental apperception determines the *material* content of an intuition by means of a determination of the sensations as *quanta continua* that have an intensive magnitude. Given that a sensation consists in being affected by a thing (B34/A20) and so concerns the correspondence to something real, the determination of sensations by transcendental apperception means that the *concept* of reality is applied to a really existing thing to which the determinate sensations correspond. We should be careful though not to conflate, as Tieftrunk appears to do (perhaps under the influence of Fichte), the positing of the existence of something x, the positing of the reality of x, x's existence and x's reality. The reality of a thing is not reducible to its being *determined* to be real, as much as the existence of a thing is not reducible to its being *determined* to exist. Nor are reality and existence the same.

Limitation also means that the determinate unity of sensations, or empirical consciousness, is delimited from all *possible* sensations, and thus all possible infinitely small degrees of consciousness that can be determined. This concerns the real as the 'one all-encompassing experience' of which any determinate object is necessarily a part, and which is 'that in which the real of all appearances

---

something a posteriori, that is, the material itself' (*Corr*, AA 12: 214, trans. mine and emphasis added; this passage is not translated in the *Correspondence* volume of the Cambridge edition).

is given' (A582/B610).[55] This all-encompassing experience, or the 'real of all appearances', which is not some phenomenalist super-experience, but should be read technically, as *possible* experience,[56] must be presupposed as 'the material for the possibility of all objects of sense', of which all determinate appearances are negations. Significantly, Kant states that 'all possibility of empirical objects, their difference from one another and their thoroughgoing determination, can rest only on the limitation of this sum total', of the infinite sphere of (empirical) reality.[57] All objects of experience presuppose 'the sum total of all empirical reality' as condition of their possibility.[58] All (empirical) realities, and hence all sensations (as the content of appearances), that can be given in space and time constitute the sum total of all possible objects of possible experience. A determination of any arbitrary object as an objectively real thing therefore rests on the determinate synthesis of a limitation of this sum total by means of negation, that is, through transcendental apperception. Put differently, the synthesis of a series of sensations in virtue of a unity of apperception constitutes the unity of the given 'thing itself (in the appearance)' (A581/B609, trans. emended), but only as a phenomenal, spatiotemporal object, or, the determinate object of perception. Note that sensations themselves are not determined as real, but that in the appearance which corresponds to sensation, that is, the thing in itself insofar as it is given in space and time, as appearance.[59] Of course, what we consider to

---

[55] Notice that the text in the original says *das Reale aller Erscheinungen*, which is wrongly translated in the Cambridge edition as 'the real in all appearances' suggesting a similarity with Kant's assertion about the constitution of 'the thing in itself (in appearance), namely the real', a few lines above the quoted passage (Kemp Smith is correct). The reality *of* all appearances, which is the whole of possible experience, and the thing in itself as the real are not the same, while it is true that the thing in itself can only be given in appearance. The sum-total of *all* reality is not reducible to the reality of the all-encompassing possible experience. See further Schulting (2017a), ch. 9.

[56] Experience for Kant is always law-governed, epistemically relevant experience, not mere psychological experience or series of inner sense experiences. Kant is an evidentialist regarding experience. All experience for which no evidence is available is excluded from *possible* experience. See Ameriks (2006: 81–2). See also Schulting (2017a), ch. 1.

[57] Heimsoeth (1956: 56) speaks of 'limitation' as 'die Gradabstufung aller endlichen Dinge, im Gegensatz zum Maximum'. See also Maier, who writes: 'Limitation ist [...] nicht einfach mit Gradation gleichzusetzen, sondern bedeutet qualitative Auswahl, Einschränkung des unendlichen Alls der Realität, und zugleich graduelle Verminderung der intensiven Größe der einzeln Realitäten. Limitatio wird daher auch mit Endlichkeit (finitudo) gleichgesetzt. Sie ist Negation + Gradation' (1930: 38).

[58] All quotations are from A582/B610.

[59] For more discussion of limitation and issues concerning Kant's idealism, see Schulting (2017a), ch. 9.

be real, and so can experience as real, is just 'the synthesis in an empirical consciousness in general' (A175–6/B217), that is, the synthesis of transcendental apperception, as we cannot go beyond our concepts to reach the 'really real' of things in themselves.

8.5 Deriving the Categories of Quality: Summary

Having expounded the arguments for deriving the categories of quality from the unity of apperception, this gives us the following additional premises of the D-argument:

> D16. Any instantiation of transcendental self-consciousness as the mode of discursive thought presupposes a sum total of sensations, all possible episodes of empirical consciousness, that have a certain degree of intensity on a scale of 0 to 1, and which correspond to the reality of all appearances, that is, of the all-encompassing possible experience.
>
> D17. Transcendental self-consciousness is the empty form of empirical consciousness, 'empirical consciousness in general', insofar as it determines or delimits a subsphere of the sum total of all sensations, all possible episodes of empirical consciousness, as a real object of experience as distinct from all other possible objects of experience.

These results show that

> D18. The category of 'reality' pertains to the identity of discursive thought and hence is analytically derivable from it.
>
> D19. The category of 'negation' pertains to the identity of discursive thought and hence is analytically derivable from it.

However, as we have seen, the categories of 'reality' and 'negation' are united, and mutually conditioning in the sense that empirical consciousness or sensation as that which corresponds to reality must be presupposed as given, as sensible material in general, while transcendental consciousness as pure form must be presupposed as the necessary condition for the possibility of applying a determinate concept of a real object to one's sensations, by means of the synthesis of the intensive magnitude of the sensations. Of course, as I have argued, it is not the case that to *have* sensations requires transcendental apperception, in contrast to what Maier and Tieftrunk suggest, let alone that transcendental apperception first generates sensation, as Tieftrunk maintains. But transcendental apperception is required in order to have a determinate grasp, by means of the category of negation, of one's episodes of empirical consciousness, one's sensations, as one's own as differentiated from the infinite sphere of the sum-total of all possible sensations (constituting the realm of possible experience). Limitation is then nothing but the unity of transcendental (negation) and empirical (reality) consciousness. By means of limitation, the transcendental unity of self-consciousness, as a qualitative unity, subdivides the infinite sphere of all possible episodes of empirical consciousness corresponding to as many possible realities, such that a determinate synthesis of sensations (or empirical consciousness) constitutes the determinate concept of an object that is a real thing (in space and time) as a subsphere of the infinite sphere of all possible realities (in space and time). The non-being or 'lack' (A575/B603) to which transcendental self-consciousness as negation or an intensive magnitude=0 corresponds is the *limitation* of all possible (empirical) realities. Hence:

> D20. The unity of transcendental self-consciousness as negation and empirical consciousness as reality constitutes the infinite sphere of the one all-encompassing experience which contains all possible (empirical) realities.

Therefore:

> D21. The category of 'limitation' pertains to the identity of discursive thought and hence is analytically derivable from it.

9 Apperception and the Categories of Quantity

9.1 Introduction

This chapter addresses the deduction of the categories of quantity ('unity', 'plurality', 'totality' or 'measure', 'quantity'[1] and 'whole' respectively, epithets that Kant adds in the *Prolegomena*). From the category of negation, which in the previous chapter had been identified with transcendental apperception as the *form* of self-consciousness, that is, as *transcendental* self-consciousness itself, we are led to the category of unity, since transcendental self-consciousness or the 'I think' is the 'analytic unity of consciousness [that] pertains to all common concepts as such' (B133n.), indeed 'the mere representation *I* in relation to all others (the collective unity of which it makes possible) is the transcendental consciousness' (A117n.). The 'analytic unity of consciousness' expresses the *numerical* unity of thought, which grounds all concepts *a priori* and hence is the *unitary* form of the *manifold* of representations in intuition. It is the categories of quantity as a whole that finally establish the thoroughgoing numerical identity of thought as including a necessary synthesis of the manifold of representations (A108, 113)—albeit again only formally in abstraction from *empirical* intuition— and hence the formal identity of the object of thought (which is of course in further need of an empirical, spatiotemporal, intuition to become the object of a genuine empirical judgement and hence an object of possible *experience*). Unlike the categories of modality and relation, but similarly to the categories of quality, with the categories of quantity we look not merely at the *act* of thought but also at the necessary form of the *manifold* of representations that is given to discursive thought (although not the a priori form of the manifold *as empirical intuition*, which are of course space and time that are not under discussion here) and how it constitutes a unity of identical units. Admittedly, as was the case with the categories of quality, the derivation of the 'mathematical' categories of quantity from pure thought in abstraction from how they are applied in spatiotemporal experience, as explained in the Axioms of Intuition, might seem very

---

[1] This points to the fact that, as argued in the Axioms of Intuition (B203), all appearances must be seen as extensive magnitudes, as quanta. 'I entitle a magnitude extensive when the representation of the parts makes possible, and therefore necessarily precedes, the representation of the whole' (A162/B203; trans. Kemp Smith). However, the categories of quantity should not be seen exclusively in the light of the Axioms of Intuition. I agree with Heimsoeth, who writes that '[d]ie reinen Kategorien müssen in ihrem ontologischen Ursprungs- und Kernsinn bei Kant immer von den schematisierten und deren Gebrauch, etwa in Grundlagen der Naturwissenschaft, sorgfältig unterschieden werden' (1956: 39 ff.).

tenuous. But I claim there is a way to see, from the evidence of the text in §§ 16–17, how they too have their seat in the pure understanding (A81/B107) or the unity of apperception itself, inasmuch as the categories of quantity correspond, although in a different order, to the quantitative functions of judgement (universal, particular and singular).[2]

In this chapter, I argue that, apart from an underlying synthetic act of apperception, which insofar as the *relational* aspects are concerned was discussed in Chapter 7, an analytic unity of consciousness that pertains to any concept requires a manifold or plurality of representations for the concept first to have application to its extension and to genuinely be the cognitive ground of an object (R2281–8, AA 16: 298–300). Further, I argue that unity and plurality together constitute a totality (totality is the unity of plurality)[3] or a whole or 'one' representation that is a bona fide concept of an object, which is the necessary correlate of what in the A-Deduction Kant calls a 'transcendental object' (A109).[4] It is important to be mindful of the fact that the unity that is a *category* of quantity is different from the qualitative unity of which Kant speaks in § 15, which concerns not the unity of homogeneous parts in a whole, but the unity of various representations in a manifold (the one in many), that is, the unity that is higher in that it forms the *ground* of the whole in which the parts are contained. The qualitative unity is a 'connection of *heterogeneous* elements of cognition into one consciousness also' (B115) (cf. Section 8.4).

Because the 'I think' of discursive thought is merely an empty representation, is 'simple', hence 'encompasses not the least manifoldness within itself' (A355)—it is 'the logical unity of every thought' (A398), and does not as such constitute a representation of a whole[5]—a content must be given to it exogenously (cf. B145). This is characteristic of human discursive cognition.[6] The content

---

[2] See Frede & Krüger (1970) and especially Longuenesse (1998: 248–9) on issues concerning the different order of the categories of quantity in relation to the order of the quantitative functions of judgement.

[3] B111: 'Thus *allness* (totality) is nothing other than plurality considered as a unity.'

[4] To be more precise: '[T]his concept [of the transcendental object] cannot contain any determinate intuition at all, and therefore concerns nothing but that unity which must be encountered in a manifold of cognition insofar as it stands in relation to an object.'

[5] The 'I' is an absolute unity, but a 'merely logical' one: '[T]he simplicity of the representation of a subject is not [...] the cognition of the simplicity of the subject itself, since its properties are entirely abstracted from if it is designated merely through the expression "I", wholly empty of content [...]' (A355).

[6] Towards the end of § 16, at B135–6, Kant contrasts the relation between the 'I' as 'simple representation', through which 'nothing manifold is given', with an 'understanding, in which through self-consciousness all of the manifold would at the same time be given'. This reflects

that must be given is an aggregate or a multitude 'of antecedently given parts' which must be taken together 'through successive synthesis (from part to part)' (B204; cf. A142–3/B182) in order to form a whole. In the Axioms of Intuition, Kant addresses this by asserting that in respect of the fact that they contain intuitions of objects in space and time all appearances must be seen as extensive magnitudes. Appearances cannot, Kant writes,

> be apprehended [...] except through the synthesis of the manifold through which the representations of a determinate space or time are generated, i.e., through the composition of that which is homogeneous and the consciousness of the synthetic unity of this manifold (of the homogeneous). (B202)

While Kant relates the thought that 'the unity of the composition of the homogeneous manifold is thought in the concept of a *magnitude*' (B203) to how intuitions as *quanta continua* in space and time must be represented, the synthesis responsible for this unity of composition has its original seat in the unity of apperception of the manifold of representations in general. In the Transcendental Deduction, Kant writes:

> [I]f I abstract from the form of space, this same synthetic unity has its seat in the understanding, and is the category of the synthesis of the homogeneous in an intuition in general, that is, the category of *quantity*. To this category, therefore, the synthesis of apprehension, that is to say, the perception, must completely conform. (B162, trans. Kemp Smith)[7]

I want here to abstract from the specificity of spatiotemporal intuition and merely look at the sheer manifold in any given intuition that is given to the mere representation 'I think' as the discursive common concept that accompanies any representation of an object. In other words, I look at 'the synthesis of the homogeneous in an intuition in general', or the concept of 'quantity' as such for any given discursive thought that requires an exogenously provided manifold.[8] What Kant means by 'homogeneous in an intuition' is that the intuition consists of a plurality of parts that are generically identical insofar as an intuition concerns a complex representation consisting of various representations. This can be a manifold of spatiotemporal units that are parts of a greater whole (space and/

---

the contrast between a discursive and intuitive understanding respectively. In the last paragraph of § 17, Kant repeats that the principle of original-synthetic unity of apperception is a principle 'only for [an understanding] through whose pure apperception in the representation *I am* nothing manifold is given at all'. See also B145.

7 Cf. R6338a, AA 18: 659, 661.
8 Cf. J. H. Tieftrunk in a letter of 5 November 1797 to Kant (*Corr*, AA 12: 212.18–32).

or time) or units of a nature other than spatiotemporal. But more in general, in abstraction from how this applies to space and time, homogeneous units in a given manifold are generically identical qua their form in that, in some sense, they share a common representation.[9]

In Section 9.2, I discuss an important distinction Kant makes between a collective unity of manifolds and discrete manifolds, a distinction whose central relevance for Kant's argument in § 16 is ignored by most commentators. This is important for understanding the specific role of the given manifold 'in a certain intuition' for establishing the category of 'totality' as 'unity in plurality'. In this context, I attend to two distinguishable types of 'accompanying' representations that Kant employs in § 16. In Section 9.3, I consider Strawson's well-known critique of sense datum experience, which illustrates how apprehension of discrete manifolds must be seen as independent of the analytic unity of apperception, that is, pure apperception. In Section 9.4, I address the issue of what it means to apply a concept to a manifold of representations. I show that, in contrast to what Hossenfelder for example believes, this can only occur by virtue of a priori synthesis of the parts contained in a manifold of representations that only *as such*, and not singly, are accompanied by an act of apperception. In Section 9.5, I address the question how the numerical identity of a manifold of representations is effectively established, which involves looking at how the categories of 'unity' and 'plurality' are linked to form a 'totality'.

9.2 'All My Representations' and 'Each Representation': About Two Types of 'Accompanying' in § 16

In Chapter 6, I argued that the 'I think' accompanies what I called P1-representations and is not instantiated for P3/P4-representations. The distinction between these types of representation can also be made clear by looking at the two types of their being 'accompanied' (*begleiten*) that Kant differentiates. P1-representations are accompanied by an 'I think', which is pure or transcendental apperception, whereas P3/P4-representations are merely accompanied by empirical apperception, which Kant distinguishes from transcendental apperception (B132). In the case of transcendental apperception the direct object concerns 'all my representations' (AA 3: 108.19), while in the case of empirical apperception the direct

---

[9] Kant uses the term 'plurality' for the category that is the counterpart of the logical function 'particular' to stress the fact that one thinks plurality without totality, since the parts *precede* the whole, which must be established or 'constructed' by means of synthesis on the basis of the antecedently given plurality of parts (see *Prol* § 20n.13, AA 4: 302).

object is 'each representation' (AA 3: 109.18–19). The standard reading of the 'I think'-proposition—'The: *I think* must *be able* to accompany **all my** representations' (B131, boldface added)—suggests that Kant *really* meant 'each' instead of 'all' (in German: *jede* and *alle* respectively). Aschenberg (1988: 58), for example, thinks that *alle* and *jede* are interchangeable. I claim that Kant specifically *means* to say *alle*, and not *jede* here at B131,[10] and specifically means *jede* at B133 (AA 3: 109.18–19), which is correlative with the *distributive* nature of the manifold (*verschiedene Vorstellungen* [109.16]) in which such singular representations occur.

The distinction regarding the use of the determiners 'all' and 'each' is important for an assessment of the scope of the 'I think' and the unity of the manifold that is accompanied by it. This involves a consideration of the deduction of the categories of quantity. My reading of the 'I think' turns on Kant's consistent use of words in the context of § 16 that express the quantitative aspects involved in transcendental apperception (e. g. *alle*, *insgesammt*, but also *durchgängig*, a term which is used by Kant in a more technical sense than usual). When he speaks of the 'I think' accompanying a manifold in intuition this manifold is a compound and not a singular representation, that is, the 'I think' is directed at the manifold collectively, not distributively. Nowhere does Kant suggest that the 'I think' could accompany a single representation as such, let alone *any* single representation, which is only consistent given his understanding of the 'I think' as a common representation contained in various representations, which *as such*, that is, *as a unified compound*, it accompanies.[11] Given the fact that an analytic unity of representations first obtains in that a synthesis of a manifold representations has been effected (cf. B133) and so does not obtain if no synthesis has been completed, it would amount to a contradiction to go on to argue as if each of these representations contained in the synthesised manifold were accompanied, *severally*, by an 'I think'-instance. The singular representations, as components of the manifold that is analytically united in having the 'I think' as their common representation, can of course be analysed regressively, but it hardly implies that each singular representation is distributively accompanied by a separate, singular 'I think', as arguing thus would reveal a misunderstanding of the special relation between representations and the 'I think' as a higher form of representa-

---

10 This contrasts with Prien (2006: 132), who in opposition to Allison's (1983: 137–40) account believes that 'das denkende Subjekt *jede* seiner Vorstellungen mit Bewusstsein begleiten können muss'.
11 See *Met-Mron*, AA 29: 888: 'A concept is the consciousness that the [same] is contained in one representation as in another, or that in multiple representations one and the same features are contained. This thus presupposes consciousness or apperception' (LM: 256–7).

tion. As Kant argues in *Anthr* § 5 (AA 7: 135 ff.), one is only mediately conscious of these representations, that is, mediately via the 'I think', and not severally, immediately conscious of them, neither through empirical consciousness nor by means of an allegedly particular instance of 'I think'. Equally, at B132 (AA 3: 109.8–9) Kant notes between parentheses that although the representations necessarily 'stand together in a universal self-consciousness' for them to be able to 'all together' (*insgesammt*), that is 'throughout', belong to me, '*I am not conscious of them as such*' (emphasis added), that is, I am not conscious of all *my* representations *severally*. That representations are accompanied severally by empirical consciousness does occur, however, in acts of *empirical* apprehension of discrete representations that are not thereby synthesised, and hence, as I shall argue, not accompanied by an 'I think' but merely by 'empirical consciousness' (cf. B133 [AA 3: 109.16–17]).

The DUDEN German grammar explains the difference between the two quantifiers *alle* and *jede* in the following manner. With regard to the quantifier *jede* ('each') it says:

> Mit *jeder, jedermann, jedweder* und *jeglicher* werden alle Wesen, Dinge usw. einer bestimmten Menge bezeichnet, jedoch nicht zusammenfassend in ihrer Gesamtheit wie mit *all*, sondern vereinzelnd, als Einzelne.[12]

With regard to the determiner *alle* DUDEN explains:

> Mit *all* wird zusammenfassend eine Menge von Wesen, Dinge u. Ä., eine Gesamtheit bezeichnet, die im Singular—etwa bei Stoffbezeichnungen und Abstrakta—ungegliedert ist (*alles Geld*) und die im Plural alle Exemplare einer gegliederten Menge ohne notwendigen Bezug auf jedes einzelne Exemplar erfasst (*alle Bäume*). Dabei nähert sich *all* im Singular der Bedeutung von *ganz, gesamt*, im Plural der Bedeutung des nachdrücklichen *sämtlich*.[13]

I believe that Kant's use of *alle* instead of *jede* in the 'I think' passage at B131 has a crucial bearing on the way the 'I think'-accompaniment must be interpreted. The fact that *alle* designates a *gegliederte Menge*,[14] a quantum consisting of parts, without a necessary relation to every single particular part, and that the

---

12 DUDEN, Bd. 4, *Die Grammatik*, 6. Auflage (Mannheim: Duden Verlag, 1998), p. 355.
13 DUDEN, Bd. 4, p. 349 ff.
14 *Menge* does not eo ipso mean, also not for Kant, 'quantity' or 'amount' in the mathematical sense. See e.g. in the early *Allgemeine Naturgeschichte und Theorie des Himmels*, where Kant speaks of a 'Menge ohne Zahl und Grenzen', 'eine wahre Unendlichkeit von Mannigfaltigkeiten und Veränderungen...' (AA 1: 309n.). 'Quantity' as 'manifold' must be distinguished from 'number'.

pronoun resembles the meaning of *gesamt* or *sämtlich*, seems to me to capture the nature of Kant's argument about the 'I think' as a 'thoroughgoing' (*durchgängige*) unity of identical representations very nicely. That the 'I think' does not accompany every single representation but only a specific manifold of representations—in its entirety (*insgesamt*) as showing a determinate set of representations—that is correlative with the 'I' as the act of *conjunctio* (B129) is conveyed by what DUDEN says to the effect that the relation is not to every single component of the class to which *alle* refers. In short, the 'I think' is not related, distributively, to singular instances of the manifold of representations that is accompanied by it. Rather, the 'I think' attaches to my representations '*conjointly*' (Van Cleve 1999: 80).[15] Nor does the 'I' relate to any arbitrary representation whatsoever. At A117n. Kant reveals that the 'mere representation *I* in relation to all others' makes possible their '*collective* unity' (emphasis added; by 'all others' Kant means those representations that are taken together, as what in B is called *insgesamt* [B132, 134]). Similarly, at A123 Kant writes:

> For the standing and lasting I (of pure apperception) constitutes the correlate of all of our representations [*aller unserer Vorstellungen*], insofar namely as it is possible [*so fern es blos möglich ist*] to become conscious of them. (trans. emended)

It is thus not as if each of any *arbitrary* representations belonged to this collective unity as a matter of course. The 'I' is the correlate of all my representations if and only if I am conscious of them as together (*insgesammt*) my representations. It is not the correlate of representations of which I am *not* conscious as *my* representations, but which may still belong to me and of which I may also be conscious in some other sense (as P3/P4-representations). Kant's main argument in these passages in § 16 is that for one's representations to be one's representations *throughout* (*insgesammt meine Vorstellungen*, with *meine* in spaced type [AA 3: 109.6]), they should be unified in one consciousness. Kant indeed talks about '*one* self-consciousness' (B132, emphasis added). The relation of the identical subject 'I think' to the manifold comes about 'only in so far as I *conjoin* one representation with another, and am conscious of the synthesis of them' (B133, trans. Kemp Smith). That is to say, the *conjunctio* (B129) does not lie in the manifold as such (B129), hence the manifold can only conjointly be seen to be related to the identical subject in that solely by means of *conjunctio* (combination, synthesis) she apperceives the manifold *as* conjoined.

---

15 See also Longuenesse (1998: 67n.13). However, Keller (1998: 66) is mistaken when he says that by the 'I think' Kant 'apparently means that all my representations, taken collectively, as well as distributively, are ascribable by me to me'.

The standard reading is that transcendental self-consciousness is the necessary formal counterpart of actual instances of empirical consciousness *in general*. Such a reading takes analytic unity of consciousness, that is the 'I think', to be 'formally implied' in empirical consciousness as such and hence in *any* manifold of representations accompanied by empirical consciousness. This reading is mistaken, as we have seen in Chapter 8, but unfortunately it is widely shared. Among others, this can be seen in the work of Stuhlmann-Laeisz (1976: 82), Baum (1986: 96–7), Mohr (1991: 127) and Deppermann (2001).[16] What are the characteristics of this kind of interpretation of transcendental self-consciousness as that which is putatively implied in any empirical consciousness or empirical apperception, which is at issue in the passage at B133 (AA 3: 109.18–19), where Kant speaks of 'accompanying each representation'? Stuhlmann-Laeisz believes that notwithstanding the fact that empirical consciousness only apprehends single instances of consciousness, all the various instances of consciousness are nonetheless *analytically,* even if not synthetically, united. In other words, all these various instances share the fact that they analytically belong to the same consciousness. Stuhlmann-Laeisz (1976: 82) glosses B133 in such a way that the *one* unitary consciousness must be seen as a consciousness that 'separates itself' (*vereinzelnt sich*) in the 'different empirical states of consciousness' without thereby having a relation to the identical self.[17] But the question then is how the one consciousness can still be seen as the *same* consciousness contained, as partial representation,[18] in all of the separate states that it accompanies, that is, how a state of consciousness A is had by the same consciousness—the 'standing or abiding self' (A107)—that is in a state of consciousness B and how both A and B share the same partial representation 'I think' *without* however having a relation to the identical subject (as Stuhlmann-Laeisz must say in conformity with B133). There is no reason to suppose that the consciousness distributed in *separate* states of consciousness, which have no relation to the identity of the subject, is the same consciousness across these states and that separate

---

16 In the older German literature, for example Heimsoeth (1956: 238) hints at a similar mutual implicatedness of empirical and transcendental apperception. See also Henrich (1976: 56 ff.). Henrich appears to connect, illicitly, Hume's bundle theory with the view that '[a]lle Gedanken gehören in der gleichen Weise zu Einem Bewußtsein in ihnen', which betrays a conflation of the objective and subjective unities of consciousness.

17 He describes this as follows: 'Im vergleichenden Durchgehen der Vorstellungen ist also das Bewußtsein als empirisches bei diesen, ohne bei sich zu sein. Aber es ist doch *eines*, es ist dasselbe in den verschiedenen Vorstellungen, die es begleitet.'

18 On the notion of 'partial representation' and 'marks', see Prien (2006: 58–67) and Stuhlmann-Laeisz (1976), ch. 5.

states of consciousness share the partial representation 'I think'. It is in fact contradictory to suppose this. The suggestion is, apparently, that the analytic unity of consciousness is somehow *prior* to the numerical identity that is established by means of a synthesis among one's representations that conjoins them. Any representation is supposedly always already, to use a hackneyed turn of phrase, analytically united with any other representation just because it is a representation.

Stuhlmann-Laeisz tries to make sense of the passage at B133 (AA 3: 109.16–20) where Kant explicitly denies any relation between a single individual representation and the identity of the subject.[19] Kant writes here:

> For the empirical consciousness that accompanies different representations is by itself dispersed and without relation to the identity of the subject. The latter relation therefore does not yet come about by my accompanying **each** representation with consciousness, but rather by my *adding* one representation to the other and being conscious of their synthesis. (underlining and boldface added)

In contrast to what Stuhlmann-Laeisz argues, whatever relation these separate or distributed instances of consciousness have among themselves, it cannot be analytical such that they share the indexical 'I'. I take Kant to say as much when he writes that they are 'without relation to the identity of the subject' (B133). Such a relation, as Kant says, does not occur when I simply accompany 'each' representation with consciousness, but *only* when I 'conjoin' one representation with the other and am conscious (even if only obscurely) of thus having synthesised these representations, and in this way 'represent to myself the *identity of the consciousness in* [i.e. *throughout*] *these representations*' (B133, trans. Kemp Smith). There is no necessary entailment relation between dispersed instances of empirical consciousness accompanying singular representations and formal unitary consciousness (analytic unity of consciousness). Therefore, I believe one is not licensed to argue, as Stuhlmann-Laeisz does, that the one consciousness that expresses analytic unity is the same in all of the dispersed representations to which Kant refers at B133.

Likewise, Mohr (1991: 149) mistakenly takes transcendental apperception as intrinsically implied (i.e. as *Implikat*) in the discrete representations that are accompanied by *empirical* consciousness. Deppermann (2001: 144) has advanced

---

19 Cf. Kant's letter to Herz of 26 May 1789, *Corr*, AA 11: 52.12–14; cf. also A107. Disconnected impressions have no relation to the identity of the subject, contrary to what Strawson suggests when he writes that '[w]e seem to add nothing but a form of words to the hypothesis of a succession of essentially disconnected impressions by stipulating that they all *belong* to an identical consciousness' (1968: 100). Strawson illicitly interprets 'belong' and 'identity' possessively.

the similar claim that self-consciousness is a *transzendentale Formimplikation* for all empirical consciousness. He cannot make much sense of the passage under discussion at B133 (AA 3: 109.16–20).[20] What these commentators misunderstand is that the analytic unity of apperception is precisely the relation to the identity of self, which presupposes the synthetic unity of apperception. The accompanying of each separate representation does not constitute a relation to the identical self, as Stuhlmann-Laeisz acknowledges (which he must in explaining the purport of the passage at B133 that is at issue), but nor does it constitute an analytic unity of consciousness with other representations, because if it did, and each representation were indeed accompanied by a discrete 'I think', it would by implication constitute a relation to the identical self, which is contradictory.

Contrary to what the aforementioned commentators maintain, the consciousness that accompanies multifarious discrete representations is not ipso facto the *one* consciousness that expresses analytic unity. In other words, the 'I think' is contained only in the manifold of representations that are *collectively* accompanied by it (viz. the 'I think'). A discrete quantum determined as such is for instance a number (*Met-L₂*, AA 28: 561). But such a manifold would ipso facto be a manifold accompanied by transcendental apperception, not by just any singular instance of empirical consciousness (or empirical apperception) that pertains to a singular representation. However, the manifold as given is not a manifold that in itself implies an analytic unity. As Reich rightly writes,

> I cannot say that the representations given me would throughout have, *as given*, the character of unity in their (possible) consciousness in relation to the representation 'I think'. (Reich 2001: 32 [27–8]; 1992: 24, trans. emended)

One should be careful to heed Kant's explicit claim that analytic unity of apperception is reciprocal with a synthetic unity among one's representations; an analytic *unity* of consciousness already implies a relation to the *identity* of the subject, namely the very 'I think' of apperception that is the common mark in the analytic unity of representations, and must not be seen as equivalent to a unity of separate instances of empirical consciousness or discrete representations. The manifold itself consists of 'different perceptions [that] by themselves are encountered dispersed and separate [*an sich zerstreuet und einzeln*] in the

---

20 See Deppermann (2001: 148). Earlier, in a note (2001: 137n.22), Deppermann expresses puzzlement over Kant's ostensible contradiction in claiming both that there is *a priori* certainty of the identity of the self (he quotes A113) and that empirical consciousness is by itself (*an sich*) dispersed and without relation to that same identity, as Kant asserts at B133.

mind' (A120) and do not share an analytic characteristic that would make them generically identical and relate them to an identical subject of representation. For one's representations to share an analytic unity of consciousness, an act of synthesis must first have been exercised (B133). This is not just the act of accompanying *each* one of the representations that I have (in the flow of representations) and that may be co-present with any other representation at any one time in my empirical consciousness. One should be careful not to conflate co-presence of representations and *unity* of representation in Kant's sense of numerical unity (or analytic unity). Transcendental consciousness is therefore not at all formally implied in any arbitrary empirical consciousness that accompanies any arbitrary singular representation or series of singular representations.[21] To argue conversely would effectively undermine Kant's call, as we have seen in Chapter 7, for a separate combinatory activity that is not yet contained in sensibility, and which establishes synthetic unity with which analytic unity is rigorously coextensive, and which first grounds the latter.

9.3 The Analytic Principle of Apperception and Sense Datum Experience

Let me consider an insight offered by Strawson's (1968: 100 ff.) critique of sense datum experience, which sheds light on the crucial difference between apperception accompanying a collective unity of representations and the apprehension of discrete representations. It is part and parcel of Strawson's construal of a transcendental argument to argue for the conceptual impossibility of something like a sense datum experience. In the hypothetical case of a pure sense datum experience (putatively a unitary consciousness of separate awarenesses at any one time) the *esse* and *percipi* of a sense datum would collapse into each

---

21 Cf. also Klemme (1996: 192ff.), who espouses the same view as the commentators discussed above. Klemme's conclusion that '[d]as empirische Bewußtsein kann nur unter der Voraussetzung eines reinen Bewußtseins als ein begleitendes empirisches Bewußtsein verstanden werden' (1996: 193) appears to me to be mistaken for the same reasons as explicated above. Klemme maintains that 'Kants subjektive Einheit der Vorstellungen einen notwendigen Bezug auf die (analytische) Identität des Subjekts hat'. This would mean that for any consciousness to occur transcendental consciousness is necessarily implied. But this conflicts with the passage at B133 that we discussed. Contrary to what Klemme (1996: 193–4) suggests, I believe that Kant's conception of empirical (i.e. psychological) consciousness has everything in common with Hume's, their differences regarding the possibility of necessary connection notwithstanding. As I have shown above, the passage at B133, which Klemme also quotes, does not license the conclusion Klemme reaches.

other. There would be no distinction between object of awareness and act of awareness in a single sense datum experience. The direct object of awareness has no existence independently of the awareness of it. By having the sense datum one would eo ipso be instantly aware of it, without however recognising that one is aware of it, for there is no web of co-referentiality within which the single datum could be contrasted with any other datum. Only the relation to an identical item over time (in a co-referential series of such awarenesses that refer to this item) saves the recognitional component from being absorbed into its object. For Strawson, evidently, this gives rise to the belief that a pure sense datum experience is intrinsically contradictory: no awareness of a separate impression (I perceive A, I perceive B, I perceive C, and so on) could occur without certain constraints that enable the recognition of the impression as that particular impression, these constraints solely being provided by the connectedness of impressions, which in turn rests on the connectedness of spatiotemporal objects. This then, presumably, invalidates the cogency of the claim that one could be (intuitively) aware of a *single* sense datum, given that by awareness one understands a bona fide consciousness of the recognitional type and not mere animal sentience. Strawson argues that

> [t]here can be no experience at all which does not involve the recognition of particular items *as* being of such and such a general kind.

And more clearly:

> It seems that it must be possible, *even in the most fleeting and purely subjective of impressions*, to distinguish a component of recognition, or judgement, which is not simply identical with, or wholly absorbed by, the particular item which is recognised, which forms the topic of judgement. (1968: 100, emphasis added)

Strawson speaks of a distinction between the *esse* of what one experiences or perceives and its *percipi*, which in the case of a putative sense datum experience would be blurred; the distinction is blurred, for the relation between the sense datum and its putatively being experienced as such is necessarily opaque as a result of the absence of the connectedness of one's sense data which would provide a ground for distinguishing the *esse* of a sense datum and its *percipi* (a putative sense datum experience is by definition a singular experience of a singular datum). Because in the putative case of a sense datum experience the *esse* and *percipi* are indistinct or indistinguishable, according to Strawson it eo ipso follows that an experience of a sense datum, which cannot distinguish itself from what it experiences, makes no sense insofar as such an experience is to

9.3 The Analytic Principle of Apperception and Sense Datum Experience — 237

provide a viable description of what is a bona fide case of experience. The notion of a sense datum experience would seem to be *conceptually* contradictory.

Pace Strawson, however, I believe the opaqueness of the relation between act and object of awareness in an ostensible sense-datum experience does not ex hypothesi invalidate the concept of a sub-recognitional relation between an act of empirical apperception and its object (I mean 'recognition' in the specific sense of conceptual recognition). One could therefore argue for the possibility of the kind of experience that is not differentiatable from *what* it experiences or apperceives (cf. B235/A190, B243/A198). Without the capacity for recognition, one could not *know that* one was severally conscious of one's sense data (the multifarious representations that one has consecutively), but even so—and this is in contrast to Strawson—one could not know that one was *not* conscious of them severally (that is, in a sub-recognitional sense).[22] This would be tantamount to the kind of experience for which there is no distinction between having the experience and that of which the experience is, but, crucially, for which also holds that no potential acknowledgement of being connected in the unity of consciousness is even required.[23] On Kant's account, sub-recognitional consciousness is surely possible, given that he associates empirical apperception with the intuitive, non-discursive consciousness of the 'I' of apprehension, viz. an accompaniment by empirical consciousness that has no relation to an 'identical subject'.[24] Wolfgang Carl (1992: 64) has rightly observed, with reference to A107,[25] that em-

---

[22] Cf. Kant's letter to Herz of 17 May 1789, *Corr*, AA 11: 52.

[23] This last specification gainsays Strawson's (1968: 100–1) solution, which he claims Kant himself must offer, for the apparent existence of disconnected experiences. That Strawson, after ostensibly having undermined the sense data theorist's line of argument, subsequently allows for experiences that altogether lack the conceptual character which would enable the distinguishability between their *esse* and *percipi*, does not help his reasoning that the premise of the Deduction's proof concerns the necessary potentiality of one's experiences being united by virtue of self-ascription. If it is necessary that experiences are at any rate unifiable and potentially show a connectedness that corresponds to an objective unity, then it seems that ex hypothesi it is not possible that in effect there are such experiences that, entirely or partially, lack the conceptual character that shows such connectedness or a potential for being thus connected.

[24] Cf. *Anthr*, AA 7: 141–2. See also his account in the letter to Herz of 26 May 1789, *Corr*, AA 11: 52. Cf. Ingeborg Heidemann, who writes that '[das empirische Ich] erlebt seine Existenz im Vollzug von einzelnem und nicht als Haben eines einzigen Ganzen, das alle Möglichkeiten einzelner Erlebnisweisen umfaßt' (1958: 160). See also Sturma (1985: 56, 117).

[25] Kant writes here: 'The consciousness of oneself in accordance with the determinations of our state in internal perception is merely empirical, forever variable; it can provide no standing or abiding self in this stream of inner appearances, and is customarily called *inner sense* or *empirical apperception*.' Prien (2006: 129) rightly points out that 'consciousness of oneself' here is not

pirical apperception, the type of accompaniment also meant by Kant at B133 (AA 3: 109.16–20),[26] is a type of empirical consciousness that is 'forever variable'. In other words, as Carl writes, 'the consciousness of apprehension is [...] a consciousness which itself changes with the change of representations'. He further notes that this kind of consciousness 'only characterises the way in which we have given representations'. Because this kind of consciousness modulates in accordance with the persistent flow or flux of representations as they are prompted, the relation between such consciousness and representations remains opaque.[27]

If we put the difference between empirical apperception and transcendental apperception in the terms of ways of 'accompanying' representations, then this means either

> 1) that the 'I think' accompanies 'all my representations' (P1-representations), in which the 'accompanying' relation between the accompanied representations and the 'I think' is clear and distinct (this is the 'accompanying' meant at B131–2) and an analytic unity between the representations is ipso facto established,

or,

> 2) an accompanying of discrete representations, in which the relation between the representations accompanied and 'empirical consciousness' remains obscure or opaque in Strawson's sense, that is, cognitively indeterminate (this is the sense of 'accompanying' meant at B133).

In the latter case, the accompaniment coalesces with the representation so accompanied. The representation's *esse* and its *percipi* collapse into one; no conceptual recognition occurs. In other words, in such a case consciousness does not differentiate itself from its representation. Kant confirms this in the following passage:

'self-consciousness' in the strict sense, although I do not concur with his view that the representations that are the object of the consciousness meant here still 'belong to the I', unless 'I' *sensu lato* is meant. If the consciousness at issue is not a self-consciousness in the strict sense, then eo ipso the representations of which one is conscious cannot said to belong to the 'I' in the strict sense. Representations can be asserted to be mine only when *I* can ascribe them to myself (cf. A122). De dicto ascription and de re possession of representations are not necessarily coextensive.

26 Cf. B235 (AA 3: 168.15–19).
27 Cf. de Vleeschauwer (1937: 106–7) and Mohr (1991: 137).

9.3 The Analytic Principle of Apperception and Sense Datum Experience — 239

> *The apprehension of the manifold of appearance is always successive. The representations of the parts succeed one another.* Whether they also succeed in the object is a second point for reflection, which is not contained in the first. Now one can, to be sure, call everything, and even every representation, insofar as one is conscious of it, an object; only what this word is to mean in the case of appearances, not insofar as they are (as representations) objects, but rather only insofar as they designate an object, requires a deeper investigation. *Insofar as they are, merely as representations, at the same time objects of consciousness, they do not differ from their apprehension,* i.e., from their being taken up into the synthesis of the imagination, and one must therefore say that the manifold of appearances is always successively generated in the mind. (B234–5/A189–90, emphasis added)[28]

What would it mean to apprehend discrete representations? Take the following case of disconnected impressions or representations. Suppose that some representer *R* is in the business of having consecutive representations, 'having sense data', which *R* might or might not relate to each other and so might or might not recognise as belonging to one, whole experience. For example, *R* looks out the window and, being in England, sees the overcast sky, is mesmerised by Karl Böhm's famous 1973 rendition of Bruckner's Fourth with the Vienna Philharmonic, smells the aroma of the espresso that is being brewed, and so on. *R* could have all of these representations or sense data consecutively or all at once, as Leibnizian *petites perceptions*, say, without explicitly recognising, even potentially, that she is having them (all together) or indeed what she is experiencing. It is full well possible that *R* does not know who Bruckner is or has never heard the Fourth before (let alone knows her Wand from her Böhm), and that *R* does not know what 'espresso' means, while her olfactory nerves and auditory organ are properly functioning nonetheless and *R* can make a distinction between what she hears and what she smells. *R* could be in a general state of mesmerisation without in the slightest having the inclination to reflect on her state or indeed knowing what causes or caused it or without being able to describe or determine the content of her experiencing the present mental state or states that she is in. But, and this relates to Strawson's point, neither does *R need* to be able to notice that regardless of representational content *she* is having those representations in order for these representations simply to occur. For

---

28 What is of importance here is Kant's remark that consciousness of representations that fall short of designating an outer appearance collapses into their apprehension. However, the quoted passage might be taken to pose a problem for my interpretation because Kant also seems to identify consciousness as such with the synthesis of imagination. Presumably, however, *reproductive* imagination is meant here, not *productive* imagination (cf. B152), which, if Kant means the latter, would appear to mean a problematic conflation of consciousness and transcendental apperception.

such a second-order reflection to take place, a condition of objective connectedness would indeed need to be fulfilled to enable R to differentiate occurring representations *as* her representations belonging to the analytic unity of her self-consciousness. There is however nothing about having sense impressions that relates them such that the condition of objective connectedness is a necessary condition *of their being had*. True, one should argue in line with Strawson's critique of sense datum experience that even if, counterfactually, R were severally conscious of individual sense data or representations, R could not occurrently *know* that she was severally conscious of her sense data, of the multifarious representations that she has, for such knowledge would require a criterion of objective connectedness. However, in opposition to Strawson one should also acknowledge that by the same token, on account of the same principle that informs Strawson's critique, R (or anybody for that matter) cannot presently know that she was *not* severally conscious of her sense data at any arbitrary time t (in a sub-recognitive sense).[29]

If it were indeed the case that *each* individual representation is accompanied by an instance of *empirical* consciousness (and this is what, in my view, Kant claims is a real possibility in the passage at B133), then ex hypothesi no relation to the identity of the subject would have been established by such accompaniment, for the empirical consciousness and the single representation so accompanied would namely collapse into each other as no unity with other representations would have been established. Identity depends on numerical unity of representation, not just an aggregate of singular, dispersed representations. As said, one could not *know* that one was severally conscious of one's sense data (the multifarious representations that I *have* consecutively), but—and, again, this is in contrast to Strawson—even so one could not know that one was *not* conscious of them (in a sub-recognitional sense). Thus, empirical consciousness accompanying representations severally is certainly possible, but this is not to say that it amounts to an inferred consciousness of the representations belonging to the compound that *has been* apperceived by a *thinking* 'I', 'the act through which it had been gradually generated'. In other words, Kant does not argue at B133 for a distributive relation among representations as such *within* the collective unity of an identical self, but he merely alludes to the possibility of a singular momentary consciousness 'in our current state' (A103).[30] The two senses of 'begleiten' at B132 and B133 respectively must therefore be kept strictly separate.

---

[29] Cf. *Corr*, AA 11: 52.6–16.
[30] With respect to the notion of 'distributivity' in regard to self-consciousness, see Thöle (1991: 68n.10). Thöle refers to R3030, where Kant writes: 'Ich verbinde [...] A mit dem Bewußtseyn.

9.4 Hossenfelder on the 'I Think' and Analytic Unity

Let me hark back to Hossenfelder's austere definition of Kant's analytic principle of apperception to stress the particular nature of the unity between the 'I think' and the manifold representations it accompanies. As we have seen in Chapter 6, Hossenfelder (1978: 100) argues that if we take the verb 'to think' to mean something else than the 'represent' that is conceptually contained in the predicate 'all my representations', then the principle would not be really analytic and would rest on a *petitio principii*. I believe this strategy is unfortunate (even though the 'I think' is in a sense a representation, albeit of a special kind), because it thus precludes the possibility of evaluating Kant's claim that an a priori synthesis necessarily underlies the analytic unity of representations and in fact makes the principle of self-consciousness as analytic possible (cf. B135). Of course, Hossenfelder, like Strawson, deliberately dissociates the so-called constitution theory—which is connected with a priori synthesis—from the putative analytic core of Kant's argument here, so it is not surprising that he reads the proposition the way he does. Given this, it is also unsurprising that he believes that Kant does not sufficiently separate the analytic and synthetic unities of consciousness or representation.

Furthermore, Hossenfelder's (1978: 101n.90) remark that the analytic principle of apperception, as he reconstructs it, would equally hold for intuitive minds disregards the fact that Kant's theory of concepts is specifically a theory for intellectual discursivity, not for intellectual intuition.[31] Since it thinks through synthetic universals (i.e. concepts that already contain the content to which they would otherwise be applicable), and not analytic universals as *conceptus communes* (cf. B134n.) or partial representations, an intuitive mind would not need a manifold of representations which it must run through and from which it must abstract concepts in order to be able to think at all, which in the case of the discursive 'I think', being an empty analytic universal, is needed to get synthetic wholes. A representation that an intuitive intellect would have,

---

Dann B [...]. Drittens die [...] Einheit beyderley distributiven Bewußtseyns in ein collectives, d.i. in den Begrif eines Dinges' (AA 16: 623). This might seem to contradict my reading of B133, as it seems to suggest that the collective unity of consciousness is just the conjoining of distributive awarenesses. Thöle even believes that Kant thinks that distributive self-consciousness is possible only if collective self-consciousness is possible (1991: 259). However, he subsequently appears to retract this statement, by saying that '[d]as bedeutet allerdings noch nicht, daß distributives Selbstbewußtsein kollektives *Selbst*bewußtsein impliziert' (1991: 260).

31 Kant clearly differentiates the two possible modes of cognition; cf. e.g. B68, B135, 139 and CJ § 77, AA 5: 407.

would not be a partial representation (representation by means of general marks or characteristics) of the whole, but would be a representation of the whole as such. Our discursive cognition is meristic, not holistic. Hossenfelder's view that the analytic principle of apperception holds for intuitive minds as well as discursive ones would appear to be hugely begging the question against Kant.[32]

Most importantly, however, Hossenfelder reads apperception in terms of PS' (as defined in Chapter 6), which shows a self-evident conceptual truth of which 'representation' is the *explanandum*, based on the assumption that with the 'I think'-proposition Kant refers to the psychological capacity for representation. Conversely, for Kant, the 'I think' as *explanans* is called upon to explain the possibility of unifying a synthetic compound of selfsame representations, representations that have a feature in common, by which they are to be taken as belonging together to the extent that they have this common feature. As we have seen in Chapter 6 in regard to the 'I think'-proposition, it is the predicate 'all my representations', that is, a manifold in the intuition that I have as a unified compound, and not each individual representation within that compound, let alone each arbitrary representation, that is the *explanandum*. In other words, the analytic relation obtains not simply between a representer (presumably the 'I') and a representation (that 'I' presumably represent) but between the 'I think', as a kind of super representation, and a certain complex or compound representation which I think *as* that compound representation, namely 'all my representations' together (in this context, Kant uses the term *insgesammt*; I return to this aspect below in Section 9.5 when discussing numerical identity). The predicate of 'I think' is 'all my representations', not 'each individual representation that I have'. Call the predicate 'all my representations' r_{all} and each representation that I have or, more accurately, each separate representation that is being represented r_{each}.

> $r_{all} = df$ a compound representation of all my representations together, which as such is accompanied by the 'I think'
>
> $r_{each} = df$ each distinct representation that is being represented by a representer R

I contend that the putative relation between the 'I think' and r_{each} as such cannot in effect be analytical (i.e. conceptual) in Hossenfelder's sense, for that relation is fundamentally asymmetrical: in the hierarchy of lower and higher representations, according to the traditional theory of concepts, the 'I think' is the higher representation, with respect to which r_{each} is the lower representation. The

---

[32] Cf. Reich (2001: 41–3 [35–7]).

9.4 Hossenfelder on the 'I Think' and Analytic Unity — 243

mark or characteristic of 'I think' is indeed analytically contained in each representation *that is part* of the compound representation in which the 'I think' is contained, namely the manifold of 'all my representations'—this compound is an r_{all}: a strict relation of identity obtains between the 'I think' and the predicate 'all my representations'. But the mark 'I think' is contained in an r_{each} only to the extent that such an r_{each} is unified with other representations r_{each} that share the same mark and so forms an analytic unity of representations with them, viz. the r_{all} that is 'all my representations' (put differently, I am not distributed in the manifold representations qua manifold, that is, discretely, but they are collectively in me as unitary representation).[33] Hence, the analytic relation is between the 'I think' and an r_{each} only if an r_{each} is part of the compound predicate r_{all} that is an analytic unity between all representations having the 'I think' as a partial representation or mark as their cognitive ground (*Erkenntnisgrund*),[34] not simply between the 'I think' and any arbitrary r_{each}. There is thus no analytic *unity*, and a fortiori no conceptual relation, between the 'I think' and any arbitrary r_{each}. Hossenfelder seems aware of this asymmetry between the 'I think' and representations as several, for that is precisely why he substitutes 'I represent' for 'I think' so as to make the relation between representer and representation clearer by making it conceptually tighter, ignoring the conceptual hierarchy between the 'I think' and a discrete representation r_{each}.

Furthermore, given the definition of discursive thought as a function of uniting different representations under a common one (A68/B93), when I am thinking I do not think, strictly speaking, each individual representation A, B, C, and so on distributively, so that the putative instances of 'I think A', 'I think B', 'I think C' collectively amount to an a posteriori unity of 'I think'-instances. This latter scenario seems to be the case on Hossenfelder's alternative reading of apperception, whereby 'represent' must be seen as substitutable for 'think'. To argue that each representation in a succession of representations is analytically related to the 'I think' to the effect that the 'I think' accompanies each of them severally would imply that we are talking about an arbitrary psychological distributive unity of representations (a unity of representations $r_{each}1...r_{each}n$, correspondent with a synthetic a posteriori unity). To argue thus would be tantamount to claiming that 'I think'-accompaniment is but an instantaneous singular apprehension (or a series of successive apprehensions) of whatever is

---

33 I can of course analyse the discrete parts of the collective unity of all the representations that I do accompany.
34 Cf. JL, AA 9: 58.

represented, and not a unified thought, which can only be a collective unity (not a mere distributive unity) (A117n; cf. A353–4).

Such successive apprehensions of singular representations would not amount to a necessary unity, a whole, of representations that first constitutes the concept (a representation r_{all}) designating an object (cf. A97 [AA 4: 76.8–11]). Moreover, if it were indeed the case that an $r_{each}1$ is a representation accompanied by an 'I think' and $r_{each}2$ is equally a representation accompanied by an 'I think' and so forth, then the *unity* of the representations $r_{each}1...r_{each}n$ so accompanied could not also be an 'I think'—or, supposedly, there are more *kinds* of 'I think', which does not make sense interpretatively.[35] Since, as Kant argues, the 'I think' is to function as the *unity* of that manifold of representations which it accompanies, the representations themselves ex hypothesi cannot *severally* be accompanied by an 'I think' on pain of circularity. Only to the extent that representations make up a unified manifold are they accompanied, *as* unified manifold, by an 'I think'. Therefore, the 'I think' is the mark of each representation that is contained in the compound representation r_{all} that it actually accompanies ('all my representations'), but the reverse does not hold: each separate representation as such (r_{each}) does not eo ipso conceptually entail an accompanying 'I think'. Put differently, it is not as separate that an r_{each} carries the mark 'I think', but only *as part of* the unified manifold to which r_{each} belongs, for an 'I think' is strictly coextensive with a collective unity of representations; this collective unity is what I called an r_{all}.

Referring to the footnote appended to B133, Kitcher adds an important reason why an r_{each} cannot in fact carry an 'I think':

> Kant's point is precisely not that someone who asserts that I am the possessor of R_1, R_2, and R_3 manages to make that claim by combining R_1 with a representation of an 'I', R_2 with a representation of 'I', and so forth. *This is not possible, because inner sense provides no 'I' representation to combine with others*, as he notes in the next paragraph: / "Through the 'I', as a simple representation, nothing manifold is given; only in intuition which is distinct from this representation, can a manifold be given" (B135). (2011: 146–7, emphasis added)

The manifold in inner sense does not provide *of itself* the criterion by means of which a transition from R_1 to R_2 is made possible such that they are necessarily combined (cf. A107). Kitcher proceeds to argue that for a combination of several

---

[35] I therefore cannot agree with the idea of several levels of 'I think'-thought advanced by Ameriks (2000b: 239–40). I agree though with the general purport of Ameriks's critique of inflated readings of apperception.

9.4 Hossenfelder on the 'I Think' and Analytic Unity — 245

representations to be possible a priori synthesis is required, which only then makes them relate to an accompanying 'I think':

> Different representations are not combined with some permanent 'I' intuition. Instead, they are combined with each other and that can come about only through an operation of synthesis that establishes their necessary connection to each other—and so their conformity to the condition for belonging to one consciousness, or an 'I'-think.' (2011: 147)

However, Hossenfelder (1978: 101–2) claims that the analytic unity of representations can be thought without contradiction *sans* a priori synthesis—so that presumably Kant's claim to the synthetic a priori as a necessary presupposition of any analytic unity, and thus of any concept as such (cf. B133n.), is an illicit assumption that has no ground in the theory of the analysis of concepts. Similarly, in his critique of Longuenesse, Cassam (2007: 141 ff.) disputes the Kantian claim that 'synthesis is necessary for analysis' (2007: 142). Cassam's main problem with this is the threat of a regress:

> [I]f pure synthesis is needed to prepare the ground of analysis, the obvious question is: what prepares the ground for pure synthesis? What ensures that the sensible given is susceptible to synthesis in the way that synthesis ensures that the sensible given is susceptible to analysis? [...] Why think that we need to *do* anything to what is given to the senses to make it possible to extract concepts from it? (2007: 143)

The regress problem that Cassam points out seems a legitimate worry. But this is only so because Cassam assumes, very much in the vein of Strawson's criticism against it, that synthesis is a subjective or psychological activity that is redundant for the explanation of the analysis of concepts. Likewise he reasons that the categories, which in some way he does accept as necessary conditions of the acquisition of concepts (2007: 144 ff.), can be separated from synthesis and can be linked more directly to analysis. But this presupposes that synthesis is something different from categories. In the present book, I argue that this is not the case and that Kant's position is in fact closer to what Cassam has in mind (at least on one construal of his main argument), namely 'that analysis itself involves thinking by means of categorial concepts' (2007: 144). Longuenesse rightly maintains that Cassam 'cannot avoid implicitly smuggling into what he calls "analysis" just those activities of combination without which no judging would take place at all' (2008: 516).

In contrast to Hossenfelder and Cassam, I contend that it is rather impossible to think an analytic unity of representations without already assuming the possibility of synthesis, that is, *a priori* synthesis (namely a synthesis that rationally grounds an analytic unity). As I pointed out above, simply to represent (and not *cogitare*, which Hossenfelder [1978: 101n.90] wrongfully conflates with representing) an arbitrary aggregate of representations $r_{each}1...r_{each}n$ does not add up to representing, or, to be more precise, thinking an analytic unity, that is, 'grasping' a concept (cf. the root form of the German *Begriff*, which is *be-greifen*, indeed 'to grasp' as in 'to understand'). When thinking an analytic unity, in that a rule is applied to a manifold of representations (by reflecting, comparing and abstracting features) so as to acquire sameness of representation that constitutes a concept, of 'apple',[36] say, it is not *merely* an analytic unity that I represent, as Hossenfelder believes. I also bring the unitary manifold of representations to [*auf*] the concept by virtue of a priori synthesis (cf. B104).

But Hossenfelder (1978: 118) thinks this bringing to concepts is still *only* analytic. It is true that in applying the concept 'apple' to the extension of the apple-like things that are thought under it (intuitions of apples), I analyse the things that fall under the concept 'apple' with respect to their shared characteristic while abstracting from the characteristics that make them different from each other and are synthetically united with this one characteristic to make up the whole representation of that particular thing (some apples are red, some are green etc.). The reflection is merely directed at the shared partial representation. But, as Kant says at B133–4n., analysis *presupposes* the synthesis among the diverse characteristics that various things also have in addition to the shared characteristic that makes them part of the analytic unity; the synthesis is not something given, but an original act by the subject of thought herself. To change given representations into concepts is an 'analytic operation'. The form of a concept is generated analytically. But being able to apply the concept to an extension of things (which one intuits) presupposes synthesis as a way of differentiating the various characteristics of the representations apprehended in intuition.

Thus, if a manifold of representations were not brought to the concept in virtue of a priori synthesis, I could not retain the features of a representation $r_{each}1$ when I represent a subsequent representation $r_{each}2$, and correspondingly the features of both $r_{each}1$ and $r_{each}2$ when I represent a subsequent representation $r_{each}3$, which whatever their material nature together share the concept that I 'apply' to the manifold $r_{each}1...r_{each}3$ (viz. the common concept r_{all} contained in that manifold as unified).[37] This involves the syntheses of reproduction and recognition.

---

36 Forming a concept occurs by taking a representation as a mark or partial representation that various things have in common. For an illuminating account of comparison, reflection and abstraction, see Prien (2006: 68–75).

37 Cf. A102–4. A concept is 'the consciousness of [the] unity of the synthesis' (A103) in the manifold of representations. Without the consciousness of synthesis 'concepts, and with them cognition of objects, would be entirely impossible' (A104).

Without the synthesis of reproduction (which is dependent on the synthesis of recognition), I would only be varying representations r_{each} without noticing their belonging together in a collective unity which is identical to an r_{all}, that is, to any arbitrary *concept* that I apply (I would have *intuitions* of apples without noticing they are all apples). Again, a posteriori synthesis is not sufficient here, for it does not provide me with the rule or criterion by means of which I can know that the representations that I apprehend and add to each other belong together necessarily in regard to their shared characteristic, rather than only contingently as would be the case in representing an aggregate of representations $r_{each}1...r_{each}n$ (cf. A100–2). Without such an a priori rule by means of which I can retain identical features of apprehended representations and 'gradually generate' a whole of representations, thus 'without consciousness that that which we think is the very same as what we thought a moment before, all reproduction in the series of representations would be in vain' (A103). All that we would have is a consecution of separate singular representations of which we might be severally conscious ('in our current state' at time t_1 and then 'in our current state' at t_2), but which will never form a whole r_{all} that is accompanied by a unitary consciousness. Now the consciousness of the rule by means of which I reproduce and recognise representations as belonging together is in fact the concept in which the manifold of representations has been united, which is what Kant means by bringing the pure synthesis of the manifold 'to concepts' (*auf Begriffe*) (B104).

9.5 Numerical Identity: 'Totality is the Unity of Plurality'

Although the 'I think' requires a manifold of representations to be given to it in order for a thought to acquire content, it is not just any manifold or indeed any of the representations of the manifold that is accompanied by the 'I think'. This has been made clear by our previous analysis of the predicate 'all my representations', indicating the collective unity of the representations. In § 16, Kant makes it clear that the manifold accompanied by apperception is one that is given 'in a certain intuition', and as such belongs to one self-consciousness (B132). The aspect of 'thoroughgoing identity' that establishes that 'all my representations' 'can stand together in a universal self-consciousness' so as to be 'my representations all together [*insgesammt*]' makes up the 'totality' of 'all my representations'. As we have seen in Chapter 7, the unity of 'all my representations' is established by means of the act of synthesis as a spontaneous act of 'self-activity'. It is this act of synthesis which establishes the thoroughgoing numerical identity of 'all my representations'. Kant says about the 'numerical unity of [...]

apperception', namely the 'I think' of apperception, which 'precedes all data of the intuitions' so as to enable 'all representation of objects' (A107) and is as such, without a manifold given to it, but a logical unity of consciousness:

> Just this transcendental unity of apperception [...] makes out of all possible appearances that can ever come together in one experience a connection of all of these representations in accordance with laws. For this unity of consciousness would be impossible if in the cognition of the manifold the mind could not become conscious of the identity of the function by means of which this manifold is synthetically combined into one cognition. Thus the original and necessary consciousness of the identity of oneself is at the same time a consciousness of an equally necessary unity of the synthesis of all appearances in accordance with concepts, i.e., in accordance with rules that not only make them necessarily reproducible, but also thereby determine an object for their intuition, i.e., the concept of something in which they are necessarily connected; for the mind could not possibly think of the identity of itself in the manifoldness of its representations, and indeed think this *a priori*, if it did not have before its eyes the identity of its action, which subjects all synthesis of apprehension (which is empirical) to a transcendental unity, and first makes possible their connection in accordance with *a priori* rules. (A108)

Here, Kant argues that appearances, 'themselves only representations' (A109), can only be seen as synthetically united if in apprehending the manifold of these representations or appearances they are apprehended, by the mind, as belonging together in 'one cognition'. The *synthetic* unity of representations is established by the mind that successively or gradually takes together, synthesises, or conjoins, the multifarious representations in the manifold and combines them 'into one cognition', which yields a concept 'of an *object*' (A108) (more of which in Chapter 10). The 'I think', in abstraction from a given manifold, is nothing but an absolute (though merely logical) simple unity (A354–5, 356). But in combination with a given manifold of representations transcendental apperception is able, by means of its inherent capacity of self-activity, to synthetically combine the manifold into 'one cognition'. This is not just a combination of representations in terms of their *analytic* unity in that they share the common representation 'I think', but also a combination of representations in terms of a *synthetic* unity in that they belong all together to the extent that they are all accompanied by the same 'I think'. One notices that one act, by virtue of the identical function of an 'I think' accompanying 'all my representations', produces 'at the same time' (A108) the numerical identity of the 'I', that is, the representation of 'the *identity of the consciousness in these representations* itself, i.e., the *analytical* unity of apperception' (B133), *and* the 'necessary unity of the synthesis of all appearances', that is, the synthetic unity of apperception. As Kant says at B134,

> [t]he thought that these representations given in intuition all together belong *to me* means [...] the same as that I unite them in one self-consciousness [...] only because I can comprehend [*begreifen*] their manifold in one consciousness do I call them all together *my* representations. (trans. emended)

Kant's use of *begreifen* in the last quote is significant, for it indicates that it is by means of the act of synthesis that not just the analytic unity of consciousness comes about but also concepts in general, to which analytic unity of consciousness always pertains (B133n.), are thus first formed from the manifold of representations. The 'numerical unity of [...] apperception', which includes or explains a synthesis, 'therefore grounds all concepts *a priori*' (A107; cf. B133–4n.).

That the manifold of representations contained in inner sense, that is, the 'different representations' that are accompanied by 'empirical consciousness' (B133), by and in itself does not amount to the totality of 'all my representations' or indeed 'the thoroughgoing identity of oneself in *all possible* representations' (emphasis added), as Kant writes less carefully at A116, is made clear in a passage at A107:

> The consciousness of oneself in accordance with the determinations of our state in internal perception is merely empirical, forever variable; it can provide no standing or abiding self in this stream of inner appearances, and is customarily called *inner sense* or *empirical apperception*. That which should *necessarily* be represented as numerically identical cannot be thought of as such through empirical data.

The 'empirical data' as such delivered in and through sensibility do not constitute a numerical identity among them, which would relate them to the 'I think' of pure apperception. Hence, Kant says that

> the empirical consciousness that accompanies *different representations* is by itself dispersed and *without relation to the identity of the subject*. (B133, emphasis added)

This does not mean that the manifold as such is completely in disarray, as the quote above might suggest.[38] Also Kant's claim, earlier in § 15, where he claims that 'the *combination* (*conjunctio*) of a manifold in general can never come to us through the senses, and therefore cannot already be contained in the pure form of sensible intuition' (B129), might seem to suggest that the manifold as such is chaotic, for since 'all combination [...], whether it is a combination of the mani-

---

[38] Perceptions that are 'unruly heaps' are in disarray to the extent that they have not been determinately connected by means of the act of synthesis, and are instead reproduced 'without distinction, just as they fell together' (A121).

fold of intuition or of several concepts [...] is an action of the understanding' (B130) the manifold prior to being combined must be wholly unconnected. But this is not the case (see Section 7.4). What Kant means, both at A107 and in § 15, is that numerical identity and combination respectively are not given with or in sensibility as a matter of course, but can be conceived as pertaining to the manifold if and only if the representations in the manifold in intuition are *taken* to be generically identical and thus to relate to the identical subject of apperception. Any combination that they might have by themselves cannot be seen as providing insight into their *necessary* identity if their combination is not grasped as such in virtue of a combinatory activity by an identical subject, for '[t]hat which should *necessarily* be represented as numerically identical cannot be thought of as such through empirical data' (A107). The numerical identity of a manifold of representations in intuition (whether this concerns an empirical sensibility or a non-sensible intuition)[39] is logically dependent on the 'identity of [the mind's] action, which subjects all synthesis of apprehension [...] to a transcendental unity, and first makes possible their connection in accordance with *a priori* rules' (A108), hence their necessary connection. Whatever other connection might hold between the representations in the manifold is not at issue in Kant's argument.

Nevertheless, in the A-Deduction account of the synthesis of apprehension in intuition, Kant might be taken to claim that a synthesis is required even to be able to conceive of the manifold, not as unified, but already purely *as* manifold. This introduces the requirement of time determination, which of course we abstracted from in our argument for the derivation of the categories from pure thought. Kant's reasoning is that if I were not able to 'distinguish the time in the succession of impressions on one another', I would not be able to represent the manifold *as manifold,* 'for *as contained in one moment* no representation can ever be anything other than absolute unity' (A99). In other words, whereas unity of apperception, and thus the synthesis of recognition in a concept establishes numerical unity in the manifold, a synthesis is also already required even to conceive of the manifold *as manifold.* Otherwise the manifold would be nothing but a series of unconnected 'now's, absolute points in time, perceptions that are 'dispersed and separate' (*zerstreuet und einzeln*) in the mind (A120), indeed 'unruly heaps' (A121) of $r_{each}1...r_{each}n$. But, also here at A99, Kant makes it clear that this is relevant for a *unified* conception of the manifold, namely a manifold 'as contained *in one representation*'. Intuition does provide the manifold (in time), even if it is true that I cannot conceive it *as such,* as *determined* in time, let

---

[39] Cf. Prien (2006: 95–8).

9.5 Numerical Identity: 'Totality is the Unity of Plurality' — 251

alone as unified, if no synthesis were added. In other words, a synthesis is not required for the manifold of representations *to be given*, to *be* a manifold, but it is required to determine or conceive of the manifold *as* manifold.⁴⁰

But Kant's most important argument concerns the requirement of a unitary act of combination of a multitude of representations by means of which the manifold 'constitute[s] a whole' (A103) that is determinately connected according to a rule, in contrast to 'unruly heaps' (*regellose Haufen*) (A121). As he argues at B133, the relation of 'thoroughgoing identity of the apperception of a manifold given in intuition' happens not simply 'by my accompanying each representation with consciousness, but rather by my *adding* [*hinzusetze*] one representation to the other, and being conscious of their synthesis'. Notice the use of the term 'thoroughgoing': the German *durchgängig* can also be translated as 'continuous' or 'constant', which should not be read as meaning literally constantly present, but in terms of a contrast to the fleeting nature of momentary apprehensions of discrete representations that do not 'gradually generate' (A103) a collective unity, and produce only 'unruly heaps'. 'Thoroughgoing identity of apperception', then, suggests the constructive nature of the act that creates or produces numerical identity among the representations apprehended. This procedure is made clear by Kant in his geometrical examples in § 24 of the B-Deduction (B154–5). In for example '*drawing* a straight line' one attends 'merely to the action of the synthesis of the manifold through which we successively determine the inner sense'. Kant employs the term 'motion' to visualise what is meant by attending to the action of synthesis and what 'first produces the concept of succession'. The combination that happens here is not something found but is 'produced' while attending to the act of, in this case, drawing itself. While drawing, the segments of the line, which are homogeneous units, are successively put together as belonging together in a quantum. At A103, Kant reasons in a similar way and uses the appropriate example of counting, which reinforces the fact that the categories of quantities are involved in the act of synthesis:

> If, in counting, I forget that the units that now hover before my senses were successively added to each other by me, then I would not cognize the generation of the multitude [*Menge*] through this successive addition of one to the other, and consequently I would not cognize the number; for this concept consists solely in the consciousness of this unity of synthesis.

In the act of counting it is obvious that quantity is involved, but the categories of quantity concern in fact *any* manifold of representations that is given to discur-

---

40 See also Schulting (2017a), ch. 6.

sive thought, which in order to be able to be *conceived of* as a numerically identical whole of representations must be recognised in a concept, that is, recognised as unified by means of apperception. A manifold must be presupposed as given, which accounts for the category of 'plurality', but for this manifold to be an r_{all}, that is, a synthetic unity of generically identical representations that have an identical subject of thought in common, the act of the mind must progress or run through the manifold representations and unite the parts of the manifold into a whole. It is only thus that a 'whole representation', the 'manifold as manifold', and hence conceptual cognition arises (cf. A120–1). This is what Kant argues at A113 when he writes that

> numerical identity [...] must necessarily enter into [*hinein kommen*] the synthesis of all the manifold of appearances insofar as they are to become empirical cognition.

The claim is put a bit awkwardly perhaps, but I take this to mean, in conformity with the argument at A107–8, that it concerns an 'identity of its action', which the mind must 'have before its eyes' in order to be able to 'think of the identity of itself *in the manifoldness of its representations*' (emphasis added). The numerical identity of the unity of representations of a self-consciousness, hence its analytic unity, is thus first established by transcendental apperception. Prior to an act of transcendental apperception (the transcendental unity of self-consciousness), which takes the manifold of representations ('plurality') together in an analytic unity ('unity'), there is no 'totality' of representations, namely representations as all together (*insgesamt*) (B132, 134) belonging to me as a unitary self-consciousness. The 'thoroughgoing identity of the apperception of a manifold given in intuition contains a synthesis of the representations, and is possible only through the consciousness of this synthesis' (B133). Since synthesis is not given in the manifold (B130), the consciousness of synthesis contained in the identity of the apperception is a consciousness of the '*identity of the function by means of which* [the] manifold is synthetically combined into one cognition' (A108, emphasis added). That is, thoroughgoing numerical identity of self-consciousness is a function of synthesis by the 'I think' which conjoins the parts of the manifold that it accompanies into a whole, the totality of its *own* representations, and thus first, not only becomes aware of its identity throughout these representations, but also 'becomes' the numerically identical subject of thought, since the identity consists precisely in the analytic identity of the function of this apperception as an action of the mind. Kant writes:

> I am therefore conscious of the identical self in regard to the manifold of the representations that are given to me in an intuition **because** I call them all together *my* representations, which constitute *one*. (B135, boldface added)

Representations are my representations if and only if they belong together to my self-consciousness, as Kant asserts at B132, but they would not belong together to my self-consciousness, and make up a transcendental unity of self-consciousness if I had not conjoined them into a whole to form this unity of self-consciousness. Prior to, or independent of, the act of combination by means of apperception there is neither unity nor identity of my self-consciousness.[41]

9.6 Deriving the Categories of Quantity: Summary

The argumentation in this chapter gives the following premises in the argument for the derivation of the categories of quantity from apperception:

> D22. The 'I think' of transcendental apperception is an analytic unity of consciousness that pertains to all concepts but is as such an empty representation that requires an exogenous content to form a concept, that is, a whole of partial representations.
>
> D23. A manifold of representations must be presupposed as given to the 'I think' to which it provides exogenous content.

These steps show that

> D24. The category of 'unity' pertains to the identity of discursive thought and hence is analytically derivable from it.
>
> D25. The category of 'plurality' pertains to the identity of discursive thought and hence is analytically derivable from it.

We have seen that a given manifold of representations must be run through by an act of synthesis that takes the manifold together to establish *one* representation that consists of various representations, that is, a determinate manifold. It is only through this synthesis that an analytic unity among the representations is established, through which they are related to the identical subject of apperception. Only unity and plurality together constitute a unified manifold that is a representation of a whole. Thus:

---

41 It is of course important to note that, as Kant points out in the Paralogisms, my real numerical identity cannot be guaranteed. The fact that the 'identity of the consciousness of Myself in different times is [...] only a formal condition of my thoughts and their connection', that is, that I am aware of myself as the same self throughout the time of which I am conscious, 'does not prove at all the numerical identity of my subject, in which—despite the logical identity of the I—a change can go on that does not allow it to keep its identity' (A363). A difference must be heeded between the de re and de dicto senses of the numerical identity of the 'I' of thought.

D26. A manifold of representations can be conceived as a manifold that belongs together throughout and thus constitutes a synthetic whole if and only if the manifold of representations is gradually synthesised in an act of synthesis by means of an analytic unity.

Therefore,

D27. The category of 'totality' pertains to the identity of discursive thought and hence is analytically derivable from it.

9.7 The Conclusion of the D-Argument

The derivation of the categories is now complete. This can be shown in a schematisation of all the aforementioned D-steps, which is meant more as a summary of the main arguments that exhibit the logical moments of discursive thought to which the categories are parallel, and is not strictly speaking a syllogistically modelled inferential link of premises. I believe a purely *formal* translation of Kant's arguments is not in principle impossible, but I doubt that it could do justice to all of the intricacies of the Deduction without becoming unwieldy.

Nevertheless, as I claimed in Chapter 3, the argumentative procedure in the Transcendental Deduction as a *transcendental* proof, which I have expounded in Chapters 6–9, and of which the D-argument is a summary, is a deduction in the specifically transcendental sense of a derivation of the logical moments of the understanding from apperception. A problem though remains regarding the connection between each of the *titles* of categories, so that it can be shown that the four titles exhaust the constitutive features of discursive thought, which is the idea behind Kant's completeness claim. Wolff (1995) has, I think, convincingly shown the completeness of the table for the functions of judgement. However, I do not make a similar claim with regard to the completeness of the table of categories insofar as the four titles are concerned. I have tried to show in the foregoing chapters the way in which each of the three *moments* within each title is necessarily implied in the constitution of transcendental apperception as the mode of discursive thought. It is a trickier proposition to argue for the necessary conceptual entailment between the four titles modality, relation, quality and quantity, although I have tried to show at least their interconnection. However, if one accepts the strict correspondence between the table of the functions of judgement and the table of the categories, and one accepts Wolff's solution for the completeness claim regarding the table of judgement, there must be a way also to prove the completeness of the table of categories for each of the four titles. Only then could Kant be thoroughly defended against Hegel's charge that he failed to derive *all* of the elementary characteristics of human discursivity

9.7 The Conclusion of the D-Argument — 255

in, to put it in Hegelian terms, a presuppositionless way, or in Kant's own words, fully a priori by means of reason's own 'self-knowledge' (Axi).

The D-argument consists of the following argumentative steps showing that the categories are derivable from the transcendental unity of apperception:

> D1. The fact of discursive thought indicates the *act* of thought or thought's actuality or *existence*, viz. the fact that *I am* the actual subject of my thought whenever I think, meaning that representations that are occurrently thought and accompanied by the identical representation 'I think' exist before the 'I'.
>
> D2. The act of thought presupposes a *possible* 'I think' accompanying all my possible representations, and hence the *possibility* of thinkingly accompanying 'all my representations', which are analytically related to the identical representation 'I' for all representations so accompanied.
>
> D3. The possibility of thinkingly accompanying 'all my representations' analytically implies the *impossibility* of thinkingly accompanying (but not of representing) representations other than 'all my representations' inasmuch as such representations that are other than 'all my representations' are not analytically related to an identical representation 'I' and so do not belong to the unity of all my possible representations.
>
> D4. The non-actuality or *non-existence* of 'I think'-thought is entailed by representations that are not contained in the unity of all my possible representations, meaning that such representations that do not belong to the unity of all of my possible representations, do not exist *before* the 'I' (they are 'nothing for me', though they could exist 'per se').
>
> D5. Therefore, the category of 'existence (/non-existence)' pertains to the identity of discursive thought and hence is analytically derivable from it. [D1, D4]
>
> D6. Therefore, the category of 'possibility (/impossibility)' pertains to the identity of discursive thought and hence is analytically derivable from it. [D2, D3]
>
> D7. Necessarily, if the 'I think' exists, then the rule that all my representations are accompanied by the 'I think' is satisfied.
>
> D8. It is contingent that for representations for which the rule that all my representations are accompanied by the 'I think' is not satisfied, the 'I think' is in fact instantiated.
>
> D9. Therefore, the category 'necessity (/contingency)' pertains to the identity of discursive thought and hence is analytically derivable from it. [D7, D8]
>
> D10. The notion of pure apperception as 'the standing and lasting I', required for the unity of representations, is that which subsists throughout (the apprehension of) my mental states, which inhere in me in that they are apperceived by me as my thoughts.
>
> D11. The subsisting 'I' is the original synthetic unity of apperception, which is that action which is the power of the self-active subject and spontaneously produces a synthetic unity among the manifold of representations.
>
> D12. Therefore, the category of 'substance' pertains to the identity of discursive thought and hence is analytically derivable from it. [D10]

D13. Therefore, the category of 'cause-effect' pertains to the identity of discursive thought and hence is analytically derivable from it. [D11]

D14. Substance and cause-effect mutually condition each other in that apperception is both the act of synthesis as an act of original self-activity which produces synthetic unity in the manifold of intuitions and that which is grounded on the synthetic unity to first constitute the identity of the function of combining representations into one cognition.

D15. Therefore, the category of 'community' pertains to the identity of discursive thought and hence is analytically derivable from it. [D14]

D16. Any instantiation of transcendental self-consciousness as the mode of discursive thought presupposes a sum total of sensations, all possible episodes of empirical consciousness, that have a certain degree of intensity on a scale of 0 to 1, and which correspond to the reality of all appearances, that is, of the all-encompassing possible experience.

D17. Transcendental self-consciousness is the empty form of empirical consciousness, 'empirical consciousness in general', insofar as it determines or delimits a subsphere of the sum total of all sensations, all possible episodes of empirical consciousness, as a real object of experience as distinct from all other possible objects of experience.

D18. Therefore, the category of 'reality' pertains to the identity of discursive thought and hence is analytically derivable from it. [D16]

D19. Therefore, the category of 'negation' pertains to the identity of discursive thought and hence is analytically derivable from it. [D17]

D20. The unity of transcendental self-consciousness as negation and empirical consciousness as reality constitutes the infinite sphere of the one all-encompassing experience which contains all possible (empirical) realities.

D21. Therefore, the category of 'limitation' pertains to the identity of discursive thought and hence is analytically derivable from it. [D20]

D22. The 'I think' of transcendental apperception is an analytic unity of consciousness that pertains to all concepts but is as such an empty representation that requires an exogenous content to form a concept, that is, a whole of partial representations.

D23. A manifold of representations must be presupposed as given to the 'I think' to which it provides exogenous content.

D24. Therefore, the category of 'unity' pertains to the identity of discursive thought and hence is analytically derivable from it. [D22]

D25. Therefore, the category of 'plurality' pertains to the identity of discursive thought and hence is analytically derivable from it. [D23]

D26. A manifold of representations can be conceived as a manifold that belongs together throughout and thus constitutes a synthetic whole if and only if the manifold of representations is gradually synthesised in an act of synthesis by means of an analytic unity.

D27. Therefore, the category of 'totality' pertains to the identity of discursive thought and hence is analytically derivable from it. [D26]

This completes the derivation of the categories from apperception. In the next, penultimate chapter, I address the ramifications of the D-argument for the reciprocity thesis, that is, the claim that the subjective conditions of the understanding are indeed the *objective* conditions of the thought or concept of an object in general, and hence of objective cognition.

10 From Apperception to Objectivity

10.1 Reciprocity Again: The Argument of § 17

In the foregoing chapters, I have delineated the way in which the categories are deducible from the very principle of apperception, from the 'I think' as an original function of thought, which formally constitutes the identity of self-consciousness. I have shown how the categories must be seen as the essential constituents of discursive thought and thus are 'determinations of our consciousness' (MFNS, AA 4: 474n.). The analysis of the categories comes to a head. What licenses Kant to posit the reciprocity thesis? What leads Kant to believe he is able to answer, or at least have the first part of an answer to,[1] the question posed at the start of the Transcendental Deduction, at B122/A89–90, that is, 'how *subjective conditions of thinking* should have *objective validity*, i.e., yield conditions of the possibility of all cognition of objects'.

I have argued that the 'identity of the function' (A108) of the original synthetic unity of apperception underpins the identity of discursive thought. The sameness of representation that establishes identity of self-consciousness, and so the analytic unity of apperception, is possible only under the condition of a priori synthesis (B133–4). I have demonstrated by means of a reconstruction of the deduction of the categories from apperception that a rigorous coextensivity obtains between the analytic and synthetic unities of apperception, which showed what logically constrains the mode of our discursive thought. This meant that a distinction must be heeded between the kinds of representation that 'belong' strictly to the identical self-consciousness and those that do not. In Chapter 6, I made a distinction between P1- and P3/4-representations, only the former of which constitute a numerically identical self to the extent that they are synthesised and thus grasped as one's own representations (argued in Chapter 9). There is nothing—or at least nothing determinable—per se that distinguishes this kind of representation, my own, from any other in an ontological respect, but epistemologically it makes all the difference in the world: representations that I do not occurrently have and apperceive as having, or that I can say de dicto that I have (A122), are not strictly speaking *my* representations (P1-representations) and as a result do not 'belong' to my identical self (notice, however, that there could still be representing going on), whereas representations that I do apperceive as occur-

---

[1] We must of course bear in mind that the Transcendental Deduction continues beyond the actual deduction of the categories, to ask the further question how the categories are actually instantiated in spatiotemporal *experience*. This question is addressed in Chapter 11.

rently having are my representations *stricto sensu* and hence 'belong' to my identity as a thinker (an 'I' that thinks). This does not mean that only *actual* representations establish my thoroughgoing identity but it means that, for all possible representations that are mine *stricto sensu*, I must attach one and the same 'I think' to them *in all its possible instantiations*. Discursive thought is thus strictly bound by the necessary conditions under which a numerically identical thought or thoroughgoing self-consciousness is possible (these binding conditions being the categories). At the same time these conditions are also *sufficient* for a numerically identical thought, for the identity of discursive thought is *merely* based on a function of synthesis; there is nothing explicitly metaphysically substantial, in the traditional rationalist sense, about self-consciousness (cf. A349–51), although Kant of course refrains from asserting metaphysical claims, negative or positive, about the ultimate self. The sufficiency claim derives from Rigorous Coextensivity, which is but another way of saying that the principle of thought or apperception is thoroughly analytic, as Kant says (B135).

Subsequently, Kant argues—and this is the claim to which many commentators take exception (see Chapter 4)—that the concept of an object is exactly congruent with the concept of an identical subject of thought (B137, B140; cf. A109). I quote again from B137:

> [I]t is the unity of consciousness that alone constitutes the relation of representations to an object, and therefore their objective validity and the fact that they are modes of knowledge [...]. (trans. Kemp Smith)

As I have argued in Chapter 4, I believe that here, together with the claim at B138 (see further below), Kant is making the claim that the necessary and sufficient conditions under which the concept of an object in general is possible are *the very same conditions* as those that constrain the identity of self-consciousness. That is, Rigorous Coextensivity underpinning the identity of self-consciousness, which rests on the function of synthetic unification of the manifold in an intuition that is given to it, translates directly into the reciprocity between the synthetic unity of consciousness and the unity of the manifold in an intuition of something=x as the *objective* correlate of the transcendental subject (self-consciousness), which makes up the concept of 'object' (B137)—in the A-Deduction this correlate is called the transcendental object (A109; cf. A104–5). Manfred Baum (1986: 28) aptly calls this notion of 'object' the *Komplementärbegriff* of the synthetic unity of self-consciousness.

Allison (2004: 478–9n.33) notes 'significant differences' between the notion of 'transcendental object' in the A-Deduction and the status of the concept of 'object' in B. But I believe there is not much difference other than in the way that Kant formulates the definition of object, whereby he might seem to suggest in A that the object is really distinct from our representations. At A104, Kant observes that 'object must be *thought of only as* something in general=X, since outside of our cognition we have nothing that we could set over against this cognition as corresponding to it' (emphasis added); that is, a *concept* of object is concerned that is *internal* to cognition. So also in A 'object' is nothing really distinct from our representations but only the *concept* of, or the way we think, that which is over against our cognition. The further definition of object as 'that which is opposed to our cognitions being determined at pleasure or arbitrarily rather than being determined *a priori*, since insofar as they are to relate to an object our cognitions must also necessarily agree with each other in relation to it, i.e., they must have that unity that constitutes the concept of an object' comports with the one given at B137. Kant's talk of transcendental object, at A109, as 'that which in all of our empirical concepts in general can provide relation to an object, i.e., objective reality', should be seen in the light of A104.[2]

So when, at B139–40, Kant speaks of the transcendental unity of apperception as an objective unity, which unites the manifold 'in a concept of the object', in contrast to a mere subjective unity of consciousness, he does not contradict his previous analyses in §16 of the constraints of self-consciousness—for the subjective unity of consciousness *is not* the same unity as the *transcendental* unity of *self*-consciousness that was expounded there; rather, a subjective unity of consciousness is the unity of consciousness that does not satisfy P1' and therefore is that kind of empirical consciousness which does not analytically relate to the identity of the subject (B133). On the contrary, when speaking of the transcendental unity of self-consciousness as an objective unity Kant articulates the reciprocity between the transcendental conditions of having an identical grasp of one's own thought, when one engages in thinking (not just representing or having some awareness), and the transcendental conditions of having a grasp of the identity of the object that one conceives of, whenever one thinks of it, regardless of further necessary (spatiotemporal) conditions under which the object of thought is cognised more concretely (that is, experienced empirically), and regardless whether this concerns my own self as object or an external object. These sets of transcendental conditions are in fact just the same set of conditions, namely the twelve categories that determine the objective validity of having a self-identical conscious grasp of oneself (P1')—rather than a mere subjectively valid awareness (P3'/P4')—as well as of thinking an object in general.

---

[2] See further the discussion in Schulting (2017a), ch. 1.

Contrary to Guyer and others who have claimed that there is an unbridgeable gap, a 'looseness of [...] connection' (Guyer 1979: 159), between Kant's argument regarding self-consciousness and his argument concerning the categories and hence objective experience (or more precisely the thought of an object), it is now clear that there is no such gap. Guyer (1992: 145–6) argued that 'even if the conditions for the possibility of apperception are also necessary conditions for the representation of objects, there must be some additional condition necessary to represent objects that is not a condition for self-consciousness as such', falsely implying that the 'conditions for self-consciousness' are different from the set of conditions for representing objects. However, this would be the case only if the conditions in question were empirical ones, which in Kant's transcendental theory of *possible* experience they clearly are not. As I have shown, Guyer's and other commentators' dismissal of Reciprocity—that is, the claim that the unity of consciousness is *necessary and sufficient* for the cognitive representation of objects—rests on a misunderstanding of the thrust of Kant's premise, issuing from a psychological reading of self-consciousness, and a misapprehension of the meaning of a transcendental deduction of the categories starting out from that premise.

If we look again at B137, where Kant writes that 'an *object* [...] is that in the concept of which the manifold of a given intuition is *united*', then it is clear that for Kant an object is not a thing in itself, but merely the objective unity of representations in a manifold of a given intuition.[3] And given that this objective unity of representations *is* the transcendental unity of apperception (B139–40), namely that unity of self-consciousness which establishes the thoroughgoing identity of a totality of representations in an intuition, Kant's reciprocity claim is sound. We must keep in mind that, as Hoppe (1983: 168) explains, the object defined as such must be understood as '*merely* the correlate of a synthesis of representations'. This ex hypothesi implies, however, as Hoppe also points out, that 'without synthesis there would not be objects for us' (1983: 168–9). As Kant puts it:

> [W]e say that we cognize the object if we have effected synthetic unity in the manifold of intuition. (A105)

---

[3] That this involves his doctrine of idealism, to which one may want to raise some independent objections, does not detract from the fact that Kant has a particular conception of 'object', which is important to recognise in order not to beg the question against Reciprocity by assuming a realist conception of object that Kant rejects. I suspect that it is precisely such a move which prevents commentators from grasping Reciprocity. See Schulting (2017a, ch 4; forthcoming).

Reference to objects and objective unity of apperception are reciprocally conditioned. But since the objects of our knowledge are mere appearances, which 'themselves are nothing but sensible representations' and are not 'objects (outside the power of representation)' (A104), the objective unity of apperception is also sufficient for the objects to *be* objects for us. This latter claim is implied by what Kant asserts at B138:

> The synthetic unity of consciousness is, therefore, an objective condition of all knowledge. It is not merely a condition that I myself require in knowing an object, but is a condition under which every intuition must stand in order *to become an object for me*. For otherwise, in the absence of this synthesis, the manifold would *not* be united in one consciousness.[4]

Before reconstructing Reciprocity, let us have a look at the main argument from § 17. Kant's own argument for Reciprocity (K) can be schematised as follows:

> **[K1]** *Understanding* is [...] the *faculty of knowledge*.
>
> **[K2]** This knowledge consists in the determinate relation of given representations to an object;
>
> **[K3]** [...] an *object* is that in the concept of which the manifold of a given intuition is *united*.
>
> **[K4]** Now all unification of representations demands unity of consciousness in the synthesis of them.
>
> **[K5]** Consequently it is the unity of consciousness that alone constitutes the relation of representations to an object, and therefore their objective validity and the fact that they are modes of knowledge;
>
> **[K6]** and upon [the unity of consciousness] therefore rests the very possibility of the understanding. (B137, trans. Kemp Smith)

Kant confirms the conclusion of K by stating that the 'first pure knowledge of understanding' is 'the principle of the original *synthetic* unity of apperception' (B137), through which 'an object [...] is first known' (B138). He then restates the controversial reciprocity claim, which was quoted above, as the corollary of K. K is the P-argument in disguise. It does not start with the 'I think'-proposition, but with the fact that the understanding is the faculty of knowledge, pointing to the R-argument, which takes experience or knowledge as the premise of the argument of the Transcendental Deduction. K concerns an analysis of the concept of knowledge, and advances the argument that based on a given definition of 'object' the necessary *and* sufficient requirements for knowledge can be

---

4 This and all following quotations in this section are from Kemp Smith.

seen to lie in the unity of consciousness, which makes representations objectively valid and hence is the condition of the understanding itself as the faculty of knowledge. The argument is fine as far it goes, but it is more of a summary of the results so far than a precise formulation of the consecutive steps that led to the conclusion of the argument that started in § 16 from the unity of consciousness (the 'I think'), not from the understanding as a faculty of knowledge. In other words, K will not do as a *proof* of Reciprocity **[K5]**, as it is clearly circular and begs the question against the derivation of the concept of object from the unity of consciousness.

In § 20, Kant gives a summary of some of the results of the 'first step' of the B-Deduction, for once in a pellucid syllogistic presentation. Contrary to the standard reading, however, I do not think that this section represents itself the *conclusion* of the so-called 'first step' of the B-Deduction so much as that it is a transitional section, together with § 21, that summarises, in argument form, the results of §§ 17–19 *to the extent that the unity of intuition is concerned* as an introduction to Kant's argument concerning the application of the categories to *spatiotemporal* intuition from § 21 onwards. In other words, § 20 does not just look back but certainly also forwards, by concentrating on the element of unitary intuition, which is important in Kant's subsequent arguments for the determination of (objects in) space and time (I discuss these in the next chapter). Of course, Kant himself (B159) refers to §§ 20–1 as giving the results of, in fact, the 'transcendental deduction' (which is remarkable as it suggests that the deduction as such is complete at that point). However, this cannot be taken to mean that the argument of § 20 is itself the conclusion, and thus part, of the P-argument, let alone the entire argument of the Transcendental Deduction as such; it is a summary of it in syllogistic form. It is noticeable that the main result of Reciprocity, i.e. that the unity of consciousness *constitutes the concept of an object in general*, argued in § 17, and which in itself is the conclusion of the argument of § 16, is not at all mentioned in § 20; this I think reinforces my belief that this section is not meant by Kant to represent the complete conclusion of all of his arguments in all of §§ 15–19 (clearly, in § 20 he does not refer to § 15 and § 16). This might be grounds for revising the received reading of the proof-structure of the Transcendental Deduction as consisting of just 'two steps'. At any rate, § 20 does not provide any concluding insight into the P-argument and hence into Reciprocity, and so cannot be seen as the overall conclusion of the P-argument or Reciprocity as such.

To return to K, Reciprocity can be vindicated only if the proof is begun with a more basic premise than that in K, which Kant in effect does in § 16, namely with the 'I think'-proposition. This is what the P-argument must do. That is, the P-argument must show that the predicates of the transcendental self, viz. the categories, which determine a priori the self's identity (qua the necessary form of discursive thought and not qua its putative, a priori knowable, de re substantial identity), are the same predicates that, by operating the same underlying a priori function of apperception, determine the identity of an object (qua the necessary form of its appearance as an object before thought, not as thing in itself) as the corresponding correlate of a unified manifold of representations in an intuition that is had by the 'same subject in which this [very] manifold is found' (B132, trans. Kemp Smith). It is in this way that the synthetic unity of consciousness, that is, the function of synthetic apperception necessarily underlying the analytic unity of consciousness, is not only necessary for objective cognition but, insofar as the necessary form of objects is concerned, also sufficient for it (as Kant claims at B138). Of course, we are only talking about logical objects here, that is, determinate objects insofar as they are *thought* (cf. B146). To be able effectively to *experience* an object sensibly as a numerically identical occupant of space and in time and consequently to have real, 'empirical cognition' (B147) of the object, a *synthesis speciosa* is required which instantiates the objectively determined intuition as a spatiotemporally determined object—this is what Kant goes on to show in the 'second step' of the B-Deduction (specifically §§ 24, 26), which will be addressed in Chapter 11. However, the fact that the knowledge of an empirical object requires a further synthesis does not detract from the fact that the understanding itself, by way of the unity of consciousness, 'causally' effects this synthesis and hence, wholly a priori, establishes an object qua object (cf. B151–2).[5]

In schematic form (reduced to its essentials),[6] this yields the following derivation of objectivity from the unity of apperception, which establishes Reciprocity:

> P1*. The analytic unity of apperception (AUA) is the analytical 'I think' which is the common representation of 'all my representations' that are united in the manifold of a given intuition by means of the synthetic unity of apperception (SUA).
>
> P2*. SUA is the necessary condition for the conception of an object, for any concept, which is a general representation of that which is common to various representations and hence is an analytic unity, rests on SUA. [from P1*]
>
> P3*. SUA is the sufficient condition of the conception of an object in general, for 'object' is merely that in the concept of which the manifold of a given intuition is united.
>
> P4*. Therefore, SUA coincides with an object understood in the formal and a priori way. [from P2*, P3*]

---

5 This was argued in Chapter 7. See also Chapter 11.
6 The actual P*-argument would have to include all the steps of the D-argument.

P5*. AUA and SUA are rigorously coextensive. (*Rigorous Coextensivity*)

P6*. Therefore, AUA corresponds with an object in the formal and a priori way. [from P4*, P5*]

P7*. Therefore, the opening statement of the D-argument (the 'I think'-proposition) is the premise of the objectivity argument and hence provides the necessary and sufficient formal conditions of objective–unitary cognition and of the objects of cognition. (*Reciprocity*) [from P1*, P6*]

These pronouncements must be further put into context, most importantly with respect to how the definition of judgement agrees with the explication of the reciprocity of synthetic unity of consciousness and the concept of an object in general, given that Kant understands the faculty of thought to be a faculty of judgement (see Chapter 5). This is what the next section addresses.[7]

10.2 From Objective Unity to Judgement: the Argument of § 19

In the intermediate § 18, Kant contrasts the transcendental unity of apperception, which was called thus 'in order to designate the possibility of *a priori* cognition from it' (B132), with the 'subjective unity of consciousness', which is 'entirely contingent' (B139–40). Only the transcendental unity of apperception is an objective unity of consciousness and is 'alone […] objectively valid', since it establishes, 'through the pure synthesis of the understanding', 'the necessary relation of the manifold of intuition to the one *I think*' (B140). What now are the ramifications for Kant's conception of judgement, which he discusses in § 19 of the B-Deduction? The argument in that section is the corollary of Reciprocity, which was argued in § 17.

Judgement, as Kant argues, is marked out as a necessary unity of given representations (or cognitions)

> in accordance with principles of the objective determination of all representations insofar as cognition can come from them, which principles are all derived from the principle of the transcendental unity of apperception (B142),

or indeed defined as

---

[7] I reflect further on the relation between apperception and object in Schulting (2017e, 2019).

the **way** to bring given cognitions to the *objective* unity of apperception (B141, boldface added);[8]

Kant's use of the word 'way' in the definition of judgement indicates that the fundamental nature of judgement lies in the use of the twelve functions of thought, which to the extent that a judgement is a claim about an object or objective event (and not just a proposition consisting of concepts or a relation of judgements) *are* the categories. The argument of the Deduction (that is, both the Metaphysical and Transcendental Deduction) has come full circle, as Kant himself concludes in § 20. That is to say, by stating that 'the *categories* are nothing other than these very functions for judging, insofar as the manifold of a given intuition is determined with regard to them (§ 13)' (B143), the 'guiding thread' offered in the Metaphysical Deduction concerning the transcendental function of the understanding operating simultaneously on the level of intuition as well as the conceptual level in a judgement has been corroborated, now that, at the end of the P*-argument of the first half of the B-Deduction, it has been shown that the categories as principles of objective determination are just the ways that manifolds of representations in an empirical intuition are determined in regard to the logical functions for judgement (B128).[9] It has also been shown that judgement itself is constituted by, and thus analytically derived from, transcendental apperception or the 'I think' itself, thus providing the a priori warrant for the guiding thread to the derivation of the categories from the functions of judgement, for both the functions of judgement and the categories derive from the transcendental apperception or the 'I think'.

We can now add the following premises to the P*-argument:

> P8*. The 'principles of the objective determination of all representations insofar as cognition can come from them, which principles are all derived from the principle of the transcendental unity of apperception' (B142), are the categories.
>
> P9*. The categories are constitutive of the objectively valid relation of representations insofar as these are necessarily united.

---

[8] For more definitions of judgement in texts prior to and contemporary with the B-Deduction, see Schulting (2017a: 102–8).

[9] Kant refers to § 13, but as Timmermann notes in his edition of the *Critique* (Hamburg: Meiner [1998], p. 186), Kant probably means § 14, where Kant gives a preliminary 'explanation' of the categories as 'concepts of an object in general, by means of which the intuition of an object is regarded as determined in respect of one of the logical functions of judgement' (B128, trans. Kemp Smith).

P10*. A judgement is an objectively valid relation of representations insofar as they are necessarily united in contrast to a merely subjectively valid relation of representations that are contingently united.

P11*. Therefore, the categories are constitutive of judgement. [from P9*, P10*]

P12*. The categories are the ways that representations are 'brought to' the objective unity of apperception. [from P8*]

P13*. Therefore, judgement is the way that representations are 'brought to' the objective unity of apperception. [from P11*, P12*]

P14*. The 'I think' is an objective unity of apperception. [from P7*]

P15*. The 'I think' is constitutive of judgement. [from P13*, P14*]

But let me expand on the relation between apperception, objectivity and judgement, in order to show their intimacy, which is at the heart of the argument of the Deduction. Kant says in the Metaphysical Deduction that 'the *understanding* in general can be represented as a *faculty for judging* [*Vermögen zu urteilen*]' (A69/B94).[10] Indeed, as Kant says, 'all actions of the understanding' can be traced back 'to judgments'. The faculty for judging, or the capacity to judge, and the faculty for thinking—which is what the understanding is (A69/B94)— are one and the same faculty operating the same function (see Chapter 5). Kant also stresses, in the Metaphysical Deduction, the fact that the faculty for thinking concerns a discursive mode of thinking, which means that to think is to cognise through concepts, which the understanding cannot employ otherwise than in judgements (A68/B93). This ties in with the fact that '[j]udgment is [...] the *mediate* cognition of an object' (A68/B93, emphasis added), because cognition through concepts is effectively the 'representation of a representation' of an object, never a direct, immediate representation of an object. Kant illustrates this mediate type of cognition in judgement with the example 'All bodies are divisible', where the concept <*divisible*> is predicable of <*body*> as one of the many other concepts of which it can be predicated, and <*body*> is in its turn related to 'certain appearances that come before us' (ibid.), and are thought under the concept <*body*>. The subject concept is the rule for the manifold of representations in intuition, *by means of* which intuited objects are subsumed under the predicate <*divisible*>.[11] The very form of judgement, which consists in the subordination of concepts, thus confirms the discursive, mediate nature of our mode

---

10 Longuenesse (1998) translates *Vermögen zu urteilen* more aptly as 'capacity to judge'.
11 All objects thought under the concept <*body*> are subsumed under the concept <*divisible*>: All bodies are divisible; x is a body; so x is divisible.

of cognition and the dependence on an immediate nonconceptual relation to given objects by means of sensible intuition.

Another element of Kant's discursive conception of judgement is the notion of the function of unity, which we already saw in Chapter 5: the concepts in a judgement are united by means of a function, which Kant defines as 'the unity of the action of ordering different representations under a common one' (A68/B93), demonstrating his basically extensional view of the relation between concepts, in contrast to the principally intensional view of judgement of his Leibnizian-Wolffian predecessors, who considered the predicate as analytically contained *in* the subject of judgement (*praedicatum inest subjecto*).

The third important element of his account of judgement is that the function of discursive thinking shows thought's spontaneity, in contrast to the receptivity of human cognition that is characterised by the affective nature of intuition.[12]

We have seen that Kant defines human cognition or thought as discursive, namely as cognition through concepts. The crucial implication of this conception of thought is that thinking is always mediate, that is, a conceptual representation is always only mediately related to the real object of intuition. This discursive aspect concerns the necessary *form* of human thought (A77/B103). However, Kant's main interest, the interest of his transcendental logic in the Transcendental Deduction and also already in the Metaphysical Deduction, explicitly so in the Third 'Clue' Section (§ 10), is to find a way to link our discursive mode of thinking to the *object* of thought, more precisely, to the immediate cognition, by means of intuition, of the object. In other words, the *content* of cognition, from which general logic abstracts (A76/B102), is the central focus of attention. As Kant points out at A69/B94, '[c]oncepts [...], as predicates of possible judgments, are related to some representation of a still undetermined object'. What is paramount, for Kant, is how to be able to determine the manner in which the relation between, on the one hand, concepts in judgement and, on the other hand, this representation of an as yet undetermined object, which occurs by means of intuition, is determined such that we have a *determinate* conception of that object. The function of unity in a judgement that subordinates concepts, by means of an analytic unity, as Kant says (A79/B105), must somehow tie in with the *immediate* representation of the object (x) in intuition. Only by explicating the link between the mediate, conceptual representation and an immediate, intuitional representation of the object are we able to answer the question of what it means to judge that some x is F.

---

[12] This element is extensively discussed in Schulting (forthcoming). See also Schulting (2017a: 114–16, 124–31).

10.2 From Objective Unity to Judgement: the Argument of § 19

Now in the so-called guiding thread (*Leitfaden*) passage in § 10 (B104–5/A79), Kant makes the prima facie startling claim that the very same function of the understanding that subordinates and unites concepts '*in a judgment*', insofar as the analytical form of conceptual relations or their logical unity (cf. A77/B103)—namely, the *analytical* subordination relation between concepts—is concerned, is *also* responsible, by 'the very same actions', for the unification of the representations '*in an intuition*' of the object, that is, for the *content* of cognition. The latter unification occurs by means of a priori synthesis, and enables the determinate representation of an object. I take this to mean that the unification on the conceptual level of a judgement and the unification on the level of the intuition do not happen separately or independently from each other.[13] Rather, the understanding itself fulfils this task for both concepts and intuition, form and content, *within* judgement.[14] A judgement is always a relation between concepts and intuition, which consists of the sensible representations that are subsumable under the subject concept of the judgement; the intuition of the object is represented by the *x* of judgement, and is the real condition of cognition. And since the understanding is the capacity to judge, the determination by the understanding of intuition must take place in judgement. Importantly, this does not imply that, necessarily, intuitions always and only occur within judgement. It means that the *determination* of intuition must always and only occur in judgement. To *have* an intuition is not dependent on the activity of judging, for, as Kant says, 'intuition by no means requires the functions of thinking' (A90–1/B123).[15]

The central remarkable claim that Kant makes in the Deduction, is that the understanding as a faculty for discursive thinking and judging is at the same time the faculty for determining objectively real things; in other words, the central claim that the subjective conditions of thought are also the objective conditions of knowledge (A89–90/B122). This is why Kant claims that the categories, which are the a priori concepts by means of which objects are determined, exactly map onto the functions of logical unity in judgement; the categories *are* those same functions of logical unity in respect of the content of judgement, namely in respect of how any judgement is intrinsically, by virtue of its very logical (discur-

---

13 However, at A78/B104 Kant writes that the synthesis of imagination is prior to bringing the synthesis '*to concepts*', which is 'a function that pertains to the understanding'. This suggests that the synthesis of the imagination in intuition operates separately from the latter function (see Chapter 5). That this is not in fact the case is argued in Chapter 11.
14 See by contrast Land (2015).
15 This topic is addressed at length in Schulting (2015b, 2017a, ch. 5).

sive) unity *in conjunction with intuition,* always already object-oriented or intentionally directed towards the object of knowledge.

However, the fact that Kant's discursive logic requires functions by means of which manifolds of representations in intuition must be united, and that such a necessary unity is required for objective knowledge, does not necessarily imply a role for self-consciousness. Functionalist theories of discursive cognition could be conceived that do not rely on a theory of self-consciousness or consciousness, so why does Kant insist on a role for apperception? It is striking that in the Metaphysical Deduction itself Kant does not refer to the unity of *apperception* or *consciousness* at all, and speaks merely of the function of unity of the understanding in general, and in the Third 'Clue' Section, where he provides the actual guiding thread to discovering the categories (see the discussion in Chapter 5), he talks about synthesis which yields the categories, but not about the synthetic unity of *apperception.* So why does Kant closely associate, if not identify, judgement with the objective unity of *apperception* in § 19 of the B-Deduction? What reasons are there for correlating the function of unity by means of which the understanding unites concepts and intuition in a judgement with the unity of self-consciousness?

In the Transcendental Deduction, Kant must demonstrate that what, by way of a promissory note, in the guiding thread passage he only submits is the case— namely that the understanding performs two tasks simultaneously—is effectively what happens in judgement by deriving the categories as the determinate a priori forms of objects *from* the unity of the understanding, that is, from the faculty of thought itself without presupposing a definition of judgement. The functions of thought must be *shown* to be those categories necessary for cognition of objects —and this is what we have done in the preceding chapters. Self-consciousness is involved to the extent that thinking is, first of all, a spontaneous activity involving a subject, which is aware of her thinking activity. (This is the 'I' which must be able to accompany all my representations introduced at the outset of § 16.) Self-consciousness is thus an inextricable element of thinking as such, and given that unitary thought is definitional of the cognition of objects (as well as of the objects of cognition) (B137), self-consciousness is an inextricable element of the cognition of objects, and hence of judgement. This is shown by the argument of the first half of the B-Deduction, which runs from the unity of apperception (§ 16) to objective unity of consciousness as the definition for 'object' (§ 17), in contrast to a merely subjective unity of consciousness (§ 18), and from thereon to the definition of judgement as the way representations are brought to this objective unity of apperception (§ 19).

One of the systematic reasons why Kant introduces self-consciousness in the context of deriving the categories of experience is the element of recognition (see e.g. A103ff.). Only what is *recognised* to be united in the manifold of one's representations counts as united in Kant's strong sense, namely as *necessarily* united. Unity of representations does not concern a unity of contingently aggregated representations, which are conjointly prompted in the mind or are conjoined in virtue of contingent, psychological laws of association. The unity of representations in objective experience concerns representations that must be united in such a way as for those representations to amount to objective experience; that is to say, a genuine *claim* about some object or objective state of affairs is at stake, and such a unity must be able to be recognised *as* objective for the claim to be an objectively valid one. Nothing counts as objective if it is not recognised as such.[16]

That in § 19 of the B-Deduction Kant speaks explicitly of an objective unity of apperception, which, in the preceding section he contrasted with a merely subjective unity of consciousness, is indicative of his intention to identify judgement, not with self-consciousness per se (in the standard psychological or introspective sense), but with the intentional stance of a judger, who is aware of the combination of, or more particularly, of her *act of combining*, concepts and sensible representations in a judgement, which constitutes a relation to an object (objective reality). A judgement is always a claim made *by a subject*, about some *objective* state of affairs, regardless of what kind of object this concerns (indeed even oneself as object in acts of self-knowledge). Kant says that the copula in a judgement indicates this contrast with a merely subjectively valid relation of representations, where for the latter there is not such a reciprocal relation between subject and object, but merely the indeterminable affective causal dependency relation of the subject upon whatever undetermined object (*Gegenstand*), which causes the affective relation (the subject is passive with regard to this; its states are causal effects of external input).

The objective validity of judgement must not be seen in terms of the truth *value* of judgement, that is, that one's judgement is either true or false, where my claim or belief expressed by it commits me in principle to giving reasons for my so claiming or believing, when asked. In the very act of my judging or claiming that G_Fx, I'm not just expressing a belief, justifiably or not, that some x is F, which is further determined as G, a belief for which I can be asked to give reasons. There is a modal element involved as well. That is, I'm also and primarily staking a claim about x's *existence*, that is, I eo ipso assert the determinate, actual existence of x (by applying the modal category of existence), as well as its objective reality (by applying the categories of quality), regardless

---

16 Further on the synthesis of recognition, see Schulting (2017a), ch. 6.

of the empirical properties F, G etc. that I attribute to it. Or in Kantian parlance, I posit x (more accurately $G_F x$) as existing, which is not just an opinion I venture or a belief I formulate about it, and which might be true or not, but a definite, 'objective holding-to-be-true' (*objectives Fürwahrhalten*) (*Logic-Vienna*, AA 24: 852 [LL: 305])[17] that is embedded in an objective network of such objective 'holdings-to-be-true' which are expressions of a true state of affairs or true states of affairs for everyone.[18] That is to say, my judgements are part and parcel of the domain of possible experience or knowledge; there is no fundamental discrepancy between all that I judge (experience, know) to be objectively true and what *is* objectively true.[19]

Hence, at B141–2 Kant mentions the copula ('is') in a basic categorical judgement, which most explicitly expresses the general objective validity of a determinative judgement, or indeed the identity that lies between the unity of consciousness and the objective unity of apperception, and between the objective unity of apperception and the object itself. At B142 Kant says that the necessary unity in the categorical judgement 'It, the body, **is** heavy' concerns the fact that these representations are 'combined in the object'. This is what marks out an objective unity of apperception in contrast to a merely subjective unity of representations. The copula 'is' designates the objective reality of something that *is* a body and *is* heavy, a fact that is objectively true, independently of anyone's particular belief. (In making any particular determinative, objectively valid judgement I may of course be mistaken if, say, the empirical evidence for my so judging is deficient, or my epistemic faculties are otherwise not properly functioning. See further below.)

That a modal element is involved in any objectively valid judgement is not to say that any judgement is eo ipso an explicit existential judgement. Existential judgements are special cases of objectively valid judgements, in which predicates are not attributed to an object, but in which an object *together with all its predicates* is just posited as existing. But this does not detract from the fact

---

[17] *Logic-Vienna*, AA 24: 852: '*Believing* is a subjectively sufficient but objectively insufficient holding-to-be-true. [...] Knowing is an objective holding-to-be-true, with consciousness' (LL: 305); JL, AA 9: 70: '*Knowing*. Holding-to-be-true based on a ground of cognition that is objectively as well as subjectively sufficient, or certainty [...]' (LL: 574).

[18] See A821–2/B849–50: 'I cannot *assert* anything, i.e., pronounce it to be a judgment necessarily valid for everyone, except that which produces conviction [*Überzeugung*].'

[19] It should be kept in mind that, for Kant, there is no distinction between experience and knowledge (cf. B147, B165–6). Attempts in the literature to differentiate 'cognition' (as a translation of Kant's term *Erkenntnis*) from 'knowledge' strictly speaking are therefore misleading and anachronistic (see Chapter 4).

that in any objectively valid judgement, a modal claim is made with regard to the actuality or existence of the object to which predicates are attributed, in the way that the modal category of 'existence' must be applied. That is why Kant emphasises the role of the copula ('is') in defining judgement in the strict sense as an objective unity of representations.

What Kant calls the objective validity of a judgement is therefore not its truth *value* per se—this one might think is the case given that Kant identifies objective validity with the truth of an empirical cognition at A125. Rather, the truth *value* of a judgement—that a judgement can be true or false—is, while certainly essential, merely a surface aspect of judgement (an aspect considered in general logic, not in transcendental logic); it is *not* what makes a judgement an objectively valid statement. I can obviously err in my believing or intending, because I might be mistaken about certain empirical facts or my empirical evidence might be deficient, but this is not a topic of transcendental logic. Hence, an analytic judgement is true or false solely on the basis of the principle of non-contradiction (B190/A151), without objective validity having anything to do with this. Truth here is logical truth in contrast to the 'transcendental' or 'material (objective)' truth that has Kant's primary interest (see B269/A222 and A60/B85), and which concerns the 'determining ground of the truth of our cognition' (B191/A152), that is, the objective validity of our empirical cognition (A125). Objective validity is not at issue in the context of determining the truth (or falsity) of an *analytic* judgement, since here the reference to an object (objective *reality*; B194/A155) is otiose (cf. A258–9); its truth can be determined solely through analysis of the subject and predicate of such a judgement. But any true *or* false *synthetic* judgement is grounded on the possible reference to an object. This does not, however, imply that a judgement's objective validity *is* its possibly being true or false (i.e. its truth value). For clearly non-objectively valid analytic judgements are also truth-apt (cf. Vanzo 2012).[20]

But the important point is that saying that there is no fundamental discrepancy between all that I *judge* to be objectively true and what *is* objectively true is of course not the same as saying, absurdly, that a particular judgement 'This easy chair is a Gispen' is always, and necessarily, a true judgement. Of course, only *if* the easy chair *is* truly a Gispen, is my judgement 'This easy chair is a Gispen' a true judgement. My judgment 'This easy chair is a Gispen' can thus evidently be false, that is, when the easy chair is by a different designer and I am mistaken in my judging. But the crucial point here is, if I make such a categorical judgement for which I have sufficient empirical evidence, by way of an empirical intuition

---

20 See also Schulting (2017f; forthcoming).

of something that has the appearance of a Gispen easy chair and given my background knowledge about furniture designed by Willem Hendrik Gispen, then there is no further question as to the truth of this judgement beyond my taking the perceptual evidence, which should be intersubjectively available,[21] as evidence for my claim. I thus cannot reach outside sensible intuition, and try and point, as it were, to the putative *fact* of the perceived object's existence, its actuality, and *see* its properties in order to establish the truth of my judgement. The correspondence between my judging (informed by my expertise) and the available perceptual evidence, received through sensible intuition, is all I have, *and need*, to establish the veridicality of my judgement.[22] No amount of pointing to an actual object *o* (or intuition of object *o*) is going to show 'more' about the correspondence between my judging and the object *o* than is determined by means of the a priori necessary rules for making an objectively valid judgement about *o*, which establish this correspondence (one of these rules being the category of actuality[23] or existence, which one applies to one's empirical intuition of *o*). The a priori, transcendental rules for objectively valid judging just establish the correspondence to, and thus the true knowledge of, the object of my judgement.[24] As Kant writes,

> [o]bjective validity and necessary universal validity (for everyone) are therefore interchangeable concepts, *and although we do not know the object in itself*, nonetheless, if we regard a judgment as universally valid and hence necessary, objective validity is understood to be included. *Through this judgment we know [erkennen] the object* (even if beyond that it remains unknown as it may be in itself) *by means of the universally valid and necessary connection of the given perceptions*. (*Prol* § 19, AA 4: 298 [TPhb: 93], trans. emended and emphasis added)

---

21 A private judgement, which rests on intuitional evidence that is available only to me, does not count as an objectively valid judgement or even as a judgement at all—although, according to the *Prolegomena* account, such a judgement could be called 'a judgement of perception'.
22 Cf. the discussion on McDowell and Sellars in Schulting (2017a), ch. 5. See also Schulting (forthcoming).
23 Kant speaks of 'actuality' at *Met-Volck*, AA 28: 397, A219/B267 and A233/B286.
24 Of course, intuitions provide the alethic modal condition for cognition, i.e. actuality, that *mere* conceptuality cannot provide; there must be a real object for there to be a possible cognition. But it is the understanding itself, by means of the application of the modal categories, in particular that of existence/actuality, which determines truth, *not* intuition or sensibility or the sheer fact of there being a real object. In other words, to put it anachronistically in contemporary jargon, the truthmaker is the understanding that judges about x, not x's existence, nor the mere intuition of x.

To mistakenly judge that *o* is *F* (e.g. mistake a fake for an authentic Gispen easy chair) comes down to having the wrong, or lacking, empirical evidence. But falsehood or possible falsehood does not detract from the objective validity of my judgement. As said, any further epistemological question concerning the *empirical* properties of the object that I judge about, and whether or not I am right about *them* specifically, lies beyond transcendental logic. The possibility of falsehood is simply not a concern of transcendental logic.[25] Objective validity, on the other hand, concerns, as the *Prolegomena* states, the universal validity and necessity inherent to *any* judgement *about an object*, more in particular, the universal and necessary relation of the given representations or concepts in a judgement (*Prol*, AA 4: 298); this relation is constituted by the categories of the understanding and the necessity of the unity of apperception (cf. B142), and in its turn establishes what it means to be related to an object.[26] *Any* empirical judgement about a given object is true *of the object*, given that I have sufficient empirical evidence for making the judgement, that is, have the requisite empirical intuition of the object that I judge about, *even if I were mistaken about the specific empirical properties of the object in question*. I can never be mistaken about the fact that, when I judge about a given object *o*, that my judgement is about *that* object *o*, namely, what is a relatively stable substance that stands in causal interaction with its surroundings in a spatial continuum, unless my epistemic abilities are not functioning properly, for example, when I'm hallucinating, or dreaming, or when I am a patient with a cognitive disorder. (But, again, this last point is not a concern of Kant's transcendental logic. Kant presumes that my epistemic abilities are working, under normal conditions.[27])

Someone might object that there is not something that is not bloody when Macbeth judges, but that there is just no dagger, bloodied or otherwise. In this case, it is not true—so the objection goes—that one cannot be mistaken about the fact that one's judgement is about *that* object, however further mistaken one is about empirical properties, for in Macbeth's soliloquy, there *is* no dagger, that is, no object, altogether. In other words, one can be mistaken about there

---

[25] The possibility of falsely claiming that there is an object at all is discussed further below.
[26] Motta (2012: 191) is therefore right to observe that judgement always has a modal component, in that its objective validity depends on a necessity that is more than a logical necessity. To judge means to connect perceptions in such a way that they are connected as necessarily belonging together and relating to an actual object, given further empirical constraints. This necessity is established by virtue of the act of apperception, which accompanies my judging.
[27] Kant considers the possibility of it not working in the *Anthropology*, when he addresses the non-objective systematicity in lunacy (*Anthr*, AA 7: 215–16). To be mistakenly judging that there is an object altogether does not amount to judging at all. It is speculating at best.

being an object in the first place. But this objection confuses hallucination for a case of judging, which, in Kant's view, the example in this case is not. Strictly speaking, determinative judgements are only claims about *given* objects; not even statements about noumenal entities, or indeed analytic judgements (see above), are determinative judgements of the kind of which Kant speaks in § 19 of the B-Deduction. It is also very doubtful whether quasi-experiential judgements, or judgements based on testimonial reports, such as 'Tongues [...] sat upon each of them' (Acts 2:3), which are prima facie not based on objectively available empirical evidence, are determinative judgements in Kant's sense. Such judgements would fall under the category of opining, belief or a *subjective* 'taking-to-be-true' (A820 ff./ B848 ff.). Also aesthetic judgements do not count as judgements as defined in § 19, for they are merely reflective judgements, and not determinative ones (see Chapter 3). In neither of the aforementioned types of non-determinative judgements or statements is objective validity involved, or at least not directly.

Kant's main point in § 19 is a point concerning what he calls 'transcendental truth' (B185/A146),[28] which is the necessary condition of what Kant calls 'empirical truth', that is, truth as correspondence to or accordance or agreement with reportable facts—transcendental truth is not a different truth, of course, but the ground of empirical truth. In judgement lies the transcendental condition of the correspondence or conformity between concept and object (which is the nominal definition of truth that Kant grants [A57–8/B82]), and by judging and thus making a claim to the truth of some state of affairs, in judgement, this transcendental condition is satisfied. The modality of the copula indicates this. In any judging G_Fx, I thereby eo ipso posit an object x both as actually existing (in the phenomenal world) and as having the empirical property F and having the further determining property G, even if I might be partly or wholly mistaken about these empirical properties. For example, in the judgement

> My Logitech mouse is anthracite-coloured

I attribute to some object x the property of being a Logitech mouse and, further, the property of being anthracite-coloured. In a merely subjectively valid statement or opinion (a belief), which does not have the form of a judgement strictly speaking, e.g.

---

[28] Cf. A221–2/B269, where objective reality is identified with transcendental truth. On this topic, see further Motta (2012: 98 ff.).

> I believe he's depressed

or,

> I prefer Joseph Hammer to Dennis Duck

no (explicit) claim is made with regard to the objective reality of any putative object or its properties, expressed in a judgement. Kant's central point is that judgement strictly speaking—i.e. a determinative judgement of which he speaks in the context of the First *Critique*—is always already intentional, directed towards the world of objects, that is, *primordially* connected to objects.

To put this more precisely still, and to underscore the difference between a Kantian view of judgement and 'realist' views of judgement, a judgement is in fact not *about* objects, but is itself objective (*Prol*, AA 4: 299), in the sense of being *constitutive of* objectivity. On Kant's view, it is not the case that there is a world of objects out there and that, independently or separately, we are free to formulate judgements or make assertions about them, whereby the objects make our judgements true. My judgement 'about' a certain object x coincides with x's existence *as object of my experience* (notice: not the existence of the putative *thing in itself* that necessarily *appears* as the object for my thought; only the determinate existence of the *appearance* is an object of my judgement).[29] If the transcendental conditions for my judgement G_Fx are satisfied, then the transcendental truth conditions for x are satisfied, where x is the object with properties F and G belonging to the realm of possible experience (the totality of all appearances). (But notice that this does not imply that the empirical conditions for x specifically *to have properties* F and G have thereby been satisfied.) Both objects and judgements 'about' objects belong to the same domain of possible experience governed by the categories. Hence, Kant says that the a priori conditions of the experience of objects are the conditions of the objects of experience (A111).

There is no fundamental discrepancy between the judgement and its object, and hence the transcendental truth conditions for a claim about object x are satisfied by the conditions for judging having been satisfied, i.e. the act of the unity of apperception, in tandem of course with the way apperception operates in sensibility by means of the productive imagination (this is to be discussed in Chap-

---

29 This ties in with a two-aspect reading of Kant's idealism concerning objects: only the phenomenal aspect of the underlying thing in itself appears as the determined object of judgement, and to this extent is the object a function of the judgement. But notice that such a reading does not necessarily imply a one-object reading of idealism. See Schulting (forthcoming).

ter 11). Because a judgement is nothing but the unity of concepts and intuition in accordance with the original-synthetic unity of apperception, and an object is defined as 'that in the concept of which the manifold of a given intuition is *united*' (B137), a judgement and its object coincide at the fundamental level. Robert Pippin is therefore entirely right to say that 'unity of apperception [...] is what establishes a possible relation to an object' and he is also right, in principle at least,[30] that conceptual unity 'achieves the unity that says how things are' (2014: 147–8). More precisely, as Pippin says elsewhere, '[t]he object just is "that in the concept of which the manifold is united"' and 'representation of an object just *is* rule-governed unity of consciousness' (2015: 71–2). In other words, the unity of apperception constitutes what an object *is*.

An objection to this might be that the earlier formulation 'unity of apperception [...] is what establishes a possible relation to an object' does not entail the strict identification of the unity of apperception with the object, what Pippin (2014) refers to, in Hegelian terms, as the identity between subject and object. For example, Allais (2015) thinks that 'relation to an object' does not imply identification with the object, but this is based on a mistaken reading of what is entailed by the unity of apperception,[31] and on the assumption that the object is something outside the relation. Of course, sensations as a result of the subject being affected by some thing still need to be presupposed as given independently, but there is no issue of our judgements having to correspond to external objects *outside* our representations or *outside* the unity among our representations, which constitutes the relation to an object (cf. A104–7).[32] There is no 'outside', with which we could compare our representations and somehow 'check' whether they are really true of the object. The fundamental correspondence relation between concepts and objects is fully 'internalised', as it were, in the unity of apperception, and hence in judgement. Therefore, the identification of the object with the unity of apperception is fully warranted. As Kant says in the conclusion to the Transcendental Deduction in its A-version:

> [A]s appearances they [a priori concepts] constitute an object *that is merely in us*, since a mere modification of our sensibility is not to be encountered outside us at all. Now even

---

[30] I say 'in principle', for one must also address the question of *how* the unity of apperception is seen to operate *in a sensible manifold*, namely in the guise of the productive imagination, which first establishes the determinate perception of *spatiotemporal* objects. Pippin pays scant attention to the need for an account of this aspect of Kant's argument in the so-called 'second step' of the B-Deduction, which is discussed in Chapter 11. Pippin's reading of Kant (and Hegel) is discussed at length in Schulting (2016b). See also Schulting (forthcoming).
[31] See the discussion in Schulting (2017a: 168ff.).
[32] See Schulting (2017a), ch. 1.

this representation—that all these appearances and thus all objects with which we can occupy ourselves are all in me, i.e. determinations of my identical self—*expresses a thoroughgoing unity of them in one and the same apperception* as necessary. (A129, emphasis added)[33]

Appearances are of course not literally, materially in us as psychological subjects, but they are in us qua 'judgers', as agents that ourselves are part of the realm of possible experience. By contrast, the things in themselves, of whose intrinsic properties we have no knowledge, are neither in us materially nor in us qua 'judgers'.

* * *

What I hope has become clear from the preceding chapters is that due to its underlying original synthetic unity in terms of a unifying activity the notion of the functional identity of the 'I think', the 'identity of apperception' (B134 [AA 3: 110.10]), which launches the progressive argument P*, has an epistemically relevant grounding function with a view to determining the specific functions—the categories—that both establish the objective validity of one's representations and so constitute an object that is before the subject of thought (the apperceiving or judging subject) *and* exhaust what constrains strict self-identical self-consciousness (P1'-consciousness), which consists in 'the necessary relation of the manifold of intuition to the one *I think*' (B140). The objective validity of apperception itself does not imply the objective validity of just any consciousness (any consciousness of the P3' or P4' kind); as Kant asserts in § 18, *subjective* unity of consciousness is explicitly excluded from the objective unity that is the transcendental unity of apperception. This should allay the worry expressed by all those who think there is a gap in Kant's 'master argument'.[34]

The a priori conditions of the identity of apperception are therefore not conditions of the capacity for mere consciousness but are in fact the categories (in their unschematised form) (B131), albeit that no cognition 'about the soul', rational or otherwise, can be derived from these 'naked concept[s]' as such (A400–1).[35] This correspondence between the characteristics of apperception

---

[33] Cf. B310/A255: "[T]he domain outside of the sphere of appearances is empty (for us), i.e., we have an understanding that extends farther than sensibility *problematically*, but no intuition, indeed not even the concept of a possible intuition, through which objects outside of the field of sensibility could be given, and about which the understanding could be employed *assertorically*" (my underlining).

[34] But for those not yet convinced, in Schulting (2017a), ch. 4, I provide a more expansive rebuttal of the objection of 'the Gap'.

[35] These 'naked concepts' can still have their indirect, symbolic function as Kant writes in *Real Progress*: '[T]he symbolization of the concept [...] is an expedient for concepts of the super-sen-

and the categories is not due to a special function of the 'I think'—an 'objectivating' feature, say—*in addition to* its own nature; rather, intentionality or, in Kant's phrasing, objective validity belongs to the very nature of discursive thought as such. That is to say, from the transcendental-logical point of view of explaining how experience in general is possible, discursive thought or the understanding *itself* must be seen as having an objective value. This explains the objective validity of the subjective conditions of thought and thus answers, at least partly (to the extent that the sensible conditions are left out), Kant's central question 'how *subjective conditions of thinking* should have *objective validity*' (A89/B122).

10.3 Kant's 'Master Argument': How the P*- and R-Arguments Interlock

In having expounded the conditions of discursive thought as having objective validity in that they are the categories of objective thought the grounds are laid for an explication of how the P*-argument from the unity of consciousness to the synthetic a priori conception of objectivity, and by implication judgement and objective experience, interlocks with the R-argument that regresses from objective experience to its necessary grounds. The *quaestio juris* that inaugurates the R-argument is fully answered—once, of course, buttressed by the arguments of the 'second step'—by means of the P*-argument, the argument that shows that a reciprocity exists between the unity of consciousness (the premise of the P*-argument) and the synthetic a priori nature of objectivity (which is the conclusion of the P*-argument that proves the legitimacy of what in the premise of the R-argument is only assumed as actual and therefore in need of such a proof as provided by the P*-argument). What in the R-argument are argued to be the a priori conditions of objective experience are shown to obtain by virtue of the P*-argument, while the premises of both arguments amount effectively to the same underlying premise, albeit seen from a different perspective: namely the possibility of conceptual representation or knowledge of objects. What I believe is at any rate evident on my reading is that Kant's claim regarding self-identity does not involve a metaphysical claim to the effect that, as Guyer has it, we have antecedent knowledge of an existential unity of all of our (possible) representations, which allegedly constitutes the self's a priori identity, from which then objective

---

sible which are therefore not truly presented, and can be given in no possible experience, though they still necessarily appertain to a cognition, even if it were possible merely as a practical one' (AA 20: 279–80 [TPhb: 370]). Cf. A96. See also Schulting (2017a), ch. 9.

knowledge would somehow have to be miraculously inferred. Therefore, the modal fallacy that Guyer imputes to Kant issues from Guyer's own misconceptions about the constituent elements of the analytic principle of original synthetic apperception as an objective unity of consciousness that establishes a necessary relation among representations. The force of the criticism that Guyer consequently levels at Kant's reciprocity claim has thereby been neutralised (see Chapter 4).

How the P*- and R-arguments actually interlock might best be demonstrated by means of the following schematisation of the R-argument as linked up with the P*-argument, with the proviso that this needs to be augmented with premises involving the argument of the 'second step'. This constitutes Kant's 'master argument' M in the Transcendental Deduction:

> M1. There is objective–unitary experience or a claim to the objectivity of our knowledge.[36] (*the premise of R*)
>
> M2. The philosophical legitimacy of objective–unitary experience or the claim to objective knowledge, which demonstrates its necessary features, cannot simply be read off from experience.
>
> M3. Therefore, an a priori ground or principle must be found which gives objective–unitary experience or objective knowledge its philosophical legitimacy. [from M2]
>
> M4. Categories are the concepts of an object in general, which establish the necessary relation and hence objective validity of representations.
>
> M5. Objective–unitary experience or knowledge is the necessary and objectively valid relation of representations.
>
> M6. Therefore, categories are necessarily applicable to objective experience. [from M4, M5]
>
> M7. Therefore, the a priori principle on which objective–unitary experience rests is provided by the categories (A95–7). [from M3, M6]
>
> M8. Therefore, objective–unitary experience is philosophically legitimated. (*conclusion of R*) [from M1, M7]
>
> M9. Transcendental apperception (original-synthetic unity of apperception) is constituted by the categories as the complete set of its a priori functions. [from D5, D6, D9, D12, D13, D15, D18, D19, D21, D24, D25, D27]

---

[36] Note again that, for Kant, experience and knowledge are more or less interchangeable terms. Knowledge is always and only knowledge of objects of possible experience, so that the class of all the objects of possible experience is the same class of all the objects that can be known. Experience in Kant's sense is not experience in a weak sense and knowledge in Kant's sense (*Erkenntnis*) is not mere cognition of logical objects. See again Chapter 4.

M10. Objective-unitary experience, and hence judgement, is a priori derivable from the principle of transcendental apperception. (*Reciprocity*) (*conclusion of P**) [from M7, M9]

M11. Therefore, transcendental apperception provides objective experience with its necessary and sufficient ground. [from M10]

M12. Therefore, the a priori derivation of the categories from the principle of transcendental apperception underwrites the philosophical legitimacy of objective experience. [from M8, M11]

M13. Therefore, P* rationally shores up R. [from M12]

Propositions M1–M8 make up R, which constitutes a non-trivially circular argument; M9 is the conclusion of the D-argument presented in Chapters 6–9; M10 represents the conclusion of P*; M11 confirms Reciprocity and M12 and M13 give support to my dual reading of the proof-structure of Kant's argument in the first half of the B-Deduction, namely as both a progressive and regressive argument. Although the intelligibility and philosophical authority of R rests on the success of P*, P* itself presupposes the generality of the thrust of R for which it provides the rational foundation. In a certain sense, R thus has primacy in that the proof of the legitimate applicability of the categories to objects, the proof that 'they must be recognized as *a priori* conditions of the possibility of experience (whether of the intuition that is encountered in them, or of the thinking)',[37] is the 'principle toward which the entire investigation [of the transcendental deduction] must be directed' (B126 ff./A94, trans. emended). This is Kant's so-called 'that'-question (MFNS, AA 4: 474n.), the question that Kant deems the most important one to be answered in the Transcendental Deduction. However, the investigation itself, that is, the philosophical proof or the explanation of *how* the categories constitute the a priori conditions of the possibility of experience,[38] requires the demonstration by means of P* (evidently augmented by the argument of the 'second step').

By reasoning in this twofold way, Kant is able to explain the possibility of experience as necessarily presupposing the categories of thought by demonstrating, rationally or a priori, that is, from within thought's own ambit, that thought

---

[37] The first disjunct of the phrase between parentheses involves, of course, the argument of the 'second step' of the B-Deduction (see Chapter 11).

[38] Carl (1992: 115n.7) points to Kant's use of the relative-interrogative adverb 'how' at A85 in his assertion that only a transcendental deduction can show 'how these concepts can be related to objects that they do not derive from any experience'. Carl further notes: 'Dieses Erklärungsziel ist nicht in Abgrenzung zu einer Begründung zu sehen, *daß* diese Möglichkeit besteht [...]; gesucht wird vielmehr eine Erklärung, die einem zeigt, wie dies möglich sein soll, d.h. aus welchen Gründen diese Möglichkeit eingesehen werden kann.' Cf. Baum (1986: 64 ff., 71 ff.).

itself is by its very nature 'intentional', 'related to an object', or objectively valid, and that it is constituted by the categories, and hence forms the formal ground of the a priori possibility of objective experience. The best construal of the Transcendental Deduction is thus to read it in terms of M, which makes the interconnection of the P*- and R-arguments visible.

10.4 The Metaphysically Modest Nature of M: The Analysis of Knowledge

I have argued that the P*- and R-arguments are inextricably entwined: there is no proof possible of the a priori applicability of categories to objects without a prior commitment to at least the actuality of objective knowledge of which the categories are the alleged pre-conditions, which is shown by a regressive argument. Kant is not out to prove the *actuality* of objective knowledge. Hence, the premise of this argument is the actuality of objective knowledge, or, experience in the 'thick' sense, as Ameriks has dubbed it, while the conclusion of that argument states that the claims in regard to it are legitimate, for the categories (and the a priori forms of intuition) are shown to be, collectively, the necessary conditions of such experience.[39] This is Kant's main argument, the objective deduction, which he stresses is his 'primary concern' (Axvii). However, there is no philosophical proof at all if the argument concerning their necessary applicability cannot be shown to be valid according to a rationally insightful method, which lends it apodicticity, or at least sufficient philosophical conviction, and universal generality, traits Kant deems to be necessary ingredients of those very a priori concepts of the understanding that cannot be abstracted from empirical experience. If he wants to show that these pure concepts are necessary (and also formally sufficient) for experience, and not instantiated in experience as a matter of course (cf. B123–4), then he needs something more than merely an

---

[39] In this way, Kant is able to establish, later in the Analytic of Principles, the legitimacy of any synthetic a priori judgement in which such an a priori notion of objectivity is primordially instantiated, and which Kant believes underlies the claim to the objectivity of cognition in experience (*Erfahrung*) as such. Kant must be taken to argue, starting from the premise that we make synthetic a priori claims with regard to object knowledge (for example, in employing the causality principle in propositions of the form 'an event B necessarily follows upon some event A'), that we are licensed to conclude that certain a priori concepts are presupposed in such claims, given that these concepts first constitute what it is first to have an intelligible grasp of causally governed objects and their objective relations. These concepts are therefore necessary constraints of experience construed as judgemental epistemic activity, which for Kant is on a par with the capacity for rational thought (cf. B106/A80–1).

'objective deduction'[40] (compare the remark at A98 about the preparatory nature of section II of the A-Deduction in contrast to the systematic exposition of the elements of the understanding in section III).

In view of this, the formal procedure of the argument in the Transcendental Deduction—at any rate the argument of the 'first step' of the B-Deduction[41]— must be considered synthetic-progressive: it concerns a 'derivation' of the 'principles of the objective determination of all representations insofar as cognition can come from them [...] from the principle of the transcendental unity of apperception' (B142) to the effect that a chain of intermediate propositions progresses from the self-confirmatory principle of the formal identity of self-consciousness (the *cogito*), whose condition is the original-synthetic unity of apperception, to a warranted conclusion regarding the synthetic a priori cognition of an object in general. The premise of this argument is apperception and synthetic a priori cognition is its conclusion.[42] The P*-argument shows, explicitly and step-by-step, how the synthetic a priori, the set of categories, is effectively drawn from the transcendental unity of apperception. It shows how the categories are those functions of thought which combine the representations in any given manifold and thus establish a relation to an object and hence an objective cognition. Kant must demonstrate that the consecutive steps of the operative P*-argument are consonant with the rules of logical reasoning. That is to say, it must be shown that the premise of Kant's operative argument is logically analytic, from which the subsequent arguments may be taken to follow according to a logical pattern. Kant proceeds from a logical basis that provides the certainty that a deductive procedure requires for it to be authoritative (see again Chapter 3). Although Kant's *modus operandi* remains largely implicit in the actual unfolding of the Transcendental Deduction—the reasoning is not according to an explicitly syllogistic schema[43]—one can discern its logic by paying close attention to the argu-

---

40 Cf. Baum (1986: 71, 64).
41 Whether the 'second step' continues the progressive line of reasoning or is an argument that is structurally independent of the P*-argument of the 'first step' is a subject for further study.
42 Note again that Strawsonians, however, depart from this scheme, for although they appear to construe the argument as a progressive one they deny the cogency of a priori synthesis altogether. Strawson (1968: 96) wants to establish 'a direct analytical connexion between the unity of consciousness and the unified objectivity of the world of our experience', thus without a priori synthesis. This makes their construal unsuitable as an interpretation of Kant.
43 This makes sense, for the a priori argument that Kant presents is a transcendental-philosophical argument that logically precedes the possibility of discursive thought and thus also the application rules of inference. The Transcendental Deduction is a piece of *prima philosophia* par excellence.

ments in respect of the constraints of what it is to think and subsequently, as explicated in the second half of the B-Deduction, to know an object.

It transpires, perhaps in too elliptical a manner that does not suit current tastes for formal rigour, that a certain circularity of reasoning informs Kant's conceptual differentiations in respect of the issues at stake. What Kant aims at is effectively nothing but an analysis of objective experience or knowledge, of which discursive thought and the object of thought are the constituent elements, premised on the *Faktum* of experience. This circularity of thought is non-trivial in that by means of it Kant is able to explain the possibility of objective experience, and so to increase our philosophical knowledge about it. At the same time, however, this explanatory circle must be capable of being shown to hold true philosophically by means of a progressively structured derivation, so that the argument is not seen to be begging the question, a charge to which a *purely* regressive construal of the Transcendental Deduction such as Ameriks's is vulnerable. A progressive rational demonstration is indispensable, even given the modest aim of Kant's basic intention to provide merely an analysis of knowledge, and not to prove that there *is* knowledge. The modesty of the aim of the proof and the rational foundation for the proof do not conflict. Only by virtue of such a rational derivation can a genuine explanation be provided that adds to our philosophical insight over and above a merely cursory account of certain presuppositions and intentions, in the same way that Kant considered his own *Prolegomena* to be mere 'preparatory exercises' (AA 4: 274) for what in the *Critique* he endeavoured to establish according to rational principles.

It is on these grounds that I think it is requisite to distinguish between the R- and P*-arguments underlying the one exposition of possible experience, each of which signals a different hermeneutical approach starting out from a different premise and hence yielding a result that is proportional to it; that is, merely analytic or regressive in the *Prolegomena* in view of its limited philosophical, popular, or didactic aim, focusing only on the global argument of the *Critique*, and in the main synthetic or progressive in the *Critique* itself, for there the account should nail down the systemic features of the Critical position—although, unsurprisingly, even in the *Critique*, in particular in the A-Deduction, Kant sometimes has explicit recourse to regressively structured arguments, such as of the *reductio* form.

Ameriks's (1978: 281–2) worry about a progressively structured argument is that it seems to bring in an unaccounted-for antecedent premise that is sub-epistemic, namely an alleged basic principle of mere representation. However, I have argued that, rather than the premise of the P*-argument being a primitive state of mind, transcendental apperception is to be regarded as expressive of the identical self-consciousness that is reciprocal to an objective unity of representations and hence to judgemental activity, given Kant's definition of judgement as 'the way to bring given cognitions to the *objective* unity of apperception' (B141); I have pointed out that the proof of the reciprocal relation between an identical self and an objective unity (what I called Reciprocity) must subsequently be seen as rationally buttressing the R-argument so as to guarantee the truth of answering the *quaestio juris*. This in no sense weakens the epistemic nature of the premise of the global argument of the Transcendental Deduction as Ameriks construes it (cf. Bxxii note).[44] There is no risk that with a properly construed progressive argument the premise of the Transcendental Deduction is taken to lie in a self-standing principle of *mere* experience or consciousness, as I have shown in Chapter 6.

Lastly, it is important to emphasise from a more conceptual-systematic point of view that, for Kant, the operative principle that launches the P*-argument (the 'I think') can never amount to an independently functioning axiom, or an immediate, intuitive evidential insight,[45] that does not have its determining reason in its conceptual contrary. An axiomatically posited principle of representation, say, would not satisfy this requirement. The operative premise, namely the analytic unity of the 'I think', which is an analytic principle, is itself contingent on a prior account of its counterpart of which Kant says that the 'I think' discloses its required 'higher' unity, namely synthesis.[46] Keeping in mind the interdependence between the unitary 'I think' and synthesis as mutually supportive conceptual contraries, which together ground the principle of thought itself that functions as premise of the Deduction, thus serves to allay Ameriks's worry about a progressively structured deduction argument from a principle.

In the Kantian scheme of things, a principle shoring up a substantive claim (which we may presume the Deduction's constitution argument or Reciprocity to be) can only really be such a principle if its grounding function can be a priori

---

[44] I take it that it is in this sense that Ameriks too allows a progressive argument (Ameriks 1978: 282; cf. 2003b: 8 ff., where Ameriks argues that the argument is neither *strongly* progressive nor *strongly* regressive). In his earlier article (1978) Ameriks already insisted that the regressive construal of the Transcendental Deduction means that 'it is not progressive in their sense', that is, in the sense that some interpreters take the Transcendental Deduction to amount to a 'radical argument from a premise not assuming the possession of knowledge' (1978: 282). From Ameriks's subsequent reading of original apperception as interchangeable with an objective unity of apperception (1978: 283) it becomes clear that his regressive interpretation can easily be aligned with my construal of the P*-argument.

[45] To this extent, Kant's argument would indeed be non-Cartesian.

[46] As Baum (1986: 88) explains, the argument in § 15 in the B-Deduction is analytic, an argument from conditioned to condition, while the argument from § 16 onwards is an argument which aims 'die zu erklärende Sache aus ihren Bedingungen wieder entstehen zu lassen'.

10.4 The Metaphysically Modest Nature of M: The Analysis of Knowledge — 287

shown in relation to what *makes* it such a grounding function (its antecedently determining reason, to speak in the terms of Kant's important early work *Nova dilucidatio*). This can only be achieved by means of contrastive conceptual differentiation of the philosophical terms that are operative in, and so in a way guide, the argument—these terms are what in the Amphiboly chapter in the *Critique* Kant calls the transcendental 'concepts of reflection', of which 'unity' and 'synthesis' are prime examples, which can be traced back to the pair 'identity–difference' (*Einerleiheit–Verschiedenheit*) that is actually listed there (cf. B317ff./A262ff.). These comparative concepts are not themselves categories but express the 'qualitative unity' (B114), the 'higher' unity (B131), that lies at their root (which is not to say that this qualitative unity is de re distinct from the categories; the unity of the 'I think' is the 'vehicle' of the categories, as Kant puts it [B399];[47] and as I argued in Chapter 8, it is the pivotal category of 'limitation' which in fact more immediately expresses the *qualitative unity* of transcendental apperception). They explain the systematic coherence of the categories. It is the interaction of these concepts of transcendental reflection that effectively articulates what can be characterised as the dynamic of explanation of possible experience, the manner in which reason itself conducts its project of 'self-knowledge' (Axi).[48]

How does Kant effect this conceptual differentiation by means of these concepts of reflection? In the text of the Transcendental Deduction itself (starting in § 15 of the B-Deduction), Kant carries out a transcendental reflection, by means of a hermeneutic re-enactment, as it were, of discursive experience itself through reason's own reflective capacity, on the concepts of unity and combination or synthesis by linking them up with the subjective source of the a priori concept of an object, namely the 'act of [the subject's] self-activity' (B130), which is the 'topic' of this concept (cf. A262/B318). In fact, transcendental reflection is of a piece with this self-acting activity (see again Chapter 7); it is the self-reflexive dynamic of reason by means of which possible experience can be explained ade-

---

[47] Interestingly, the great theologian Karl Barth (1985: 254) noted in the context of his interpretation of Kant's philosophy of religion that the source of the term 'vehicle' in its eighteenth-century use is pharmaceutical, so that 'vehicle' was what we would call the excipient of a pharmaceutical drug, in contrast to its active ingredient. Barth renders it *Leitmittel*. In today's German one would call this the *Wirkstoffträger*, which still reflects the older term *Vehikel* (*veho* in Latin meaning 'to carry'). Where the 'I think' is the vehicle or bearer of the active agents, the categories must be seen as the active ingredients or agents.

[48] Cf. A849/B877, A735/B763 and R4284, AA 17: 495; see also *Prol* § 35, AA 4: 317. For discussion, see Schulting (2009a: 49–51, 62–4). On the connection between the concepts of reflection and the Transcendental Deduction, see also Banham (2006: 77–9).

quately and coherently. Kant performs such a reflection—which is in effect a reconstruction of the self-reflection of reason—by contrasting unity with synthesis while simultaneously linking them as conceptual contraries that necessarily presuppose each other in virtue of a certain higher synthetic unity underlying the capacity of thought itself, that is, of the act of judging, or, transcendental apperception; this almost dialectical capacity of thought is consistent with reason's self-reflective reenactment of experience before the 'tribunal [of] reason' (Axi–xii, trans. Kemp Smith), by way of a transcendental reflection on the legitimacy of the categories as the necessary conditions of experience.

In § 16, in the context of the P*-argument proper, the basic idea of synthetic unity (and synthesis) that has been reflectively devised or conceived, as it were, in the foregoing section then 'appears' more concretely, or is made explicit, through the function of 'pure apperception' (B132). That is to say, it is made explicit in the analytical representation 'I think'. In this way, Kant appears to indicate that the formal identity of 'I'-thought (the identity of the 'transcendental subject of thoughts' [B404]), which as analytic proposition serves prominently as the premise of the P*-argument, does not come out of thin air, so to speak. The 'I think' is not a self-standing principle. It has its methodical warrant in that it itself flows, almost teleologically, from the implicit reflection, in § 15, on the conceptual requirement of synthetic unity for the possibility of an objective-referential combination of one's representations, a unity that is conceptually underpinned by, and so calls for, a 'higher' kind of unity that is the 'I think'. (Notice that the argument regarding this requirement for the possibility of combinatory representation is itself regressive structurally,[49] which implies that the ground of the premise of the P*-argument, the 'I think' of § 16, is the conclusion of a regressive argument set out in the preceding section, of which the possible representation of an object is the premise.)

It is for the above reasons, which point to the fundamental intentionality or objective validity of thought, that I believe that reading transcendental apperception in terms of a basic principle of representation *simpliciter*, from which what Ameriks (2003b: 8) rightly dismisses as a 'super-deduction' would putatively be launched, has no warrantable basis in Kant's text. Given further that, as is textually evident from the section that is the antecedent of the P*-argument from § 16, Kant already quite explicitly alludes to the possibility of object cognition, not mere experience (in the Strawsonian sense), the most charitable interpretation of Kant's operative premise of the P*-argument would be to consider it in conformity therewith, that is, as *already* having an unmistakably epistemic pur-

---

49 See again Baum (1986: 88).

10.4 The Metaphysically Modest Nature of M: The Analysis of Knowledge

port and therefore as implying a restrictive scope of transcendental apperception in regard to the representations that are subject to it. This is of a piece with my central claim that the analytic unity of consciousness (the formal 'I think' of apperception) is rigorously coextensive with the original-synthetic unity of apperception (a priori synthesis) and the further claim that this coextensivity underpins the dual nature of the Transcendental Deduction as both regressive and progressive. If, then, the premise of the P*-argument (the 'I think') is interpreted in accordance with this construal of the relation between § 15 and § 16 of the B-Deduction, additional weight is given to the soundness of Reciprocity, namely Kant's persistently disputed claim that the transcendental apperception, the 'Radicalvermögen aller unsrer Erkenntniß' (A114), alone establishes the objective validity of our experience of objects and, given that the sufficient condition of solely the *a priori form* of objectivity is at issue, indeed of these objects themselves as objects of our experience.

11 On the 'Second Step' of the B-Deduction

11.1 Introduction

In this last chapter, I address Kant's argument in the B-Deduction about how figurative synthesis (*synthesis speciosa*) or transcendental imagination accounts for the possibility of perceptual knowledge of spatiotemporal objects. I delineate Kant's main argument in the 'second step' of the B-Deduction, which shows that perceptual knowledge requires figurative synthesis, a.k.a the transcendental synthesis of the imagination. This involves the question of the determination of the spatiotemporality of objects. I concentrate on space, although time is a vital element in the act of determining space (B155n.; cf. A412/B439, B48–9).

Of course, *that* figurative synthesis is an integral element of Kant's account of perceptual knowledge is no news to attentive readers of the B-Deduction, but the question of *how* in fact figurative synthesis is supposed to ground perceptual knowledge has been less emphasised in commentaries (Friedman 2012 is one of few exceptions). What I mean by this is that, though there have been many interpretations of the general role for figurative synthesis, it has rarely been examined in detail how figurative synthesis precisely accounts for the possibility of perception.

Here, I attempt to get a better picture of why and how Kant thinks that this specific type of synthesis is indispensable for enabling perceptual knowledge, specifically by addressing the relation between figurative synthesis and the determination of space or, more precisely, the determination of spaces. I focus on the main issues and shall not consider in scholarly detail tricky interpretative questions that have to do with the so-called 'two-step' structure of the B-Deduction per se, although my reading of figurative synthesis can be seen to provide a means of how finally to solve the riddle of the 'two-step' structure in B. Without engaging the literature on this last point, the methodical issues pertaining to the B-Deduction will briefly be discussed in Sections 11.2 and 11.3, and then later in Section 11.7.

Here's a summary of this chapter. In Section 11.2, I rehearse Kant's goals in the Transcendental Deduction (henceforth 'the Deduction', 'the B-Deduction', or abbreviated as TD), while in Section 11.3, the 'two-step' procedure is briefly addressed. In Section 11.4, I expand on the themes of figurative synthesis, geometry and the a priori possibility of representing a particular. Then, in Section 11.5, I discuss figurative synthesis in relation to the sui generis unity of space. In Section 11.6, the distinction between metaphysical and geometric space, which Kant makes in a late unpublished essay on the mathematician Abraham Kästner, is highlighted as an aid to understanding the argument of the B-Deduction. In Section 11.7, I address the question of what Kant has actually proven in the 'second step' of the B-Deduction. Finally, in Section 11.8, I briefly consider the perplexing question of Kant's claims about the *idealism* of nature.

11.2 Kant's Goals in the Deduction

As I made clear in Chapter 4, Kant's goals in the Deduction are multifaceted and it is not always crystal clear, from reading the text, what the relation is between those goals and whether they do not conflict. At least three aims can be differentiated:

> 1) Kant wants to show that the categories are justifiably used in experience (TD, § 13). (*justification or legitimation*)
>
> 2) Kant wants to derive or deduce the categories as objective conditions of experience from the subjective conditions of thinking itself, or from a principle (B90–2/A65–7). (*ostensive proof*)[1]
>
> 3) Kant wants to show that experience is possible only on condition of the instantiation of the categories, so that there cannot be any experience without involvement of the categories (e.g. A95–6). (*transcendental argument*)

But a further issue arises regarding the third of the above set of goals: Kant can be said to argue in the Deduction for either the claim (3*) that the categories are the conditions *that* there *is* experience (de re), or the claim (3**) that the categories explain *how* experience is possible, *given* that there is experience. Although one would think that, on Kant's account, without categories there would not be objects much less experience of them (see e.g. *Met-Schön*, AA 28: 476–7; *Corr*, AA 11: 313–14), it is not as if Kant argued that experience is first *generated* by the categories, or that the objects are somehow *existentially created* by the categories. In the introductory section of the *Critique*, right at the outset, Kant expressly says that knowledge starts with experience, i.e. with sense impressions as impingements on the mind from empirically real objects (B1). This suggests that he takes experience as a given, and by implication it also suggests the fact of there being such empirically real objects that involuntarily prompt sensations in us, and thus exist externally to our minds. The experience meant here is experience in a different sense than experience defined as the 'sum total [*Inbegriff*] of all our objects' (*Met-Schön*, AA 28: 477, trans. mine), which is dependent

---

[1] I mean ostensive proof in the sense that Kant indicates at A789/B817.

for its possibility on the categories. The former type of experience concerns experience *quoad materiale* or sense experience. Let's call this type of experience S-experience. S-experience is not generated or even as such conditioned by the categories, whereas experience that is governed by the categories, namely the '*Inbegriff* of all our objects', is in a way generated by them, namely, insofar as the form of experience is concerned. Call this latter type C-experience. In the Deduction, Kant is interested in demonstrating the possibility of C-experience, not the possibility of S-experience. The categories enable the former, not the latter.

Whereas on this reading (3**), the Deduction *starts* with the premise that S-experience, and so the object(s) that cause(s) it, is given and unproblematic, another reading (3*) does not see the Deduction as starting with this premise, but sees the argument in the Deduction as starting from a more minimal basis, that is, the *mere* having of representations (as mere mental states), which must be justified with recourse to an analysis of the categories as conditions of such mere having. That there are objects, which cause representations in us, must thus first be shown to follow from that more minimal premise. On this second reading, the categories are seen as the conditions that are constitutive of experience *simpliciter*—without making a distinction between S-experience and C-experience. On the former reading (3**) the account of the categories has just an explanatory role to play, namely to explain the extent to which and the sense in which from given S-experience there arises C-experience. A crucial difference between 3** and 3* is that on the latter view we cannot assume the *fact* that we experience *objects* (rather than just our own subjective inner states), and thus the fact of either S-experience or C-experience. That fact must first be demonstrated.[2]

These different ways of reading Kant's argument reflect the well-known discussion whether the argument in the Deduction is either regressive or progressive. I do not want specifically to delve again into that question here (see Chapter 4). I do not think, though, that there should be any doubt about the general underlying assumption, for Kant, that S-experience is a given and not in need of any justification or proof. I thus endorse reading 3**. Whatever the constitutive role of the categories might be, neither is the particular goal in the Deduction to argue, in an anti-sceptical fashion, that we are licensed to conclude that we do have experience or knowledge of external spatiotemporal objects starting from the premise of the mere having of representations; that is, to argue that any *mere having* of representations already implies the necessary obtaining of physical objects that exist independently of these representations, and that thus, by

---

[2] See e.g. Carl (1989: 11).

way of a progressively structured argument, the existence of objects is proven—the fact alone that I could have representations that are not veridical disproves this type of argument. This implies that the argument also cannot be to claim, in the conclusion of the Deduction, that the categories even apply to the mere *having* of perceptions (cf. B164), ruling out strong forms of conceptualist readings of the Deduction (see Schulting 2017, ch. 5). At any rate, transcendental arguments of the broadly Strawsonian sort (that is, refutations of the sceptic) are not Kant's business in the Deduction.³

There is the further issue of whether the argument concerns the possibility of *either* experience *or* knowledge, i.e. empirical knowledge, or even just scientific knowledge. But, leaving aside the controversial neo-Kantian view that solely scientific knowledge is the object of analysis, Kant is quite clear that he means *C*-experience and empirical knowledge to be equivalent (B147). It is fairly well-established that Kant's definition of 'experience' (*Erfahrung*) is different from what the English expression 'experience' denotes, which is closer to Kant's *Wahrnehmung*, i.e. perception (*mit Empfindung begleitete Vorstellung*; B147), or, perhaps indeed equivalent to *S*-experience. 'Experience' in Kant's narrower sense (*C*-experience) denotes a higher form of perception, which is formed by means of the forms of judgement, that is, through a connection among perceptions (B218, *Prol*, AA 4: 298 [§ 19], A110, A200/B245, A764/B792; cf. B161). Nevertheless, we should be careful not to think that this implies that Kant allows room for lower-level 'experience', in the sense of the English term, which can be expressed in propositions with a subject-predicate form or by means of demonstrative thought, as a way of direct reference, but which is not yet *C*-experience (see Schulting 2017a: 198–212). Some Kant commentators believe that, at least in the *Prolegomena*, Kant allows for this kind of experience, namely as what he himself calls 'judgements of perception'. However, whatever the case may be regarding the account of judgements of perception in the *Prolegomena*, I do not think that in the B-Deduction Kant still adheres to it, given his very precise definition of judgement as being equivalent to *objectively* valid knowledge, or experience in the sense of *Erfahrung*, i.e. *C*-experience.⁴

Lastly, a crucial aspect of the Deduction's goal, in particular, the 'second step', is to show the conformity between the specifically spatiotemporal form of our intuition and the categories. Therefore, not just the legitimation or justification of the use of the categories is called for in the Deduction, but also of the concept of 'space' itself (cf. B120/A88), which enables not only geometrical sci-

---

3 For a critique of Strawson's construal of the Deduction, see Schulting (forthcoming).
4 Cf. Pollok (2008).

ence, but also the perceptual cognition of objects in empirical or physical space (what Sellars [1992: 53 ff.] calls 'coarse-grained' space). The legitimation of the use of the categories coincides with showing this conformity, more specifically, the conformity between the unity of space and the unity of apperception. The former unity cannot be analytically deduced from the unity of apperception. Hence, the 'first step' of the B-Deduction, in which Kant argues for the necessity of the unity of apperception and its instantiation in any unified manifold of representations, is not sufficient for showing that the categories apply to specifically *spatiotemporal* manifolds of representations. The subsumption of empirical manifolds of representations of objects, which are characterised by their own spatiotemporal structure, under the categories, by means of the unity of apperception, is thus a further task for the 'second step', which is expounded in § 26 of the B-Deduction.

To return to the first and second aspects of Kant's goal in the Deduction, as formulated above: does the argument concern merely a legitimation of the categories, more precisely, showing their justified use (Aim 1)? Or does Kant also want to provide a proof of how they are derived from their subjective origin in thought (Aim 2)? Again, this relates to the question of whether the Deduction concerns a regressive analysis or a progressive synthetic argument, where the latter addresses the constitutive role of the categories, and the former merely their explanatory role. If one thinks the Deduction is *either* regressive *or* progressive, then one cannot claim that both the legitimation and an a priori proof are at issue.[5] Most commentators, however, have indeed claimed that the proof procedure is either of the two, not both; on the regressive reading, for example, it would make sense to say that merely a legitimation of the use of categories is concerned, since a proof of their subjective a priori origin is not at issue—just as Kant suggested in the A-preface (Axvi–xvii). A regressive reading starts, not with the subject, but with the fact of objective experience, and then regresses to its conditions. There is the further issue of whether the legitimation of the categories applies to how metaphysics is possible as a science of synthetic a priori knowledge (which seems to be how the *Prolegomena* portrays it) or how again experience or empirical knowledge itself is possible. These two approaches are

---

5 That is, on a regressive reading that takes experience (as knowledge) as a premise in the argument the argument cannot be a priori strictly speaking, in the sense that an a priori argument is one that is mounted completely independently of experience. Of course, the regressive argument is still a priori in another sense of being part of a transcendental analysis, rather than an inductive analysis *based on* experience. A regressive argument in the transcendental vein still seeks to provide certainty about the categories' applicability, but it is not an ostensive proof that is strictly a priori from a pure principle of thought.

not unrelated, since showing that the categories are metaphysical concepts justifiably employed in synthetic a priori propositions means at the same time showing that they can only justifiably be used in empirical experience, given that synthetic a priori propositions are about possible experience. The claim regarding synthetic a priori knowledge and the one concerning empirical knowledge hang together.

Without rehearsing the earlier proposed solution to the aforementioned issues (see Chapter 10), I am going to assume that in the Deduction Kant argues for the explanation of the question of *how* experience or knowledge is possible, not *that* there is such experience or knowledge (cf. *Prolegomena*). So, more precisely, I consider the general argument to be grounded on the unproblematic assumption that there is S-experience (3**), but also already, inchoately, that there is C-experience or knowledge (B147), namely, the fact that synthetic a priori claims to knowledge are generally being made—this is especially clear from the *Prolegomena* account.[6] We should keep in mind, though, that in the *Critique* itself, for the purposes of delivering a philosophical proof of the justified use of the categories, Kant does not accept as a given the actuality of C-experience, but wants the proof of the possibility of such experience to start from a principle of thought (Aim 2). But, at any rate, S-experience is never the object of proof in the Deduction, and so does not function in any way as a premise in that proof. At least one argument can be provided that demonstrates that Kant's argument *cannot* in fact be such as to show that S-experience is possible. This concerns the relation between *natura formaliter spectata* and *natura materialiter spectata* (which is discussed in Section 11.8). For if to prove that S-experience is possible were indeed (part of) his argument, it would mean that Kant would have to engage in a phenomenological study of the constitution of the a posteriori nature of experience and, more in particular, its dispositions (*natura materialiter spectata*), i.e.: first, how natural kinds are *empirically* presented in space and time, secondly, how things are ontologically or dispositionally constituted so as to be objects of our experience, and thirdly, how we would be *physiologically* disposed to being in reception of sense stimuli from objects, which empirically enables S-experience. This is however completely beyond the scope of the transcendental investigation of the Deduction.[7] It would also appear to mean that we would be

---

6 That also C-experience is already implicitly claimed to exist concerns the fact that, to some extent, Kant is a common sense realist (see Ameriks 2005), namely, in the way that he accepts the *fact*, not just of there being S-experience, but also of there being scientific (mathematical, natural-scientific) knowledge.
7 Kant of course considers, in the Appendix to the Transcendental Dialectic in the *Critique* and later in the Third *Critique*, the question of how natural kinds must be seen as organised in such a

able to describe the *transition* from *natura materialiter spectata* to *natura formaliter spectata*, and thus in fact to beg the question against a transcendental investigation, which is concerned solely with an investigation of *natura formaliter spectata*. I leave here aside the question to what extent the argument of the Deduction is nonetheless also a progressive synthetic argument in the sense of a derivation of the categories from discursive thought itself (Aim 2). We have addressed the derivation question in the preceding chapters, and it is not required to consider it for our purposes here, which is an account of the 'second step', which takes the derivation question to already have been answered (cf. B159).

11.3 The 'Two-Step' Argument

In the conclusion to the first part of the B-Deduction, i.e. the 'first step', Kant argues he has shown (§ 20) that

> 1. unity of intuition is possible only on condition of the subsumption of the manifold of representations in any sensible intuition that requires a discursive running through, under the unity of apperception;
>
> 2. the combined set of logical functions of judgement is defined by the act of the understanding which brings the manifold under the unity of apperception;
>
> 3. therefore, the manifold stands under the logical functions of judgement insofar as 'it is given in a unitary empirical intuition' (B143);
>
> 4. the logical functions of judgement, insofar as the manifold in a given intuition is determined in accordance with them, are the categories;
>
> 5. therefore, the manifold of a unitary intuition stands under the categories.

In short, Kant's main argument is that the categories, which are employed in judgement, enable the *unity* of the manifold of representations in *any* sensible intuition given for a spontaneous discursive mind. This is in very broad terms the upshot of the 'first step' of the B-Deduction (see Chapters 6–10). What Kant does *not* do in the 'second step', then, is to say simply that, since, as shown in the 'first step', the manifold of representations in *any* unitary given intuition (for a spontaneous discursive mind) requires the categories, so also the manifold of a given *empirical* intuition, namely an intuition of spatially located

---

way as to be perceivable and knowable by us in accordance with regulative principles. But these principles, and the account thereof, are still a priori, and transcendental, and do not concern any examination of the constitution of the a posteriori, empirical nature of objects of experience per se. See also OP, AA 22: 502; cf. Mathieu (1989).

objects, requires the categories. That implication is of course trivially true, but in making such a claim there is nothing in the way of showing *why* that would be true. Kant must show *how* the categories must be seen to apply to an empirical intuition of spatial objects too, and *this*, the manner of their application, cannot be analytically inferred from the conclusion of the 'first step'. That is, Kant must show *how* an empirical intuition that has the specific characteristic of spatiotemporality for human receptivity, which was argued in the Transcendental Aesthetic, is in fact brought under the unity of apperception by the understanding in general, as the seat of the categories (since the act of the understanding is the function of unity in a judgement; B143, A68/B93). This is where figurative synthesis comes into the picture. As I shall point out later below, figurative synthesis is the effect of the understanding itself, or the act of apperception, *in* sensibility, and is in fact the act of the mind that 'applies' the categories within the domain of spatial objects (i.e. the domain of sensibility). I shall explain how this 'application' works in due course.

In the transitional section to the 'second step' (§ 21), Kant makes a few cryptic remarks about what he aims to do in the 'second step'. He writes:

> In the sequel (§ 26) it will be shown from the way in which the empirical intuition is given in sensibility [*aus der Art, wie in der Sinnlichkeit die empirische Anschauung gegeben wird*] that its unity [*die Einheit derselben*] can be none other than the one the category prescribes to the manifold of a given intuition in general according to the preceding § 20 [...]. (B144–5)

The phrase 'from the way in which the empirical intuition is given in sensibility' might be taken to mean that showing that the manifold in intuition owes its unity to the understanding (categories) is to show that *its receptivity* is somehow dependent on the understanding. That would mean, in the most radical reading, that the forms of intuition—space and time as forms of our receptivity—are themselves, in some sense, products of the understanding. This is not such an odd view. Longuenesse (1998, 2005: 34) believes this is what Kant means, and that it is indeed Kant's aim in the 'second step' to retake the claims of the Aesthetic, and somehow to blur the boundary between the forms of sensibility and the forms of the understanding, or at least in terms of their constitutive origins. This is all put a bit crudely, but I come back to this further below, when I address the convoluted passage in the note to B160–1 (§ 26), where importantly Kant distinguishes between space as 'form of intuition' and as 'formal intuition', a distinction the relevance of which is downplayed by Longuenesse.

Notice also that from the above-quoted passage from § 21, it could be inferred that 'unity' is not a characteristic of intuition, but is something that the understanding uniquely brings to it, by synthetically uniting the manifold in intuition (through categorial unity), so that mere intuition has no unity *whatsoever.* First, such a reading assumes that categorial unity, which is a necessary unity, is the same as contingent unity, the unity of the array in which representations are prompted in the mind, say, which is not at issue in the Deduction (B140). Secondly, it would be a mistake to conflate the sui generis unity of space and categorial unity (I discuss the distinction further below). The goal of the Deduction is to show that the unity of a spatial manifold is correspondent with a categorial unity, but not that the categorial unity and spatial unity are qualitatively identical.[8]

From what Kant says subsequently, in the next section (§ 22, B146–7), it is already clear that not receptivity *simpliciter,* or the forms of receptivity, space and time, are at issue, but the possible a priori knowledge of objects (in geometry) by means of the determination of 'pure intuition', as Kant says, *and not* of 'the empirical intuition of what, in space and time, is immediately given as real [*wirklich*], by means of sensation' (trans. emended). Of course, objects in space and time are given only insofar as they are perceived, and hence the determination by the understanding results in knowledge of objects only if the categories are applied to *empirical* intuition, that is to say, when sensations are given. (Even in pure geometry, sensations are presupposed in the distal background as the given material for the construction of geometric objects.)[9]

But the important point to note here, is that the categorial determination does not concern the question of how empirical intuitions are immediately given, necessarily in space and time, but how by means of the application of the categories to those empirical intuitions, formal *unitary* intuitions of spatially located and distinct *particulars* are first formed, on the basis of which there can be empirical knowledge of spatiotemporal objects (and also geometrical knowledge). The distinction between how, on the one hand, indeterminate objects (*Gegenstände*) are *given* in space and time, and how space and time itself, as forms of sensibility, are given with their sui generis unity and, on the other, how the understanding determines our intuition of them, which generates distinct particulars (*Objekte*) in bounded space, is never blurred. This then is my main thesis: The central claim of the 'second step' concerns the analysis of the possibility of spatiotemporally determinate and distinct *particulars* in space and their percep-

---

8 One could argue that, though spatial unity and categorial unity are indeed not to be identified, spatial unity is dependent on a unity that is different from categorial unity, namely, the synthetic unity of the imagination, or the synthetic unity of apperception. But this move presupposes that categorial unity and the synthetic unity of the imagination come apart.
9 See Butts (1981).

tion, *not* how space and time themselves, and thus the forms of intuitions, and whatever objects are *empirically* given in it, are (metaphysically) possible.

11.4 Figurative Synthesis and the A Priori Possibility of Representing a Particular

The approach delineated in the last section is confirmed in the section in the B-Deduction where the notion of a figurative synthesis is first introduced, namely § 24. Figurative synthesis is the synthesis of the manifold of *given* representations in a sensible intuition. Through figurative synthesis the categories 'acquire objective reality' (B150), that is, through it they get applied to spatially located particulars given in sensible intuition.[10] This synthesis is called 'figurative' so as to distinguish it from the *mere* categorial synthesis 'in regard to the manifold of an intuition in general', which is the 'combination of the understanding' or '*synthesis intellectualis*'. Intellectual synthesis is what is thought in the mere categories in regard to an intuition in general (given for a discursive mind), or, 'the merely intellectual combination' (B151). That is, intellectual synthesis is in fact an *abstraction* from the synthesis that take places in the sensible manifold, which is then called figurative synthesis, when an empirical judgement is made about some object. Both figurative and intellectual syntheses are transcendental and a priori.

---

[10] Friedman (2012: 248) is wrong to separate the transcendental synthesis of the imagination from the categories. He emphasises that the former 'precedes' the latter, apparently based on what Kant writes in the B160–1 note (although Kant says about the 'unity of space', not the synthesis, that it precedes concepts). But if at all there is an issue of the imagination 'preceding' the schematised categories, this should be read in terms of the imagination being the transcendental-logical condition of the schematisation of the categories, not in terms of the imagination coming before the categories in time. There is of course no schematisation of the categories without the imagination. But nor is it true to say that one can have the imagination without the (schematised) categories, or put differently, without it ipso facto resulting in the schematising of the categories. For the transcendental act of the synthesis of imagination *is* the act of schematisation of the categories, the pure concepts of the understanding, in the domain of sensibility. Since the transcendental act of the synthesis of imagination *is* the pure act of intellectual synthesis insofar as it is enacted in sensibility (as the synthesis of apprehension; see A120), and given that the 'synthetic unity' in a manifold, 'if I abstract from the form of space, *has its seat in the understanding*', namely, '*is the category* of the synthesis of the homogeneous in an intuition in general' (B162, emphasis added), it is hard to see how synthesis 'precedes' the categories, as if synthesis could take place *without* involvement of the categories—which is what Friedman appears to believe.

Figurative synthesis is also called the 'transcendental synthesis of the imagination', and since it 'can give a corresponding intuition to the concepts of understanding' (B151), i.e. the categories, Kant says it belongs to sensibility. Unlike concepts, the act of transcendental imagination makes it possible to represent a particular, by means of construction through a successive synthesis of representations given in sensibility. However, though operating in the domain of sensibility, figurative synthesis or transcendental imagination is the a priori *determining* factor in sensibility, not *that which is determined*, the determinable, i.e. the manifold of representations. It can therefore not be equated with or seen as constitutive of sensibility itself, in terms of that which is *given* in and through the senses, nor with the pure forms of sensibility as such (space and time). Transcendental imagination is 'a faculty for determining the sensibility *a priori*', and is '*an effect of the understanding on sensibility* and *its* first application [...] to objects of [...] intuition' (B152, emphasis added). Neither the understanding nor transcendental imagination, as an effect of the understanding, turn out to be constitutive of the forms of intuition, as Longuenesse suggests they are. Thus, contrary to what seemed at first to be suggested (§ 21), the issue here is not how objects or particulars are first *given* in receptivity, or presented to us *simpliciter*. Rather, Kant wants to examine the way *objects are first constructed in sensibility by us as particulars or singular objects that are spatially distinct*.

Recently, Thomas Land (2014: 530) has interpreted the above-quoted passage at B151—namely, that the synthesis of the imagination 'can give a corresponding intuition to the concepts of understanding'—as saying that the productive synthesis of the imagination first 'generates' the intuitions of space and time, and thus '*generates* sensible representations' (2014: 541). Crucially, Land differentiates between the *structure* of space as intuition and its *unity*, where its unity is dependent on the understanding (by way of the imagination) but its structure ('strict logical homogeneity') is not. But he also says that 'the actualization of the capacity for having outer intuitions nonetheless depends on acts of the intellect, the capacity for concepts and judgement' (Land 2014: 535).

This would appear to imply that, on Land's account, I cannot *have* intuitions unless they depended on an act of the understanding (by means of a spontaneous act of the imagination), which is a broadly conceptualist standpoint (cf. Schulting 2017, ch. 5). As said, Land distinguishes between the structure and the unity of an intuition, whereby the former is independent of spontaneity and the latter is not. But given that Land means by 'the unity of a complex representation [...] the fact that it is represented *as* complex', and that 'the actualization of the capacity for having outer intuitions [...] depends on acts of the intellect' (2014: 535), he has no means of interpreting the intuition's structure, which on his own account is independent of conceptuality, as bona fide intuitional. It is odd to talk about an intuition that is not in any straightforward sense an intuition, independently of the understanding's role in determining its unity.

This ties in with Land's view that what he calls 'a merely receptive capacity for representation' (2014: 537) is not the capacity that typifies human sensibility, but rather a kind of notional contrast to the receptivity that human sensibility is, since such a *merely* receptive capacity excludes the spontaneity on which human sensibility is absolutely dependent (cf. Aportone 2014: 203). But I believe Land just begs the question here whether our human sensibility is absolutely dependent on spontaneity. It seems that Land excludes the possibility, for human sensibility, of a receptivity that '*merely* represents the here and now', which is '"locked into" its current location and the present moment' and does not 'grasp that location or this moment as one in a system of locations or a continuous series of moments' (Land 2014: 537); as Land rightly says, 'if sensibility were a merely receptive capacity, it would represent the here and now, but not *as* the here and now' (2014: 538). It is indeed correct to say that a 'merely receptive consciousness' would not be able to represent a manifoldness *as* manifoldness, *as* complex, and would be '"locked into" each moment' (Land 2014: 538). The manifold would not be represented *as* a manifold of representations, but there would just be (many) consecutive representations. But, Land says, for Kant 'spatial representation [...] is not like that' (2014: 538), and he seems thereby to exclude the possibility, for humans, of having a manifold of representations of a spatially located object which is short of representing that object *as* located in space. In other words, Land seems to exclude the possibility of *merely* intuiting the object that is in space, without thereby representing something *as* in space, that is, grasping it as located 'in a system of locations' (2014: 537).

On Land's account, then, intuition is always already a representation of the manifold as complex. But surely, an infant or animal, say, should be able to represent something *in* space by merely being affected by it, in that a variety of impressions from 'outside' are involuntarily 'impressed' on their sense organs, and thus to have a sense of spatiality, without thereby representing it *as* in space, i.e. by having an 'awareness of complexity', and not 'merely a succession of impressions' (Land 2014: 538). And if it can represent something in space by merely being affected by it, then it must intuit in space, since space is the necessary form of everything *represented in* space. So, on this account, intuition is not always already a representation of the manifold *as* complex, contrary to what Land argues.

Take the example of an elephant calf taking a shortcut through the wooden fence of the elephant sanctuary in a Ugandan wildlife reserve, rather than entering through the open gate, when it returns to its stable from a day out in the African wilderness, together with its mother, who instead enters through the gate.

The elephant calf intuitively knows it can leap between the rails of the fence, because it has an immediate, instinctual sense of its own small size relative to the open space between the rails of the fence. It does not need to have an awareness of spatial complexity that is borne of the human adult capacity for imaginative synthesis or understanding, i.e. to ratiocinate—schematise concepts—whether or not it should be able to squeeze itself through the fence. An elephant calf's sense of spatiality is purely intuitive.

However, Land might be thought to have a point in saying that the mere succession of impressions, in whatever array they might be prompted, does not add up to a *representation of* space, which therefore 'cannot be the product of a merely receptive capacity of representation' (2014: 538) but is the product of receptivity *plus* the understanding by means of the productive imagination. However, Kant says that space is the form of outer receptivity (A26/B42), and *not* that space is the form of outer receptivity *and* 'something else', namely the understanding. If beings such as infants (as well as animals, such as the elephant calf in the example above), who do not employ the understanding in their merely receptive capacity for being affected, are affected by spatial things, do they then not have spatial representations in the sense of representing things in space, on Land's account?

I believe, for philosophical as well as textual reasons, that we must distinguish between representing *in* space, being able to orient oneself in a particular direction, as a result of e.g. a sudden noise coming from the left, or noticing some indistinct object in the distance (cf. JL, AA 9: 33), and the representation *of* space or spatial objects, which latter is tantamount to the representing of something spatial as complex, namely, as located adjacent to something else and at some specified distance outside of me. Orienting oneself towards a sound coming from a particular direction requires spatial location, representing something that is still indeterminate *in* space, but the very act of directing one's head left or right upon hearing a noise does not yet require the capacity to determine that indeterminate something *as object*, *as* 'a determinate space' (B138), that is, as locatable in a specific place at a specific distance. Moreover, Land appears to conflate the complexity of, on the one hand, a homogeneous quantum such as space, which is the pure form of any intuition, and is independent of any conceptualising or unifying act of the understanding, and, on the other, the *awareness* or *representation* of that complexity, that is, the determination of distinct spaces, which as different quanta constitute that complexity; it is this determination that first requires a spontaneous act of unity that unites the manifold parts in an intuition into a synthetic (finite) homogeneous whole.

Grasping a manifold as a complex spatial quantum happens by means of *figurative* synthesis and the act of constructing geometric objects is typically such

11.4 Figurative Synthesis and the A Priori Possibility of Representing a Particular — 303

an act of synthesis. In § 24, Kant gives some paradigm examples of the construction of geometric objects or figures by means of figurative synthesis. For example, the drawing in thought, or on paper, of a straight line means that we are aware of the act in accordance with a rule of successively synthesising segments or parts of space from an initial given point (cf. B291–2); or the describing of a circle, which comes down to the operating of 'a function which takes an arbitrary point and line segment having this point as one of its endpoints as input and yields the circle with the given point as center and the given line segment as radius as output' (Friedman 2012: 237). Similarly, in describing the three dimensions of Euclidean space, one imagines '*placing* three lines perpendicular to each other at the same point' (B154). Kant associates this description of space with motion, as 'a pure act of the *successive* synthesis of the manifold in outer intuition in general through productive imagination' (B155n., emphasis added). It is in this respect that time is an indispensable element of determining space, for the movement in the act of successive synthesis is a process over a timespan t_1–t_2, corresponding to the successively added parts of the spatial object, such as a line or circle (cf. A412–13/B439–40).

Now of course, in the Deduction Kant is not primarily interested in the possibility of *geometrical* objects or figures per se, or indeed geometric concepts, but rather in the possibility of *empirical spatiotemporal* objects. But the claim is, I contend, that the possibility of spatiotemporal objects and their determination is grounded on the objective determination or limitation *of space as such*, given that, as per the argument of the Aesthetic, outer objects that are accessible for human intuition must be spatial, and thus have space as their condition of possibility. Indeed, as Kant suggests at B138, the act of the synthesis of imagination first generates an object as 'a determinate space' itself within the larger space in which it is contained, from which it is delimited by means of the categories of quality in particular.[11] The unity of the act of synthesis, in the imagination, defines an object, and hence the *possibility* of empirical spatiotemporal objects. He writes:

> Thus the mere form of outer sensible intuition, space, is not yet cognition at all; it only gives the manifold of intuition *a priori* for a possible cognition. But **in order to cognize something in space**, e.g., a line, I must *draw* it, and thus synthetically bring about a determinate combination of the given manifold, so that the unity of this action is at the same time the unity of consciousness (in the concept of a line), and **thereby is an object (a determinate space) first cognized** [*erkannt*]. (B137–8, boldface mine)

---

[11] The act of the synthesis of imagination does not first generate intuitions, such as Land (2014) argues (see above).

The determination or perceptual knowledge of objects is first made possible by the determination of space itself as the 'mere form of outer sensible intuition', which is initially only given as the manifold of intuition 'for a possible cognition' (B137). Spatiotemporal objects are discriminated, or delimited, from the larger space in which they are necessarily perceived, in virtue of delimiting space itself in smaller partitions of itself. Unbounded space is the single domain in which all bounded particular spatial objects must be able to be located. Hence, the possibility of determinate spatiotemporal objects is grounded on the a priori determination of space itself by means of the figurative synthesis. This happens by means of the categories of quantity and quality.[12]

This, then, is what Kant aims to show in the 'second step': how the synthetic unity of apperception, by means of the transcendental synthesis of the imagination, determines a manifold of representations as given in space as an object, which, in virtue of that determination by the act of synthesis, is itself 'a determinate space' within the larger space, in which it is contained. The distinction between the first and second steps thus concerns the distinction between defining the unity of consciousness as an object in general (in the 'first step'), and defining the unity of the synthesis of imagination in the sensible manifold (in apprehension) as an object as 'a determinate space' within space ('second step'). By showing that the unity of the synthesis of imagination determines the unity of space and is thus definitional of a spatially bounded object, and given that the synthesis of imagination is an effect of the understanding on sensibility, and hence an act of apperception, Kant thus shows that the unity of space corresponds to the unity of apperception, insofar as a part of space is delimited as *a* determinate space, a 'something', that is, an object.

The main goal of the 'second step' is to point out that the way a priori concepts, categories (in particular, the categories of quantity and quality), are indeed the functions which subsume empirical intuitions under concepts has to do with pointing out how the unity of space (and, equally, time), as the a priori form of intuition, corresponds to the unity bestowed on the sensible manifold by the understanding by virtue of the categories—this latter unity is the 'qualitative unity' of which Kant speaks at B131 (see Chapter 8), not just the *category* 'unity'. The way to show this correspondence is by showing that the successive synthesis of the manifold of representations in an empirical intuition is required so as to produce or construct a synthetic unity of representations as a 'whole', in the sense of a 'whole of compared and connected representations' being the definition of a 'cognition' (*Erkenntniß*) (A97), within the realm of space as infinite given

---

[12] For more detail, see Onof & Schulting (2015: 41 ff.).

magnitude, which first enables the determination of spatial objects (cf. A224/B271).

11.5 Figurative Synthesis and the Sui Generis Unity of Space

Does this mean that Kant wants to say that the understanding or the unity of apperception is responsible for, indeed generates by construction, the sui generis unity of space, as some might think on the basis of what Kant appears to be saying in the notoriously difficult note at B160–1n. (see e.g. Friedman 2012: 247–8)?[13] This would mean that space (and time), as given infinite magnitudes, as singular and all-encompassing, itself are first generated by the understanding, or at least by the figurative synthesis a.k.a the transcendental imagination (Longuenesse 1998: 219, 223; 2005: 34), and that therefore space (and time) would seem to be conceptual, given that the way the understanding operates is by means of the application or, through the imagination, schematisation of a priori concepts (the construction occurs in accordance with a priori rules, these being the categories). Figurative synthesis is often thought to be an operation that is pre-conceptual—in the sense that it is itself not conceptual and that it does not require concepts (i.e. categories) (see Schulting 2017a, chs 5 and 6), but that it is (merely) a necessary condition for conceptuality and/or the catego-

---

13 Friedman writes: 'What unites this totality [of possible perspectives from which the subject can be affected by outer objects] into a "single all-encompassing" space [...] is the transcendental unity of apperception, which entails that any possible outer object is in principle perceivable by the *same* subject' (2012: 247); and: '[T]he synthesis responsible for the characteristic unity and singularity of space (as the pure form of outer sensible intuition) does indeed belong to the understanding' (2012: 248). See also Bauer (2012: 229). Bauer believes that '[s]patial unity just is a specific instance of categorial unity, which means that the objects we intuit in space will already be conceptually determined by [the] understanding'. This view might seem to be bolstered by Kant's claim, in the very passage from §21 that we quoted earlier, namely, 'that its unity [i.e. of empirical intuition] can be none other than the one the category prescribes to the manifold of a given intuition in general'. However, reading this passage as saying that spatial unity simply reduces to categorial unity begs the question against the very goal of the Deduction, specifically the 'second step', namely how two *heterogeneous* unities, the unity of intuition and conceptual (categorial) unity, can be said to correspond such that cognition of spatiotemporal objects is made possible. Only categorial unity can guarantee this conformity between intuition and concept. Hence, the categorial unity prescribed to the manifold corresponds to the spatial unity in the manifold; the former unity thus produces the manifold *as* synthetically united manifold, but it does not *generate* the sui generis unity of space, which is not a synthetic unity (see further below). For different viewpoints on space and unity see also Messina (2014) and Land (2014), whose reading was discussed above.

ries, or that it requires the categories in a Pickwickean sense, such as Longuenesse's (2005) view that there is a 'first application' of the categories, or in terms of the categories being merely obscure concepts, as Grüne (2009) argues. And since figurative synthesis is pre-conceptual, arguing that the unity of space itself is dependent on figurative synthesis would then not conflict with Kant's thesis that space (and time) are intuitions and not concepts, and the putatively Kantian thesis that space is dependent on figurative synthesis.

There are at least two main problems with this reading. First, it presupposes that figurative synthesis is pre-categorial, which begs the question of how it relates to the understanding. Kant clearly states that figurative synthesis is 'the effect *of the understanding*' (B152, emphasis added), and hence not something that takes place independently of it. At B164, Kant says that with respect to the unity of the intellectual synthesis *of a sensible intuition*, the imagination 'depends on the understanding'. If figurative synthesis is the effect of the understanding and given that the categories are the pure concepts of the understanding, it is hard to conceive of a way in which figurative synthesis could be said not to involve the categories. As Kant often says, synthesis is the unification of a manifold in accordance with a priori rules. These rules *are* the categories (e.g. B162). Also, in a note to B162, Kant explicitly says that the 'synthesis of apperception, which is intellectual [...] is contained in the category completely a priori [*gänzlich a priori in der Kategorie enthalten*]' (trans. Kemp Smith). I take this to mean that the intellectual synthesis of apperception fully coincides with the categories. And given that, as Kant says in that note, the 'synthesis of apprehension, which is empirical, must necessarily be in agreement with the synthesis of apperception', the synthesis of apprehension must necessarily agree with the categories. There is no ambiguity about the meaning of the agreement here. It means strict correspondence. For in the main text Kant explicitly says that the 'synthetic unity, [...] if I abstract from the form of space, has its seat in the understanding, and **is** the category of the synthesis of the homogeneous in an intuition in general, i.e. the category of *quantity*' (B162, boldface mine). That the synthesis of apprehension happens in separation from the categories, or that the synthetic unity in the manifold is not yet categorially determined, is thus interpretatively difficult to maintain.

When Kant writes in the note to B160 that the synthetic unity of intuition a priori belongs to space and time, not to the concept (note the singular!) of the understanding, he implicitly refers back to B131, where it is made clear that the unity of apperception is concerned, not the *category* 'unity'. But this does not imply that in the unification of space and time under transcendental apperception by virtue of figurative synthesis, the categories (as a whole) are not involved, as Friedman (2012) claims. The determinate synthetic unity of space

11.5 Figurative Synthesis and the Sui Generis Unity of Space — 307

and time, as produced by means of apperception, is not literally pre-categorial, in the temporal sense of prior. What Kant means to say is that the unity of apperception, which establishes the unity of space (in terms of geometrical space or determinate space) and time, is the necessary a priori *condition* for determining spaces as parts of space. The original synthetic unity of apperception is not the category of unity nor simply the sui generis unity of space (and time), but it is the mediating unifying ground, or 'qualitative unity' (B131) which binds the two, and thus allows simultaneously, and originally, the schematisation of the category of unity and the determination of the sui generis unity of space (and time).

But also philosophically Friedman's reading is in trouble, since if figurative synthesis—which is an a priori and transcendental act as much as the intellectual synthesis—were independent of the understanding and of the categories, one wonders which further synthesis is required to bind figurative synthesis and the categories. The problem here is what Hanna (2013) has recently aptly called the 'schmimagination' problem in response to a critique of mine (Schulting 2010); if transcendental imagination as one kind of a priori synthesis, namely figurative synthesis, happens separately from the other kind of a priori synthesis, namely intellectual synthesis, then a third kind of a priori synthesis—let's call it 'schmimagination'—is required that connects the first two. But then a fourth kind of a priori synthesis is required to connect the third with the first two etc. The threat is one of an infinite regress, when we should in fact have realised that a priori or original synthesis was precisely designed by Kant in order to block further questions concerning the constitutive ground of experience, and ex hypothesi exists only as *one* kind (cf. B145–6). The view that figurative synthesis is pre-conceptual and hence prior to the categories compromises the main claim of the Deduction to find the common ground between determinate intuitions and concepts. This problem is not solved by a Longuenessian approach of distinguishing between the supposedly first and second applications of the categories, whereby in some deflationary sense the dependency relation between figurative synthesis and the categories is kept intact; for the 'schmimagination' problem would now relate to how the first and second *application* of the categories originally relate to each other (namely, how is the second application effected?), apart from the fact that Longuenesse's reading lacks textual evidence and faces some other inconsistency problems.[14]

---

14 As others have pointed out (Allison 2000), it is difficult to conceive of a consistent way whereby, as Longuenesse argues, the categories both *are* the rules that govern the synthesis which, on the other hand, first *leads to the very formation* of the categories as such analytical rules (concepts). Moreover, how can figurative synthesis be the ground of intellectual synthesis

The second problem concerns space. Kant appears to be saying that the 'unity of space' presupposes a synthesis, which most likely would be figurative synthesis. He says this in B161n.[15] But it should be noted that Kant here makes an important distinction between space as 'form of intuition' and space as 'formal intuition', where only the latter provides the unity of space in terms of a unity applied to a spatial manifold through the unity of apperception. Hence, space as *formal intuition* presupposes a synthesis. By contrast, space as pure form of intuition *does not* presuppose a synthesis. The manifold of intuition as such does not contain any unity in the sense that Kant means here (in conformity with the main claim of § 15). However, confusingly Kant does also say in the note that in the Aesthetic he counted this unity of space as belonging to sensibility, and not as a unity that is imposed from the outside by the understanding, or an external act of synthesis. Aside from the question regarding what Kant means to say by saying that the unity belongs to sensibility—also because in the main text he says that it is not given *in* but only *with* the intuition (B161)— one wonders how such a synthetic unity is related to space. In the note (B160n.), Kant clearly says that form of intuition 'merely gives the manifold', and that the unity is only contained in the *formal intuition*. There is thus reason to believe that, since he claims that in the Aesthetic unity was counted as belonging to sensibility, Kant there does not make a distinction between form of intuition and formal intuition. Given the focus on the specific features of space (and time) in the Aesthetic, independently of the role of the understanding in cognitively determining space—a task reserved for the Analytic—that would make sense (see Onof & Schulting 2015).

Now, to return to the second problem more in particular: if the 'unity of space' that Kant counted as belonging to sensibility in the Aesthetic, is the unity imposed on the manifold by the understanding from the outside, as it were, then the question is what the role of space as 'mere manifold' can still be. That is, if formal intuition gives the unity of space, how much of space is there in the 'mere manifold', and what could that mean?[16] At issue here is the phenomenological character of space. Indeed, Longuenesse (1998: 219, 222–3) has claimed that Kant's distinction in the note between form of intuition and formal intuition is not a meaningful distinction. The two are all but the same. Secondly, if the unity of space is the same unity that is established by figurative synthesis (and a fortiori the understanding), then there is at least the threat of a

---

if it is rather the latter which is more general than the former, corresponding to the 'two-step' structure of the B-Deduction?

15 For extensive discussion, see Onof & Schulting (2015).
16 See again the discussion of Land (2014) above.

reduction of space as intuition to a concept, precisely what Kant argues against in the Aesthetic. Of course, one could still insist that figurative synthesis is a preconceptual operation and thus fully compatible with the view that space is *not* a concept or category (cf. Friedman 2012: 248). But above I have pointed out the philosophical and interpretative problems with the view that figurative synthesis is not a (conceptualising, i.e. categorial) act of the understanding. Friedman maintains that

> the same original synthesis precedes all (schematized) categories or pure concepts of the understanding, and therefore precedes all (schematized) concepts whatsoever […] none of which are identical with the 'action of the understanding on sensibility' that first gives both space and time their characteristic unity and singularity. (2012: 248–9)

The problem with Friedman's reading is twofold: (1) he mistakes the sui generis unity of space and time for the unity of apperception (original synthesis), and (2) he mistakenly interprets the 'action of the understanding on sensibility', which supposedly on his reading generates the unity of space, as somehow operating independently of or separately from the action of the schematisation of the categories. This violates against the *Leitfaden* argument and it begs the question of how 'the action of the understanding on sensibility' is related, and by what means, to the schematisation of the categories if the categories are precisely nothing but the a priori concepts *of the understanding*. (See the earlier discussion in this section.)

11.6 The Distinction Between Metaphysical and Geometric Space

I propose that we read the distinction between space as form of intuition and as formal intuition differently.[17] That is, we should distinguish between the sui generis unity of space and the synthetic unity bestowed on the spatial manifold from the side of the subject. The sui generis unity of space cannot be reduced to the synthetic unity that the understanding generates, although of course it is precisely the goal of the Deduction to show that the sui generis unity of space and the synthetic unity produced by the understanding correspond insofar as the *determination* of the unity of space is concerned, but not to the extent that space as a whole is concerned (the unity of space as a whole is and remains underdetermined). This differentiation between the sui generis unity of space and

---

[17] For this section, I rely on the account that is given in Onof & Schulting (2014).

the synthetic unity due to the understanding corresponds to the distinction that Kant makes, in his unpublished tract *On Kästner's Treatises*, between metaphysical space and geometric space. Figurative synthesis is responsible for the generation of geometric space, but not metaphysical space, not even the latter's sui generis unity, as Land (2014) suggests (see Section 11.4 above). So any sui generis unity that metaphysical space has is not one that is due to the operation of the understanding by means of the transcendental imagination, but is rather intrinsic to space itself and independent of any unifying act of the understanding (i.e. a priori synthesis).

Before we go into detail about the sui generis unity of space, what does Kant mean by the distinction between metaphysical and geometric space? Very succinctly put, metaphysical space is a given absolute infinite magnitude, as Kant defines space in the Metaphysical Exposition of the Aesthetic (A25/B39–40). Geometric space, on the other hand, is a potential infinite. Space *stricte dictum* is metaphysical space, 'i.e. originally, nonetheless merely subjectively given space'. This is space as pure intuition, which is a singular representation (OKT, AA 20: 421), 'cannot be brought under any concept', and 'contains the ground of the construction of all possible geometrical concepts' (OKT, AA 20: 420), Euclidean or non-Euclidean ones. Metaphysical space is 'the pure form of the sensible mode of representation of the subject' (OKT, AA 20: 421). Geometric space, by contrast, is in fact not a single space, but rather a plurality of spaces or subspaces that are defined by the conceptual determinations of regions of metaphysical space; metaphysical space, on the other hand, is 'space [...] considered in the way it is **given**, *before all determination of it*' (OKT, AA 20: 419, italics added; cf. B41, Prol § 9, AA 4: 282).

The possibility of, for example, extending a straight line indefinitely, i.e. 'successively generating all its parts from one point' (A162/B203) is *grounded on* the givenness of infinite space. This is what the term 'metaphysical space' indicates. The 'many spaces' of which Kant speaks in the Kästner essay concern the geometrical determinations or constructions—by means of the successive synthesis of the imagination—that are to be thought of as 'parts of the unitary original space' (OKT, AA 20: 419), i.e. 'a proper subset of the determinations of the single metaphysical space' (Patton 2011: 282–3). As Kant points out, the fact that I can extend a line to infinity is made possible by the fact that 'the space in which I describe the line, is greater than every one line which I may describe in it' (OKT, AA 20: 420). Metaphysical space is originally *given* as infinite, and is always already greater than any subset of geometrical determinations of space; by contrast, geometric space is 'made' (a term Kästner himself uses) or constructed by means of the synthesis of the imagination and so finite with respect to metaphysical space. Therefore, metaphysical space, original unitary given space, cannot be dependent on, and be generated by, the synthesis of imagination, since the latter is the act of construction, hence the determining factor in determining a finite space, not the determinable given space. The possibility of the synthetic act of constructing a space is grounded on the prior givenness of metaphysical space. It is an analytic truth that *the act of construction cannot generate that on which what is generated by it is grounded*.

Now to the unity of space. The sui generis unity of space, as expounded in the Metaphysical Exposition of the Aesthetic, is contrasted with conceptual unity, which is a unity of a multiplicity of representations contained under a higher representation (A69/B94, A78/104). The representation of space is just the representation of a unique, single space, which is not subsumable under a higher space, as it would be if space were a concept. Rather, the sui generis unity of space is the unity *in* which the multiple parts are contained, and is the 'single all-encompassing space' whose parts are 'only thought *in it*' (A25/B39). The unity of space is an absolute unity, or a *totum analyticum* (R3789, AA 17: 293), so not a synthetic whole, which is based on the combination of given parts.[18] All parts or regions of space share the same analytical feature of belonging to the same unique, originally given space. In contrast to conceptual unity, the sui generis unity of space is defined by its singularity (uniqueness), mereological inversion (the whole precedes its parts, implying infinite divisibility), and infinity (B39–40).

To mark the difference between the synthetic unity conferred on the manifold by the understanding through the transcendental synthesis of imagination, and the sui generis unity of space, this spatial unity can be called 'unicity'. The 'unicity' of space is, as said, defined by the essential characteristics of space: its (1) singularity; (2) infinity; and (3) mereological inversion. Further topological characteristics of space are: (4) its continuity (no gaps in space; and its absence cannot be represented); (5) externality (relation between parts of space); (6) its homogeneity (the 'outside another' relation applies to all parts of space, which are only numerically different; mutual exteriority of the components of a partition of space) and (7) centred externality (space is represented outside *me*, i.e. it is the form of outer sense). These characteristics of space form the basis of all possible spatial determinations.[19] The 'unicity' of space and the unity of the understanding, by virtue of the unity of apperception, must some-

---

18 Synthesis always proceeds part to whole, hence space and time cannot be generated by synthesis, since their parts are posterior to the whole (A24–5/B39, A77/B103, A169–70/B211, A438/B466; cf. KU, AA 5: 407, 409, OKT, 20: 419, and R5248, AA 18: 130–1; to this last reference I was directed by Fichant 1997: 31).
19 For more discussion see Onof & Schulting (2015).

how be shown to match, thus enabling perceptual knowledge of spatiotemporal objects, but the former ('unicity') is at any rate not claimed by Kant to be reducible to the latter unity.[20] Neither is it the case that the 'unicity' of space is due to figurative synthesis, since, as I have said above, this synthesis is a determining[21] act of the understanding on inner sense and hence cannot do justice to the unique phenomenological features of space, i.e. its character as infinite given magnitude, and as singular. The determining and the determinable must be kept apart, on pain of making Kant into a German Idealist who confuses transcendental and existential conditions.[22] As I argued earlier, the understanding cannot generate space as a single all-encompassing magnitude, which as Kant says in the Kästner piece is 'the original representation of a unitary, infinite, *subjectively given* space', not 'the geometrically and objectively given space', which is always finite, since 'it is only given through its being *constructed [gemacht]*' (OKT, AA 20: 420). Such a claim—that synthesis generates space as a single all-encompassing magnitude—would also imply a conflation of Kant's explicit distinction between the roles of the two types of space, metaphysical and geometric space(s).

However, for the unicity of space to be grasped *as* a unity for the understanding, that is, grasped by the understanding by means of the unity of apperception, the unicity or unity of space presupposes a synthesis, as Kant says in the B160–1 note. This brings us to the key point of the 'second step' argument, namely: *What does it mean for the unicity of space to be grasped **as** a unity for the understanding?*

The unicity of space defines space as the horizon of all possible empirical objects, given that all the space that such objects occupy must be part of the one single space. The synthesis of the series of parts of space is however never complete, but can only take place in terms of a *progressus in indefinitum* (A511/B539); space is intrinsically underdetermined. But given the infinite divisibility of space, infinitely ever smaller objects can also be determined (a *regressus in infinitum*). The synthesis of apprehension of the manifold in a given empirical intuition enables us to perceive the given manifold of sensations as a

---

20 Longuenesse (1998: 83, 2005: 36) also emphasises this unicity, but for her both the unity and unicity of space are brought about by the understanding, whereas I contend that space's unicity is precisely not brought about by the understanding but characterises space essentially, wholly independently of the understanding.
21 Longuenesse claims that there is a pre-conceptual determining role for the understanding (1998: 222–3, 245), but this view is based on a mistaken distinction between the categories (intellectual synthesis) and figurative synthesis (see Section 11.5).
22 See Schulting (2016b).

unity defining a determinate spatiotemporal object, as part of geometric space (A120), against the background or horizon of the unity (i.e. unicity) of metaphysical space. Of course, geometric space and metaphysical space are in fact the same infinite space in which empirical objects can be perceived. The difference lies in the fact that geometric space is *determinate* space (and in fact consists of a plurality of spaces), for which figurative synthesis is the determining factor, and which enables us to locate and track empirical objects in space as well as construct geometrical figures in space; metaphysical space, on the other hand, is *determinable* space, space *simpliciter*, as the subjective condition of representing objects as spatial in the first place. When we determine the unity (i.e. unicity) of space as a unity for the understanding, by means of the unity of apperception, we of course do not determine space *qua* metaphysical space, with its sui generis unity (i.e. the unicity which defines space, as described earlier). Rather, we determine a particular space as a bounded object in geometrical space, and thus, through limitation, we determine space as consisting of an infinite unified plurality of spaces.

11.7 What Has Kant Actually Proven in the 'Second Step' of the B-Deduction?

To return to the topic of the goal of the Deduction: on my reading, the premise of the Deduction was the assumed *fact* of 'experience' in the strong sense of perceptual knowledge (C-experience), as well as the unproblematic fact of S-experience. This is not put to doubt by Kant. Neither one is the object of proof. But nor is even the *possibility* of S-experience at issue (as reading 3* believes). Only the *possibility* of C-experience is the object of proof, hence C-experience features as the premise of the Deduction (reading 3**). If this is true, then although this might appear exactly what Kant is claiming in § 26, Kant's conclusion cannot be that even perception itself, 'perceptually seeing or sensing' rather than 'perceptually knowing', is only possible due to the functions of the understanding. The conclusion of the proof cannot demonstrate more than what was assumed to be true in the premise. Kant, then, argues for the necessary (transcendental) conditions of C-experience, that is the possible perception of *objects*, not the necessary conditions of *mere* sense perception, in the sense of single instances of perceiving that are not combined into a unity with other such instances.

Kant says at the start of § 26:

> Now the possibility of cognizing *a priori through categories* **whatever objects *may come before our senses*, not as far as the form of their intuition but rather as far as the laws of their combination are concerned** [...] is to be explained. (B159, boldface mine)

This clearly demarcates the scope of the argument of the 'second step' to the possibility of the knowledge of *objects* that appear before our senses. Clearly, it is not the *mere intuition* of spatiotemporal objects that is to be explained here, as this has already been done in the Transcendental Aesthetic. However, in the next sentence of this passage (at B160), Kant seems less precise in defining the goal of the 'second step's argument:

> For if the categories did not serve in this way, it would not become clear why *everything that may ever come before our senses* must stand under the laws that arise *a priori* from the understanding alone. (B160, emphasis added)

This passage might be, and indeed has been, read as implying that Kant does after all strive to explain how perception itself (in its broadest sense) is possible. This appears to be confirmed by a passage further on in the section, at B161, where Kant says that '[c]onsequently all synthesis, *through which even perception itself becomes possible*, stands under the categories' (emphasis added). Kant appears to be arguing that

1. all synthesis of the manifold representations in a sensible intuition stands under the categories;

2. perception is grounded in a synthesis of the manifold of representations;

3. hence, perception stands under the categories;

4. experience is cognition through the connection of perceptions;

5. hence, experience stands under the categories.

But if this were indeed what Kant is arguing, then one is bound to conclude from this that Kant wants to prove that perception *simpliciter* requires the categories, and that a fortiori there is no intuition that does not entail categorial determination (if we take perception *simpliciter* to be identified with intuition; see the *Stufenleiter* at A320/B376–7). In this way, one is apt to believe Kant has shown, in the 'second step' of the B-Deduction, that the possibility that intuitions are not determined in accordance with the categories, has hereby been excluded. Kant has thus exorcised the possibility of 'transcendental chaos' (Allison 2012: 184), by showing that *all* intuitions whatsoever, and thus all possible perception,

11.7 What Has Kant Actually Proven in the 'Second Step' of the B-Deduction? — 315

are amenable to categorial determination. However, the use of the term 'perception' in Kant's text, and in the above argument, is ambiguous between *mere* perception and perception of objects, i.e. objective perception (A320/B376–7) (There remains a further question, which many point out is related to the modality of Kant's argument at B131, as to whether it is in principle possible that intuition or perception is not de facto categorially determined but should at least be *amenable* to categorial determination, but it is unclear to me what it could mean to have a perception that is not de facto categorially determined but must at the same time *be able* to be categorially determined, that is, to claim that perception per se has merely a necessary disposition to being categorially determined.)

But what does Kant in fact prove in the 'second step'? In the A-version of the Deduction, at A120, Kant provides an important clue as to how to read the link between the figurative synthesis of § 24 and the a priori synthesis of apprehension in § 26. Kant says namely, at A120, that the transcendental imagination is the faculty 'whose action exercised upon perceptions I call apprehension'. That is, the synthesis of apprehension is not a faculty distinct from transcendental imagination, but rather is the imagination *in* perception, more precisely, insofar as perceptions are synthetically united into one representation of an object. It is the *combination* of perceptions, not perception *simpliciter*, that is necessarily dependent on the categories. This is made clear by Kant in § 26 again and again:

> [T]he possibility of cognizing a priori *through categories* whatever objects *may come before our senses*, **not as far as the form of their intuition but rather as far as the laws of their combination** are concerned, [...] is to be explained. (B159, boldface mine)

> Thus even *unity of the synthesis* of the manifold, outside or within us, hence also **a combination with which everything that is to be represented as determined in space or time** must agree, is already given a priori, along with (not in) these intuitions, as condition of the synthesis of all *apprehension*. (B161, boldface mine)

> As mere representations [...], they stand under no law of connection at all except that which the connecting faculty prescribes. Now that which connects the manifold of sensible intuition is imagination, which depends on [the] understanding for the unity of the intellectual synthesis of the intuition and on sensibility for the manifoldness of apprehension. (B164, trans. emended and emphasis added)

> Now since all possible perception depends on the synthesis of apprehension, but the latter itself, this empirical synthesis, depends on the transcendental one, thus on the categories, all possible perceptions, hence everything that can ever reach empirical consciousness, i.e., all appearances of nature, *as far as their combination* is concerned, stand under the categories [...]. (B164–5, emphasis added)

In each of these passages, one notices a constraint on the claim advanced, namely, that *insofar as the combination of the manifold of representations or percep-*

tions is concerned, the manifold is subject to the categories. This fully comports with the line of reasoning starting in § 13 of the Deduction, which I discussed in detail in Schulting (2017, ch. 5),[23] and shows that Kant is committed to what I defined there as argument **M*** (not to be confused with argument M in Chapter 10), which shows a modal constraint on the claims Kant puts forward in the Deduction. **M*** says:

> Necessarily, *if* intuitions are to be seen as contributing to possible knowledge of objects, *then* intuitions are subsumed under the categories as the conceptual conditions under which knowledge of objects is possible.

We should heed the fact that the 'transcendental action of the imagination' is the 'synthetic influence of the understanding on the inner sense', which latter is itself just the mere manifold of representations ('the mere *form* of intuition') and in and of itself does not contain a combination of that manifold (B154). As was already made clear in § 15 of the B-Deduction, combination (*Verbindung*), hence synthesis, is not given in the manifold:

> Yet the *combination* (*conjunctio*) of a manifold in general can never come to us through the senses, and therefore cannot already be contained in the pure form of sensible intuition. […] [A]mong all representations *combination* is the only one that is not given through objects but can be executed only by the subject itself […]. (B129–30)

Equally, in the notorious note to B160, Kant makes it clear that the form of intuition does not yet contain the '*comprehension* [*Zusammenfassung*] of the manifold'; it 'merely gives the manifold', but not yet 'unity of the representation'. Thus, in the conclusion to the B-Deduction, in § 26, Kant is not suddenly claiming that mere sense perception, indeed the very form of intuition as the merely given manifold, is after all united *per se*. If it were indeed the case that Kant argues in the concluding section of the B-Deduction that, necessarily, all intuitions or perceptions in the broadest sense stand under the categories and are thus synthetically united, then this plainly contradicts his earlier statements that intuition or perception does not in and of itself contain the element of combination, namely a priori synthesis.

What Kant instead shows in the 'second step' of the B-Deduction is what it means for us to grasp the unicity of space *as* a unity for the understanding. It is shown in §§ 24 and 26 specifically that by virtue of the very same act of spontaneity that enables any discursive thinker to combine the manifold of representa-

---

[23] See also Schulting (2015b).

tions in any arbitrary sensible intuition (human or other), as was shown in the 'first step' of the B-Deduction, the unity (i.e. unicity) of *space* (and time) can be determined objectively through the understanding, by means of the categories, in virtue of the unity of apperception. Kant wants to say that despite the absolute, irreducible distinction between the forms of sensibility and the forms of the understanding, i.e. the categories, which shows their reciprocal irreducibility, we are capable of grasping space and time as objects for the understanding, not *qua* space and time, that is, *qua* infinite given magnitudes, but in terms of bounded objects *in* space and time (i.e. determinate spaces and times).

This fundamental grasp of, or, acquaintance with what is the opposite of our conceptuality, namely, the pure intuitions space and time, and every object which is contained in it, is shown to obtain by showing how the transcendental unity of apperception unites the manifold of representation in a spatiotemporal intuition, by virtue of the synthesis of apprehension. We have an intimate grasp of empirical objects in space and time, not because space and time itself are first generated by the understanding, or by the synthesis of the imagination, as Friedman, Land, Longuenesse and others claim, but because we know, in virtue of the fundamental structure of our thought—i.e. in virtue of the fact that it is governed by characteristic functions—what it means to determine, by means of these same functions, which are then called categories, objects in space and time (cf. *Prol*, AA 4: 318). We do not just encounter these objects in space and time and then happen to be able to determine them logically. How would we be able to know that we determine them correctly if this were indeed the manner in which we were confronted with objects? We are rather intimately familiar with them at the most fundamental level, in our sensible relation to them, because by virtue of the transcendental unity of apperception, through its 'synthetic influence [...] on the inner sense' (B154), by combining the given manifold in *an empirical* intuition, objects are first determined as bounded objects in space as a unitary whole of which the bounded object is a constituent part. This determination has an epistemic and ontological aspect, as we shall see in the next section. Spatiotemporal objects themselves, not just their knowledge, are in some sense first constituted by the transcendental synthesis of the imagination, in contrast to space and time *qua* space and time (*qua* infinite given magnitudes), which as such are and remain fully independent of any subjective act of synthesis.

Combination of intuitions, not mere intuition, is what is argued, in § 26, to be wholly dependent on the subjective agency of synthesis. The conclusion of the Deduction is thus that knowledge of objects, which consists in the connection of perceptions (B161), essentially and wholly depends on subjective functions of thought or the capacity to judge by virtue of transcendental apperception, given sensory input, which is the thesis of radical subjectivism I argued for in Schulting (2017a). It is difficult to *understand* though, for a human being endowed with the capacity to judge, what it could mean for one to have intuitions that are *not* synthesised, that is, to have 'merely [a] manifold' (*bloß Mannigfaltiges*) (B160n.) of representations. It would be less than perception of determinate spatial objects, since, given the absence of any synthesis of the aggregate parts of the manifold representations, the categories enabling the determination of such objects would be lacking. One would merely be varying representations in time, though one would of course oneself still be located in space, and be able to have perceptions. But any unity between oneself, as the one who has the intuition or intuitions, and the sui generis unity of space, would be contingent—which does not mean that the empirical (causal etc.) laws governing one's bodily movements would not apply; it just means that in the case of arbitrarily varying one's representations, the rules governing one's movements *have not been determined as* necessarily applying, since the unity of apperception is ex hypothesi not involved.

Kant's goal in the Deduction is to show that insofar as the determinate perceptual knowledge of spatially located objects and their very objectivity in space is concerned, our intuitions necessarily entail a priori synthesis (the transcendental unity of apperception) and thus the categories. However, he does not (and cannot) exclude the real possibility that occurrent intuitions or perceptions do not agree with figurative synthesis and hence with the transcendental unity of apperception, in which case no perceptual knowledge would result and no objectivity could be established, but nor would we even be aware of them *as* our intuitions. As Kant says in the A-Deduction, at A116:

> All intuitions are nothing for us and do not in the least concern us if they cannot be taken up into consciousness, whether they influence it directly or indirectly, and through this alone is cognition possible.

11.8 The Idealism of Nature

There is one remaining element in the concluding § 26 that may arouse puzzlement. Kant writes that

> laws [of appearances in nature] exist just as little in the appearances, but rather exist only relative to the subject in which the appearances inhere, insofar as it has understanding, as appearances do not exist in themselves, but only relative to the same being, insofar as it has senses. (B164)

11.8 The Idealism of Nature

What Kant seems to be committed to here is the plainest form of reductive phenomenalist idealism: the laws of nature do not exist in the objects of nature themselves, or in nature itself, but are entirely due to the experiencing subject who imposes them on the objects. The objects of nature are lawfully governed and connected *only insofar as* the subject has knowledge of them *and senses them*. In fact, as Kant says, nature 'depends' upon the categories, 'as the original ground of its necessary lawfulness' (B165). It is the subject that makes and prescribes laws to nature (cf. B159–60), rather than nature being that which is given prior to, and independently of, the subject's sensory experience of it.

Similarly, in the A-Deduction at A114, Kant says that 'nature should direct itself according to our subjective ground of apperception, indeed in regard to its lawfulness even depend on this'. This is what amounts to Kant's idealism about nature itself. Nature *itself* is ideal, not just our experience of it. In the A-Deduction version of the argument, this is made very explicit:

> [I]f one considers that this nature is nothing in itself but a sum of appearances, hence not a thing in itself but merely a multitude of representations of the mind, then one will not be astonished to see it [i.e. nature] *solely in the radical faculty of all our knowledge*, namely, *transcendental apperception*, in that unity on account of which alone it can be called object of all possible experience, i.e., nature. (A114, trans. emended and emphasis added)

This raises the question of how we should understand the claim that the categories make nature possible, to the extent that nature depends on them. Kant writes:

> Categories are concepts that prescribe laws *a priori* to appearances, thus to nature as the sum total of all appearances (*natura materialiter spectata*), and, since they are not derived from nature and do not follow it as their pattern (for they would otherwise be merely empirical), the question now arises how it is to be conceived that nature must follow them, i.e., how they can determine *a priori* the combination of the manifold of nature without deriving from the latter. (B163)

What should be clear from the start is that Kant makes a distinction between nature seen from a material or empirical perspective (*natura materialiter spectata*) and nature considered from a formal or transcendental perspective (*natura formaliter spectata*; B165). Further, nature is never just an aggregate of things. In the *Prolegomena*, Kant writes that '[n]ature considered *materialiter*' amounts to the '*totality of all objects of experience*' (*Prol*, AA 4: 295), or as Kant puts it here in the *Critique*, 'the sum total of all appearances' (B163; cf. A114). But, at the same time nature in the formal sense 'is the *existence* of things, *so far as it is determined according to universal laws*' (*Prol*, AA 4: 294, emphasis added); it 'denotes the conformity to law of the determinations of the existence of things *generally*' (*Prol*, AA 4: 295, emphasis added). Thus, while the *whole of material nature* is subject to determination by the a priori laws that are prescribed by the categories, as Kant says in the above quote from B163, it is not *qua* the material existence of empirical or physical nature, that is, the *fact* that it exists, but only insofar as material objects are 'combined', i.e. determined, in accordance with these a priori laws, that nature is so subject. It is thus only under the formal perspective (*formaliter spectata*) that nature stands wholly under, and is dependent on, the categories. These laws of nature are a priori general laws, to which all objects are subject insofar as objects obey universal principles such as that 'substance is permanent', or 'every event is determined by a cause according to constant laws' (*Prol*, AA 4: 295), including the laws that a priori determine, by means of the categories of quality, the intensive magnitude of spatial objects, the *material stuff* that nature is made of.[24] The categories only prescribe an a priori lawfulness that describes how objects in nature obey a certain rule-governedness in general, namely, to the extent that objects in nature, and thus nature as the whole of objects, are such objects only as determined, in their very givenness, by the unity of apperception, that is, are permanent phenomenal substances, which are bound by the law of causality, interact in a community of distinct objects, and are spatially located and bounded. The a posteriori element of experience of nature, and so the a posteriori element of empirical nature itself—that is, the very *fact* of there being *particular* natural objects and events—can be established and determined only by means of experience itself: 'Experience must be added in order to come to know *particular laws*' (B165). The understanding thus cannot prescribe a lawfulness for objects in terms of *particular* empirical natural laws, which cannot as such be derived from the categories and are 'only particular determinations of the pure laws of the understanding' (A128; cf. A126).

This then could be called the 'idealism' of nature: nature *in general*, and its lawfulness *in general* is constituted by, and thus wholly dependent on, the 'subjective laws, under which alone an empirical cognition of things is possible', but

---

24 The distinction between *natura materialiter spectata* and *natura formaliter spectata* should not be read as if it suggested that the *matter* of nature is not subject to the ideal subject's faculty of determining nature formally. The matter of nature is as much ideal as is its form, insofar as matter is that to which our determinable sensations refer. Rather, Kant speaks of a dual *perspective* (hence *spectata*) from which nature can be seen: looking at nature from the material perspective means to look at it merely empirically (as what physical scientists do), while looking at it from the formal perspective means to look at it in terms of explaining its general metaphysical grounds of possibility (*metaphysica generalis*). However, nature as a whole, *including its particular laws*, is ideal, for particular natural laws are just 'particular determinations of the pure laws of the understanding' (A128), and thus are, qua laws, ultimately *grounded on* the a priori laws that make nature ideal.

also 'hold good of these things as objects of possible experience (not as things in themselves [...])' (*Prol*, AA 4: 296). These a priori laws of nature are subjective, not because they concern psychologically necessary laws of the *experience* of nature or 'rules of the observation of a nature that is already given', whereby the possibility of experience is already presupposed, but they are subjective because they *first constitute* nature itself and the very possibility of the experience of nature (*Prol*, AA 4: 297). If the laws of nature were contained in the objects themselves, and Kant's analysis would concern the study of these laws by means of experience, then those laws would not be *a priori* laws (cf. *Prol*, AA 4: 297, A125). They would not tell us anything about nature *qua* the very conception of nature, and its very possibility—what it means to conceive of nature at all, and as a result no natural science would be possible. Kant writes in the *Prolegomena*:

> There are many laws of nature which we can only know by means of experience; but conformity to law in the connection of appearances, i.e., nature in general, we cannot discover by any experience, because experience itself requires laws which are *a priori* at the basis of its possibility. *The possibility of experience in general is therefore at the same time the universal law of nature, and the principles of experience are the very laws of nature.* For we know nature as nothing but the totality of appearances, i.e., of representations in us; and hence we can only derive the law of their connection from the principles of their connection in us, that is, from the conditions of their necessary unification in a consciousness, which constitutes the possibility of experience. (*Prol*, AA 4: 318–19, emphasis added)

The 'highest legislation of nature', as Kant says, 'lie[s] in ourselves', in the conditions of possible experience, that is, the forms of space and time and the categories, as the 'principles of [the] connection' of appearances or representations (*Prol*, AA 4: 319). The understanding itself is the 'legislation for nature' and 'the source of the laws of nature', and 'without understanding there would not be any nature at all'. The a priori rule-governedness of nature lies in the 'synthetic unity of the manifold of appearances in accordance with rules', hence, since the necessary synthetic unity of the manifold is first established by an act of transcendental apperception, Kant is licensed to claim that it is the 'unity of apperception [that] is the transcendental ground of the necessary lawfulness of all appearances in an experience', that is, of nature itself (all quotations from A126–7). Only in this manner, by taking nature as grounded on the unity of apperception, is it possible to determine something a priori of nature. The pure or universal laws of nature are not drawn from experience through observation, but both they and our experience of law-governed nature are first constituted by the conditions of possible experience. Indeed, nature and possible experience are quite the same, and as the conformity to law in the latter depends upon the necessary connection of appearances in experience (without which we cannot cognize any object whatever in the sensible world), consequently upon the original laws of the understanding, it seems at first strange, but is not the less certain, to say: *the understanding does not derive its laws (a priori) from, but prescribes them to, nature.* (*Prol*, AA 4: 320)

In a word, 'the understanding is the origin of the universal order of nature' (*Prol*, AA 4: 322). Thus, it is 'we ourselves [that] bring into appearances that order and regularity in them that we call *nature*' (A125). It is the very subjective ground of experience and its objects, i.e. the 'unity of apperception', which is 'the transcendental ground of the necessary lawfulness of all appearances in an experience', hence of nature itself, which, to be sure, receives merely its 'formal possibility' from it, not its material possibility (A127). This claim reinforces my thesis about Kant's deduction of the categories as conditions of possible experience *from* apperception.

Bibliography of Secondary Literature

Allais, L. (2009) 'Kant, Non-Conceptual Content and the Representation of Space', *Journal of the History of Philosophy* 47(3): 383–413.
—. (2015) *Manifest Reality. Kant's Idealism and his Realism* (Oxford: Oxford University Press).
Allison, H. (1983) *Kant's Transcendental Idealism. An Interpretation and Defense* (New Haven: Yale University Press).
—. (1996) *Idealism and Freedom. Essays on Kant's Theoretical and Practical Philosophy* (Cambridge: Cambridge University Press).
—. (2000) 'Where Have All the Categories Gone? Reflections on Longuenesse's Reading of Kant's Transcendental Deduction', *Inquiry* 43(1): 67–80.
—. (2001) *Kant's Theory of Taste. A Reading of the 'Critique of Aesthetic Judgment'* (Cambridge: Cambridge University Press).
—. (2004) *Kant's Transcendental Idealism. An Interpretation and Defense*, revised and enlarged edition (New Haven: Yale University Press).
—. (2012) *Essays on Kant* (Oxford: Oxford University Press).
—. (2015) *Kant's Transcendental Deduction. An Analytical-Historical Commentary* (Oxford: Oxford University Press).
Ameriks, K. (1978) 'Kant's Transcendental Deduction as a Regressive Argument', *Kant-Studien* 69(3): 273–87.
—. (1983) 'Kant and Guyer on Apperception', *Archiv für Geschichte der Philosophie* 65(2): 174–86.
—. (2000a) *Kant's Theory of Mind*, new edition (Oxford: Clarendon Press).
—. (2000b) *Kant and the Fate of Autonomy. Problems in the Appropriation of the Critical Philosophy* (Cambridge: Cambridge University Press).
—. (2001a) 'Kant on Science and Common Knowledge', in E. Watkins (ed.) *Kant and the Sciences* (New York: Oxford University Press, 2001), pp. 31–52.
—. (2001b) 'Text and Context: Hermeneutical Prolegomena to Interpreting a Kant Text', in D. Schönecker & Th. Zwenger (eds) (2001) *Kant verstehen/Understanding Kant. Über die Interpretation philosophischer Texte* (Darmstadt: Wissenschaftliche Buchgesellschaft), pp. 11–31.
—. (2003a) 'Problems from Van Cleve's Kant: Experience and Objects', *Philosophy and Phenomenological Research* 66(1): 196–202.
—. (2003b) *Interpreting Kant's 'Critiques'* (Oxford: Clarendon Press).
—. (2005) 'A Commonsense Kant?', *Proceedings and Addresses of the American Philosophical Association* 79(2): 19–45.
—. (2006) *Kant and the Historical Turn* (Oxford: Clarendon Press).
Aportone, A. (2009) *Gestalten der transzendentalen Einheit. Bedingungen der Synthesis bei Kant* (Berlin/New York: de Gruyter).
—. (2014) *Kant et le pouvoir réceptif. Recherches sur la conception kantienne de la sensibilité* (Paris: L'Harmattan).
Aschenberg, R. (1988) 'Einiges über Selbstbewußtsein als Prinzip der Transzendentalphilosophie', in Forum für Philosophie Bad Homburg (ed.) *Kants transzendentale Deduktion und die Möglichkeit von Transzendentalphilosophie* (Frankfurt a.M: Suhrkamp), pp. 51–69.

Balfour, A. (1878) 'Transcendentalism', *Mind* 3(12): 480–505.
Banham, G. (2006) *Kant's Transcendental Imagination* (Basingstoke/New York: Palgrave Macmillan).
Barth, K. (1985) *Die protestantische Theologie im 19. Jahrhundert* (Zürich: Theologischer Verlag).
Bauer, N. (2010) 'Kant's Subjective Deduction', *British Journal for the History of Philosophy* 18 (3): 433–60.
—. (2012) 'A Peculiar Intuition. Kant's Conceptualist Account of Perception', *Inquiry* 55(3): 215–37.
Baum, M. (1986) *Deduktion und Beweis in Kants Transzendentalphilosophie* (Königstein/Ts: Athenäum).
—. (2001) 'Systemform und Selbsterkenntnis der Vernunft bei Kant', in H. Fulda & J. Stolzenburg (eds) (2001) *Architektonik und System in der Philosophie Kants* (Hamburg: Meiner), pp. 25–40.
Beck, L. W. (1978) 'Did the Sage of Königsberg Have no Dreams?', in L. W. Beck, *Essays on Kant and Hume* (New Haven: Yale University Press, 1978), pp. 38–60.
—. (1984) 'Kant's Theory of Definition', in M. Gram (ed.) (1984) *Kant: Disputed Questions*, 2nd edition (Atascadero: Ridgeview), pp. 291–303.
—. (1989) 'Two Ways of Reading Kant's Letter to Herz: Comments on Carl', in E. Förster (ed.) (1989) *Kant's Transcendental Deductions. The Three 'Critiques' and the 'Opus postumum'* (Stanford: Stanford University Press), pp. 21–6.
Bird, G. (2006) *The Revolutionary Kant. A Commentary on the 'Critique of Pure Reason'* (Chicago/LaSalle, IL: Open Court).
Brandt, R. (1991) *Die Urteilstafel. Kritik der reinen Vernunft A67–76;B91–101* (Hamburg: Meiner).
Brandt, R. & W. Stark (eds) (1987) *Neue Autographen und Dokumente zu Kants Leben, Schriften und Vorlesungen*, Kant-Forschungen, Band 1 (Hamburg: Meiner).
—. (eds) (1994) *Autographen, Dokumente und Berichte*, Kant-Forschungen, Bd. 5 (Hamburg: Meiner).
Brook, A. (1994) *Kant and the Mind* (Cambridge: Cambridge University Press).
Butts, R. (1981) 'Rules, Examples and Constructions. Kant's Theory of Mathematics', *Synthese* 47(2): 257–88.
Callanan, J. (2006) 'Kant's Transcendental Strategy', *Philosophical Quarterly* 56: 360–81.
—. (2011) 'Normativity and the Acquisition of the Categories', *Bulletin of the Hegel Society of Great Britain* 63: 1–26.
Carl, W. (1989a) *Der schweigende Kant* (Göttingen: Vandenhoeck & Ruprecht).
—. (1989b) 'Kant's First Drafts of the Deduction of the Categories', in E. Förster (ed.) (1989) *Kant's Transcendental Deductions. The Three 'Critiques' and the 'Opus postumum'* (Stanford: Stanford University Press), pp. 3–20.
—. (1992) *Die transzendentale Deduktion der Kategorien in der ersten Auflage der 'Kritik der reinen Vernunft'. Ein Kommentar* (Frankfurt a.M: Klostermann).
—. (1998) 'Die transzendentale Deduktion in der zweiten Auflage (B129–169)', in G. Mohr & M. Willaschek (eds), *Klassiker Auslegen: Immanuel Kant, Kritik der reinen Vernunft* (Berlin: Akademie Verlag, 1998), pp. 189–216.
—. (2007) 'Das Subjektive als Bedingung des Objektiven', in J. Stolzenburg (ed.) (2007) *Kant in der Gegenwart* (Berlin/New York: de Gruyter), pp. 113–29.

Cassam, Q. (1987) 'Transcendental Arguments, Transcendental Synthesis and Transcendental Idealism', *Philosophical Quarterly* 37: 355–78.
—. (2007) *The Possibility of Knowledge* (Oxford: Oxford University Press).
—. (2008) 'Reply to Longuenesse', *Philosophy and Phenomenological Research* 77(2): 525–31.
Castañeda, H.-N. (1990) 'The Role of Apperception in Kant's Transcendental Deduction of the Categories', *Noûs* 24(1): 147–57.
Cohen, H. (1907) *Kommentar zu Kants Kritik der reinen Vernunft* (Leipzig: Meiner).
—. (1987) *Kants Theorie der Erfahrung*, 1918 edition (Hildesheim: Olms).
Collins, A. (1999) *Possible Experience. Understanding Kant's 'Critique of Pure Reason'* (Berkeley: University of California Press).
Conant, J. (2016) 'Why Kant is not a Kantian', *Philosophical Topics* 44(1): 75–125.
Deppermann, A. (2001) 'Eine analytische Interpretation von Kants "Ich denke"', *Kant-Studien* 92(2): 129–52.
Dickerson, A. (2004) *Kant on Representation and Objectivity* (Cambridge: Cambridge University Press).
Di Giovanni, G. & H. S. Harris (eds) (2000) *Between Kant and Hegel*, revised edition (Indianapolis: Hackett).
Düsing, K. (2010) 'Apperzeption und Selbstaffektion in Kants *Kritik der reinen Vernunft*. Das Kernstück der "transzendentalen Deduktion" der Kategorien', in N. Fischer (ed.) *Kants Grundlegung einer kritischen Metaphysik. Einführung in die 'Kritik der reinen Vernunft'* (Hamburg: Meiner, 2010), pp. 139–53.
Dyck, C. (2014) 'The Function of Derivation and the Derivation of Functions: A Review of Schulting's *Kant's Deduction and Apperception*', *Studi kantiani* XXVII: 69–75.
Edwards, J. (2000) *Substance, Force, and the Possibility of Knowledge* (Berkeley/Los Angeles: University of California Press).
Erdmann, B. (1878) *Kants Kriticismus in der ersten und in der zweiten Auflage der Kritik der reinen Vernunft* (Leipzig: Leopold Voss).
Falkenstein, L. (1996) 'Review of Klaus Reich, *The Completeness of Kant's Table of Judgments* (Stanford: Stanford UP, 1992)', *Kant-Studien* 87(4): 455–77.
Fichant, M. (1997) '"L'espace est representé comme une grandeur infinie donnée": La radicalité de l'esthétique', *Philosophie* 56: 20–48.
Forster, M. (2008) *Kant and Skepticism* (Princeton: Princeton University Press).
Frede, M. & L. Krüger (1970) 'Über die Zuordnung der Quantitäten des Urteils und der Kategorien der Grösse bei Kant', *Kant-Studien* 61(1): 28–49.
Friedman, M. (2012) 'Kant on Geometry and Spatial Intuition', *Synthese* 186(1): 231–55.
—. (2015) *Kant's Construction of Nature. A Reading of the 'Metaphysical Foundations of Natural Science'* (Cambridge: Cambridge University Press).
Golob, S. (2016) 'Why the Transcendental Deduction is Compatible with Nonconceptualism', in D. Schulting (ed.) *Kantian Nonconceptualism* (London/New York: Macmillan), pp. 27–52.
Gram, M. (1984) 'Do Transcendental Arguments Have a Future?', in M. Gram (ed.) (1984) *Kant: Disputed Questions*, 2nd edition (Atascadero: Ridgeview), pp. 133–66.
Greenberg, R. (2001) *Kant's Theory of A Priori Knowledge* (University Park, PA: The Pennsylvania State University Press).

Grüne, S. (2009) *Blinde Anschauung. Die Rolle von Begriffen in Kants Theorie sinnlicher Synthesis* (Frankfurt a.M: Klostermann).
Guyer, P. (1979) 'Review of D. Henrich, *Identität und Objektivität: Eine Untersuchung über Kants transzendentale Deduktion* (Heidelberg: Carl Winther, 1976)', *Journal of Philosophy* 76(3): 151–67.
——. (1980) 'Kant on Apperception and *A Priori* Synthesis', *American Philosophical Quarterly* 17(3): 205–12.
——. (1987) *Kant and the Claims of Knowledge* (Cambridge: Cambridge University Press).
——. (1992) 'The Transcendental Deduction of the Categories', in P. Guyer (ed.) (1992) *The Cambridge Companion to Kant* (Cambridge: Cambridge University Press), pp. 123–60.
——. (2001) 'Naturalizing Kant', in D. Schönecker & Th. Zwenger (eds) (2001) *Kant verstehen/Understanding Kant. Über die Interpretation philosophischer Texte* (Darmstadt: Wissenschaftliche Buchgesellschaft), pp. 59–84.
——. (2003) 'Review of Karl Ameriks, *Kant and the Fate of Autonomy* (Cambridge: Cambridge UP, 2000)', *Mind* 112: 87–94.
——. (2006) *Kant* (London/New York: Routledge).
——. (2010) 'The Deduction of the Categories: the Metaphysical and Transcendental Deductions', in P. Guyer (ed.) (2010) *The Cambridge Companion to Kant's 'Critique of Pure Reason'* (Cambridge: Cambridge University Press), pp. 118–50.
Hanna, R. (2011) 'Kant's Non-Conceptualism, Rogue Objects, and the Gap in the B Deduction', *International Journal of Philosophical Studies* 19(3): 399–415.
——. (2013) 'The Togetherness Principle, Kant's Conceptualism, and Kant's Nonconceptualism', *Stanford Encyclopedia of Philosophy*, ed. E. Zalta, http://plato.stanford.edu/archives/fall2013/entries/kant-judgment/supplement1.html.
Heidegger, M. (1991) *Kant und das Problem der Metaphysik*, Gesamtausgabe, I. Abteilung, Bd. 3 (Frankfurt a.M: Klostermann).
——. (1993) *Sein und Zeit* (Tübingen: Niemeyer).
——. (1995) *Phänomenologische Interpretation von Kants Kritik der reinen Vernunft*, Gesamtausgabe, II. Abteilung, Bd. 25 (Frankfurt a.M: Klostermann).
Heidemann, I. (1958) *Spontaneität und Zeitlichkeit* (Cologne: Kölner Universitäts-Verlag).
Heimsoeth, H. (1956) *Studien zur Philosophie Immanuel Kants*, Gesammelte Abhandlungen, Bd. I (Cologne: Kölner Universitäts-Verlag).
——. (1963) 'Zur Herkunft und Entwicklung von Kants Kategorientafel', *Kant-Studien* 54(4): 376–403.
——. (1966) *Kants Transzendentale Dialektik. Ein Kommentar zu Kants Kritik der reinen Vernunft*, Bd. I (Berlin: de Gruyter).
Henrich, D. (1967) *Fichtes ursprüngliche Einsicht* (Frankfurt a.M: Klostermann).
——. (1976) *Identität und Objektivität: Eine Untersuchung über Kants transzendentale Deduktion* (Heidelberg: Carl Winter Verlag).
——. (1988) 'Die Identität des Subjekts in der transzendentalen Deduktion', in H. Oberer & G. Seel (eds) *Kant. Analysen—Probleme—Kritik* (Würzburg: Königshausen & Neumann), pp. 39–70.
——. (1989) 'Kant's Notion of a Deduction and the Methodological Background of the First Critique', in E. Förster (ed.) (1989) *Kant's Transcendental Deductions. The Three 'Critiques' and the 'Opus postumum'* (Stanford: Stanford University Press), pp. 29–46.
——. (1998) 'Subjektivität als Prinzip', *Deutsche Zeitschrift für Philosophie* 46(1): 31–44.

Hogan, D. (2010) 'Kant's Copernican Turn and the Rationalist Tradition', in P. Guyer (ed.) (2010) *The Cambridge Companion to Kant's 'Critique of Pure Reason'* (Cambridge: Cambridge University Press), pp. 21–40.
Hoppe, H. (1983) *Synthesis bei Kant. Das Problem der Verbindung von Vorstellungen und ihrer Gegenstandsbeziehung in der 'Kritik der reinen Vernunft'* (Berlin/New York: de Gruyter).
—. (1991) *'Forma dat esse rei.* Inwiefern heben wir in der Erkenntnis das aus der Erfahrung nur heraus, was wir zuvor in sie hineingelegt haben?', in Forum für Philosophie Bad Homburg (ed.) *Übergang: Untersuchungen zum Spätwerk Immanuel Kants* (Frankfurt a.M: Klostermann), pp. 49–63.
Hossenfelder, M. (1978) *Kants Konstitutionstheorie und die transzendentale Deduktion* (Berlin: de Gruyter).
Houlgate, S. (2006) *The Opening of Hegel's Logic* (West Lafayette, IN: Purdue University Press).
Hurley, S. (1994) 'Kant on Spontaneity and the Myth of the Giving', *Proceedings of the Aristotelian Society*, vol. XCIV: 137–64.
Keller, P. (1998) *Kant and the Demands of Self-Consciousness* (Cambridge: Cambridge University Press).
Kemp Smith, N. (1999) *A Commentary to Kant's Critique of Pure Reason*, 1923 edition (Amherst: Humanity Press).
Kitcher, P. (1982) 'Kant on Self-Identity', *Philosophical Review* 91(1): 41–72.
—. (1984) 'Kant's Real Self', in A. Wood (ed.) *Self and Nature in Kant's Philosophy* (Ithaca: Cornell University Press), pp. 113–47.
—. (1990) *Kant's Transcendental Psychology* (New York: Oxford University Press).
—. (1999) 'Kant on Self-Consciousness', *Philosophical Review* 108(3): 345–86.
—. (2006) 'Kant's Philosophy of the Cognitive Mind', in P. Guyer (ed.) (2006) *The Cambridge Companion to Kant and Modern Philosophy* (Cambridge: Cambridge University Press), pp. 169–202.
—. (2011) *Kant's Thinker* (New York: Oxford University Press).
Klemme, H. (1994) 'Subjektive und objektive Deduktion. Überlegungen zu Wolfgang Carls Interpretation von Kants "Deduktion der reinen Verstandesbegriffe" in der Fassung von 1781', in R. Brandt & W. Stark (eds) (1994) *Autographen, Dokumente und Berichte*, Kant-Forschungen, Band 5 (Hamburg: Meiner), pp. 121–38.
—. (1996) *Kants Philosophie des Subjekts* (Hamburg: Meiner).
—. (2001) 'Perspektiven der Interpretation: Kant und das Verbot der Lüge', in D. Schönecker & Th. Zwenger (eds) (2001) *Kant verstehen/Understanding Kant. Über die Interpretation philosophischer Texte* (Darmstadt: Wissenschaftliche Buchgesellschaft), pp. 85–105.
Krüger, L. (1968) 'Wollte Kant die Vollständigkeit seiner Urteilstafel beweisen?', *Kant-Studien* 59: 333–56.
Kuehn, M. (2001) *Kant: A Biography* (Cambridge: Cambridge University Press).
Land, T. (2014) 'Spatial Representation, Magnitude and the Two Stems of Cognition', *Canadian Journal of Philosophy* 44(5–6): 524–50.
—. (2015) 'No Other Use Than in Judgment? Kant on Concepts and Sensible Synthesis', *Journal of the History of Philosophy* 53(3): 461–84.
—. (2018) 'Review of D. Schulting, *Kant's Deduction and Apperception. Explaining the Categories* (London/New York: Palgrave)', *Kantian Review* 23(1): 145–51.

La Rocca, C. (2008) 'Der dunkle Verstand. Unbewusste Vorstellungen und Selbstbewusstsein bei Kant', in V. Rohden et al. (eds) *Recht und Frieden in der Philosophie Kants. Akten des X. Internationalen Kant-Kongresses* (2005) (Berlin/New York: de Gruyter, 2008), vol. 2, pp. 457–68.
Longuenesse, B. (1993) *Kant et le pouvoir de juger* (Paris: PUF).
—. (1998) *Kant and the Capacity to Judge* (Princeton: Princeton University Press).
—. (2005) *Kant on the Human Standpoint* (Cambridge: Cambridge University Press).
—. (2006) 'Kant on a priori Concepts. The Metaphysical Deduction of the Categories', in P. Guyer (ed.) (2006) *The Cambridge Companion to Kant and Modern Philosophy* (Cambridge: Cambridge University Press), pp. 129–68.
—. (2008) 'Cassam and Kant on "How Possible" Questions and Categorial Thinking', *Philosophy and Phenomenological Research* 77(2): 510–17.
Maier, A. (1930) *Kants Qualitätskategorien* (Berlin: Pan Verlag Metzner).
Mathieu, V. (1989) *Kants Opus Postumum* (Frankfurt a.M: Klostermann).
McLear, C. (2015) 'Two Kinds of Unity in the *Critique of Pure Reason*', *Journal of the History of Philosophy* 53(1): 79–110.
Messina, J. (2014) 'Kant on the Unity of Space and the Synthetic Unity of Apperception', *Kant-Studien* 105(1): 5–40.
Mohr, G. (1991) *Das sinnliche Ich. Innerer Sinn und Bewußtsein bei Kant* (Würzburg: Königshausen & Neumann).
Motta, G. (2007) *Kants Philosophie der Notwendigkeit* (Frankfurt a.M: Peter Lang).
—. (2012) *Die Postulate des empirischen Denkens überhaupt* (Berlin/Boston: de Gruyter).
Muralt, A. de (1958) *La conscience transcendantale dans le criticisme kantien. Essai sur l'unité d'aperception* (Paris: Aubier).
Natorp, P. (2000) *Philosophische Systematik* (Hamburg: Meiner).
Neuhouser, F. (1990) *Fichte's Theory of Subjectivity* (Cambridge: Cambridge University Press).
Onof, C. & D. Schulting (2014) 'Kant, Kästner, and the Distinction between Metaphysical and Geometric Space', *Kantian Review* 19(2): 285–304.
—. (2015) 'Space as Form of Intuition and as Formal Intuition. On the Note to B160 in Kant's *Critique of Pure Reason*', *Philosophical Review* 124(1): 1–58.
Patton, L. (2011) 'The Paradox of Infinite Given Magnitude: Why Kantian Epistemology Needs Metaphysical Space', *Kant-Studien* 102(3): 273–89.
Pereboom, D. (1995) 'Self-Understanding in Kant's Transcendental Deduction', *Synthese* 103 (1): 1–42.
—. (2001) 'Assessing Kant's Master Argument', *Kantian Review* 5: 90–102.
—. (2010) 'Kant's Metaphysical and Transcendental Deductions', in G. Bird (ed.) (2010) *A Companion to Kant* (Oxford/Malden, MA: Wiley-Blackwell), pp. 154–68.
Pippin, R. (1997) 'Kant on the Spontaneity of Mind', in R. Pippin, *Idealism as Modernism. Hegelian Variations* (Cambridge: Cambridge University Press), pp. 29–55.
—. (2014) 'The Significance of Self-Consciousness in Idealist Theories of Logic', *Proceedings of the Aristotelian Society* 114(2), part 2: 145–66.
—. (2015) 'John McDowell's Germans', in R. Pippin, *Interanimations. Receiving Modern German Philosophy* (Chicago: University of Chicago Press), pp. 63–90.
Pollok, K. (2008) '"An almost single inference"—Kant's Deduction of the Categories Reconsidered', *Archiv für Geschichte der Philosophie* 90(3): 323–45.
Prauss, G. (1971) *Erscheinung bei Kant* (Berlin: de Gruyter).

Prien, B. (2006) *Kants Logik der Begriffe* (Berlin/New York: de Gruyter).
Proops, I. (2003) 'Kant's Legal Metaphor and the Nature of a Deduction', *Journal of the History of Philosophy* 41(2): 209–29.
Puntel, L. (2001) 'Über das komplexe Verhältnis der Philosophie zu ihrer Geschichte', in D. Schönecker & Th. Zwenger (eds) (2001) *Kant verstehen/Understanding Kant. Über die Interpretation philosophischer Texte* (Darmstadt: Wissenschaftliche Buchgesellschaft), pp. 132–58.
Quarfood, M. (2004) *Transcendental Idealism and the Organism. Essays on Kant* (Stockholm: Almqvist & Wiksell).
—. (2011) 'Discursivity and Transcendental Idealism', in D. Schulting & J. Verburgt (eds) (2011) *Kant's Idealism. New Interpretations of a Controversial Doctrine* (Dordrecht: Springer), pp. 143–58.
—. (2014) 'A Note on Schulting's Derivation of Contingency', *Studi kantiani* XXVII: 87–93.
Reich, K. (1986) *Die Vollständigkeit der Kantischen Urteilstafel*, 3rd edition (Hamburg: Meiner).
—. (1992) *The Completeness of Kant's Table of Judgments*, trans. and ed. J. Kneller & M. Losonsky (Stanford: Stanford University Press).
—. (2001) *Gesammelte Schriften*, ed. M. Baum et al. (Hamburg: Meiner).
Robinson, H. (1988) 'The Priority of Inner Sense', *Kant-Studien* 79: 165–82.
Rosefeldt, T. (2000) *Das logische Ich. Kant über den Gehalt des Begriffes von sich selbst* (Berlin: Philo).
Sassen, B. (ed.) (2000) *Kant's Early Critics* (Cambridge: Cambridge University Press).
Schulting, D. (2008) 'On Strawson on Kantian Apperception', *South African Journal of Philosophy* 27(3): 257–71.
—. (2009a) 'Kant's Copernican Analogy: Beyond the Non-Specific Reading', *Studi kantiani* XXII: 39–65.
—. (2009b) 'Review of K. Westphal, *Kant's Transcendental Proof of Realism* (Cambridge: Cambridge UP, 2004)', *Kant-Studien* 100(3): 382–5.
—. (2010) 'Kant, non-conceptuele inhoud en synthese', *Tijdschrift voor Filosofie* 72(4): 679–715.
—. (2012a) 'Non-Apperceptive Consciousness', in P. Giordanetti, R. Pozzo & M. Sgarbi (eds) *Kant's Philosophy of the Unconscious* (Berlin/New York: de Gruyter), pp. 271–302.
—. (2012b) *Kant's Deduction and Apperception. Explaining the Categories* (Basingstoke/New York: Palgrave Macmillan).
—. (2015a) 'Transcendental Apperception and Consciousness in Kant's Lectures on Metaphysics', in R. Clewis (ed.) *Reading Kant's Lectures* (Berlin/Boston: de Gruyter), pp. 89–113.
—. (2015b) 'Probleme des „kantianischen" Nonkonzeptualismus im Hinblick auf die B-Deduktion', *Kant-Studien* 106(4): 561–80.
—. (2016a) 'In Defence of Reinhold's Kantian Representationalism: Aspects of Idealism in *Versuch einer neuen Theorie des menschlichen Vorstellungsvermögens*', *Kant Yearbook* 8: 87–116.
—. (2016b) 'On an Older Dispute: Hegel, Pippin, and the Separability of Concept and Intuition in Kant', in D. Schulting (ed.) *Kantian Nonconceptualism* (Londen/New York: Palgrave Macmillan), pp. 227–55.

—. (2017a) *Kant's Radical Subjectivism. Perspectives on the Transcendental Deduction* (London/New York: Palgrave Macmillan).
—. (2017b) 'Analyticity, Analytic Philosophy and Kant's Synthetic A Priori: Comments on Robert Hanna's *Cognition, Content, and the A Priori*', *Critique* (May), https://virtualcritique.wordpress.com/2017/05/27/dennis-schulting-on-robert-hannas-cognition-content-and-the-a-priori/.
—. (2017c) 'Apperception, Self-Consciousness, and Self-Knowledge in Kant', in M. Altman (ed.) *The Palgrave Kant Handbook* (London/New York: Palgrave Macmillan), pp. 139–61.
—. (2017d) 'The Unity of Cognition and the Subjectivist vs. "Transformative" Approaches to the B-Deduction. Comments on James Conant', *Critique* (October), https://virtualcritique.wordpress.com/2017/10/04/the-unity-of-cognition-and-the-subjectivist-vs-transformative-approaches-to-the-b-deduction-comments-on-james-conant/.
—. (2017e) 'Gap? What Gap?—On the Unity of Apperception and the Necessary Application of the Categories', in G. Motta & U. Thiel (eds), *Immanuel Kant: Die Einheit des Bewusstseins* (Berlin/Boston: de Gruyter, 2017), pp. 89–113.
—. (2017f) 'Reply to Robert Watt: Epistemic Humility, Objective Validity, Logical Derivability', *Critique* (November), https://virtualcritique.wordpress.com/2017/11/11/reply-to-watt-epistemic-humility-objective-validity-logical-derivability/.
—. (2018a) 'Gaps, Chasms, and Things in Themselves: A Reply to My Critics', *Kantian Review* 23(1): 131–43.
—. (2018b) 'The Current Status of Research on Kant's Transcendental Deduction', *Revista de Estudios Kantianos* 3(1): 69–88.
—. (2018c) 'Why Kantian Nonconceptualists Can't Have Their Cake And Eat It—Reply to Sacha Golob', *Critique* (May), https://virtualcritique.wordpress.com/2018/05/21/why-kantian-nonconceptualists-cant-have-their-cake-and-eat-it-reply-to-sacha-golob/.
—. (2019) 'Apperception and Object. Comments on Mario Caimi's Reading of the B-Deduction', *Revista de Estudios Kantianos* 4(1).
—. (forthcoming) *Reflexivity and Representation. Essays on Kant and German Idealism.* (Berlin/Boston: de Gruyter)
Sedgwick, S. (2000) 'Longuenesse on Kant and the Priority of the Capacity to Judge', *Inquiry* 43(1): 81–90.
Seeberg, U. (2006) *Ursprung, Umfang und Grenzen der Erkenntnis. Eine Untersuchung zu Kants transzendentaler Deduktion der Kategorien* (Hamburg: Philo).
Sellars, W. (1992) *Science and Metaphysics. Variations on Kantian Themes* (Atascadero: Ridgeview).
Stapleford, S. (2008) *Kant's Transcendental Arguments. Disciplining Pure Reason* (New York/London: Continuum).
Stephenson, A. (2014) 'A *Deduction* from Apperception?', *Studi kantiani* XXVII: 77–85.
Strawson, P. (1968) *The Bounds of Sense*, 2nd printing (London: Methuen).
—. (1989) 'Sensibility, Understanding, and the Doctrine of Synthesis: Comments on Henrich and Guyer', in E. Förster (ed.) (1989) *Kant's Transcendental Deductions. The Three 'Critiques' and the 'Opus postumum'* (Stanford: Stanford University Press), pp. 69–77.
Stuhlmann-Laeisz, R. (1976) *Kants Logik* (Berlin: de Gruyter).
Sturma, D. (1985) *Kant über Selbstbewußtsein* (Hildesheim: Olms).
Thöle, B. (1991) *Kant und das Problem der Gesetzmäßigkeit der Natur* (Berlin/New York: de Gruyter).

—. (2001) 'Kants Systemidee. Bemerkungen zu Karl Ameriks' "Kant's Notion of Systematic Philosophy"', in H. Fulda & J. Stolzenburg (eds) (2001) *Architektonik und System in der Philosophie Kants* (Hamburg: Meiner), pp. 92–105.
Vaihinger, H. (1881) *Commentar zu Immanuel Kants Kritik der reinen Vernunft*, Bd. 1 (Stuttgart: Spemann).
Van Cleve, J. (1999) *Problems From Kant* (New York: Oxford University Press).
Vanzo, A. (2012) 'Kant on Truth-Aptness', *History and Philosophy of Logic* 33(2): 109–26.
Vinci, T. (2015) *Space, Geometry, and Kant's Transcendental Deduction of the Categories* (New York: Oxford University Press).
Vleeschauwer, H. J. de (1937) *La déduction transcendantale dans l'oeuvre de Kant*, vol. 3 ('s-Gravenhage/Antwerpen/Paris: Nijhoff/De Sikkel/Leroux).
Warren, D. (2001) *Reality and Impenetrability in Kant's Philosophy of Nature* (New York/London: Routledge).
Watkins, E. (2005) *Kant and the Metaphysics of Causality* (Cambridge: Cambridge University Press).
—. (2010) 'The System of Principles', in Guyer (ed.) (2010) *The Cambridge Companion to Kant's 'Critique of Pure Reason'* (Cambridge: Cambridge University Press), pp. 151–67.
—. (2011) 'Making Sense of Mutual Interaction', in L. Thorpe & C. Payne (eds) *Kant and the Concept of Community* (Rochester, NY: University of Rochester Press), pp. 41–62.
Watson, J. (1880) 'The Method of Kant', *Mind* 5: 528–48.
Watt, R. (2017) 'Robert Watt on Dennis Schulting's *Kant's Radical Subjectivism*', *Critique* (November), https://virtualcritique.wordpress.com/2017/11/07/robert-watt-on-dennis-schultings-kants-radical-subjectivism/
Williams, J. (2018) 'Kant on the Original Synthesis of Understanding and Sensibility', *British Journal of the History of Philosophy* 26(1): 66–86.
Wolff, M. (1995) *Die Vollständigkeit der kantischen Urteilstafel* (Frankfurt a.M: Klostermann).
Wolff, R. (1973) *Kant's Theory of Mental Activity*, 2nd printing (Gloucester, MA: Peter Smith).
Wunderlich, F. (2005) *Kant und die Bewußtseinstheorien des 18. Jahrhunderts* (Berlin/New York: de Gruyter).

Index of Names

Allais, L.   116 f., 278
Allison, H.   vi, xvi, 3, 5, 7, 16, 20, 41, 44 f., 55, 62, 67, 70, 78, 82, 86, 131, 147, 150, 153, 182, 184, 208–211, 213 f., 229, 259, 307, 314
Ameriks, K.   11, 22, 65, 73, 81–85, 91, 94 f., 97–100, 108, 110, 139, 141, 148, 173, 207, 211, 222, 244, 283, 285 f., 288, 295
Aportone, A.   5, 14, 55, 72, 112, 121, 301
Aristotle   29, 72, 88
Aschenberg, R.   229

Balfour, A.   83
Banham, G.   10, 67, 287
Barth, K.   287
Bauer, N.   3, 305
Baum, M.   5, 14, 19, 31, 67, 73, 92, 151, 232, 259, 282, 284, 286, 288
Baumgarten, A.G.   209
Beck, J.S.   93, 125, 146, 207
Beck, L.W.   20 f., 73, 210
Bird, G.   10
Brandt, R.   v, 5
Brook, A.   147, 206
Bruckner, A.   239
Butts, R.   298

Callanan, J.   xv, 29, 57, 60 f.
Carl, W.   vi, 16, 20, 24 f., 54, 65–67, 70, 78, 93, 172, 237 f., 282, 292
Cassam, Q.   28, 65, 82, 85, 131, 137, 245
Castañeda, H.-N.   207
Cohen, H.   93
Collins, A.   78, 82, 207 f.
Conant, J.   v f.
Crusius, C.A.   24, 61

Deppermann, A.   139, 232–234
Descartes, R.   39 f., 95–97, 99–103, 106 f., 133, 148, 156, 286
Dickerson, A.B.   207

Düsing, K.   1, 5
Dyck, C.   ix, xvi

Edwards, J.   193
Erdmann, B.   74, 93, 97, 126

Falkenstein, L.   5
Fichant, M.   311
Fichte, J.G.   11, 15, 97, 150, 220 f.
Forster, M.   5
Frege, G.   87
Friedman, M.   xiv, 290, 299, 303, 305–307, 309, 317

Golob, S.   10
Gram, M.   37, 83
Greenberg, R.   6 f., 67, 114
Grüne, S.   xii, 306
Guyer, P.   vi, 1 f., 16 f., 20, 63, 65–72, 78, 81 f., 85, 93, 95, 97, 101–108, 110, 123 f., 129–131, 133–135, 138, 143, 148, 159, 206, 261, 280 f.

Hanna, R.   xii, 67, 307
Hegel, G.W.F.   viii, xvii, 11–15, 39, 54, 254 f., 278
Heidegger, M.   31, 153
Heidemann, I.   184, 237
Heimsoeth, H.   16, 166, 179, 181, 193, 196 f., 199, 222, 225, 232
Henrich, D.   vi, xv, 15, 17, 30–34, 38, 41, 67, 69, 92, 97, 101 f., 104, 107 f., 120, 130, 132, 134, 143, 147, 160, 191, 232
Herz, M.   14, 17, 20–26, 36, 40, 74, 166, 207–209, 233, 237
Hogan, D.   24, 61
Hoppe, H.-G.   67, 78, 108 f., 135, 150, 188 f., 191, 207, 261
Hossenfelder, M.   68, 102 f., 139 f., 228, 241–243, 245 f.
Houlgate, S.   12–15
Hume, D.   ix, 60 f., 77, 120, 182, 232, 235
Hurley, S.   109

James, W. 188

Kästner, A.G. 290, 310, 312
Keller, P. 147, 231
Kemp Smith, N. 85, 207
Kitcher, P. 16, 33, 82, 150, 154, 172, 208, 215, 244
Klemme, H. 11, 66f., 78, 138f., 146, 187, 235
Krüger, L. 13–15, 226
Kuehn, M. 20

Land, T. xiif., xvi, 269, 300–303, 305, 308, 310, 317
La Rocca, C. 207, 215
Leibniz, G.W. 39, 53, 75, 105, 154, 166, 209, 215, 239
Locke, J. ix, 51, 53–58, 145, 208, 215
Longuenesse, B. v, xii, xv, 5, 17, 24f., 30, 41, 44–60, 62, 118f., 193, 195–197, 199, 213, 217, 226, 231, 245, 267, 297, 300, 305–308, 312, 317

Maier, A. 16, 196–200, 214, 216–218, 220–223
Mathieu, V. 296
McDowell, J. 74, 274
McLear, C. v
Meier, G.F. 215
Mendelssohn, M. 199, 201
Messina, J. v, 305
Mohr, G. 78f., 210–212, 232f., 238
Muralt, A. de 205, 211

Natorp, P. 124
Neuhouser, F. 150

Onof, C. v, xiii, 304, 308f., 311

Patton, L. 310
Pereboom, D. 2, 17, 68f., 73
Pippin, R. 154, 184f., 208, 215, 278
Pistorius, H.A. 12
Plato 22, 24
Pollok, K. 49, 293
Prauss, G. 84

Prien, B. 4f., 51, 68, 76, 114, 119f., 229, 232, 237, 246, 250
Proops, I. xv, 29, 34, 54–56
Puntel, L. 11

Quarfood, M. xvi, 23, 50f., 57, 61, 128, 166, 183

Reich, K. v, viii, 4–7, 9, 111, 121, 124, 126f., 141, 234, 242
Reinhold, K.L. 11, 211
Robinson, H. 188
Rosefeldt, T. 135, 138, 142, 148

Schelling, F.W.J. 11, 15
Schultz, J.F. 45, 49, 164
Sedgwick, S. 51f., 62
Seeberg, U. xv, 15, 30–32, 34, 41
Sellars, W. 274, 294
Spinoza, B. de 39
Stapleford, S. 38, 99
Stephenson, A. xvi
Strawson, P.F. vii, 74, 81–85, 89, 93–98, 101–103, 108–110, 123f., 137–139, 228, 233, 235–241, 245, 284, 288, 293
Stuhlmann-Laeisz, R. 114, 232–234
Sturma, D. 212, 237

Thöle, B. 67, 84, 91, 95, 188, 212, 240f.
Tieftrunk, J.H. 125f., 218, 220f., 223, 227

Vaihinger, H. 84f., 95
Van Cleve, J. 207, 231
Vanzo, A. 273
Vinci, T. v
Vleeschauwer, H.-J. de 70, 238

Warren, D. 195–197, 199, 217–219
Watkins, E. 10, 141, 182f., 192f.
Watson, J. 82f.
Watt, R. xvi
Williams, J. v
Wolff, C. 36, 166, 268
Wolff, M. v, viii, 4f., 7, 9, 13f., 26, 111–114, 121, 155, 165, 254
Wolff, R. 207f.

Wunderlich, F.   1, 130, 146, 151, 160, 191, 201, 215

Index of Subjects

acquisition (of the pure concepts)   xi, 17, 28–30, 41, 51–53, 57 f., 62, 245
– derivative (*acquisitio derivativa*)   57 f.
– original (*acquisitio originaria*)   xi, 17, 28–30, 41–51, 57 f.
action   32, 58, 77, 113, 115, 117, 121, 132, 145, 153, 171, 181–183, 185 f., 189, 191, 194, 248, 250–252, 255, 267–269, 303, 309, 315 f.
actuality   83–85, 88, 92, 124–126, 156 f., 163–167, 170, 190, 196–198, 255, 273 f., 283, 295; see also existence
A-Deduction   vi f., xv, 3, 16, 45, 48, 50 f., 64, 69, 87, 97, 101, 105, 115, 130 f., 134 f., 178, 198, 203, 210, 213, 226, 250, 259, 284 f., 318 f.
affection   17, 22, 113, 218
affinity   36, 179, 188–190, 193
– material   189 f., 193
Amphiboly of Concepts of Reflection   53, 287
analysis   x, 6, 8 f., 18, 37–40, 47, 52, 72 f., 77, 81, 83, 91, 108, 115, 141, 146, 172, 205, 245 f., 262, 273, 283, 285, 292–294, 298
– of the faculty of understanding   xi, 2, 6, 40, 115
Analytic of Concepts   6
Analytic of Principles   10, 29, 61, 71, 283
Anticipations of Perception   195, 199 f., 214, 219
anti-sceptical, see scepticism
appearance(s)   xi f., 21, 25, 42, 46, 50, 58, 66, 74, 77, 86, 88, 93, 104, 114, 118, 131, 134 f., 145, 148 f., 152 f., 171 f., 178, 181, 187 f., 196 f., 199–201, 213, 216 f., 221–223, 225, 227, 237, 239, 248 f., 252, 256, 262, 264, 267, 277–279, 315, 318 f., 321 f.; see also object
– swarm of   149, 188
apperception   v–xvi, 1–6, 9 f., 15–19, 34, 38 f., 41, 46–50, 59 f., 62 f., 65–72, 75–82, 86 f., 89 f., 93–95, 97, 101–111, 116–124, 126–156, 160 f., 168–172, 174, 176–179, 182, 185, 189–196, 198, 200–212, 215, 219–223, 225, 227–229, 231–235, 237–239, 241–244, 247–262, 264–267, 270–272, 275, 277–279, 281 f., 284, 286–289, 294, 296–298, 304–309, 311–313, 317–322
– as analytic principle   vii, 81 f., 90, 101, 106 f., 129, 235, 241 f., 281
– analytic unity of   6, 75, 90, 120, 130, 153, 168, 228, 234, 258, 264
– empirical   17, 48, 147, 178, 198, 203, 206, 228, 232, 234, 237 f., 249
– objective unity of   v, viii, 4, 6, 16, 41, 46–50, 60, 77, 94, 262, 266 f., 270–272, 286
– as self-ascription of representations   82, 89, 93 f., 102, 109, 137–140
– as synthetic principle   131
– synthetic unity of   xiii f., 39, 49, 75–77, 90, 119 f., 129–131, 143, 151, 153, 182, 191 f., 194, 227, 234, 248, 255, 258, 262, 264, 270, 278, 281, 284, 289, 298, 304, 307
– thoroughgoing identity of   128 f., 146, 152, 155, 251 f.
– transcendental unity of   xi, 1, 48, 67 f., 70, 141, 248, 255, 260–261, 265 f., 279, 284, 305, 317 f.; see also self-consciousness
apprehension   45, 51, 115, 132, 134, 171, 178, 194, 205, 214, 218, 220, 227 f., 230, 235, 237–239, 243 f., 248, 250 f., 255, 299, 304, 306, 312, 315, 317; see also synthesis
a priori concepts   4, 6 f., 20, 25 f., 29, 37, 42, 53, 55 f., 58, 60–62, 83, 85, 88, 91 f., 115, 269, 278, 283, 304 f., 309; see also category, categories; concept
– birthplace of   2, 6, 126
archetypal   22–25, 99; see also ectypalism
– *cognitio prototypa*   22

Index of Subjects

B-Deduction   v–viii, xiii, xv, 1–3, 16–19, 24f., 29, 33, 35, 46, 48f., 63–68, 70–72, 86, 116, 123, 126f., 136, 168, 177, 186, 192, 198, 251, 263–266, 270f., 276, 278, 282, 284–287, 289–291, 293f., 296, 299, 308, 313f., 316f.
- 'first step' of   vf., viii, xiii, 18f., 47, 64, 81, 86, 118, 126, 177, 263, 284, 294, 296f., 304, 317
- 'second step' of   vf., vii, xiii–xv, 3, 18f., 64f., 71f., 81, 264, 278, 280–282, 284, 290–294, 296–298, 304f., 312–316
belief   73, 83–85, 96, 98f., 104, 271f., 276

capacity to judge   xi, 7, 9, 44f., 80, 98, 115, 121f., 267, 269, 300, 317f.
category, categories   *passim*
- as ancestral concepts   165
- a priori origin of   26, 294
- derivation of   v, viii–xi, xiii, xvf., 1f., 4–7, 9–12, 14–16, 18, 30, 40, 55, 63, 92, 97, 108, 110f., 122, 124, 129, 154–156, 163, 168, 195, 198, 225, 250, 253f., 257, 266, 282, 296
- entitlement (or right) to use of   29f., 32, 37, 91
- justification/legitimation of   29, 31, 35, 38, 60–62, 91, 291, 293
- legitimacy of   10, 17, 25, 28f., 34f., 54f., 60, 62, 72, 83, 85, 288
- of modality   124f., 154–157, 163, 165, 190, 197, 225; see also actuality, modal, necessity, possibility
- as necessary conditions (of possible experience)   xiv, 3, 17, 71, 91f., 207, 245, 283, 288 *et passim*
- as principles of objective determination   1, 265f., 284
- of quality   16, 73, 195f., 198, 200, 202, 204, 213f., 223, 225, 271, 303, 320; see also limitation, negation, quality, reality
- of quantity   125, 144, 225f., 229, 251, 253, 304; see also plurality, quantity, totality, unity
- of relation 16, 168f., 171f., 190, 194, 225; see also cause-effect, community, substance
- schematisation of   6, 42, 71, 125, 200, 216, 225, 279, 299, 302, 305, 307, 309
- table of   viii, xvi, 4, 7f., 13, 18, 111f., 254
- as titles of self-perception   70
causality   10, 161, 168, 170, 177, 180–183, 190, 192f., 283, 320
cause-effect   24, 168, 180, 190, 194, 256
certainty   35–37, 86, 88, 96f., 102, 106, 134, 234, 272, 284, 294
- apodictic   35
- a priori   102, 106, 234
- Cartesian   102
- comparative   36f.
- discursive   35, 37
- intuitive   35, 37
- logical   96
- mathematical   35, 86
- philosophical   88
clue (*Leitfaden*)   viii, x, 4f., 7–9, 18, 49, 111–122, 130, 266, 268–270, 309
combination (*conjunctio*)   xiif., 48f., 58, 77, 112, 114f., 122, 126, 130, 135, 146f., 159, 161, 164, 168, 183, 186–191, 193, 209, 231, 244f., 248–251, 253, 271, 287f., 299, 303, 311, 314–317, 319; see also synthesis
community   168, 186, 190, 192–194, 256, 320
- as mutual interaction   190, 193
- of apperception   193
comparison/reflection/abstraction (CRA)   44, 46–48, 51–53, 56–59, 246; see also reflection
complex, complexity   22, 98, 106, 122, 144, 148, 168, 213, 227, 242, 300–302
concept(s)   *passim*
- acquired (*notiones acquisitae*)   3, 51, 54, 57–59
- as *conceptus communis*   58f., 241
- empirical   xi, 42f., 46, 51, 53, 56–58, 116, 260
- innate   57f.
- original   56, 59, 164
- as partial representation   113, 232, 241f., 246, 253, 256
- pure   ix–xii, 2, 6–7, 14, 23f., 30, 40, 53f., 56f., 64, 85, 91, 114, 117, 126, 156,

199, 202, 283, 299, 306, 309; *see also* category, categories
consciousness   vi f., xi, xiv, 1, 9, 13, 28, 44, 48–50, 59, 63–65, 68–71, 74–79, 86, 89, 94, 99, 102, 106, 108 f., 111–114, 117–120, 123, 128, 132–134, 138 f., 141 f, 144–147, 149–154, 156, 160, 165, 168, 171–174, 178 f., 182–184, 189 f., 193, 196, 198, 200–227, 229–241, 245–249, 251–253, 256, 258–265, 270–272, 279–281, 284, 286, 289, 301, 303 f., 315, 318, 321
– analytic unity of   xiv, 49, 59, 75–77, 86, 131, 138, 151 f., 154, 168, 225 f., 232–235, 249, 253, 256, 264, 289
– empirical   141, 146, 149, 153 f., 189, 196, 198, 201–206, 209, 213, 217–221, 223 f., 230, 232–235, 237 f., 240, 249, 256, 260, 315
– first-order   196, 208, 210, 212 f.
– objective unity of   vi, 48 f., 65, 71, 77 f., 129, 190, 193, 265, 270, 281
– obscure   154, 201, 215, 233, 238
– (original-)synthetic unity of   64 f., 69 f., 74–76, 79, 123, 259, 262, 264 f.
– sub-cognitive   147
– subjective unity of   49, 70, 77, 190, 193, 206, 260, 265, 270 f., 279
– transcendental (self-)   xiii, 10, 17, 78, 93 f., 93, 109, 128, 139, 146, 149, 153, 160, 189, 202–205, 210, 213, 215, 217, 219, 221, 223–225, 232, 235, 256; *see also* self-consciousness
– unconsciousness   203, 208 f., 212–216, 219
construction   73, 82, 298, 300, 303, 305, 310 f.
contingency   125, 166 f., 255
Copernican hypothesis   20, 35, 100 f.
copula   155, 157, 271–273, 276
Critical philosophy   5, 36, 199

deduction (*deductio*)   viii–x, xiii–xvi, 1–6, 8, 10, 12–15, 17–19, 25 f., 28–35, 37, 40, 49, 51, 53–56, 58, 62, 65, 72, 79, 81, 88, 91–93, 95, 121, 144, 155, 172, 220,

225, 229, 254, 258, 261, 263, 282–284, 286, 288, 322
– of the categories   xiii–xv, 4, 12, 15–18, 26 f., 53, 79, 81, 91–93, 121, 144, 172, 225, 229, 258, 261, 322
– empirical   ix, 53–55
– juridical usage of   32
– legal   17, 31
– as a logical derivation   ix, xiii, 12, 14 f., 18
– objective   93, 283 f.
– subjective   2 f., 92 f.
Deduction
– Metaphysical   4–7, 10, 13, 17 f., 34, 55 f., 90, 111, 114, 121, 124, 195, 266–268, 270
– Transcendental   v, viii, xiii–xvi, 1–4, 7 f., 10 f., 16–19, 21, 28–35, 38–41, 47, 50 f., 55, 59, 61, 63–65, 67 f., 70–72, 75, 77, 81–85, 88, 90–93, 95–97, 99–101, 103, 107, 110, 112, 117 f., 121, 123, 125, 128, 132, 172, 178, 183, 189, 192, 198, 200, 213, 221, 227, 254, 258, 261–263, 266, 268, 270, 278, 281–287, 289–291; *see also* A-Deduction, B-Deduction
– explanatory role of   10, 17 f., 28 f., 39 f., 292, 294
– as a progressive argument   18, 40, 81–83, 85, 88 f., 99, 102, 167, 279, 286
– as a regressive argument   17–19, 40, 84, 91 f., 110, 189, 282 f., 288, 294
– revelatory role of   28, 85
– validatory role of   17 f., 28 f., 41, 85
Deduktionsschriften   32–34
demonstrative thought   293
determination   xi, 1, 3, 13, 23, 35, 37 f., 41, 44–47, 50–52, 60, 73, 87, 117 f., 125, 135 f., 154, 156, 158, 161 f., 166, 169, 171, 175, 178 f., 182, 185, 191, 193, 195, 197 f., 202, 210, 215, 217–222, 237, 249 f., 258, 263, 265 f., 269, 279, 284, 290, 298, 302–305, 307, 309–311, 314 f., 317–320
discursivity   viii f., 121, 241, 254
– discursive thought   ix, 4, 7–11, 16 f., 46, 71, 75, 80 f., 90, 96, 98, 121, 124, 128, 141, 144, 148, 150, 155, 158, 163–165,

167f., 184, 194, 196, 223–227, 243, 251–256, 258f., 264, 280, 284f., 296
– discursive understanding   xi, 23, 113f., 128, 183f.
Duisburg Nachlass   vi, 16, 20, 26, 66f., 94, 171f.

ectypalism   22f.
– *cognitio ectypa*   22
epigenesis   10, 25f., 51, 57, 61
– epigenetic system   57
existence   2, 24, 50, 63, 68, 73f., 85f., 93f., 97, 101, 108f., 124f., 141, 156–159, 161–165, 169f., 174, 177, 180–182, 185, 196–198, 213, 216, 220f., 236f., 255, 271, 273f., 277, 293, 319f.
experience (*Erfahrung*)   75, 82, 91 et passim
– actuality of   83–85, 92, 295
– C-experience   292f., 295, 313
– common (sense)   83, 85, 91, 95, 99f., 149
– fact of   65, 91, 93, 285
– justification/legitimation of   190, 291
– objective   xiv, 4, 8, 10, 17f., 28, 39, 45, 47, 63, 65f., 73, 78, 83, 85f., 91–93, 95f., 98–100, 149, 190, 198, 213, 261, 271, 280–283, 285, 294
– possible   3f., 7f., 10, 15f., 25, 29f., 35, 37f., 64f., 71, 79, 84f., 88, 92, 96, 125, 157, 159, 203, 217, 222–225, 256, 261, 272, 277, 279–281, 285, 287, 295, 319, 321f.
– *quoad materiale*   84, 292
– S-experience   292f., 295, 313
– in 'thick' sense   83, 283
– in 'thin' sense   92, 95
– as 'third thing'   38

force   47, 50, 181; *see also* power
forms of judgement, *see* judgement
freedom   39, 185
– transcendental   185
– of a turnspit   183, 185
functions of thought, *see* judgement

generatio aequivoca   26, 57

geometry   100, 290, 293f., 298
guiding thread (*Leitfaden*), *see* clue

holding-to-be-true (*Fürwahrhalten*)   272
hyperphysical influx   24

idealism   11, 24f., 65, 93, 199, 222, 261, 277, 291, 318–320
– Refutation of Idealism   99, 182
identity   67f., 71, 74, 76f., 86f., 88–90, 92, 94, 97, 102–109, 112–114, 119f., 123, 128–138, 140–146, 148–150, 152–155, 160, 162–164, 167, 174, 180–182, 192, 194, 205f., 209, 223–225, 228, 232–234, 240, 242f., 247–256, 258–261, 264, 272, 278–280, 284, 287f.
– of apperception   129, 131, 138, 155, 192, 251, 279
– numerical   74, 102–107, 120, 128, 133f., 143f., 148–150, 174, 177f., 193, 225, 228, 233, 242, 247–253, 258f., 264
– of self-consciousness   76, 86, 88, 97, 104, 128f., 131, 137, 152f., 205f., 252, 258f., 284
– thoroughgoing   97, 128f., 131, 133–137, 141, 146, 152, 155, 162f., 206, 247, 249, 251f., 259, 261
imagination   xi–xiii, 43f., 48, 50, 52, 61f., 115f., 118, 149, 187, 209, 218, 220, 239, 269, 277f., 290, 298–300, 302–307, 310f., 315–317; *see also* synthesis
– as effect of the understanding   62, 297, 300, 304, 306
– schmimagination   xiif., 307
– transcendental   50, 62, 116, 290, 299f., 304f., 307, 310, 315, 317
infinite, infinity   214, 217, 222, 224, 256, 304f., 310–313, 317
innate, innatism   xi, 56–58, 95; *see also* concepts
inner sense   48, 135, 141, 153, 171, 178f., 184, 187, 200, 204, 209, 212f., 222, 237, 244, 249, 251, 312, 316f.
intensive magnitude, *see* magnitude
intuition   vf., viii, xii, 6, 18, 20, 22f., 25f., 42, 44, 47–49, 51f., 64, 72, 74, 78, 81, 86, 93f., 97, 100, 106, 111–119, 121f.,

125–138, 142 f., 146 f., 150–152, 154 f., 157, 159, 161, 165, 173, 175–177, 182, 184–187, 192–196, 198–204, 211 f., 218 f., 221, 225–229, 241 f., 244–252, 256, 259, 261–270, 273–275, 278 f., 282 f., 293, 296–310, 312, 314–318
– a priori   114, 165
– empirical   25, 42, 51, 81, 94, 126, 129, 135 f., 143, 159, 175, 177, 184 f., 198, 201, 204, 218, 225, 266, 273–275, 296–298, 304 f., 312, 317
– formal   297, 308 f.
– form of   100, 112, 199, 218, 283, 297, 299 f., 304, 308 f., 316
– intellectual   20, 23, 95, 128, 241
– manifold (of representations) in/of   xii, 49, 64, 72, 97, 112, 114–119, 121, 126–134, 136–138, 146, 150, 152, 154, 161, 177, 182, 185 f., 192 f., 225, 227–229, 242, 250–252, 256, 259, 261 f., 264–267, 270, 278 f., 296–299, 303–305, 308, 312, 314 f., 317; *see also* manifold
– non-sensible   186, 250
– pure   81, 116, 202, 219, 298, 310, 317
– sensible   xii, 6, 26, 48 f., 114, 187, 203, 249, 268, 274, 296, 299, 303–306, 314–317
– unity of   263, 296, 298, 305 f.

'I think'   vi, viii f., xi, xv, 6, 34, 39, 47 f., 70 f., 75, 77, 79, 81 f., 90, 96 f., 105, 107 f., 110, 122–124, 127–129, 131, 136–167, 171–176, 179 f., 182–184, 191 f., 202–206, 210, 225–234, 238, 241–245, 247–249, 252 f., 255 f., 258 f., 262–267, 279 f., 286–289; *see also* apperception, self-consciousness
– accompanying, accompaniment by   77, 89, 128 f., 136, 140–152, 154 f., 157–163, 165–167, 173–175, 179 f., 184, 192, 203–206, 210, 228–235, 238, 241–245, 248, 252, 255, 270
– as vehicle of the categories   127, 160, 175, 287

judgement   vii f., xi–xiii, xv, 3–10, 13, 16–18, 30, 38 f., 41–50, 52 f., 55 f., 58–62, 65, 69 f., 73–75, 85, 88, 90, 98, 111–119, 121 f., 124, 148 f., 155, 157, 172, 175, 193, 195, 202, 225 f., 236, 254, 265–278, 280, 282 f., 286, 293, 296 f., 299 f.
– aesthetic   43 f., 46 f., 59, 62, 276
– analytic   273, 276
– determinative   41 f., 44 f., 50, 59 f., 62, 272, 276 f.
– empirical   16, 47, 52, 59 f., 225, 275, 299
– of experience   45, 48 f., 52
– forms of   9, 293
– (logical) functions of   xi, xv, 4, 6, 8–10, 14, 38, 44, 112, 117 f., 121, 124, 165, 184, 195, 228, 266, 296
– merely reflective   46, 276
– of perception   45, 48 f., 52, 149, 274, 293
– power of   42–44, 46, 58, 60 f.
– reflective   17, 30, 41, 45 f., 59, 62, 276
– table of   5–8, 13, 17 f., 111 f., 114, 254
– teleological   46
justification   11, 17, 28 f., 31, 33, 35, 38, 60–62, 85, 91, 96, 100, 291–293

knowledge (cognition)   79 f. *et passim*
– a priori   20, 22, 29, 33, 61, 67, 84, 87, 92, 97, 102–106, 133, 135 f., 143 f., 159, 166, 294 f., 298
– discursive   135
– empirical   81, 91, 99 f., 293–295, 298
– intellectual   17, 20, 26
– objective   84, 86, 91, 96, 270, 281, 283
– perceptual   18, 290, 304, 312 f., 318
– self-   xvi, 17, 32, 39, 255, 271, 287

lawfulness   32, 43, 319–322
laws   viii, ix, xiv, 2, 26, 29, 32, 38, 40, 42 f., 58, 60, 158, 248, 271, 314 f., 318–322
– empirical   xiv, 42 f.
– natural   32, 320
– of nature   187, 319–321
– particular   320
– transcendental   43 f., 60
limitation   195 f., 202, 216 f., 219–222, 224, 256, 287, 303, 313
logic   9, 12–15, 36, 38 f., 48, 58 f., 75, 89, 97, 270
– discursive   270
– general   8 f., 61, 118, 268, 273

- transcendental   6, 8f., 40, 61, 114, 118, 268, 273, 275, 280, 299
logical function(s)   xi, xv, 4, 6, 8–10, 14, 38, 44, 112, 117f., 121, 124, 165, 184, 195, 228, 266, 296; see also judgement
- (completeness of) the table of   5–8, 13, 17f., 111f., 114, 254

magnitude   154, 196, 198, 200–203, 213f., 216–221, 223–225, 227, 305, 310, 312, 317, 320
- extensive   196, 198, 200, 202f., 213, 218, 225, 227
- intensive   154, 196, 198, 200–203, 213f., 216f., 219–221, 223f., 320
manifold(ness)   xif., 33, 42f., 47, 49, 64, 72, 74, 77, 97, 104–106, 108, 112, 114–119, 121, 126–138, 141, 143, 146, 150–154, 156, 161, 165, 176–178, 182–194, 201f., 207, 210, 213, 219, 225–232, 234, 239, 241–244, 246–256, 259–262, 264–267, 270f., 278f., 284, 294, 296–306, 308f., 311f., 314–319, 321; see also intuition, plurality
matter   29, 86, 93, 114, 159, 197, 199f., 203, 213f., 218, 220, 320
memory   145, 148
mereological inversion   311
Metaphysical Deduction, see Deduction
method   vi, 4, 10, 32, 34, 36, 39, 83, 92, 95f., 98, 100, 107, 121, 283, 288, 290
- dogmatic   36
- transcendental   39
modal, modality   11, 19, 65, 73, 79, 103, 108–110, 123–126, 141f., 154–158, 163–165, 167f., 190, 196–198, 204, 221, 225, 254, 271–276, 281, 315f.; see also category, categories

nature   xv, 19, 42f., 60, 62, 185, 187, 193, 196, 228, 291, 296, 315, 318–322
- *formaliter spectata*   42f., 295f., 319f.
- idealism of   291, 318–322
- *materialiter spectata*   295f., 319f.
- nomothetic of   43
- purposiveness of   43
- technique of   43

necessity   x–xii, 12–15, 22, 30, 43f., 61, 82f., 88f., 93, 102, 104f., 107f., 125f., 130, 133, 137, 139, 141, 149f., 157, 161, 164–167, 190, 255, 275, 294
- absolute   105, 107f., 133, 166
- conditional   88, 104, 107f., 130, 149
- de dicto   137
- hypothetical   166
- ontological   139
negation   154, 169, 195f., 200–202, 213, 216f., 219, 221–225, 256

object   *passim*
- concept of   25, 43f., 47, 51, 63f., 69, 81, 93, 100, 122, 189, 224, 226, 257, 259f., 263, 265, 287
- definition of   73f., 90, 260
- of experience   20, 24f., 30, 37, 71, 74, 83, 91, 100, 112, 155, 158, 178, 200, 217, 222f., 256, 277, 296, 319
- in general   25, 38, 47, 51, 63f., 71–73, 81, 100, 116, 123–125, 155, 170, 189, 195, 201, 257, 259f., 263–266, 281, 284, 304
- relation to   3, 24, 69, 129, 219, 226, 260, 271, 278, 284
- transcendental   xi, 94, 226, 259f.
- 'in the weighty sense'   93f.
objective validity   ix, xi, xiii, 2, 6–8, 16, 21, 28, 30, 37f., 44f., 48–50, 52f., 54, 58, 64, 68, 70f., 79, 81, 86, 88, 94, 98, 104f., 111, 119f., 122, 129f., 149, 155, 186, 190, 213, 258–260, 262f., 265–267, 271–276, 279–281, 283, 288f., 293
objectivity   25, 48, 62f., 70–76, 78f., 82f., 86, 89f., 92f., 98, 102, 106, 109f., 123, 130, 258, 264f., 267, 277, 280f., 283f., 289, 318
ontological, ontology   19, 21, 66f., 87f., 104, 139, 141, 155, 161, 172, 195, 225, 258, 295, 317
outer sense   207, 213, 311

Paralogisms   66, 90, 124, 126f., 169, 171f., 174, 177, 184, 199, 204, 253
perception (*Wahrnehmung*)   xiii, xv, 18f., 23, 44f., 47–49, 51f., 54, 64, 66, 70,

75, 78, 81, 86–88, 94, 114, 127, 130, 132, 135, 145, 147–149, 153, 159, 178, 183, 188, 193, 196 f., 200–204, 208 f., 211, 213–215, 221 f., 227, 234, 237, 239, 249 f., 274 f., 278, 290, 293, 313–318
phenomenal (world)   xiv, 21, 222, 276
plurality (category)   198, 201, 225–228, 247, 252 f., 256, 310, 313; *see also* manifold
positing   136, 156 f., 198, 220 f.
– absolute   156 f.
– relative   157
possibility (category)   124–126, 135, 141–150 *et passim*
– logical   155, 158, 165 f.
– material   322
– real   88, 145 f., 149 f., 159, 208, 240, 318
possible experience, *see* experience
Postulates of Empirical Thought   125 f.
power   47, 170, 183, 185, 190, 194, 201; *see also* force
Principles of Experience   xiv, 10, 29, 35, 61, 71, 168, 195, 202, 213, 219, 283, 321
proof   vi, xiii, 4, 10, 12, 17–19, 26, 28–40, 50, 54 f., 81, 83–85, 88, 90, 92, 95 f., 98 f., 110, 121 f., 125, 155, 190, 199, 201, 212, 237, 254, 263, 280, 282 f., 285 f., 291 f., 294 f., 313
– apagogic   36, 38
– apodictic   31, 35, 92
– direct   35, 37 f.
– genetic   37
– mathematical   31, 34
– ostensive   xiii, 28, 31, 36 f., 40, 291, 294
– philosophical   10, 31, 35, 37, 88, 95 f., 282 f., 295
– syllogistic   33
– transcendental   33, 35–40, 83, 190, 254
pure concept(s)   54, 56 f., 64, 91, 283; *see also* category, categories

quality   16, 73, 124 f., 195 f., 198, 200, 202, 204, 213 f., 217 f., 220 f., 223, 225, 254, 271, 303 f., 320
– categories of   16, 73, 124 f., 195 f., 198, 200, 202, 204, 213 f., 217, 220 f., 223, 225, 254, 271, 303 f., 320; *see also* magnitude
quantity (*quantitas*)   124 f., 144, 198, 203, 218, 225–227, 229 f., 251, 253 f., 304, 306
– categories of   124 f., 144, 225–227, 229, 253 f., 304, 306; *see also* magnitude
quantum, quanta   200, 218–221, 225, 227, 230, 302, 234, 251, 302
– *quanta continua*   219, 221, 227
quidditas   197
quid facti (*quaestio facti*)   xv, 28 f., 31, 34, 54–56, 214
– and empirical deduction   54–56
quid juris (*quaestio juris*)   xv, 28–31, 35, 37, 41, 54 f., 73, 85, 121, 280, 286

reality   21, 34, 88, 171, 173, 176, 181, 189, 193, 195–202, 204, 213 f., 216–224, 256, 260, 271–273, 276 f., 299
– objective   xi, 88, 173, 189, 193, 198 f., 213, 260, 271–273, 276 f., 299
– *realitas evanescens*   217
– *realitas noumenon*   197, 199 f.
receptivity   112, 183–186, 192, 199, 268, 297 f., 300–302
reciprocity   xiii f., 2, 17 f., 28, 63, 68, 70–72, 75, 77–79, 81, 85 f., 89 f., 92 f., 95, 98, 101, 103, 105–108, 110, 119 f., 123 f., 129, 168, 189 f., 257–265, 280–282, 286, 289
reference   29, 72, 104 f., 110, 140, 145, 188 f., 262, 273, 293
reflection   vii, xv, 25, 29, 31, 33 f., 38 f., 40 f., 43–46, 48, 52–56, 58–60, 62, 72, 97, 104, 142, 150 f., 154 f., 172, 208, 215, 239 f., 246, 287 f.; *see also* comparison/reflection/abstraction (CRA)
– logical   41, 44, 59, 62
– psychological   142
– self-   288
– transcendental   34, 38–40, 59, 72, 155, 287 f.
relation   *passim*
– categories of   16, 168 f., 170–172, 190, 194

- necessary   131, 194, 230, 265, 275, 279, 281
representation   *passim*
- partial   76, 113, 146, 232f., 241–243, 246, 253, 256
- power of   183, 190, 262

scepticism, sceptical   61, 83f., 85, 98, 292f.
Schematism   42, 195f., 198f., 201, 218
self-activity   10, 39, 168, 177, 182f., 186, 189f., 194, 247f., 256, 287; *see also* spontaneity
self-consciousness   vii, xiii, xvi, 10, 13, 15, 17f., 47, 63–65, 67–71, 73, 75–78, 82, 86, 88, 93f., 97, 101–104, 109, 120, 125, 127–129, 131–141, 145–147, 151–154, 159–161, 172, 176f., 179, 182f., 189, 191–193, 195, 202–206, 209f., 213, 217, 220, 223–226, 230–232, 234, 238, 240f., 247, 249, 252f., 256, 258–261, 270f., 279, 284f.
- transcendental (unity of)   xiii, 10, 17, 69f., 76–78, 93f., 109, 128f., 139, 159–161, 179, 189, 191, 193, 202–204, 206, 210, 213, 217, 223–225, 232, 252f., 256, 260
sensation (*Empfindung*)   113, 149, 155, 171f., 196–202, 204–206, 211, 213f., 216, 218–224, 256, 278, 291, 293, 298, 312, 320
sense datum/sense data (experience)   109, 166, 208, 228, 235–237, 239f.
sensibility   18, 20f., 25, 62, 79, 95, 99, 113f., 126, 149, 153, 171, 183, 185f., 196, 204, 209, 220, 235, 249f., 274, 277–279, 297–301, 304, 308f., 315, 317
soul   97, 115, 149, 170f., 173–177, 179, 193, 201, 279
- and gradual remission of its powers   201, 214
space   v, 17, 19f., 35, 57, 72, 86, 94, 100, 113f., 121, 193, 196, 198, 200f., 203, 217–219, 222, 224f., 227f., 263f., 290, 293–295, 297–313, 315–318, 321
- determinate   227, 302–304, 307, 313, 317
- determination of   290, 304, 310

- geometric   290, 307, 309–313
- metaphysical   310f., 313
- unicity of   311–313, 316f.
- unity of   290, 294, 298f., 304–312, 318
spatiotemporal(ity)   xv, 19, 72, 81, 94, 113f., 129, 193, 196, 219, 222, 225, 227f., 236, 258, 260, 263f., 278, 290, 292–294, 297f., 303–305, 312–314, 317
spontaneity   xi, 39, 112, 114, 124, 156, 160, 168, 177, 182–186, 220f., 268, 300f., 316
- absolute   183–186
- of Reason   186
- relative   184f.
- of the understanding   177, 184, 186
subject   *passim*
- absolute   171–173, 175f., 181
- transcendental   94, 155f., 170, 174, 185, 209, 259, 288
subsistence   170
substance   16, 70, 97, 126f., 150, 168–182, 184, 190–192, 194, 201, 255f., 275, 320
the substantial   169–171, 173
synthesis   *passim*
- a posteriori   247
- of apprehension   45, 115, 132, 227, 248, 250, 299, 306, 312, 315, 317
- a priori   xiif., 48, 53, 69, 74, 82, 94, 96, 101f., 105–107, 110, 115, 118f., 123, 130f., 135, 138f., 153, 228, 241, 245f., 258, 269, 284, 289, 307, 310, 315f., 318
- figurative   v, 114, 116, 290, 297, 299f., 302–310, 312f., 315, 318; *see also* imagination
- of (the) imagination   xi, 52, 62, 116, 118, 239, 269, 290, 299f., 303f., 310f., 317
- intellectual (*synthesis intellectualis*)   xiif., 114, 116, 299, 306f., 312, 315
- necessary   xii, 77, 120, 225
- pre-discursive   45
- of recognition   115f., 247, 250, 271
- of reproduction in the imagination   115f., 247
- *speciosa*   xii, 52, 213, 264, 290
- successive   198, 200, 218, 227, 300, 303f., 310
- threefold   xv, 45, 51

synthetic a priori   16, 37, 40, 47, 83f., 86, 89, 99f., 103, 121, 123, 159, 245, 280, 283f., 294f.

thing in itself, things in themselves   25, 75, 157, 197–200, 214, 222f., 261, 264, 277, 279, 319, 321
totality   142, 159, 225f., 228, 247, 249, 252, 254, 256, 261, 277, 305, 319, 321
Transcendental Aesthetic   vf., 99, 114, 128, 199, 202, 297, 303, 308–311, 314
Transcendental Analytic   vi, 6f., 24, 308
transcendental argument   82f., 98, 100, 110, 235, 291, 293
transcendental chaos   314
Transcendental Deduction, *see* Deduction
transcendental matter   199f.
tribunal/court of justice   32, 288
– critique of pure reason as   288
truth   12, 36–38, 87–89, 93, 96, 99, 273f., 276f.
– as correspondence   87, 89, 276
– material   88f., 273
– objective   88, 273
– transcendental (*veritas transcendentalis*)   88, 96, 276f.
– value   98, 271, 273

(the) understanding   *passim*
– pure concepts of, *see* category, categories; concept
unicity, *see* space
unity   *passim*
– of apperception, *see* apperception
– as category   225, 228, 252f., 256, 287, 297, 304, 306 *et passim*
– collective   205, 225, 228, 231, 235, 240f., 243f., 247, 251
– conceptual   278, 311
– of consciousness, *see* consciousness
– distributive   243f.
– higher   155, 192, 286f.
– of intuition, *see* intuition
– qualitative   221, 224, 226, 287, 304, 307

www.ingramcontent.com/pod-product-compliance
Lightning Source LLC
Chambersburg PA
CBHW020326240426

43665CB00044B/671